Bargaining on Europe

Bargaining on Europe

Britain and the First Common Market, 1860–1892

Peter T. Marsh

Yale University Press
New Haven and London

Copyright © 1999 by Peter T. Marsh

Set in Ehrhardt by Best-set Typesetter Ltd, Hong Kong
Printed in Great Britain by Biddles Ltd, Guildford and King's Lynn

Library of Congress Cataloging-in-Publication Data
Marsh, Peter T.
    Bargaining on Europe: Britain and the First Common Market.
  1860–1892/Peter T. Marsh.
    Includes bibliographical references and index.
    ISBN 0–300–08103–0 (cloth: alk. paper)
    1. Free trade – Europe – History – 19th century.   2. Free trade –
Great Britain – History – 19th century.   3. Protectionism – Europe –
History – 19th century.   4. Protectionism – Europe – History – 19th
century.   5. Great Britain – Commercial policy – History – 19th
century.   6. Great Britain – Commercial treaties – History – 19th
century.   I. Title.
HF2035.M37   1999
382.4041 – dc21   99–33406
                                                                    CIP

A catalogue record for this book is available from the British Library.

10 9 8 7 6 5 4 3 2 1

To Andrea

Contents

Acknowledgements   ix

1   Tools for Bargaining   1

2   Ambivalent Inauguration: The Anglo–French Treaty of 1860   8
     a. *The British Initiative*   8
     b. *Bradford and the British Mercantile Response*   17
     c. *The High Politics of the European Market*   23

3   The Construction of the Network, 1861–1866   28
     a. *The Belgian Treaty*   28
     b. *The Italian Treaty*   36
     c. *The Prussian Treaty*   40
     d. *Inquest on the British Approach*   45
     e. *The Austrian Treaty*   49
     f. *The Benefits*   52

4   Dividends in Wartime, 1866–1872   62
     a. *The Austro-Prussian War*   63
     b. *The Franco-Prussian War*   79

5   The Impact of Depression, 1873–1879   88
     a. *The Onset of Depression*   89
     b. *The First Governmental Responses*   93
     c. *The Renegotiations of 1877*   103
     d. *The Departure of Germany*   109

6   Disengagement between Britain and France,
     1879–1882   117
         a. *Lord Salisbury's Discontent*   119
         b. *Say's Mission and Gladstone's Budget*   124
         c. *The Dilke–Tirard Discussions*   129
         d. *Waiting for Gambetta*   132
         e. *Impasse*   140

7   The Quandary over Commercial Policy,
     1883–1888   148
         a. *The European Market after 1882*   150
         b. *The Stalemate over Spain and the Depression*   153
         c. *The Franco-Italian Tariff War*   164

8   The Transformation of the Network, 1889–1892   172
         a. *The French Retreat*   174
         b. *A Constructive German Aberration*   181
         c. *The Continental Line-Up*   189
         d. *Implications for Britain*   192
         e. *The Spanish Sequel*   195

9   In Retrospect   207

     Note on Documentary, Periodical and Archival Sources
     (with Abbreviations)   212

     Notes   214

     List of Secondary Sources   237

     Index   241

Acknowledgements

This venture into economic history has taken me to new places and introduced me to new friends. Peter Cain was particularly helpful, reading much of the initial draft of this work, pointing out pertinent sources of information and ideas past and present, and fortifying my hunches. Andrew Marrison helped me with the final revision, particularly in locating and digesting needed statistical information. John Davis, Sabine Freitag and Fred Marquardt helped me appreciate the predominantly political dimensions of German tariff policy – as did my former colleague at the University of Saskatchewan, Ivo Lambi, when I rediscovered his book on Bismarck's policy. Frank Trentmann and Michael Dintenfass gave me stimulating advice on early chapters. My colleagues in the Global Political Economy Consortium at Syracuse University's Maxwell School – particularly Dave Richardson and Mary Lovely in Economics, Beverley Mullings and Richard Grant in Geography, and Richard Sherman in Political Science – helped me look at my story from different disciplinary perspectives – as did David Lazer. I am also indebted to the students in my graduate seminar on the European Union who alerted me to the affinity between its current concerns and the commercial diplomacy of Europe in the nineteenth century. Ian Mason and his colleagues at the West Yorkshire Archive Service led me into the richly detailed records of the Chamber of Commerce in Bradford. John and Derick Behrens, Michael Buneman and Lady Flowers responded cordially to my queries about Sir Jacob Behrens.

I wish to acknowledge the permission of Her Majesty Queen Elizabeth II to quote from the papers of Queen Victoria, and of Brian L. Crowe to quote from letters and writings of Sir Joseph Archer Crowe in the National War Museum and the British Library. On the nomination of the University of Birmingham, the Leverhulme Foundation granted me a visiting fellowship and Syracuse University an accompanying sabbatical leave, which enabled me to complete the research for and to write this book much sooner than would otherwise have been possible. A concluding word of thanks is due to Robert Baldock of Yale University Press in London for his counsel and encouragement.

Chapter 1

Tools for Bargaining

'Put your principles in your pocket, and aim only for the lowest duties which will let you sell the most stuff.'

Richard Cobden to Jacob Behrens, October 1860

More than a century ago, during the 1860s, Britain co-operated with France to spread a network of tariff-reducing treaties across Western and Central Europe. The British objective was to open the markets of Europe to international commerce and thus to promote broader co-operation and peace. Though the government of France under the emperor Napoleon III hoped through these treaties to draw the continent into its embrace, it sympathised with the economic philosophy of the British. After reaching an agreement to lower the tariff between themselves, the two powers negotiated tariff-reducing treaties with other European states. These treaties were linked together through most-favoured-nation clauses that entitled each signatory to the lowest customs duties to which any other signatory states had agreed. The resulting treaty-made or, as it was called, 'conventional' tariff gave the countries of Europe more open access to each other's markets than they had ever enjoyed before.

That was what they all wanted. The participating states hoped to increase the wealth of their people and thus to strengthen themselves by extending their trade beyond their borders. They had no agreed political objective beyond the growth of their common market. And grow it did through the 1860s into the 1870s. But thereafter, when falling prices and profits brought about a protracted depression, the states on the continent adjusted their tariffs to give more protection to domestic producers while retaining some measure of access to neighbouring markets. Britain, which also suffered from the depression, was shocked by this departure in policy but found, when it tried to resist, that it lacked the power to do so.

Tariff-reducing treaties could not be made without tariffs. Tariffs were the bargaining chips or levers of negotiation with which those who sought to reduce the barriers to trade between nations had to work. These seeming truisms presented the government of Britain with a problem because they ran counter to several principles and predilections of the commercial policy that it had adopted, which was based on the classical economic teaching that tariffs only hurt the country that imposed them. Tariffs clearly raised the cost of imports, a costly drawback for a country that could not produce enough food to feed itself or the raw materials needed to sustain its manufacturing industry. So deeply were British policy-makers convinced of this truth that they recoiled from anything that looked like bargaining for tariff reductions with other countries for fear that it might set them a bad, misleading example. The economic liberals who were in charge of British policy in the second half of the nineteenth century concluded that tariffs were best set unilaterally by each country in its own interest, which made them reluctant to reach and renew tariff-reducing treaties. Their disinclination was deepened by the further principle that the tariff should be stripped of all protective and discriminatory provisions and reduced to a few items solely for the purpose of generating governmental revenue.

The British governments of the 1860s reconciled these principles with their negotiation of commercial treaties by making their tariff reductions applicable to all countries and by reducing the number of items subject to customs duties to little more than a dozen. The British tariff was confined to things not produced in Britain in hopes of placing the tariff beyond suspicion of protecting British industry. But these principles and practices almost eliminated Britain's international bargaining power on tariff matters. Furthermore, the customs duties that it retained proved highly lucrative to the Treasury, a result that deepened the government's aversion to any bargaining for their reduction. A civic ethic raised these commercial principles almost beyond challenge. Detachment from tariff-making was praised for elevating the conduct of government above sordid private interests. The limitation of the tariff to a very few items was commended as a benefit to the people as a whole because everyone was a consumer. These ethical perspectives made highly principled ministers like Gladstone unwilling to recognise that some of the remaining customs duties, particularly that on wine, worked in a discriminatory and protective way, and hence prevented them from making candid use of these effects in their commercial diplomacy.

For more than 30 years, during the 1860s while Britain tried to keep up with France in extending the network of treaties, and later when Britain strove to prevent an upward revision of the conventional European tariff, British ministers found themselves without the tariff leverage they needed to secure their objectives. At last in 1892, after Britain had been marginalised and France had withdrawn from the group that they had created, the Prime Minister Lord Salisbury told his supporters that the commercial policy Britain had followed since 1860 'may be noble, but it is not business.'[1] Yet the British electorate refused to sanction a change in policy. Though continental Europe remained its largest market, Britain turned its commercial attention elsewhere.

The following chapters trace the story of that perplexing experience. Their focus rests primarily on the relationship between Britain and continental Europe rather than on the formulation of British policy or on the worldwide pre-eminence, overseas activity and internal balance of the British economy in the nineteenth century. Historians have already looked at the primarily British dimensions of this economic subject, including the policy of free trade, the trade and finance of Britain as the first industrial nation, and its policy as the predominant or hegemonic power of the nineteenth century, setting the pattern for the United States in the twentieth. Those stories overlap with the narrative here. Anthony Howe's recent study, *Free Trade and Liberal England, 1846–1946*,[2] deals extensively with the commercial treaty-making on which this book concentrates. But our two books tell different tales, in part because the rival merits of free trade and protection in the nineteenth century looked, and indeed continue to look, quite different on the two sides of the Channel.[3] The free-trade treaties imposed by Britain on less developed economies overseas served a quite different purpose and had to be negotiated quite differently from the treaties of the European network.[4] It is, furthermore, not hard to see how Britain's interests in the global market and insistence upon framing economic questions in universal terms kept it from grasping the requirements of commercial diplomacy in continental Europe. Economic historians nowadays are inclined to play down the impact of tariffs,[5] in part because it is difficult to distinguish from the multitude of other influences at work in the market. Yet nineteenth-century governments regarded tariffs as one of their main tools for economic regulation, at once indispensable from a continental perspective but pernicious to the British.

Apart from Anthony Howe's book, a few articles and unpublished dissertations,[6] and some studies of the 1860 treaty between Britain and France,[7] little attention has been paid to Britain's participation in the nineteenth-century network of commercial treaties in Europe.[8] Yet, aside from its intrinsic historical importance, this body of experience is surely pertinent to the problematic relationship that Britain has had with the European Community and Union in the latter half of the twentieth century. Like the twentieth-century Community, the nineteenth-century network embraced virtually all of Western and Central Europe. Both aspired to the creation of a common European market that would transcend the essentially national confines of customs unions such as the German Zollverein. The concept of 'common market' can be applied to both the nineteenth-century network and the twentieth-century Community in another sense. The members of both sought access to each other's markets while continuing to think of their domestic markets and economies separately, in national terms. All that the British wanted from the later Community was the common market they had endeavoured to open up a century earlier. The reluctance of nineteenth-century British Liberals to allow continental countries any hand in the shaping of the British tariff is, furthermore, akin to the aversion of Conservatives at the end of the twentieth century to any diminution of British sovereignty.

There are, of course, fundamental differences between the nineteenth-century network and its twentieth-century incarnation. The nineteenth century treaties of commerce were negotiated bilaterally, though often with other partners or competitors in mind; and the participants in the network had no collective political goal. These characteristics stand in contrast to the multi-lateral proceedings of the European Union as it presses towards an 'ever closer union'. Even so, the Belgians, and particularly their leading contributor to the European movement, Paul-Henri Spaak, were quite aware of the connection between the earlier network of commercial treaties and the union they strove to build a century later.[9] The British were not conscious of that connection. But a faint echo of the old commercial treaty network lingered in the cataloguing practices of the Foreign Office. Not sure how otherwise to deal with the documents on the birth and infancy of the European Community in the 1950s, the filing clerks at the Foreign Office placed them under the heading of 'commercial policy'.[10] That way they were at any rate easier to find than the host of Foreign Office papers on nineteenth-century commercial issues involving more than two countries, which were filed and then forgotten under the unhelpful heading of 'general'.

While British historians have not paid much attention to this European story, political scientists have treated it as illustrating one way in which a pre-eminent or hegemonic power can stabilise the international political economy of its era. Prompted by Charles Kindleberger's analysis of the depression in the 1930s,[11] political scientists have elaborated a theory of hegemonic stability according to which Britain, in adopting its policy of unilateral free trade, underwrote the international economic order in the nineteenth century. Kindleberger suggested that the inability of Britain and the unwillingness of the United States to perform this function between the two world wars did much to produce the depression of the 1930s. Political scientists have used this line of thought to provide a rationale for the economic policies pursued by the United States since World War II as leader of the Western world.

But the theory is more applicable to the United States in the latter half of the twentieth century than to Britain in the latter half of the nineteenth; and it works much better in the realm of finance, which Kindleberger places at the centre of his analysis, than for international trade. Those who focus on nineteenth-century European tariff-making find that hegemonic stability theory raises more questions than it answers.[12] The capital market and financial services provided by the City of London along with British adherence to the gold standard undoubtedly lubricated the international economy while accentuating Britain's ascendancy within it. But when the theory is applied to the realm of trade and industry rather than to finance, it does not fit the facts or correspond with the experience of British commercial policy-makers. After the initial treaty between Britain and France in 1860, France set the pace in the creation of the trade-treaty network, while Britain lagged plaintively behind. British pre-eminence generally diminished after 1870 when the United States and Germany with their larger home markets began to flex their industrial muscles. Salisbury later tried to reactivate British commercial policy, but this proved effective only when accompanied by German initiatives. British Foreign Secretaries discovered to their dismay that power in the political economy of Europe was more widely diffused than Britain's early ascendancy in industry and subsequently in finance would suggest.

This book looks across the Channel, not across the Atlantic. In the second half of the twentieth century the attraction of the United States for Britain has rivalled, when it has not exceeded, that of continental Europe. But during the 1860s the Civil War disabled the United States and focused British attention on Europe; thereafter the increasing level of the US tariff limited the appeal of its market as an alternative to the European. US protectionism made remarkably little impact on British commercial policy in spite of the speed with which the US economy grew after 1870. The US example was a great anomaly to the makers of British commercial policy. Far from prompting British free traders to question their faith, the United States as the supplier of foodstuffs and raw materials for Britain served as the clearest proof of how suicidal it would be for Britain to raise its tariff. Those who dissented from this orthodoxy and sought to restore Britain's capacity to bargain for better terms of access to the European market had to accept the inapplicability of their proposals to British trade with the United States.

The account presented in this book is European as much as British. It explores the participation of Britain in the attempt to open up the European market, an attempt that proceeded rapidly in the 1860s and with palpable rewards but then foundered when the latter diminished. The British set the process going and believed that they also set its guiding principles. But when continental Europeans moved away from those principles or interpreted them differently and subverted British objectives on the continent, the British still clung to their principles. Faced with a choice between these principles and the ongoing struggle for access in the European market, Britain turned away from Europe.

The business community in Britain accepted this decision. Chambers of Commerce gave the original treaty with France a warmer reception than did the House of Commons. Until the mid-1870s Chambers of Commerce harried the Foreign Office to intensify its efforts to open the continental market. But the businessmen who led this effort were disappointed and in some cases disillusioned by their inability to persuade their continental counterparts to go on widening instead of narrowing British access to their market. This experience hardened the commitment of some businessmen to unilateral free trade and turned others into sceptics or outright opponents. Thus divided, the business community was in no position to change the commercial policy of the country.

Richard Cobden, the Englishman responsible for the 1860 treaty with France, had raised the hopes and earned the lasting gratitude of British businessmen by involving some of them in working out the detailed implementation of that treaty. His selection of them over diplomats was just one of the anomalous features of the model of commercial diplomacy that he created in 1860. The greater anomaly was that Cobden shared responsibility with Gladstone for the budget that accompanied the treaty with France and that eliminated so much of the tariff that British commercial diplomacy thereafter was ineffective. The combination of budget and treaty in 1860 has a better claim than the repeal of the Corn Laws in 1846 to be considered the measure that established what the British meant by free trade. Yet even the label of 'free trade' was paradoxical because the customs duties that remained after 1860 contributed a hefty proportion to the revenue on which the British government relied, a much higher proportion than was the case, for example, in Germany and France.[13] There was yet another inconsistency. Cobden and Gladstone sought a commercial treaty with France for primarily political reasons, to be discussed in the next chapter. But these two men and those in Britain who continued their work failed to recognise the political agenda of the friends of free trade on the continent.

Two more observations need to be made about the terms that appear frequently in the following pages. The first concerns 'free trade'. The meaning that Cobden and Gladstone attached to this term did not apply in continental Europe. Many continental Europeans identified themselves with the greatest possible freedom of international trade, but singularly few of them favoured depriving the industry of their countries of all tariff protection. In the following pages, therefore, the label of free trader will be applied as far as possible only to the British, while the continental advocates of tariff reduction will be called commercial liberals.

Finally a word on the term 'most-favoured nation'. Its unconditional application to international trade came to be regarded as the most valuable, and was certainly the most durable, achievement of the nineteenth-century network of commercial treaties. But businessmen in Britain discovered that this provision in the treaties of the 1860s did not work in a neutral fashion. The prescribed tariffs were usually designed to promote the goods only of the two signatory states in each case, to the detriment of competing countries even when they were entitled to most-favoured-nation treatment. Accordingly, the most-favoured-nation clause became a bone of contention. The British Foreign Office valued it after 1882 as providing Britain with its only means of access to the conventional tariff of Europe. The Spanish charged, on the other hand, that the most-favoured-nation clause promoted imports from abroad at the expense of domestic production. The German Chancellor Caprivi, who reconstructed the network in 1892, regarded the power to shape the tariff to which the most-favoured-nation clause applied as the greatest benefit that this diplomatic achievement gave Germany against its commercial rivals, particularly Britain and France.

That was just one of the costs of the British commitment to unilateral free trade. However much it enhanced the financial interests of the country, Britain's abandonment and continuing rejection of a tariff for negotiating purposes proved costly to trade, especially in Europe. That is the theme of this book. Free trade has been a commitment of US commercial policy in the second half of the twentieth century as much as it was of British commercial policy in the second half of the nineteenth. But the free traders who have shaped the commercial policy of the United States since World War II did not work in terms of unilateral tariff disarmament; they negotiated aggressively in the interests of their own trade and industry. Such behaviour would have horrified those who laid down the basic terms of the British commercial policy that began with the Anglo–French treaty of 1860.

Chapter 2

Ambivalent Inauguration:
The Anglo-French Treaty of 1860

'It is really a great European operation!'

Gladstone to his wife, January 1860

a. The British Initiative

A quarter of a century afterwards, Gladstone recalled 1860 as 'one of the most perplexed and critical [years] of our recent parliamentary history.'[1] At the head of the questions that combined to create that crisis, he listed the commercial treaty with France along with the issues in foreign and defence policy that revolved around it. The crisis had arisen in midsummer the previous year. In June 1859, Napoleon III of France revived the fears that Europe associated with his dreaded uncle by invading, in alliance with the King of Sardinia, the territories controlled by Austria in northern Italy. The French and Sardinians beat the Austrians twice, at Magenta and Solferino. Meanwhile, between those two battles, elections in Britain brought Lord Palmerston back for the last time as Prime Minister and reinstated Gladstone as Chancellor of the Exchequer. Alarm about the intentions of France, which had strengthened its navy with iron-clad vessels, prompted Palmerston to press for the fortification of the British coast, the cost of which in turn jeopardised Gladstone's ambition to complete the reform of British governmental finance by discarding the remaining protective tariffs.

Cobden, an independent friend of the new government, intervened to suggest that Britain reach a commercial treaty with France. In making the proposal Cobden deviated from the policy that had made him famous; but he did so in order to pursue a higher goal. His name was synonymous with the unilateral free trade that he had induced Britain to adopt in the 1840s, a policy seemingly confirmed by the prosperity of the 1850s.[2] The Board of Trade noted with satisfaction at the end of the decade that the total volume of Britain's international trade and the tonnage of British shipping had more than doubled since 1842 when Sir Robert Peel launched Britain on the path towards free trade.[3] But peace ranked higher in Cobden's hierarchy of values than prosperity. He had advocated free trade as the best way to promote peace as well as prosperity, both at home and abroad. Once Britain embraced his policy for trade and commerce by repealing the Corn Laws and Navigation Acts, he redirected his energies to attack all expressions of belligerence in Britain's conduct overseas. In 1857, when a British force bombarded Canton to protest against the refusal of China to open its markets to British exports, including opium from India, Cobden induced the House of Commons to censure the action.

In the ensuing elections he was repudiated by his textile-making former supporters in West Yorkshire. They favoured a more aggressive assertion of the interests of their country and its commerce than he could approve. But electoral defeat did not diminish Cobden's commitment to the pursuit of peace. The thriving economy reduced his concern about prosperity; he worried on the contrary that Britain might have too much of it, that the expanding demand for its exports would encourage labour to demand higher wages and thus threaten Britain's international competitiveness. When the general election of 1859 that returned Palmerston and Gladstone to office also returned Cobden to the House of Commons, he was prepared to modify the way he pursued his objectives, to be flexible in applying the doctrine of unilateral free trade if it reduced the risk of war.

He was induced to do so by two free-trading friends. John Bright, his closest colleague in the crusade against the Corn Laws, referred to free trade in the most elevated terms as 'the Faith'.[4] Yet it was Bright who first suggested in the new parliament that, in order to relieve tension between the two countries, Britain should reduce the 'extraordinarily heavy'[5] duty it imposed upon wines and other luxury articles from France. His proposal strained but did not violate the principles of unilateral free trade since it did not insist on reciprocal French tariff reductions. Bright trusted that the British offer would encourage the French to respond, also unilaterally, with reductions of their own. It was a French friend, Maurice Chevalier, who persuaded Cobden to translate Bright's suggestion into the form of a treaty. Chevalier was one of the foremost advocates of free trade in France. He had welcomed Cobden to Paris after his triumph in Britain over the Corn Laws and had kept in touch with him ever since. Chevalier understood that there was a need for strong executive leadership in the fight for free trade in France. Protectionism there rested on a broad popular base among the land-owning peasantry and enjoyed extensive support among industrial producers, who were more interested in their large home market than in the intensely competitive market for exports. Hence, Chevalier had welcomed Napoleon's seizure of power in 1848/52 and his insistence on the right to make commercial treaties without legislative approval. In the wake of Bright's speech in 1859, Chevalier travelled to England to see Cobden. When they failed to meet, Chevalier made his case by letter.

Cobden at first recoiled from the notion of a tariff treaty. He had always argued that free trade was a universal good of which every country should avail itself. That truth would be obscured if one country offered tariff reductions to another in the context of a treaty, thereby implying that the tariff reductions were somehow a concession requiring compensatory reductions by the other party. Previous offers to reduce its tariff in return for reciprocal reductions had made continental states suspicious that Britain was seeking to take advantage of their lower levels of economic development to flood their markets with the often technologically superior yet cheaper products of British industry. But the prosperity that Britain enjoyed at the end of the 1850s enabled Cobden to argue that it did not need new markets and hence that, in seeking tariff reductions, it was not seeking its own selfish advantage. As he told Chevalier: 'I feel no present solicitude for an extension of our foreign trade, in so far as the material or pecuniary interests of this country are concerned. We have as much to do as we can accomplish. It is very difficult to manage matters with the working classes owing to the great demand for their labor. I am afraid we shall have "strikes" in all directions . . . Therefore, I repeat, we have no necessity for opening new markets in France or elsewhere with a view to promoting our material prosperity.' Cobden hoped that this lack of economic interest would reduce the practical difficulty of negotiating a tariff treaty with France. To have any chance of success with the French, he needed to be able to assure them that he was 'not a *commis voyageur* travelling abroad for the sale of British fabrics'.[6]

Confidence that he could convey that assurance cleared Cobden's mind about the route to his political objective. He was readily convinced that there was no way other than a tariff treaty to bring about 'any permanent improvement in the political relations of France and England'. The focus of such a treaty on trade could take things out of the hands of aristocratic diplomats, whom he suspected of an appetite for conflict, and direct attention instead to middle-class men of commerce, whom he believed to be inherently pacific. Cobden believed further that the road to peace could be secured only when the people of each nation learnt to be interdependent by supplying each other's material needs. 'There is no other way of counteracting the antagonism of language and race,' he wrote. 'It is God's own method of producing an *entente cordiale*.'[7] Moreover, a tariff treaty need not involve a clear violation of unilateralism. Chevalier showed Cobden that the unilateral reductions that Bright proposed might constitute the British side in a tariff treaty with France; Britain could make its reductions applicable to all countries, even if France confined its reductions initially to Britain.[8]

Once he began to take Chevalier's argument seriously, Cobden took counsel with Gladstone. The two Englishmen shared the same concerns, though with significant differences. Gladstone was if anything more worried than Cobden about the deviation from the doctrine of free trade that a tariff treaty implied. His anxiety on this score was reduced, not as with Cobden by the buoyant economy, but rather by the recollection that Sir Robert Peel had retained some

duties, including that on wine, in hope of negotiating tariff reductions, particularly with France. Yet as Chancellor of the Exchequer Gladstone was loath
to lose much of the revenue from the wine duty and the related duty on spirits.
Though he shared Cobden's faith in the pacific potential of commerce, Gladstone's international objectives were more sophisticated. As a member of the
cabinet he bore responsibility for the main lines of British foreign and defence
policy. He was obliged to think in terms of the great power politics that so
repelled Cobden, though Gladstone too found them distasteful. The victories
of France and Sardinia over Austria in northern Italy created a dangerous situation. They released indigenous forces for the unification of Italy in a way that
unsettled Napoleon's ambitions for France while leaving Austria anxious to
repair its fortunes. The leading members of the British cabinet, including
Palmerston and the Foreign Secretary Lord John Russell as well as Gladstone,
sympathised with the movement for Italian unification, but they were apprehensive of Napoleon's intentions in that connection. One way for Britain to
curb his ambitions would be to ally itself with France as a friend of Italian unification, a ploy Britain had used successfully *vis-à-vis* Russia over the independence of Greece. The government recoiled from a straightforward political
alliance, but a commercial treaty might serve its purpose without over-
committing it. And it could achieve some other, even more important goals so
far as Gladstone was concerned. It would reduce if not eliminate the need for
the costly coastal fortifications sought by Palmerston, and would thus enable
Gladstone to start his term as Chancellor by completing the reform of the
British tariff begun by Peel.

Assured of Gladstone's sympathy, Cobden headed for Paris on an unofficial
mission, of which the British government was kept nonetheless fully aware, to
see whether the French Emperor would agree to such a treaty. The venture was
momentous. If successful, it would mark a change in commercial policy for
Britain and France; it might also signally ameliorate the international climate
as well as trade throughout Europe. Since 1846, after the failure of earlier
efforts to reach tariff-reducing treaties with other European states, Britain had
acted strictly on its own in reforming its tariff, discarding many items from the
list of dutiable articles and lowering the rate on others. France, on the other
hand, despite occasional attempts, had done little to reduce the high, often prohibitive import duties with which it protected its domestic market.[9] And what
better way was there to begin improving the political climate in Europe than
with the relationship between the two great powers that had been at each other's
throat for most of the past two centuries?

Cobden threw himself into the mission, and he carried it out with remarkable success. From the start, however, there was something deeply ambivalent
about the enterprise. Cobden and also Gladstone did not recognise the means
that made the mission to Paris successful; and they did away with those means

as part of the eventual agreement. Gladstone later recalled approvingly how, within months of concluding the treaty with France, Cobden had withheld his approval from 'the principle of commercial treaties'. Cobden argued that what he had concluded with the French was not a treaty in the usual sense of the word: 'The arrangement lately contracted with the French Government is not in its old and exclusive sense a commercial treaty, but is a simultaneous movement on the part of the two Countries in the direction of freedom of trade.'[10] He claimed, in other words, that the Anglo–French treaty did not involve reciprocal bargaining, with two parties making what they regarded as concessions to each other. He had simply persuaded the French to proceed alongside Britain in reducing their customs duties for their own good. Yet the French government had won things, including acceptance of its annexation of Nice and Savoy, that the British would not have given so readily without reduction in the French tariff. And Gladstone bargained stiffly with the French through Cobden to minimise the reduction of the wine duties and hence the loss to the Treasury.

Only by interpreting the negotiations as Cobden did could he and Gladstone remain true to the creed they had professed since the 1840s. That set of principles had been hammered out in the parliamentary debates leading up to the repeal of the Corn Laws. The consensus that emerged in favour of free trade had been challenged by a maverick economist, Robert Torrens,[11] who advocated what was called reciprocity.[12] That is to say, Torrens argued that Britain should reduce its tariffs only in exchange for the reductions in tariff that it wanted another country to make. Those who espoused classical economic theory scorned this suggestion. Torrens's argument was, however, sound enough theoretically to win endorsement from John Stuart Mill, though *only* as a theory. Mill recoiled from the practical application that Torrens wished to give his argument. Having proved in the abstract that the unilateral reduction of tariffs by one country could turn the terms of trade in its disfavour, Torrens pressed the British government to reduce the tariff only if its trading partners made reciprocal reductions and to threaten them with stiff retaliation if they refused. He contended, with Mill's reluctant agreement, that a policy of insistent reciprocity might benefit British trade, though it would reduce world trade as a whole. Mill laid stress on this worldwide cost. The difference in emphasis reflected a difference in priorities between the Liberal free traders with whom Mill was aligned and Conservatives such as Disraeli who sympathised with Torrens's standpoint. Yet the champions of the national interest were not all on Torrens's side. No one beat the patriotic drum more loudly than Lord Palmerston, but he insisted upon setting the tariff unilaterally as Britain's sovereign right.

The case against Torrens and reciprocity was essentially practical. Britain had tried since the Napoleonic Wars to reach tariff-reducing treaties with its trading partners, and had little to show for its efforts. By 1840 this experience suggested 'that there was little to be gained by commercial negotiations, other than reciprocity in navigation', and that tariffs were not of much use as bargaining counters.[13] Continental countries were too fearful of the industrial might of Britain to open their doors to its products. Sir Robert Peel accordingly resolved in 1846 'that we would no longer injure the people of this country by debarring them from foreign articles, because foreign countries would not enter into reciprocal treaties with us.'[14] Furthermore, reciprocity might not even be necessary. Cobden was utterly confident that other countries would follow once Britain gave them the lead. He assured the House of Commons at the beginning of the debates on repeal that, 'if you abolish the Corn-law honestly, and adopt Free Trade in its simplicity, there will not be a tariff in Europe that will not be changed in less than five years to follow your example.'[15] Though that prophecy was remembered against him, there were some signs of movement in a liberal direction on the continent over the next few years. By 1859 Cobden was disappointed but not disillusioned by the slowness of the foreign response. He interpreted the 1860 Anglo-French treaty in such a way as to reaffirm his faith: the French would come to see the wisdom of the tariff reductions they had made alongside the British. Continental countries would witness the prosperity and harmony that accompanied commercial liberalism, and would be persuaded to proceed further along the path to free trade.

The outlook of the man to whom Cobden presented his proposal was deliberately unclear. Napoleon III was an opportunist and man of action who rarely chose to explain himself. He remains an enigma to historians. Yet it was the practice of Napoleon's government after 1860, rather than the principles of Cobden, that animated the commercial treaty network initiated by the two men. Napoleon had displayed serious economic intentions when he seized power in France. He secured the right to make commercial treaties on his own authority, without reference to the legislature, and made some attempt thereafter to lower the French tariff. But when the legislature resisted these efforts, he did not resort to his treaty-making powers – until Cobden counselled him. Napoleon kept his international ambitions even more obscure than his economic inclinations for fear of arousing opposition before he was ready to meet it. But his name and the trappings of empire with which he surrounded himself were quite enough to make Europe apprehensive. He left little doubt that he aimed to revise the settlement imposed on France in Vienna at the end of the Napoleonic Wars and to reassert French leadership on the continent.

After the decade of political brinkmanship that reached its climax at Magenta and Solferino, Napoleon III stood at the height of his power. But what he intended to do with this power remained uncertain. To the intense disappointment of Sardinia, he declined to impose a victor's settlement on the defeated Austrians. His restraint accomplished little. The Austrians were not mollified. Nor were the Italian nationalists subdued: Napoleon's victories excited a movement that he could not thereafter subordinate to his purposes. Indeed, the speed with which Italy proceeded to unify itself, and the consequent threat to the political autonomy of the Pope in Rome, opened a rift between Napoleon and French Catholics.

Needing to reduce the alarm that his Italian campaign had aroused, he therefore welcomed the overture that Cobden made to him in the autumn of 1859. Napoleon had no wish to add Britain to his adversaries; he saw that as his uncle's fatal mistake. The enmity of Britain was not a necessary consequence of his own continental ambitions. Moreover, while a commercial treaty need not greatly fetter his freedom of diplomatic manœuvre, it could serve to extend the sway of France as possessor of the strongest economy and largest national market on the continent. Napoleon was also inclined to believe, though never in a doctrinaire fashion, that lower tariffs would increase the competitive stimulus to French industry and also improve the standard of living of the working classes by lowering consumer prices. But what made an Anglo–French agreement not merely appealing but urgent was the impending announcement that, as a result of his support in their summertime campaign, Napoleon had induced Sardinia to cede the provinces of Nice and Savoy to France – news that would awaken old fears of French expansionism. If a commercial agreement could be reached before the announcement was made, it would offset British fears by indicating that Napoleon wanted good relations with them and that his ambitions were not directed across the Channel. His cessation of the Italian war after Solferino had left him with unspent money in his war chest, funds he could use to reduce French opposition to a treaty by financing loans 'to help out the industries most harmed (or most likely to complain of harm) by the sudden removal of prohibitions and to encourage modernization of plant and equipment to make French industry more competitive . . . the bulk going to textiles, metallurgy, and mining.'[16]

For three months Napoleon kept his intentions veiled while encouraging Cobden to negotiate clandestinely with those in the French ministry who favoured freer trade. The need to work in secret so as not to arouse the protectionist interests in France prematurely amused rather than angered Cobden. He had long inveighed against the evils of secret diplomacy, but now it served his cause. He kept the British government informed about the progress of the discussions. Russell at the Foreign Office followed them sympathetically, Palmerston less so, though he welcomed the prospective improvement in relations with France.

Still, for fear of the risk to the Treasury, Gladstone took issue with 'one of the essential bases' that Cobden offered Napoleon, 'the lowering of duty of 1s.

per gallon on all French wines which entered into general consumption'.[17] The interest that many governments – though not the French – took in tariff talks had almost as much to do with revenue as with regulation, the issue with which the manufacturing and mercantile community was preoccupied. The concession the French most wanted from Britain was in the duty on their wine, which at nearly six shillings a gallon effectively excluded it from the British market. Cobden offered a reduction to a single shilling, as the French wished. He described his proposal as giving the French government a 'moral claim' on the British, but Gladstone refused to honour it fully because of the impact it would have had on the revenue the Treasury received from the duty on spirits even more than from the wine duty, for the former was assessed in proportion to the latter. Gladstone could make a principled defence for his refusal. Mill had argued that, when it came to revenue duties as distinct from protective duties, 'considerations of reciprocity' could fairly be taken into account. 'A country', Mill explained, 'cannot be expected to renounce the power of taxing foreigners, unless foreigners will in return practise towards itself the same forbearance.'[18] Gladstone replaced the uniform duty that Cobden had offered Napoleon with a graduated one based on weight or alcoholic strength. The eventual scale imposed a duty of 1s. on the weakest wines, 1s. 9d. on heavier wines, 2s. 5d. on the still heavier, and 2s. 11d. on those close to spirits in strength.

The trouble with this scale was that it discriminated in favour of the light yet often expensive wines of France and against the heavier yet often cheaper wines of the Mediterranean. That regional favouritism ran contrary to Gladstone's economic principles. It also preserved some bargaining power for the British, a dividend from which he recoiled. He boasted, particularly after the enactment of his budget for 1860, that Britain admitted imports on an absolutely non-preferential basis, without regard to the country of origin. His graduation of the wine duties belied his boast. While France was disappointed that some of its wines would not enjoy the lowest duty, it drew satisfaction from the knowledge that little of the wine from the other producing states of the Mediterranean would do so. Gladstone described this discrimination quite candidly when he first outlined his scheme to the House of Commons.

Britain and France interpreted the balance in the concessions which they made to each other quite differently. The British denied that they were making concessions at all. Most of the changes in the British tariff were put into effect unilaterally in the budget for the year, which Gladstone presented to parliament after the signature of the treaty; and they applied to every country regardless of its tariff. The British government was ready to admit that it reduced the wine duty further than the Treasury would have liked in order to meet the French demand. The other obvious British concession to the French lay in the agreement of both parties not to prohibit or lay any duty on their export of coal, an issue of military importance to the French who were large coal importers. Otherwise the British were anxious to deny that they had done anything specially for France, putting the emphasis instead on all they were doing for free trade. Gladstone's budget slashed the number of articles in the British tariff from 419 to 48, bringing to a climax the long line of reductions begun by Peel in 1842 when the tariff extended to more than 4,000 articles. Britain sought, as Gladstone later put it, 'to show the world that, while it is a good to substitute low duties for high duties, to change low duties into no duties at all is, in the view of national wealth, a still greater good.'[19] The government trusted that, within a very few years, as France began and Britain continued to prosper, the wisdom of free trade would ignite a bonfire of tariffs throughout the trading world.

From the French point of view, the reductions in their tariff under the treaty of 1860 constituted a much greater and more daring departure in policy than did the British. In those terms the French were right. Their former tariff had been not just protective but often prohibitive, reducing British trade with France to minuscule proportions. Now that the policy had been reversed, the benefit that British merchants expected worried the French. Cobden might not care about widening foreign markets for British goods, but it was that prospect that made British manufacturers strong supporters of his treaty and alarmed their French counterparts. There was nothing in the French experience to foster confidence in the consequences of free trade.

Wisely as it turned out, though to Gladstone's occasional dismay, Cobden framed the treaty so as to give the French plenty of time to ascertain the specific needs of key industries and then to test the impact of the first tariff reductions before making further ones. So long as the French would agree to an initial maximum for their industrial tariffs of 30 per cent, Cobden was happy to allow them the best part of a year for commissions of inquiry to set the particular rate for each industry, and another four years before lowering the maximum rate to 25 per cent. These rates were higher and extended to a much wider range of goods than in the British tariff. British commentators dwelt on these disparities in their reaction to the treaty. The French, however, argued that they were making a much greater change in policy than the British, who were merely completing a reform already well advanced.[20] France was transforming its whole approach to international trade and recasting its entire tariff. It was abandoning an often prohibitive tariff for a selectively protective one and holding out hope of substantially lower rates of duty on manufactured goods in the near future. The treaty, moreover, explicitly envisaged extending this policy to the other trading partners of the two signatory states. The French proceeded to honour the spirit as well as the letter of these commitments to an extent that delighted but eventually disconcerted the British.

b. Bradford and the British Mercantile Response

The financial interests of the City of London, as voiced by *The Economist*, responded coolly to the news of the treaty. They were more concerned about the loss of revenue the government would incur from the slashing of the British tariff than gratified by the widened market for British goods. Though Walter Bagehot, who began to assume control of *The Economist* in 1860, was a liberal internationalist in his sympathies and not insensitive to the needs of trade, his heart lay in the banking world of Lombard Street. Striking a note that was to differentiate British devotees of free trade from commercial liberals on the continent, *The Economist* drew an invidious distinction between British producers, meaning manufacturers, and the common interest of the entire nation as consumers: 'no doubt manufacturers are pleased at the prospect of a wider market for such goods as England can best supply. But English producers are comparatively a small class, and by no means a depressed class. Their gain is to some extent, no doubt, the gain of the whole community; but still this is an indirect and gradual process.'[21] The reduction of foreign tariffs would benefit British consumers only slowly, as it led to an increase in manufacturing capacity. Consumers would benefit more quickly from the reduction in Britain's own tariff, which would immediately lower the cost of imports from France; but the loss of revenue to the Treasury would have to be made good somehow.

The treaty received a more cordial welcome from British manufacturers, especially from the woollens industry of West Yorkshire and particularly Bradford. For a peculiar mixture of reasons, woollens proved to be the pivotal sector of British industry, and Bradford played the premier role among British manufacturing centres in the creation and then preservation of the European commercial treaty network inaugurated in 1860. Hitherto both woollens and Bradford had played secondary parts in the industrialisation of Britain. Cottons rapidly outstripped woollens as the leading sector in the textiles industry during the first half of the nineteenth century, joining iron and steel as one of the engines of British industrialisation. Furthermore, Bradford played second fiddle to Leeds among the centres of the woollens industry in West Yorkshire until mid-century. That Bradford rather than Leeds provided leadership in the second half of the century was essentially a matter of personnel, but the importance of woollens to the commercial diplomacy of Europe after 1860 was built on more substantial foundations.

The manufacture of woollens was deeply rooted in the economy of Europe generally. Woollens had constituted one of the great staples of the European market since the Middle Ages. Continental producers worked more skilfully with this familiar fibre, well suited to their cold winters, than with foreign-grown cotton. Concentrated in Lancashire, the ascendancy of Britain in the manufacture and merchandising of cottons was further fortified by the position of Liverpool as the port of entry for raw cotton to the entire European market. The competition that the cotton masters of Lancashire feared came mainly from India, whereas the most serious rivalry to the British woollens industry in the nineteenth century came from continental Europe; production in the United States was small.[22] The comparative importance of woollens to the European market was increased in the early 1860s by the interruption of the cotton supply from the southern United States as a result of the Civil War. Still cotton so dominated the British conception of the textile industry that the British Foreign Secretary at the time, Lord John Russell, continued to use the word 'cotton' to mean all textiles.

Continental woollens producers were stimulated as well as alarmed by the general economic ascendancy Britain acquired in the first half of the nineteenth century, and they strove hard to preserve their share of the market. Competition in this sector was particularly fierce between Britain and France: hence the pivotal role of woollens in all the tariff talks of the 1860s. The French could make headway in this area without the amount of tariff protection they required in cottons. They were less interested in the other engine of British industrial dominance, in iron and steel, than were the Germans. French skill in the manufacture of fine textiles – silks and muslins as well as woollens – was unrivalled in Britain. The British advantage in textile production generally lay at the lower end of the market, in the production of cheap but serviceable goods for the mass market abroad as well as at home. Cotton cloth found its best market in hot climates, above all in Asia.[23] Woollens looked to states with cool climates, much the most populous of which lay in Europe. The woollens manufacturers of West Yorkshire came up with a host of measures to cheapen their wares without damaging their utility. One way, with which Bradford was particularly associated, was to interweave cotton fibres, which were inexpensive, with wefts of wool, which was most costly.[24] The combination resulted in not only cheaper but more durable fabric. Bradford manufacturers also introduced mohair and alpaca to the world of textiles, producing fabric with a sheen that appealed to the tastes of the moment.

Bradford's interest in Europe had been further quickened since the 1830s with the arrival of German traders, familiar with the opportunities as well as risks of the continental market. This addition to the entrepreneurial mix in Bradford was inseparable from its leading figure, Jacob Behrens. He was to become the most influential merchant in the formulation of British commercial policy for the next half-century. The extent of that sway is reflected in the remarkable set of annual reports, minute books and printed correspondence preserved by the Chamber of Commerce in Bradford under his leadership. So rich are those records that they leave an undoubtedly exaggerated impression of the impact Behrens and Bradford had on British response to the commercial treaty network created in the 1860s. Yet the proceedings of the national association of Chambers of Commerce and the official correspondence of those responsible for commercial diplomacy at the Foreign Office provide ample evidence of their reliance on Behrens's grasp of the intricacies of the treaty system and of the needs of his town and industry in shaping their policy.

Behrens was born in 1809 into a Jewish textile-making family in Pyrmont, a small town 40 miles south of Hanover and 100 miles south of Hamburg.[25] In the heady aftermath of the Napoleonic Wars, the family relocated to Hanover so that their business could expand. But they found that the move increased their costs more than their sales. Consequently, as the eldest son Jacob had to give up his schooling at the age of thirteen and devote himself to the family business.

They bought mainly woollen cloth, in part from English producers, and sold it at the fairs and markets of the chief northern German towns. Once his father had familiarised him with these markets, Jacob took over the travelling and soon increased their sales. He took advantage of the widened market opened by the German customs union, or Zollverein, formed under the leadership of Prussia. Behrens pressed on to the port cities on the Baltic and into Berlin with such success that he exhausted his supplies at Hamburg and had to hurry off orders to England. This introduced him to the limitations of British enterprise. His supplier would not furnish him with the kind of finish on goods and the smaller bales that German buyers preferred, nor would he answer Behrens's letters. In the summer of 1832 Behrens travelled to Leeds, then the centre of the English woollen trade, to meet his supplier. His mission was kindly received but fruitless. A return mission in 1833 met with only partial success.

Behrens took matters into his own hands, and in doing so made a fundamental change in the European textile trade. He stayed on in Leeds and opened up an establishment of his own to meet his packaging needs. He was not the first German merchant in the woollens trade to open up a branch in England, but he was the first to proceed independently of his German base. Bypassing Hamburg, he sold what he packaged in Leeds to German importing merchants and soon, circumventing them, directly to their customers. As he saw it, 'the commission-merchant on the spot in England, buying for foreign customers, with expert knowledge and at market prices, had obvious advantages over the stock-holding merchant on the Continent who – far from knowledge or control of his source of supply – bought from one or two manufacturers at whatever rates they chose to fix.'[26] The woollens merchants of Yorkshire with whom he now competed did not welcome this development, but Behrens was nonetheless able to establish himself thanks to the orders he received from the textile houses of Hamburg.

One more move completed the change in the organisation of the trade. Leeds had established itself as the English trading centre, but most of the woollen textiles on the Leeds market were made nine miles away, in Bradford. This distance deprived merchants of familiarity with manufacturers' costs and capacities, knowledge they needed in order to price their wares effectively. The merchants of Leeds recoiled at the thought of moving: Bradford was an ugly town that had sprung up from almost nothing at the beginning of the century and still lacked the cultural amenities that the Leeds merchants were creating for themselves. Behrens appreciated these considerations; but economic logic drove him to Bradford in 1838. The ties of friendship and culture of which he was once again depriving himself quickened the civic spirit that he brought to his new home. He determined to do all he could to serve the needs of the town and industry that gave him his wealth.

The move to Bradford placed Behrens at the most sensitive point of conflict between British and French industry. Bradford brought together all the resources needed for the production of low-priced woollens. It owed its ascent as an industrial town to some natural advantages and the skills already possessed by nearby labour, drawn together by entrepreneurs. The town stood at the confluence of three valleys,[27] beneath which lay soft water that was good for washing wool. Ironstone, building-stone and seams of coal lay nearby for the construction and fuelling of the mills. The surrounding hills contained a population familiar with the elementary skills of spinning and weaving wool and desperate to raise their standard of living. The population of Bradford soared from some 13,000 at the beginning of the nineteenth century past 100,000 at mid-century, making it one of the fastest-growing towns in Britain. As the town expanded, railways converged upon it. A canal linked it to Hull on the east coast and Liverpool on the west. The product for which Bradford became particularly famous was worsted[28] woollens. Worsteds were tightly woven from wool that had been spun to ensure the maximum length and parallelism in the fibres.[29] Worsteds were not fulled, that is to say thickened through washing and pressure, after being woven. They often contained other fibres such as cotton or silk interwoven with the wool. The best-known manufacturers of Bradford, men such as Titus Salt and S.C. Lister, made their names through technological innovation, whether of cost-cutting machinery, improved dyeing systems, the incorporation of new fibres or salvaging usable fibres from scrap.

In the 1850s, however, the expansion of Bradford slowed down, partly because of machinery that reduced the need for additional manpower, but also because of a stagnant market across the Channel. Behrens extended his operations into the Low Countries, Italy and further afield, though never, significantly, to the United States. He and his fellow merchants were especially frustrated by their failures to penetrate the richest continental market of all, the French, from which they were excluded by the prohibitive tariff. The businessmen of Bradford organised themselves at the beginning of the decade into a Chamber of Commerce to work out a common response to their problems, including the restricted continental market. At the end of the decade, delegates from many of the other Chambers of Commerce in Britain converged upon Bradford to form a national association.

Maurice Chevalier looked to Bradford for support in the autumn of 1859 when trying to induce Cobden to seek a commercial agreement with France. Once Cobden had secured it, he and the Board of Trade asked the Bradford Chamber of Commerce, among others, for help. The negotiators remaining in Paris wanted assistance from people familiar with the costs and requirements of the branches of industry most affected by the tariffs that French commissions of inquiry were to make more specific under the general provisions of the treaty. Cobden and the Board of Trade sent their requests to representatives of other industrial sectors; but it was from Bradford that they received the most eager and informative response.

This involvement of Chambers of Commerce in the work of commercial treaty-making opened a new chapter in the always uneasy relationships involved in this kind of diplomatic activity. There were tensions within government as well as between government and commerce. The aristocratic Foreign Office relied but looked down upon the commercial fact-gathering responsibilities of the Board of Trade, while the business community was suspicious of the competence and intentions of any governmental office but especially of the Foreign Office when it came to the regulation of commerce. Cobden approached his negotiations with France as a friend and admirer of business. Bradford and to a lesser extent other centres of manufacturing industry embraced his approach with enthusiasm, but the Foreign Office never warmed to it.

Bradford was concerned about the nature and basis as well as about the level of the French tariff. The French insisted on specific duties, based on the weight and composition of the fabric. Bradford called for a 10 per cent *ad valorem* tariff, based on the fabric's value. Cobden fought hard for *ad valorem* duties before discussion was opened up to representatives of British business. When he failed, he urged the latter to accept the inevitable. The delegation from Bradford refused. There were several points to their argument, one that applied to all textiles, the others peculiar to worsteds. Specific duties based on weight would discriminate against the heavy but cheap stuffs that British textile-makers, whether of cottons or woollens, marketed well for working-class consumption. The problem with specific duties was compounded for worsteds because of 'the endless variety of textures & of mixtures of materials'[30] with which they were made. This variety affected prices, which differed still further as new fibres were introduced. The pains the Bradford committee took under Behrens's leadership in preparing their case and their lucidity in presenting it delighted Cobden. 'Well,' he told them, 'if you go before the French government, and show them, clearly and distinctly, that it is impossible, from the nature of the materials used and their combination, to fix a specific duty, then, I have no doubt the Emperor and his government will make an exception in your case.'[31] When H.W. Ripley, the dye-maker who was president of the Bradford Chamber of Commerce, questioned his confidence in the good faith of the French government, Cobden replied that these suspicions were unfounded. He underscored his faith in the French authorities by predicting that they would not levy the duty at the full 30 per cent allowed by the treaty and were unlikely to set the duty on yarns above 10 per cent.

Encouraged by Cobden, the Bradford Chamber persuaded *The Economist* to take a more hopeful view of the treaty and to support their stance on how the French textile duties should be levied.[32] The Chamber's tariff committee prepared themselves well for the French. There were two sets of meetings. In July 1860 a five-man delegation persuaded French manufacturers that it was impossible to devise a system of classification for worsteds detailed enough to serve as a satisfactory basis for specific duties. Back in Bradford, the delegates reported that the Frenchmen in charge of revising their tariff were 'steadily and conscientiously working to arrange such duties as will allow a large importation of English goods and produce a good revenue from the custom-house, while still affording a protection to the French producer.'[33] In October a smaller delegation under Behrens's chairmanship returned to Paris at Cobden's behest and worked closely with him for the best part of a month. Joined by a deputation from Leeds and Huddersfield, they thrashed out the different needs of worsted and other woollen fabrics. Their objective was to secure a specific scale of duties as close as possible to the *ad valorem* tariff they always preferred. At one point, when the French brought in a greatly improved proposal and the Bradford delegates still objected in the name of free trade, Cobden advised them to 'Put your principles in your pocket, and aim only for lowest duties which will let you sell the most stuff.'[34] It was a remarkable statement from the chief apostle of free trade; it might have served beneficially as the first commandment to all British negotiators through the subsequent history of the European commercial treaty network.

Ad valorem duties were, of course, no more consistent with free-trade theory than specific duties. But theory was not the point. The concrete criticisms the Bradford delegates brought to bear on every proposal for specific duties finally wore the French down. To the delighted surprise of Behrens and his friends, they secured a 15 per cent *ad valorem* duty for most textiles, to be reduced to 10 per cent in 1864, though specific duties were applied to the finer yarns. The French commissioners set the customs dues for most sectors of French industry to begin substantially below the 30 per cent that the treaty allowed. The new tariff averaged 20 per cent for cutlery, 10 per cent for glassware, china and earthenware, between 10 and 12 per cent for tools, and between 10 and 15 per cent for chemicals, while industrial raw materials were admitted free of duty.

Cobden shared the special pleasure of the men from Bradford at this outcome. Thereafter he and they regarded the way they had worked together in Paris as the model for all tariff treaty negotiations. Cobden was only sorry that the cotton masters of Manchester had not followed Bradford's example – Manchester paid for its lack of diligence when the French tariff proved less favourable to cottons than to woollens. Behrens looked back afterwards on his three and a half weeks with Cobden as the highlight of his life. The two men had approached the negotiations in the same frame of mind, rooted in and informed by business, which they regarded as the best agency for building peaceful relations between nations. Cobden took an almost paternal pleasure in Behrens's knowledge of his branch of industry. In turn he tried to teach Behrens a little of what he knew about handling men in government, but in the process imbued him with his own impatience at the impeding practices and incomprehension of commerce that characterised the Foreign Office. British commercial diplomacy would continue to be fractured by a lack of sympathetic understanding among those who sought to direct it.

c. The High Politics of the European Market

Cobden conducted the negotiations with France with more astuteness and to greater effect than the British were to display again in their commercial diplomacy for a very long time. Yet neither he nor the ablest practitioners of traditional diplomacy at the Foreign Office grasped all that the Anglo-French treaty might mean for the international order of Europe.

As it happened, the agent who would be called upon in the 1880s to deal with the collapse of the agreement as Britain's first Commercial Attaché for Europe, Joseph Archer Crowe, received his appointment to government service while Cobden was negotiating in Paris. Crowe's appointment as British consul-general for the kingdom of Saxony gave him an early glimpse of the imperial policy upon which Napoleon III embarked in concluding his treaty with Britain. Crowe was posted in Leipzig, a good vantage-point from which to observe the emergence of the German power that would eventually take over the leadership of the commercial treaty network that France and Britain set up.

He received conventional instructions for a consul-general, to devote himself 'to the encouragement of British Trade with Leipzig and to furnishing Her Majesty's Government with useful and interesting information relating to Commerce, Navigation, Agriculture and any other branch of Statistics.'[35] As was usual in the diplomatic service, Crowe possessed no familiarity with the world of commerce or other qualification for this assignment beyond a general sympathy with the movement for free trade. He had, however, a gift for languages, a ready pen and an eye for significant detail. Born in 1825 to a struggling Whig journalist who sought to escape from the high cost of living in London, Crowe was brought in infancy to Paris: indeed, French was his first language. As he grew older, he became acquainted with French friends of his father such as Thiers and Barthélemy St Hilaire who would be prominent in the Third Republic when he came to deal with its commercial policy.

But his deepest love was for art. His eventual distinction as a connoisseur earned him a welcome in the aristocratic world of diplomacy which he would not otherwise have received. When his drawing skills as a youth proved unequal to the higher demands of art, he deployed them as an art historian. Crowe and a young Italian nationalist, Giovanni Battista Cavalcaselle, met in 1847 as they travelled through northern Germany in search of works from the different parts of Europe where the Renaissance had begun. Animated by their common fascination with the work of painters both famous and forgotten, the two men devoted their lives, Cavalcaselle entirely and Crowe as much as the other demands upon him would allow, to the preparation and publication of studies of Renaissance art. They committed themselves to the painstaking observation of works of art long advocated by art historians[36] but as yet scarcely put into practice. Crowe's work as a connoisseur sharpened his skills of observation, gave fluency to his pen and made him a respected visitor to the great houses where the rulers of Europe displayed their grandeur through their collections of art.

But that was not what drew Crowe to the attention of Lord John Russell, who as Foreign Secretary was responsible for the appointment to Leipzig. Russell knew of Crowe as a war correspondent: and in this capacity Crowe had developed still other skills that would serve him well in the consular and diplomatic service. In 1843, when his father became a leader-writer for the *Morning Chronicle*, Crowe, then a young man of 18, had followed him back from Paris to London and into journalism. He was aided here by his artistic skills. The *Illustrated London News* sent him to draw as well as report on the Crimean War. Subsequently *The Times* asked him to cover another war – that between France and Austria in northern Italy which led to Cobden's treaty.

Crowe's involvement in commercial diplomacy thus arose very differently from Cobden's, and the difference never ceased to colour the commentary Crowe offered on the commercial treaty network that Cobden inspired. *The Times* was dissatisfied with the war reports it was receiving from the Austrian side, and despatched Crowe by way of Vienna to the headquarters of the emperor Francis Joseph at Verona. Crowe's fluency in German, his ease in the saddle and familiarity with the ways of war enabled him to ride with the small party that accompanied the Emperor as he witnessed the defeat around the hilltop tower of Solferino. Crowe's vivid portrayal for *The Times* of the scenes prompted Russell to send him afterwards on an unofficial mission of inquiry into the repercussions of the Austrian defeat on the divided and demoralised states of Germany. While sympathetic to Italian unification, Russell did not know what to make of Germany, split as it was between conservative Austria, a confused Prussia and the lesser German principalities, united only by the all-German Diet at Frankfurt.

Hence, while Cobden completed his negotiations in Paris, Crowe travelled in Central Europe, mainly to the secondary German states about which Russell knew least. Napoleon III provided a common denominator in these contributions to foreign policy-making, Crowe's in Germany as well as Cobden's in France. In the aftermath of the Italian war, Napoleon probed Germany, looking for opportunities to extend French influence over the Rhine. The great underlying issue was the settlement that the powers that defeated the first Napoleon had imposed on France in 1815 at the Congress of Vienna. The defeat at Solferino of Austria, the chief guardian of the Vienna settlement, opened up an opportunity for release from its constraints. Italy was already taking advantage of the chance to throw off the Austrian yoke and unite. The only doubt regarding Napoleon III was how far he would go to break through the barriers that the Congress of Vienna had erected against French expansionism. About the aspirations of the divided Germans, on the other hand, there was complete uncertainty.

Crowe moved readily among the middle rank of the German governing and mercantile classes to whom Russell discreetly introduced him. By upbringing, as Russell knew, Crowe was a thoroughly English Liberal. He interpreted the Germans accordingly. The situation he discovered was such as to tempt Napoleon into rather than to deter him from stretching his tentacles over the Rhine. In a report that was passed on to the Queen, Crowe observed that 'The weakness of Prussia . . . the prostration of Austria & the symptoms of aggressive tendencies on the part of France, all this has tended to create anxiety & depression amongst all the classes of the people. . . . I have myself heard respectable men of the middle & working classes discussing the question as to whether it would not be better to live under a powerful monarchy like that of France, rather than remain in the hands of such weak & selfish princes as now.'[37] Personally Crowe sympathised with the Protestant liberals of the National verein and their allies among the German princes[38] who looked to the unification of Germany and the enlargement of commerce through a parliamentary style of governance under the direction of Prussia. He received a particularly cordial welcome from the Duke of Saxe-Coburg-Gotha, the brother of Prince Albert. With flattering candour, the Duke made Crowe aware of his anger as well as disappointment at the failure of the Prussian monarchy to provide liberal nationalists in Germany with a resolute lead against the pretensions of reactionary Austria. The conversation and confidences that Crowe enjoyed with his German hosts led him to report with assurance on the cast of mind of the German people, though his acquaintance excluded much of the highest and all of the lowest social strata. Still, when Russell passed Crowe's reports on to Windsor, Prince Albert judged them to be the ablest British report he had yet read on the situation in Germany.

Crowe regarded his ensuing appointment to Leipzig as in some measure a continuation of his unofficial assignment in Germany. During his first months at his new post, he reported on the rival manoeuvres of Prussia and Austria, on debates in the Nationalverein, on contests between princes and parliaments and concordats with the papacy in the minor states, on attempts by Napoleon III to extend his power into the German vacuum, and on German nationalist reaction against the Danish attempt to absorb the duchy of Schleswig. But the paucity of the response he received on these issues from the Foreign Office indicated to him that his primary responsibilities lay elsewhere; and thenceforth he paid increasing attention to the Central European market.

Leipzig was the site of one of the great fairs of Central Europe. Three times a year the primarily agricultural producers to the east, from Russia and the Balkans, came to Leipzig to exchange their wares for the manufactured goods, mainly textiles, produced in the mills of Saxony and the more industrial parts of Western Europe. The British had a substantial interest in the Leipzig market. After a year's observation of the non-German presence at the fairs, Crowe estimated that 'Of Woollen manufactures $\frac{9}{10}$ are British, $\frac{1}{10}$ French. Of Iron manufactures, the whole import is British. Of leather manufactures $\frac{9}{10}$ are British – of linen yarn . . . $\frac{9}{10}$ are English – of woollen yarn $\frac{9}{10}$ are British and of the remainder, Great Britain furnishes on an average about $\frac{5}{10}$. England's share in the imports of Leipzig in 1860 may thus be taken at about 2 millions sterling.'[39] But the Leipzig fairs had already passed their heyday. Merchants like Behrens of Bradford sold manufactured goods directly to wholesalers all over the continent, bypassing Leipzig. The railways being constructed across Europe assisted this new trade, as did the gradual freeing of the great continental waterways from the tolls imposed by each state through which they flowed. Crowe reported on how Prussia urged other states along the Rhine to consolidate and simplify their toll collection, since otherwise the railway network in France and Belgium would continue to divert traffic away from the German states.

The prospective lowering of the French tariff under Cobden's treaty chilled the Leipzig fair in the autumn of 1860. Buyers held off in expectation of lower prices once the talks in Paris were complete. Here was the first faint sign of the French power and ambition that lay behind the treaty with Britain. Napoleon hoped that it would strengthen the economic muscle of France and thus help to extend French influence across the continent. Cobden never thought in those terms. He believed 'that the Emperor has renounced the policy of war & conquest & that instead of the sword of the great Napoleon, he will wield the pen of Sir Robert Peel.'[40] But the commercial treaty-making of the next half-dozen years was to involve considerations of empire and state-building that Cobden clearly never anticipated when he initiated the process.

Chapter 3

The Construction of the Network, 1861–1866

'Every new Commercial Treaty was at once a model and a starting point, a pattern for imitation and a basis for further development.'

Lord Napier to Lord Russell, 24 Mar. 1865

The most remarkable thing about the Anglo-French treaty of 1860 was the chain reaction it produced. Within six years, France had signed up another 11 commercial treaty partners and Britain another four. These made further agreements among themselves and also brought additional states into the network until it embraced all of Western and Central Europe. The treaties were interlocked through most-favoured-nation clauses that entitled the signatories to the lowest duties to which any two of them had agreed. Thus, although every treaty was bilateral in form, the resulting network was effectively multilateral. Even more important than the formal shape were the consequences of the network. Each new treaty further lowered the tariff barriers that had fragmented the European market from time out of mind.

It might all have looked like the fulfilment of Cobden's dream of a world that embraced free trade, a world where tariffs fell away like scales from its eyes as it perceived the truth first illuminated by the British example; but already, by the time that his treaty with France was completed, Cobden was disappointed by Britain's suspicion of Napoleon's ambitions. In a variety of ways, the rivalries that divided Europe politically were intensified as much as alleviated by the process of commercial negotiation initiated by Cobden. Moreover, Gladstone's elimination of all but a handful of duties deprived Britain of the weapons it needed to obtain as good terms as France secured in constructing the network foreshadowed in their treaty.

a. The Belgian Treaty

Russell, Foreign Secretary and now an earl, moved to obtain commercial treaties with other European countries even before Cobden had finished work on the initial treaty in Paris. Though sceptical about their value, as an archetypal Whig Russell was happy to wrap himself in a progressive mantle that promised to please the industrial community at home and promote good relations abroad. In June 1860 he asked his office and also the Board of Trade for draft treaties with Spain, Portugal and Austria.[1] But he did not press the mater. Though informed that France had already begun commercial discussions with Belgium, Russell did not follow suit until those two countries opened formal treaty talks at the end of the year.

Belgium, the only country on the continent that approached Britain's level of industrialisation, was France's third largest supplier,[2] with strengths that complemented more than they competed with the French. France hoped not just to improve market access over its northern border but in a sense to incorporate Belgium into its economic realm, an objective fully consonant with Napoleon's political ambitions. To the Belgians, that prospect had attractions as well as dangers. Their country made economic sense only in association with its immediate neighbours, including Rhineland Prussia and the Netherlands as well as Britain and France. Yet it was also their battlefield. It owed its political independence, barely 30 years old and still precarious, to a treaty that most of its neighbours had accepted with reluctance. The independence of Belgium marked the first rupture of the Vienna settlement: it separated itself from the kingdom of the Netherlands, which had been enlarged at Vienna to strengthen the barrier against French expansion to the north. The objective of Belgium in its trade negotiations was, accordingly, to strengthen its political independence through economic development in co-operation with its neighbours.

British merchants were irritated by Belgium's preferential treatment of France even before the new treaty was signed. Belgium already gave France special favours in its tariff in order to reduce the French duty on the import of linens, long vital to the Belgian economy. In its negotiations with Belgium at the end of 1860, the French government sought to maintain and improve upon these privileges, while Belgium sought admission to the benefits of the French treaty with Britain. Belgium expected to open parallel negotiations with Britain. But France bargained stiffly, harder than the Belgians had anticipated, delaying the opening of these talks. France extracted substantial concessions from Belgium, on wine, brandy and silks. In return, France granted Belgium some improvement on the terms of the Anglo-French agreement, particularly on linens.[3] The Belgian government, with its liberal trade minister Frère-Orban, welcomed the treaty. They attempted to minimise protectionist criticism by submitting the treaty to the legislature for approval shortly before it was scheduled to recess. The Belgian protectionists, who were particularly strong among the manufacturers of cotton goods in Ghent, were roused too late to block it. They took out their frustration on the subsequent treaty with Britain.

This turn of events took Russell by surprise. He had expected an agreement with Belgium to fall into Britain's lap as a natural sequel to its treaty with France; he had never imagined a Franco-Belgian agreement that might work against British interests. But the interests of Belgium and Britain, though closely tied together, were no more identical than were those of Britain and

France. Nor did the economic interests of any of these countries necessarily point in the same direction as its political concerns. The political economy of tariff treaty-making was more complex than the official British understanding of free trade allowed.

The merchants of Bradford, who naturally focused on their particular interests, were much more clear-sighted about the trade talks with Belgium than Russell. They had struggled to secure a market there and, despite stiff Belgian competition, had managed to make woollens the most valuable Belgian import from Britain. In order to make the most of this market, the Bradford Chamber of Commerce had for years been demanding that the Foreign Office do something about the unfairness of the Franco-Belgian tariff, but to no avail. The Bradford Chamber feared that the existing inequality would be compounded by any new agreement negotiated between Belgium and France unless immediately accompanied by a treaty between Belgium and Britain. The Chamber urged the Foreign Office to keep abreast of the Franco-Belgian negotiations, as the Belgians had done with the Anglo-French talks: again to no avail. The treaty that Belgium and France signed at the end of April 1861 confirmed all the Chamber's fears. Understandably, Bradford accused the Foreign Office of negligence. The Bradford Chamber had been pleasantly surprised the previous year when the Board of Trade had sought its input in the negotiations with France. But after the French agreement was secured, the government apparently reverted to its old practices and seemed reluctant even to respond to letters from the Chamber.

In fact, Russell had forwarded these letters to the Board of Trade for its commentary. The Board not only confirmed Bradford's complaint of Belgian discrimination against British goods, but pointed out concrete ways in which a tariff treaty between Britain and Belgium could lessen the imbalance.[4] But the fears of the Board were allayed and Russell was comforted by reassurance from Lord Howard de Walden, the British minister in Brussels, that the Belgian government had every intention of admitting British goods on the same terms as French goods. Bradford remained suspicious; and when the terms of the Franco-Belgian treaty were finalised and published, Bradford turned out to be a better judge than Lord Howard de Walden of the Belgian government's commercial intentions.

The Belgian ministers took care always to speak to the British in the language of free trade. But they were commercial liberals of the continental sort, more concerned to strengthen their state through economic development than to liberate individual enterprise on the British model. When pressed by industrial interests within its own borders, the Belgian ministry responded protectively, if indirectly. They agreed whenever the British argued that protective tariffs would ultimately hurt the people they were supposed to help, but the Belgian government nonetheless felt obliged to protect its own political position against opposition in the legislature to tariff reductions affecting major local industries, particularly the cotton textiles makers of Ghent. Lord Howard de Walden discovered to his dismay that the industrial interests hostile to an agreement with Britain were emboldened by the 'consideration that they are actually in enjoyment of all the benefits conferred by the British tariff as well as of the protection still afforded under the Belgian tariff against the competition of British manufactures.'[5] The opposition from Ghent underlined the fragility of Belgium as a still unproven state divided in religion and language as well as economic interests. In order to convince the legislature and electorate that they stood up for Belgium, the ministry sought some concession beyond what Britain had granted France. After all, the French had just granted Belgium better terms on textiles than they had granted the British. Belgium wanted Britain to follow suit. Russell found himself confronted with a demand for what the Belgians called 'compensation' – concessions that could be presented to the Belgian legislature as payment before British goods could be admitted on the same terms as French ones to the Belgian market.

Talk of compensation struck Russell as outrageous. Under Gladstone's tariff of 1860, Britain already gave Belgium along with the rest of the world free admission for most of its exports, far better terms than Belgium had from France even under their new treaty. Why should Britain pay more to enjoy simple parity with France in the Belgian market? Belgium's preference for France was all the more galling because Britain was the chief guarantor of the independence of Belgium, upon which France looked with predatory eyes. Russell's reaction held up agreement with Belgium for a long time.

Blame for the delay fell more on him than on the Belgians. The manufacturers and merchants of Bradford, ably led by their Member of Parliament, W.E. Forster, who was himself in the woollens industry, charged the Foreign Office with a lack of commitment to the advancement of Britain's industrial interests. This suspicion, founded on past experience, was borne out by the eagerness with which the Foreign Office embraced the doctrine of free trade and its corollary insistence that public servants distance themselves from private interests. Forster reacted as indignantly as Russell to the Belgian demand for compensation. The businessmen of Bradford were confident that the expertise that they had put so effectively at Cobden's disposal in Paris could have worked with similar success in Brussels, if only the Foreign Office had deigned to call upon their help. The Foreign Office did not request assistance, however, and so did not receive it. Yet the Foreign Office could not simply walk away from the controversy. Too much was at stake, as the Board of Trade pointed out, 'considering the great importance to the trade of the United Kingdom generally of securing access to the markets of Belgium on favourable terms.'[6] However angrily Russell reacted to the demands of the Belgian ministers, ultimately he had to do as they bade.

The Board of Trade woke up to the situation earlier than the Foreign Office, and tried to heighten Russell's sense of the significance of the continental market. The mutiny in India and the Taiping rebellion in China focused attention on the safer markets across the Channel. Evidence of protectionist sentiment in Britain's self-governing colonies added to the Board's uneasiness at the outlook overseas. Those disturbances compounded the greatest upheaval of them all, the American Civil War. It undermined what had been the largest single national market for British goods and interfered massively with the supply of cotton. The 'cotton famine' was the main source of disturbance in the European economy through the first half of the 1860s when the European commercial treaty network was put together.[7] The Civil War and the construction of the European network began and ended together. As the divided United States slid towards war, the Board of Trade warned the Foreign Office that 'free access to the markets of Europe at the present time is an object of grave importance . . . for some years to come greater attention must be paid to our commercial relations with European countries than has hitherto been deemed necessary.'[8]

Gloom reigned at the Board of Trade. Even before Belgium signed its agreement with France, the Board feared that the grip France was taking on the Belgian market would prove 'difficult to weaken even if we hereafter secure similar advantages.' Putting pressure on Russell that he came to resent, the Board urged the Foreign Office to behave more proactively elsewhere, in particular in the markets of Prussia, Austria and Italy. These were the countries with which the British government concluded trade treaties over the next five years. But it never moved as fast or as widely as its French counterpart.

In view of the virtual impossibility of reductions in the tariff, the Belgian government suggested other sorts of concession that Britain might make. One was to include its colonies within the scope of the treaty, something not done in Britain's treaty with France. Belgium had a keen interest in colonies generally in view of its small size, and had its eye particularly on the market in British India. That interest was sharpened by envious Belgian recollection of the extensive colonial possessions of the Netherlands in South-East Asia, access to which Belgium had lost when it gained its independence.

Rivalry with the Netherlands dictated another concession Belgium asked of Britain. Here, as was so often the case, the commercial treaty-making of the 1860s had to do with nation-building. The Dutch controlled the mouth of the River Scheldt through which the trade of Flanders reached the sea. In order to compensate themselves for the loss of Belgium and to ensure that Belgium paid for its share of the previously united kingdom's debt, the Dutch insisted that a toll be imposed on shipping at the mouth of the Scheldt. Belgium had undertaken to pay that toll for all foreign as well as Belgian shipping in order to encourage use of its commercial lifeline, and also to help the Scheldt port of

Antwerp, which had suffered particularly badly in the struggle for independence. Belgium's undertaking proved all too successful. Freed of tolls and fuelled by the growth of Belgian industry, foreign commerce along the Scheldt expanded so much that the burden of paying the tolls alarmed the Belgian Treasury. Belgium therefore sought an international agreement among the countries whose commerce profited from use of the Scheldt to capitalise the tolls, that is to replace them with a lump sum payment to the Netherlands. Belgium asked Britain, as by far the greatest foreign user of the Scheldt, to initiate that change.

The British government did not want to make either of these concessions because they violated the principles of free trade as they understood it. While the government said little about the inclusion of the colonies because as yet no great and obvious material issue was at stake, capitalising the Scheldt tolls would cost money. Britain favoured freeing the waterways of Europe from impediments to commerce; but the commerce of the Scheldt was already free, so far as foreign traders were concerned. Gladstone had been willing to sacrifice the revenue interests of the British Treasury over the wine duty in order to open up the market with France, but he saw no reason to comply with the Belgian demand.

Meanwhile the merchants of Bradford lost patience with the government's handling of the matter. Forster, Behrens and the president of the Chamber of Commerce, H.W. Ripley, worked closely together; Forster was in touch with the political and administrative realities of Westminster and Whitehall, Behrens with businessmen in Belgium who gave him information of a kind not available to the Foreign Office, and Ripley acted as the Chamber's forthright public spokesman. By the summer of 1861, this trio had recognised an institutional problem in London and knew what they wanted done about it. The Foreign Office was responsible for the conduct of negotiations with other countries on all matters, including trade. But it received its information on British and international commerce from the Board of Trade, which rarely turned for information to spokesmen for the private sector who were familiar with the needs of local industry. The only person the merchants of Bradford knew to be capable of cutting through the maze of divided relationships within government and between government and commerce was Richard Cobden.

When Forster could not get a satisfactory reply in parliament about the Belgian negotiations, Ripley led a large deputation from Chambers of Commerce all over the United Kingdom – from Batley, Belfast, Birmingham, Bradford, Bristol, Coventry, Dewsbury, Dover, Dundee, Edinburgh, Galashiels, Glasgow, Gloucester, Hawick, Huddersfield, Hull, Kendal, Leeds, Leicester, Liverpool, Manchester, Newcastle, Norwich, Nottingham, Sheffield, Southampton, the Staffordshire Potteries, Wolverhampton and Worcester – to Lord Palmerston as Prime Minister. This pressed for Cobden's reappointment as the chief British trade negotiator with Belgium and also Prussia. However prominent the leadership provided by Bradford, it undoubtedly spoke on this occasion for the commerce of the country as a whole. The members of the deputation understood that Prussia was 'on the eve of concluding a treaty of commerce with France upon a basis similar to that which has been concluded between Belgium and France.'[9] They believed, also with good reason, that France was pressing for treaties with other countries including Switzerland and Spain. After the presentation of their case to the Prime Minister the Bradford delegation saw Cobden himself. Although he was ailing, he conveyed his willingness to serve as they wished.

But Russell as Foreign Secretary, to whom Palmerston referred the deputation, indicated that the government was uneasy about reappointing someone not in regular government service. Instead, Russell selected the member of the consular service with the most experience of continental commerce, John Ward – Crowe's predecessor at Leipzig and now consul-general for the Hanse towns – to attend to the Belgian and German negotiations. The Bradford wool merchants accepted Ward's appointment as a second best until they found out that he was not expected to gather information from industrial sources in Britain, not at any rate until he had proposals from the continental countries to communicate. Ward handled his assignment passively. He did not attempt to shape either the foreign proposals or the British response as Cobden had done.

Bearing out Bradford's gloomiest predictions, the Franco–Belgian agreement that came into effect in October subjected British woollens and silks entering the Belgian market to more than twice the duty levied on French goods. *The Economist*, though generally opposed to reciprocal bargaining in tariff treaty negotiations, shared Bradford's anger at this discrimination.[10] This intensified with the discovery that, while the existing trade treaty with Belgium did not entitle Britain to the benefits of the Belgian treaty with France, those benefits were extended under current agreements to a long list of other countries, Liberia, Chile, Nicaragua, Costa Rica, Honduras, Venezuela, Guatemala, the United States, Italy, Russia, Greece and Peru, and to which a few months later Mexico and Turkey were added. It was little consolation to learn that the benefits of the Franco–Belgian treaty did not extend to Austria, Denmark, Hanover, the Roman States, or Tunis, even though they too, like Britain, had trade treaties with Belgium.

The impasse between Britain and Belgium stretched on for a year, exhausting the loyalty of the officials at the British embassy in Brussels to the orthodoxy of free trade. Lord Howard de Walden was anxious to offer any reasonable concession in return for Belgium's agreement to a treaty, but because he never quite grasped the commercial alternatives at issue his advice was easy to ignore. The secretary at the British mission in Brussels, H.P.T. Barron, prepared two able analyses of Anglo-Belgian trade and the barriers to its growth. He concluded with a plea for 'a temporary *discriminating tariff on our side*. . . If we are supposed to have played our last card, and to be *utterly powerless to give or to withhold anything*, we cannot expect to make much impression on a selfish world. A sense of equity may do us some good, but a sense of interest would do us more.'[11] Barron, however, presented his reports in the spring and summer of 1862, too late to have an impact on the thinking of the Foreign Office, if indeed that would ever have been possible.

What broke the stalemate was the cotton famine, deepened by the continuing war in the United States. It confronted the people of Ghent with destitution which it was beyond the capacity of their charitable institutions to alleviate; there was nothing in Belgium like the English Poor Law to fall back on. The plight of the inhabitants of Ghent had nothing to do with tariffs; however, the prospect of increased competition from British cotton textiles intensified their fear and made their cry politically irresistible. The British government could appreciate the political necessity without admitting its logic. What the Belgian government requested, and what the British government proved willing to concede, was deferment of the reduction in the Belgian duty on cottons until cessation of the American war brought the cotton famine to an end. The postponement extended to worsted woollens with warps that included cotton. The two governments disposed of the question of the Scheldt tolls simply by mentioning it in their treaty in the knowledge that nothing could be done until Belgium and the Netherlands agreed on the amount at which the tolls should be capitalised. Belgium's desire to reach agreement with Britain increased sharply when the King fell ill and the monarchs of France and the Netherlands met to discuss (so rumour had it) the possibility of dividing Belgium between them. As the Belgian Prime Minister observed to Lord Howard, 'Certes ce n'est pas le moment de nous bouillir avec l'Angleterre' ('This is definitely no time to embroil ourselves with England').[12]

Britain and Belgium finally signed their treaty at the end of July 1862. Preoccupied by the dearth of cotton from the United States, Lancashire paid little attention to deferment of the lowering of the Belgian tariff. The treaty gave other sectors of British industry what they expected in equity with the French. The inclusion of the colonies in its terms ruled out preferential tariffs among the member states of the British Empire; but that too awakened little concern as yet, and it passed unnoticed in Britain. There was nonetheless one more hiccup before the matter was finally settled: the Belgian legislature insisted on temporarily still better terms, in other words less reduction in their tariff, on cotton thread; again the British gave way.

Framed thus, the treaty did not make much of an impression in Britain. It had exposed the powerlessness of the government in commercial diplomacy, though the lesson was slow to sink in. France was clearly setting the pace, and a fast one, in the extension of commercial agreements envisaged in the initial treaty. Though the most-favoured-nation clause in that treaty had been worded in precedent-setting unconditional terms, it did not seem automatically to guarantee enjoyment of tariff reductions granted by third parties to the original signatories. The Bradford Chamber of Commerce raised a further point that the Foreign Office and the Board of Trade were slow to grasp. The tariff reductions that France negotiated with third parties in the interests of its trade and industry did not always suit, indeed rarely suited, the particular needs of British trade and industry.

This outcome deepened the ambivalence of the British government concerning trade treaties with continental countries. The Foreign Office might have done nothing more, had it not been for the merchants and manufacturers. It was the latter, together with the French, who kept up the pressure on the British government, so much so that the Foreign Office and the Board of Trade began to blame each other for tardiness. In a speech to the annual meeting of the Bradford Chamber of Commerce in 1863 that *The Times* singled out for commendation,[13] Forster accused the government of having surrendered the initiative to France. He rejected the argument that Britain 'had lost the opportunity of making any bargain with foreign governments, that we had already given everything to them, and therefore could give nothing in return, and that therefore our government might hold their hands.' The government, he insisted, could accomplish a lot simply through propaganda for free trade, instilling the lesson that countries damaged themselves with tariff protection because it raised consumer prices, dampened industrial initiative and reduced governmental revenue.

And propaganda was not Britain's only weapon. The Belgian case demonstrated the effectiveness of the demand for equity, or so Forster thought. Belgium had found that it could not afford to discriminate against one ally in favour of another. Extending that point, Britain ought to be able to argue effectively that it should not be punished for giving every country free access to its market. Forster later goaded Lord Palmerston by saying that 'it did not become him, as the protector of British interests, to hand over to France the direction of that free-trade movement which was originated by England, or to follow with faltering footsteps the movements of France.'[14] Forster applied his argument to Italy, the country to which Britain next turned when its trade talks with Prussia experienced even longer delays than had those with Belgium.

b. The Italian Treaty

Italy was to validate Forster's argument but also to expose its limitations. The demand for equity with France proved effective with countries anxious to treat both Britain and France as allies, but it gave Britain equity only in form, not in substance. The Anglo-Italian treaty was to be the first of the network agreements of the 1860s in which the benefits to Britain were restricted essentially to a most-favoured-nation clause, which enabled Britain to enjoy the tariff reductions that France negotiated in its treaties. But Britain found itself unable to obtain any other reductions to ensure that the needs of British industry were as well served as those of France.

Like Belgium, Italy was a new and unsettled state set up in an alteration of the Vienna settlement, and which had received crucial support at its birth from Britain as well as from France. The predominantly pre-industrial economy of Italy did not pose any competitive challenge to the British, who looked to it as an opportunity, expanded by unification, for capital investment as well as trade, and as a source of mainly agricultural produce. The secretary of the British embassy in Turin reported glowingly that 'A vast market has been opened to Europe in Italy, and the demand for foreign goods will increase every year.'[15] Under the leadership of the first Prime Minister, Cavour, Italy had modelled its commercial policy explicitly on Britain's. A policy of reducing trade restrictions served the purposes of the new nation by overcoming its former internal divisions as well as by stimulating economic development. In these circumstances, the British government hoped to secure a treaty comparable to the one France was negotiating with Italy. Russell compiled a list of the further tariff adjustments Britain would need to achieve substantial parity of treatment.

But no new country anxious to assert its legitimacy and strengthen its economy could afford to be meek in representing the concerns of its citizens or offer generous terms of trade to the great economic powers of Europe. The cotton spinners and weavers of Genoa voiced the same fear of inundation from Lancashire as had their counterparts in Ghent. Trade talks with the Italians were subject to a host of delays. Even the French found their negotiations more difficult and slower than with Belgium because of the competitive agricultural interests of the two Mediterranean economies, including the always vexed subject of wine. They were further hampered by the rudimentary infrastructure of the national government that the Italians had hastily cobbled together. It proved hard, for instance, to find out what exactions the Italians currently imposed on trade. The British had to obtain the terms of the eventual Franco-Italian treaty from their embassy in Paris because the Italian government lacked facilities for quick copying. Meanwhile Italy entered into trade talks with other countries, including Sweden, which had to be interrupted because of the dearth of competent Italian trade negotiators. The difficulty in obtaining information from Italy also increased the impediments to communication within Britain between the Foreign Office, the Board of Trade and the various Chambers of Commerce.

British hopes for an agreement with Italy rose in the spring of 1862 with the despatch of an Italian commissioner to London. News soon followed about the general basis on which Italy and France were negotiating. They kept fairly closely to the terms of the French treaty with Belgium, 'with a few exceptions in favour of special products of Italy, such as olive oil, preserved fruits, oranges, lemons, &c.'[16] Britain was not much interested in the reduced duty for silks on which the French insisted; on woollens, French demands matched the expectations of Bradford, which told the Foreign Office that it would be satisfied with Italian duplication of the terms of Cobden's treaty with France. But though France and Italy signed a navigation treaty towards the end of June, they failed to reach agreement on the tariff and suspended their talks. The prospect was no more promising on the British side since the Italian commissioner was pressing for further reductions in the remaining British tariff on 'wines, confectionery, and other articles, which could not have been granted without a considerable loss of revenue'.[17] There was nothing offensive about the Italian demand at this stage, before Italy and France had reached an agreement to which Britain could claim equitable entitlement. The revenue considerations were nonetheless enough to prompt a British refusal, and the Italian commissioner returned home. Thereupon Bradford accused the Foreign Office of negligence: the Foreign Office had certainly failed both to keep Chambers of Commerce abreast of proceedings and to put the Italian commissioner in direct touch with them.

The Foreign Office again lapsed into inactivity until the beginning of 1863 when Italy and France reached their tariff agreement. Russell was willing to settle for simple most-favoured-nation access to its benefits. L.S. Sackville West, the British chargé d'affaires at Turin, handled most of the negotiations in Italy, while the staff at the Foreign Office put itself in closer touch with the Board of Trade. But no matter how ably conducted, this triangular relationship was bound to produce irritation and delay. The intergovernmental situation was aggravated by pressure from the Board of Trade for consultation with the Chambers of Commerce and the opportunity to consider 'any further modifications which may be urgently required by British commerce'[18] before any treaty was signed.

The most important benefits of the treaty Italy eventually concluded with France were the phasing-in over five years of reduced duties on textiles of flax, silk or jute, tanned hides, chemicals, crystal and pottery. But the Italians proved unwilling to extend these benefits to Britain unless Britain offered 'compensating advantages'[19] – again that infuriating demand for compensation. Though this provided the British government with an opportunity to consult interested Chambers of Commerce,[20] their response only added to the problem by putting forward further demands rather than forms of compensation for Britain to make. Bradford might have been content with the terms of the Franco-Italian treaty, but Birmingham was disturbed by the increases in the new treaty tariff over the previous one, which had been low because there was so little Italian metal manufacturing to protect. Lancashire, on the other hand, hoped for as good terms for cottons as Bradford had secured for its woollens under the 1860 treaty with France.

Exasperation with the prolonged fruitlessness of the government's endeavours provoked a parliamentary debate on their intrinsic weakness. Having given up what Gladstone had called 'the rags and tatters of protection', Britain had to look for other inducements to improve its access to the market in other European states. One MP described Britain's prospects in this endeavour as 'absolutely hopeless'.[21] Disraeli accentuated the dilemma in which the government found itself. He insisted that the dilemma was of the government's own making but that there was now no escape. Harking back to the debate of the mid-1840s over reciprocity, he suggested that the decision to abandon that policy in favour of one based on unilateral free trade and the renunciation of most tariffs had been rash and mistaken. Yet he accepted and even exaggerated that decision. 'You have resolved that the means which only can bring about these arrangements should be surrendered. . . . You gave them up without condition, and it is impossible now to resume the position you have lost. . . . By accident certain articles were excepted, and two years ago you used them as the means of negotiating a treaty of commerce with [France]. . . . You have played all your cards.'[22] The government did not dispute Disraeli's assessment and welcomed his acceptance of the irreversibility of its commercial policy. All that Britain could hope for was most-favoured-nation access to the tariff reductions that France, but no longer Britain, had the leverage to secure. The president of the Board of Trade, Milner Gibson, distanced the British government from the whole business of commercial treaty-making. 'I do not', he admitted, 'think tariff treaties in themselves desirable, speaking abstractly, or that any country should shackle itself by engagements with other countries as to the particular mode in which it would raise its own revenue.'[23]

In May, anxious on their side about the time the negotiations were taking, the Italians dropped their request for compensation and offered to settle for a most-favoured-nation agreement, to be presented to their parliament along with or right after the treaty with France. Though Russell refused to meet the Italian timetable, he pulled the British response together. Working at last in close collaboration with the Board of Trade, he boiled the recommendations the Board collected from the Chambers of Commerce down to three points where the Franco-Italian treaty could damage British interests. They included earthenware, on which the Italians had agreed to a tariff that would help fine French porcelain as against the cheaper produce of the Staffordshire potteries, mixed fabrics and jute, where the Italian duty remained high because France did not produce it.[24]

These three requests did not threaten any Italian economic interest; Russell therefore hoped that Italy would not call for any reciprocal British concessions. But his proposals put the negotiations back into a bargaining mode. The

Italians now requested a reduction in the two British duties that affected Italian interests, on dried fruit as well as wine. The British refused for fear of the loss of revenue. The Treasury was growing ever more dependent upon the remaining customs duties, not just because they were so few in number but also because they were proving ever more lucrative as British commerce and consumption soared up on the wings of free trade and reduced duties. The British still found it hard to believe that the Italians would decline to offer them anything beyond strict most-favoured-nation equality with France. At the prompting of the Board of Trade, Russell therefore pressed the Italian government at least to include his three proposals in its next revision of the general Italian tariff, but the Italians refused to promise anything without a matching concession from Britain. Lacking leverage, Britain could do nothing more than decline to gratify the Italian desire for a speedy conclusion of their treaty, but any delay might leave British goods liable to adverse tariff discrimination after the French treaty had been submitted.

Once the Italian government indicated that exports from Britain would indeed pay that penalty, Russell hastened to settle for most-favoured-nation treatment. Even so, the insecurity and concern for status of the new Italian kingdom caused another delay before its treaty with Britain could be concluded. Russell wanted the treaty to include a guarantee of religious liberty in Italy. Its component states had treated foreign Protestants harshly in the era before unification, behaviour that Russell as an inveterate anti-clerical and anti-Catholic Whig could not forget. But there was no such guarantee in Britain's treaties with France or Belgium or, as the Italians indignantly pointed out, with any 'civilized state'.[25] Italy rejected what 'would almost amount to a slur upon her reputation, her policy and her institutions'.[26] Sticking to the language of reciprocity, the Italian Foreign Minister offered the simple assurance that British citizens in Italy would continue to enjoy the same 'parfaite reciprocité' of religious treatment that the citizens of Italy enjoyed in the United Kingdom.[27] (Was he thinking of Ireland?) Russell was willing to settle for that assurance, assuming that it would be embodied in a formal exchange of notes. After an unexplained delay of nearly two months, the Italian ambassador in London received authorisation to sign the treaty. But 'no note or Declaration about Religion' accompanied his instructions.[28] Russell was dismayed to learn that the Italian government 'never meant to propose a more solemn exchange'.[29] He had to settle for the insertion of a reference to the Italian Foreign Minister's earlier assurance in the protocol that preceded ratification.

c. The Prussian Treaty

Despite this experience, the British government clung to the hope that considerations of equity would convince other commercial treaty-making countries in Europe to treat Britain as well as they treated France. The British also assumed that, though of course there were political implications, commercial treaties were mainly about commerce. Prussia approached the subject from a completely different standpoint.[30] The government of Prussia and indeed of most other German states assumed that commercial treaties were methods of state-building and that the objective in making these treaties was not equity between states but ascendancy.

Everything in Germany revolved around the rivalry between Prussia and Austria for ascendancy in Central Europe. Britain was to discover how that rivalry could hold up its own access to the benefits of the commercial treaty that France, still setting the pace, reached with Prussia. But the British never grasped that, so far as Prussia was concerned, the case for equity did not apply to Britain in the way it did to France. The latter was more important to Prussia for a mixture of reasons. France was an immediate neighbour; it possessed the largest domestic market in Europe; and it aimed to spread its ascendancy across the centre of the continent. Furthermore, Prussia and indeed most Germans resented Britain's opposition to German nationalist aspirations over Schleswig-Holstein when Britain had so obviously sympathised with the Italian desire for Venetia: so much for equity.

Trade policy was of enormous importance for Prussia politically, much more so than for Britain. Over the preceding 15 years the politically significant classes in Britain had come to a consensus that assigned the development of the economy to the wonderfully productive energies of private enterprise, leaving government simply to establish the ground rules. Prussia, on the other hand, used trade policy to extend its orbit in Germany, particularly through leadership of the Zollverein. This customs union had been formed after the Napoleonic Wars to remove the internal barriers to trade which separated Prussia from the other German states and to strengthen these states under Prussian leadership with a common external tariff. The economic success of the scheme enabled Prussia to extend the customs union until, by 1860, it embraced most, though still not all, of the German states, with the deliberate exception of Austria. In a twist of policy that was diabolical from the British standpoint, 'Free Trade was to be the most potent weapon employed by Prussia in her effort to exclude Austria from the future German Empire.'[31] Prussia kept the Zollverein tariff comparatively low because such a practice was intolerable to Austria, which clung to old-fashioned protectionism. Metternich, the Austrian chancellor who dominated the politics of continental Europe until the revolutions of 1848, had paid little heed to economic matters. Prussia exploited that blind spot. By removing tariff barriers inside the Zollverein and lowering them outside, Prussia appealed to those Germans who hoped that the resulting growth in their economy might compensate for their enfeebling political divisions. The dashed political hopes of the bourgeois revolutionaries of 1848 only increased the temptation. Bismarck continued to use the policy when he came to power in Berlin in 1862 as a way to offset the unpopularity of his aggressively illiberal political prescriptions.

The commercial treaty that Prussia concluded with France in 1862–63 served all of these political purposes; and it attracted more attention in Germany than even Cobden's treaty with the French had done in Britain. The Franco-Prussian treaty had, of course, its economic objective, which the British assumed to be of primary importance. The Cobden treaty had given Britain privileged access to a market in which the neighbouring German states, including Rhineland Prussia, had previously been more significant traders. Crowe reported from Frankfurt that, within a few months of the completion of the Anglo-French treaty, the iron and steel of the Zollverein had been driven out of the French market by superior competition from Britain. Napoleon's intention was, however, to widen the market rather than merely replace one supplier with another; even before the negotiations with Britain were complete, France had opened discussions with Prussia. This displacement from the French market enabled Prussia to warn the associated principalities in Germany that 'unless a speedy arrangement be come to between the States of the Zollverein and France a similar result will be produced as regards other products and manufactures.'[32] The agreement Prussia sought with France had other economic implications, but they divided Germans politically. An agreement to reduce the tariff would appeal to the liberally inclined industrial community of western and central Prussia and to the wheat-exporting Junkers of east Prussia who provided commercial liberalism with its staunchest support. But it alarmed the protectionist business interests which were especially strong in the south, notably cotton spinning in Württemberg and the glassworks of Bavaria.

This division coincided with the conflict in the Zollverein between those states, led by Bavaria and Württemberg, that continued to lean towards Austria and those that gravitated towards Prussia. Debate focused on this political question more than on any economic consideration. Though Prussia negotiated on its own with France, any tariff agreement that those two states reached would require unanimous approval from the rest of the Zollverein. If members insisted on going their separate ways in tariff agreements with foreign states, the union would break up. There was an alternative to an agreement with France, and that was an agreement with Austria. Austria was anxious to extend the limited agreement it had reached with Prussia in 1853, but was not willing to reduce its tariffs as far as the treaties that France had reached with Britain and Belgium would require, to say nothing of the further reductions Prussia sought in its negotiations with France.

The Franco-Prussian negotiations did not proceed smoothly. Prussia, with the Zollverein behind it, was able to put up a stronger resistance to French pressure than Belgium had managed. The negotiations revolved, as was usual on the French side, around wine and silks. The Prussians were mainly concerned about iron and steel and their heavier textiles that aimed at the lower end of the market. Pleased with the rewards of reciprocal bargaining for tariff reductions with the British, Belgians and Italians, France pressed for lower tariffs than Prussia was happy to concede. Rather than give way, Prussia threatened to retaliate by 'creating differential duties against such states as are not in relation to the Zollverein on the footing of the most favoured nation'.[33] Yet, particularly under Bismarck, Prussia resisted the universalising of its tariff concessions through the unconditional most-favoured-nation clause. The talks seemed to collapse after six months. Neither side was willing to break them off completely, however, and they finally reached agreement in the spring of 1862.

In the event, Prussia did well for itself. The treaty offered Prussia and the Germans better terms of access to the French market than the British and Belgians currently enjoyed, with the further concession that Prussia could phase in the lower tariffs to which it agreed on iron and steel over three years. The Franco–Prussian treaty aroused more concern in Britain than the Franco–Italian agreement because German manufactures were beginning to compete with British ones in foreign markets. In a pattern of trade similar to the British, German producers competed with British exports at the low end of the market in textiles,[34] with coarse materials for working-class consumption, and at the higher end in metal manufactures. The Board of Trade was also increasingly impressed with the magnitude of the German market. Britain had been slow to appreciate this, partly because the Board's trade figures for the Hanseatic ports were collected separately from those for the Zollverein and failed to distinguish what remained in the ports of entry from what then passed through to inland states. But after Prussia and France had endorsed their agreement, the Board stressed to the Foreign Office that 'It is difficult to overestimate the value of obtaining for the trade of this country a freer access to the markets of the Germanic Union. The states composing it contain a population of 33,000,000 steadily advancing in wealth and civilisation, and it is easy to foresee that even if the governments of the vast contiguous empires of Russia and Austria should refuse to adopt similar reforms, the manufactures of Western Europe once allowed to circulate freely throughout the heart of Germany, would soon find their way . . . to the countries which lie beyond its frontier.'[35] There was some fear too that a Franco–Prussian treaty might reverse the movement towards ever lower tariffs begun in the treaties with Britain and Belgium. Since the existing tariff of the Zollverein on textiles was lower than the French, the Bradford Chamber of Commerce worried that France would agree to an increase. British anxieties were magnified by the secrecy with which Prussia and France surrounded their talks, though Crowe's friends in Saxony and the Nationalverein gave him a glimpse of Prussia's reports to the Zollverein.

When the terms of the treaty, which was signed in 1863, were divulged, they turned out to be as acceptable to Britain as the Franco-Italian treaty had been. Of course, they left something to be desired. But the Chambers of Commerce in Britain that had followed this commercial diplomacy had moderated their expectations; and the British government had learnt from its Italian experience to present its requests for further tariff adjustments almost *pro forma*, without serious hope of acceptance. Irritation, however, replaced anxiety when Prussia declined to open talks for a treaty with Britain until the Zollverein had given its approval to the treaty with France.

Prussia's demand for this approval placed the survival of the Zollverein in question. The reductions in the Franco-Prussian agreement threatened – the Prussians might have said promised – to deepen the estrangement of Austria which the southern states in the Zollverein were anxious to overcome. Bavaria and Württemberg favoured the inclusion if not indeed the leadership of Austria in the co-operative arrangements of Germany. Saxony, which stretched between the borders of Prussia and Austria, swung back and forth to maximise its leverage; and on the issue of the Franco-Prussian treaty, it sided with the southern states and Austria. The weight of opposition was so heavy that Prussia threatened to dissolve and reconstitute the Zollverein, excluding the recalci-trant states. The force behind this threat was economic. However much Bavaria and Württemberg would have preferred the political leadership of Austria, its economy was comparatively small and stagnant; and they were not prepared to do without the benefits of economic affiliation with industrialising Prussia and its associates.

Britain made its bid for a treaty with Prussia just as this controversy broke out within the Zollverein, and in the event compounded Prussia's problem. The French treaty was bad enough from the standpoint of the southern German states; a parallel treaty with Britain would make it intolerable. The industrial might of Britain increased their protectionist fears, for they were not strong enough to hold their own against it. Prussia therefore tried, politely, to hold the British at bay with an assurance that they would be welcome to share the benefits of the Franco-Prussian tariff once the Zollverein had acceded to it. The treaty could not, in any case, take effect until the next revision of the Zollverein tariff, which was scheduled for 1865.

The Foreign Office did not appreciate these excuses. Nor did it understand the resentment Germans felt over the opposition from Britain to their desire to absorb the duchies of Schleswig and Holstein. The reluctant but unanimous approval that the Zollverein eventually gave the French treaty did not dispel the suspicion between Britain and Germany. Instead of settling promptly for the most-favoured-nation agreement that Britain expected, Bismarck acted unilaterally. Using the Zollverein to account for his reluctance to offer most-favoured-nation treatment, he proposed to incorporate the terms of the French treaty in the revision of the German tariff in such a way as to make them available to free-trading states like Britain and the Netherlands, which already gave Germany what it wanted, and to other states that would offer to do so.

Bismarck's proposal would give Britain substantially what it wanted. The unilateral approach that he wished to take, leaving each country free to decide its own tariff, was just what the purest British free traders wanted Britain to do. This was the approach Britain had taken when it repealed the Corn Laws without bargaining for other concessions from wheat-exporting states. Voices inside and outside the Board of Trade continued to bemoan Cobden's departure from this approach in his treaty with France. Few free traders of any stripe in Britain were prepared to face up to the reciprocal bargaining that commercial treaty-making required. The British government, ministers and permanent officials alike, nevertheless clung to the assumption that the unconditional most-favoured-nation clause was a good substitute for bilateral bargaining and could bring Europe ever closer to the bliss of completely free trade. Perhaps because Bismarck's liberal trade ministers sympathised with these beliefs, Russell was able to obtain the most-favoured-nation treaty he now desired. In his haste to secure it, he disregarded the possible effects of the application of the Anglo-Prussian treaty to the British colonies, a concession so far given only to Belgium and in less extended terms. Lord Napier, the British ambassador in Berlin, remarked with surprise that, while exports from the Zollverein would be given most-favoured-nation status in Britain, they would be treated even better in the British colonies, as if they came from the mother country:[36] but Russell did not object.

Bismarck's conduct in these negotiations was a harbinger of things to come. It was not just a matter of the unilateral approach, to which he would revert in 1879. Prussia opened talks with a range of other states including Switzerland, Sweden, Italy and Belgium as well as Austria, all of which sought to adjust their commercial relationship with Prussia and the Zollverein in the wake of the French treaty. Prussia entered these discussions from a position of strength and adopted a demanding stance. A new power was making its debut in the commercial diplomacy of Europe. Hitherto there had been two European powers with hegemonic aspirations: Britain and France. Now there were three. But neither Britain nor France immediately recognised the new arrival.

d. Inquest on the British Approach

The meagre achievements and lacklustre performance of the British officials in charge of commercial negotiations after the Anglo-French treaty had drawn criticism, especially from those businessmen who had worked closely with Cobden in 1860. Cobden was in poor health, but that did not account for the persistence with which the government passed over him in its commercial diplomacy. Russell, by his own private admission, was prodded into action on trade matters by agitation in the business community. Yet the Foreign Office was reluctant to look outside its own ranks, let alone outside the civil service, for assistance in commercial matters. This bureacratic prejudice was reinforced by old-fashioned aristocratic disdain for trade and a new-fangled ethic that regarded public service as distinct from and superior to private enterprise. The gospel of free trade intensified this ethic by insisting on the removal of government from the regulation of international commerce and by decreeing that it was improper for public servants to concern themselves with the advancement of private business interests.

The fruits of these prejudices and principles were apparent to the Associated Chambers of Commerce in the failure of Lord Palmerston's government to keep up with France and advance the interests of British exporters by opening the continental market through commercial treaty. The Bradford Chamber summarised the previous few years' experience in a memorial, which the national association unanimously agreed to present to the government with a demand for a parliamentary inquiry. The memorial deplored the fact, with regard to Italy, that 'we have been obliged to accept a mere reciprocity treaty, while France has been engaged in minute and protracted discussions upon the details of the future Italian tariff.'[37] The memorial admitted that 'The English government may not have had the power, and decidedly never had the desire to bargain in the same manner as France for commercial advantages; but there cannot be a doubt that it is the duty of government to watch the negociations [sic] between friendly powers from their very commencement, with the view of preventing, by every legitimate means, such tariff rates as might otherwise be agreed upon to the injury of British interests.' It blamed the government for 'a great want of efficiency' in its commercial diplomacy, and traced the cause of this inefficiency 'to the double machinery and the divided responsibility of the departments now entrusted with the duty of protecting England's commercial interests.'

Working in co-operation with the Manchester Chamber, Ripley of Bradford obtained a preliminary interview with the Prime Minister. But Palmerston, who had made his reputation at the Foreign Office, 'pooh-poohed the whole matter', stating, as Ripley reported, that the arrangements between the Foreign Office and the Board of Trade were 'perfect'.[38] For all the supposed popularity of Palmerston's chauvinism in international affairs, he did not go down well among the working people of Bradford, and they greeted him with stony silence when he came to lay the cornerstone of the Wool Exchange.[39]

W.E. Forster, the rising Bradford MP, fared better when he moved in the House of Commons for the inquiry sought by the Associated Chambers of Commerce. Replying for the government as undersecretary at the Foreign Office, A.H. Layard displayed all the traits of the arrogance that businessmen so resented in the Foreign Service. He attacked the Chambers of Commerce for suggesting, in their demand for tariff reductions abroad, that Britain might have some self-interested objectives in pressing foreign governments to adopt free trade.[40] But Forster's request for an inquiry received a more cordial reception everywhere else in the House, to the point where the government was induced to accept it. Cobden, in one of his last appearances in parliament, reiterated his claim that the agreement with France for which he was responsible was not a treaty in the usual sense. 'It so happened – opportunely happened – that we had considerable reforms of our tariff still to accomplish . . . it so happened, fortunately, that the French Government was just in the disposition to make the first great step in the path of commercial freedom in that country. The two Governments were enabled with much more ease and advantage to perform these two operations together than they could have done separately.' Yet he urged the government to persevere in its commercial treaty-making rather than rely on other countries spontaneously to follow the good example Britain had set in embracing free trade. 'Did the Government remain passive with other countries after we had abolished the slave trade? On the contrary, they made it the constant object of their diplomacy abroad to induce other countries to follow in the same enlightened and humane course.' He did his best to dispel any doubts about the failure of the Foreign Office to encourage interest in commercial matters: 'if our diplomatic representatives knew that by exerting themselves in the cause of free trade abroad they would be as likely to get the decoration and rank of G.C.B. as if they had been successful in assisting at the ceremony of a dynastic treaty or some Court marriage, I think you would very soon find these young gentlemen begin to take an interest in commercial questions.'

The House accepted Forster's motion without a division. The Foreign Office then scrambled to mount a defence. Russell sent telegrams to his embassies across Europe, requiring summary information by telegram and more detailed but still speedy reports by letter on the relationship between foreign ministries and ministries of commerce on the continent. Summing up British practice with a condescending turn of phrase, he explained, 'As a general rule it is held that the Board of Trade, being fully conversant with the commercial interests of the country, and being in constant communication with the industrial classes, is most competent to form a just opinion upon matters of trade, and to determine how far it may be expedient to suggest to the Foreign Office to call the attention of a foreign Government to any special subject connected with them.'[41]

The replies Russell received suggested that, though practice varied among continental participants in the treaty network, they gave commerce a higher priority and integrated it more firmly into their other diplomatic concerns. French practice was closest to the British. But the French Foreign Office was a kind of super-ministry; it acted in concert with other ministries, including Commerce and Finance, the Interior, Public Works, and Marine, insofar as their concerns were at issue in the foreign relations of the country. Hence, the French Foreign Ministry was well placed to control all dealings with foreign states and representatives. Prussia's Foreign Office, furthest from Britain's in practice, divided its business functionally between political and commercial departments rather than geographically as the British did. Within that overarching structure, the Prussian Foreign Secretary co-operated closely with the Minister of Commerce in handling commercial matters, including consular appointments. Though all correspondence with consuls was handled by the Prussian Foreign Office, its staff included officers as competent and well trained to handle commercial questions as those in the Ministry of Commerce. The Prussians always included commissioners from both ministries in their negotiating team for commercial treaties. Belgium was too small and new a state to have elaborated such a structure. But the economic concerns of Belgium were so wrapped up with its foreign relations that its Foreign Ministry handled most of the responsibilities assigned to Ministries of Commerce elsewhere.

Still, the ambassador in Berlin belittled the difference between Prussian and British practice. Russell and his officials saw no need for change, and they tried to resist the parliamentary committee of inquiry's demand to see the correspondence that had passed between the Foreign Office and the Board of Trade on the treaties with Belgium and Italy. The parliamentary committee was able to overrule them, however, and it extended its questioning to include those officials who were currently negotiating with Prussia. It emerged quite dissatisfied with the relationship between the two departments engaged in the conduct of commercial diplomacy, a dissatisfaction that was shared by the Board of Trade. But the members of the parliamentary committee were not sure what to put in the place of the existing arrangement. They ended up, in a modest approximation to Prussian practice, by recommending the establishment of a commercial department in the Foreign Office to gather the information that it needed to discuss tariffs and trade with other countries. There was some regret about the loss of contact that this arrangement would entail with the Board of Trade, whose officers were more in touch with and sympathetic to the industry and commerce of the country than was the Foreign Office.

The reception of the report of the inquiry in the House of Commons did not bode well for British commercial treaty-making. Robert Lowe, one of the ablest but most academic of free traders, delivered a classic denunciation of the pretensions of commercial diplomacy in any shape or form. He insisted that 'the entire business which the Government have with the trade of the country might be described by the pithy axiom of Lord Melbourne, "Why can't you let it alone?"' Now that Britain had got rid of all but revenue-producing tariffs, it was in no more of a position to negotiate tariff treaties than a person who 'should go into a shop to purchase goods for ready money, but should first throw his purse into the Thames'. Furthermore, in entering into commercial treaty negotiations, Britain taught foreigners false economic principles. 'Political economy says, "Lower your duties in order that you may get the productions of other nations as cheaply as possible". . . . But what do we virtually say when we negotiate a commercial treaty? . . . We say to foreign countries, "Allow us to export to you, and we will allow you to export to us" . . . we teach them to believe that the wealth of nations consists not in what we get, but in what we send away. Thus we are leading foreign countries to suppose that our advantage and their advantage are very different things, instead of being one and identical.'[42] That was not how the exporters of British manufactured goods thought of free trade; they thought of it as meaning the removal of tariff barriers to entry into foreign markets. But Layard of the Foreign Office followed Lowe in accusing these manufacturers and merchants of 'stupendous ignorance'.[43] (The person he had particularly in mind was Ripley of Bradford.) It was Layard to whom the new commercial division at the Foreign Office would report. He told the Commons that he 'would always be ready to receive commercial gentlemen who came to the Foreign Office to consult on matters of business'.

That prospect could scarcely have encouraged these commercial gentlemen to come to call. The Foreign Office prepared to implement the organisational recommendations of the parliamentary inquiry grudgingly. Yet, even before it did so, a beneficial impact was evident in what Ripley described as 'amazingly increased activity'[44] at the Foreign Office on commercial matters. This heightened concern showed itself during the proceedings of the inquiry, when the Foreign Office asked the Chambers of Commerce whether they would like the appointment of an agent to watch the commercial discussions going on between France and the Netherlands. But the main evidence of the British government's new attentiveness to commercial matters came in its almost frantic wooing of Austria, an effort that nonetheless continued to expose the infirmity of Britain's commercial diplomacy.

e. The Austrian Treaty

Britain had no clearly defined or compelling reason to seek a commercial treaty with Austria beyond a general desire to open up the European market.[45] The attractions of Austria in the 1860s, whether economic or political, were faint or failing; and there was not the competitive goad here of a preceding Austrian treaty with France. Despite the enormous population of the Austrian empire, it had hitherto proven no larger or more lucrative for British purposes than the market in Belgium; and it displayed none of the Italian founders' faith in commercial liberalism. The British ambassador in Berlin described Austria as 'an embarrassed State with a permanent deficit . . . a depreciated paper currency' and an empire that contained 'vast primitive populations still living on indigenous vegetable diet and clad in home made fabrics or sheepskins'.[46] As for its political weight, though until recently it was the most formidable of the continental powers, Austria was debilitated rather than roused by the challenge of Italian nationalism and incipient German unification.

This floundering on the Austrian side was matched by fitfulness and misinterpretation on the British. While the government gave the subject only spasmodic attention, the organs of financial opinion in Britain tended to misunderstand the available evidence on the Austrian economy. *The Economist* compared the figures for British trade with Austria and with the Hanseatic ports on the Baltic to the advantage of the latter. 'At present, while our imports from Austria stick fast at an annual value between 800,000 *l* and 1,000,000 *l*, and our exports thither – *including* even the foreign and colonial produce, which merely passes through England – are valued at about half as much again, the value of our trade with the Hanse Towns is in imports about 7,000,000 *l*, and in exports (including again the foreign and colonial produce) about 17,000,000 *l*.'[47] This calculation ignored the function of the Hanse towns as gateways for onward trade by land to Austria as well as the rest of Germany. Given this misleading assessment, together with the lack of firm pressure from Austria, British commercial policy was dictated by pressures at home. The debate in Britain turned into a contest over control and competency in the negotiating process, while the eventual treaty was drained of all commercial value.

The British government had shown interest in a commercial treaty with Austria when Napoleon III annexed Nice and Savoy. Palmerston considered offsetting the extension of French power with a limited commercial agreement to help Austria sustain its remaining presence in Italy. He contemplated a further reduction in the wine duties to benefit Austria in exchange for a reduction in the Austrian export duty on rags, a commodity important to Britain's paper industry, and on timber for maritime use. Such a narrowly defined possibility did not, however, excite either nation; and the idea was set aside. British interest in an agreement revived when Prussia concluded its treaty with France and Austria sought trading agreement with the southern states of the Zollverein. But the British hoped for too much from this development. Exaggerating the extent to which Austria was likely to reduce its tariff to woo the Zollverein, Britain sought terms on a par with those in its treaty with France.

When it became apparent that Austria had no intention of lowering its tariff walls that far, the Foreign Office allowed its critics in the Associated Chambers of Commerce to try their hand. The leaders of the Chambers of Commerce had fewer illusions about the commercial inclinations of the Austrian government. Behrens recognised that Austria was unlikely to change its protectionist spots. Still he thought that 'there was something brewing'. Whether or not the rewards to be found in the Austrian market were substantial, he wanted the British government to move promptly so as 'not to let the French government make treaties for us'.[48] Confident that the best hope for commercial agreement lay with the men of commerce, the Associated Chambers proposed to send a delegation of its ablest spokesmen to meet the leaders of the Chambers of Commerce in Austria and persuade them that lower tariffs were profitable. Four men were sent: Behrens; another German, Max Liebmann of Huddersfield; Francis Prange of Liverpool; and an MP, Somerset Beaumont of Newcastle, who became the most enthusiastic advocate of the cause.

Once they reached Austria, they were shocked to discover that the businessmen there were even more opposed than the governing aristocracy to any loss of tariff protection. The Austrians, like the French, were capable of fine work in the higher grades of textiles, but the industrial base was too small and undeveloped to encourage its leaders to stand up to foreign competition. The British delegates returned home disillusioned, willing to let the Foreign Office resume responsibility for the thankless work of commercial diplomacy.

Still, their experience in Austria did not resolve the underlying conflict between the Chambers of Commerce and the Foreign Office. It flared up when the next opportunity to renew negotiations with Austria presented itself. British hopes for a treaty were raised in the spring of 1865 by the unexpectedly large majority by which the Austrian legislature gave its approval to the commercial treaty that the Austrian ministry finally reached with the Zollverein after it adopted the Franco-Prussian tariff. But Russell made no attempt to join forces with the Chambers of Commerce in pursuit of a treaty. Gratified by the failure of their delegation in 1864, he resisted the inclusion of Somerset Beaumont in the commission that the Foreign Office proposed to set up for the talks with Austria. Beaumont, backed by the Associated Chambers, finally gained a place, but Russell abandoned the commission altogether when the Austrian ministry indicated that it would rather proceed via a different forum in order to circumvent the opposition from its business community.

The Foreign Office wanted to prove that it was fully competent in every field of diplomacy, including commerce. To that end it recruited the ablest person in the Board of Trade for this sort of work. Louis Mallet had worked with Cobden in Paris in 1860 and had since been the Board's most ardent advocate of commercial treaties. The negotiations in Vienna proved harder than they had anywhere else, because the Austrians kept backing away from tentative agreements. Rather than abandon the talks, however, the British tried to make the most of each diminished proposal from Austria, only to find it again backing away. Dashing British hopes for terms as good as those in the 1860 treaty with France, Austria offered either a maximum 15 per cent tariff with a long list of exceptions or a 25 per cent maximum without exception. Gladstone at the

Exchequer advised acceptance of the latter terms. Then it became apparent that the Austrian ministry was not interested in any sort of tariff treaty unless it secured the large loan needed to shore up the country's tottering finances. Beaumont, who maintained a lively interest in the negotiations, was astonished at the Austrian assumption that the British government could control the capital market. Still, he made good use of the unwillingness of the leading private bankers, Barings and Rothschilds, to lend to any impoverished government that refused to stimulate the commerce of its country through lowered barriers to trade.

The two countries finally settled upon an agreement at the end of 1865, alongside an agreement between Austria and France. Though France was not ahead of Britain this time, once again it was the treaty with France that defined the new tariff. The Anglo-Austrian treaty did not amount to much more than a most-favoured-nation agreement. The main addition was Britain's agreement to reduce its duty on wine in bottles to equal that on wine in wood, while Austria undertook to reduce its maximum tariff to 25 per cent, though not until 1867, with a further reduction to 20 per cent in 1870. Austria's treaties with Britain and France gave those two states most-favoured-nation benefits that they valued. France enjoyed the further reduction in the British wine duties, while Britain enjoyed the relaxation France had obtained in the Austrian navigation laws. However, the Anglo-Austrian agreement of 1865 was described as 'a preliminary treaty' since the Austrian commitments had yet to be defined in working detail. That was work of the sort Mallet and Behrens had participated in alongside Cobden during the autumn of 1860. In other words, Austria gave Britain nothing more substantial in 1865 than guidelines for action in the future.

f. The Benefits

Britain's agreement with Austria brought the network of commercial treaties near to completion. The Anglo-Austrian treaty had yet to be made operational; and France was still to reach agreement with Portugal. Otherwise the components of the network were in place by the end of 1865, and its main features were established. In commercial terms the accomplishment was substantial, and Prussia and Italy reaped significant political rewards. Yet the achievement was strangely equivocal for the initiating powers, Britain and France. As free-trade purists in Britain had predicted, the process of constructing the network confirmed the reciprocal nature of commercial treaty-making. Britain could not keep continental Europeans from thinking of lower tariffs in terms of concessions. The example that Britain set in scuttling most of its tariff found few continental admirers and all but destroyed Britain's bargaining power. As for France, it suffered from other illusions. Napoleon's hope for a peaceful extension of French influence over neighbouring states through commercial treaties was not to be fulfilled.

The extent and interlocking character of the network were nevertheless extraordinary, unprecedented in European history and unsurpassed until the creation of the European Economic Community after 1957. Once Austria had joined, it embraced virtually all of Western and Central Europe. In addition to the states with which Britain reached agreement, France concluded treaties with Switzerland in 1864, with the United Kingdoms of Sweden and Norway, the Hanse towns, Spain and the Netherlands in 1865, and with Portugal in 1867. Belgium, the most avid of the treaty-making states, reached a host of agreements in 1863, with Switzerland, Prussia, Italy, the Hanse towns, the Netherlands, Sweden and Norway, and Denmark. Many, though not all, of the treaties included further tariff-cutting provisions, to the benefits of which the contracting parties' earlier treaty partners were then entitled through the unconditional most-favoured-nation clause. These were designed to benefit the particular commercial interests of the two contracting parties in each treaty, and were often of little use, and occasionally of some harm, to their other most-favoured-nation treaty partners. On the other hand, some states accompanied their bilateral tariff agreements with unilateral reductions in their general tariff, especially for imports of needed raw materials. Aside from such unilateral reductions, the network extended a uniform 'conventional' tariff across Europe, with duties averaging from 8 to 15 with a maximum of 25 per cent.[49]

By the end of 1865, there was something truly approaching a European common market. Separate from the network of tariff treaties but reinforcing it, France and its closest affiliates, Belgium, Switzerland and Italy, set up a Latin Monetary Union. The barriers to trade on the great waterways of the continent, including the Scheldt and the Rhine, were dismantled. Of still greater importance, the continent was laced with railways in the middle third of the nineteenth century, even more densely in Belgium than in Britain, proliferating across Germany into the pre-industrial empires and principalities of Eastern Europe. Railways provide more than swift land transport. Wherever they were built, they broke the cake of custom and stimulated enterprise.

But the emerging community did not look at all like the paradise of liberated individual enterprise that Cobden and British free traders had envisaged. The construction of the commercial treaty network in the 1860s strengthened the new nation states, as they meant it to do, and increased their capacities for rivalry instead of lessening governmental intervention in economic matters. The British spoke of free trade in the universal terms of economic science and moral values, but each continental state pursued its own distinctive commercial policy, tailored to its particular industrial needs and political ambitions. British economists insisted on the primacy of the consumer, who would always benefit from lower prices, whether for domestic produce or imports cheapened by lower tariffs. In the governing discourse of Britain, producers' interests were suspect as selfish. But producer-interest reigned supreme on the continent, where it was associated with the sinews of power. British trade policy thus turned out to be as nationally idiosyncratic as that of the continental states, indeed more so because it had less in common with them than they had with each other. Britain's insistence that its policy was framed for the good of world trade rather than in the national interest was dismissed by continental trade negotiators as one more manifestation of British hypocrisy.

It was still too soon, at the end of 1865, to assess the economic benefits of the network. Most of its components had just been put in place or had yet to become fully operative. The statistics on commerce were still rudimentary and unrefined, even in the most advanced economies. Even if these statistics documented, as they did, a great expansion of trade between the members of the network, it was not clear how much of the credit for this growth should go to their lowered tariffs. The heat of argument had magnified the significance of tariffs, but there were other obvious contributory factors: for instance, improved transport, diversion of trade away from the United States and China, and the increase in the worldwide supply of gold. Considerations such as these have led economic historians to agree that tariff reductions made only a marginal contribution to the expansion of international trade in the 1860s; commentators also point out that the growth had begun already in the 1850s and at a higher rate than in the ensuing decade. Historians are impressed by the diffused prosperity of Europe in the 1860s, but the truth is that the economic well being looked more impressive in retrospect, particularly amidst the long depression that set in during the final quarter of the century, than it actually felt at the time under the impact of the cotton famine.

There were, nevertheless, remarkable figures on trade, particularly between the original pair of treaty partners. Gladstone calculated later that trade between Britain and France almost doubled between 1859 and 1864.[50] The figures issued by the Board of Trade at the time put British exports to France for 1861 at £8,896,282, up from £5,249,980 in 1860, with spectacular increases in railway components and in woollens and worsteds. Milner Gibson as president of the Board gave the trade with France much of the credit for the prosperity Britain enjoyed in spite of the American Civil War. The initially sceptical *Economist* admitted that even the 'most sanguine advocates of the French treaty hardly expected so much'.[51] There was a further increase in the exports to France in 1862, not as much as for the preceding year but again particularly great in woollens and worsteds. Over the next two years there was a slow decline from the high-water mark of 1862, but by then the benefits from the more recent trade treaties were taking effect. Milner Gibson pointed out that the cumulative effect of Belgium's treaties with France and then Britain was to reduce the duty on the British export of textiles to Belgium by 30 per cent.[52]

More generally, because the terms of the 1860 treaty between Britain and France formed the basis on which the subsequent treaties built, 'the Treaty Tariff of Europe was, in effect, settled, both as to the classification of goods and rates of duty, with especial reference to the requirements of the trade of the United Kingdom.'[53] After 1860, however, this advantage to Britain diminished as France refined the treaty tariff of Europe in its particular interest.

The reservations the Treasury had felt at the revenue implications of the tariff reductions of 1860 were dispelled by the substantial income it drew from the remaining duties on imports of consumer goods, which the prospering British, enticed by the reduced price, bought in ever-increasing amounts. The government continued indeed to derive a greater proportion of its revenue from customs dues than did most protectionist nations. Nearly one-third, or £21,707,000, of the total Treasury revenue of £69,196,478 in 1865 came from the customs.[54] Table 3.1 indicates that this proportion diminished only slowly in the ensuing decades, as did the contribution of the wine and related spirit duties so important in commercial diplomacy:

Table 3.1 Amount of Revenue of the United Kingdom for Selected Years, in Millions of Pounds[55]

	1876	1878	1880	1882	1884	1886
Customs revenue	20	19.9	19.3	19.2	19.7	19.8
Wine duties	1.7	1.6	1.3	1.3	1.2	1.1
Spirits duties	6.1	5.5	4.6	4.2	4.2	4.1
Total revenue	67.3	69.2	70.2	74.2	75.1	78.2

Even so, it was British trade and industry rather than the Treasury that reaped the greatest rewards from the opening of the European market. Its importance for British trade is indicated in Tables 3.2 and 3.3. Rarely in the last 40 years of the nineteenth century did continental Europe absorb less than a third of British exports; rarely in the same period did continental European countries supply less than 40 per cent of what Britain imported. These proportions were far higher than for any other continent. Only in imports from North America and then only once, around 1880, did the proportional shortfall in the comparison with the other continents dip below 10 per cent.

The fact of the primacy of the European market for Britain throughout the lifetime of the basically Anglo-French network of commercial treaties,

Table 3.2 United Kingdom Exports by Continents, 1860–1900 (Percentage of Total Exports)[56]

Year	Europe	Africa	Asia	North America	South America	Australia
1860	36.0	5.1	20.2	19.1	12.4	7.2
1865	38.3	6.1	18.4	16.8	12.3	8.1
1870	39.7	6.8	18.9	18.1	11.5	5.0
1875	42.1	4.9	19.5	14.2	10.6	8.7
1880	35.9	5.9	23.4	17.9	9.4	7.5
1885	36.1	5.2	23.3	14.1	9.4	11.9
1890	34.8	6.7	21.8	15.7	12.2	8.8
1895	36.5	8.5	20.2	15.5	11.5	7.8
1900	41.0	9.5	21.0	10.3	8.8	9.4

Table 3.3 United Kingdom Imports by Continents, 1860–1900 (Percentage of Total Imports)[57]

Year	Europe	Africa	Asia	North America	South America	Australia
1860	40.7	7.9	13.9	24.7	9.7	3.1
1865	41.2	10.5	20.9	11.6	11.9	3.9
1870	43.7	7.1	14.8	19.3	10.4	4.7
1875	42.4	5.6	15.7	21.5	9.1	5.7
1880	39.1	4.9	14.1	29.5	6.1	6.3
1885	42.4	4.9	15.2	26.3	4.9	6.3
1890	44.4	4.7	13.3	26.2	4.4	7.0
1895	46.3	4.7	11.3	24.1	5.5	8.1
1900	42.4	4.3	9.9	30.9	5.7	6.8

from 1860 to 1892, does not indicate how or even whether the treaty network contributed to that primacy. All that Tables 3.1, 3.2 and 3.3 make clear is the supreme importance for Britain of the European portion of its worldwide trade. But that point was obscured for Britain when its economic supremacy stood at its height worldwide. It was further obscured by the deviation of the British economy from the European norm. The British economy was decidedly less dependent on the European market than were the economies of the continental states, as Table 3.4 indicates:

Table 3.4 Comparison of the Geographical Destination of Exports of Europe, the United Kingdom and Continental Europe, 1860–1910 (in Percentages of Total Exports; Three Years' Annual Average)[58]

		Europe	North America	South America	Asia	Africa	Oceania
1860							
	Europe	67.5	9.1	7.7	10.0	3.2	2.5
	UK	34.3	16.6	12.0	25.7	3.2	8.2
	Continent	82.0	5.8	5.8	3.1	3.2	0.1
1880							
	Europe	72.2	8.4	6.0	8.6	2.5	2.3
	UK	35.6	15.9	10.2	25.4	4.3	8.4
	Continent	85.0	5.8	4.5	2.8	1.8	0.1
1910							
	Europe	67.9	7.6	7.5	9.8	4.8	2.4
	UK	35.2	11.6	12.6	24.5	7.4	8.6
	Continent	78.0	6.4	5.9	5.2	3.9	0.5

Moreover, the dependence of the continental states on the European market increased during the life of the Anglo–French network of commercial treaties,[59] while the degree of British dependence remained fairly stable.

Joseph Chamberlain, who was to turn away from free trade towards the end of the century, began by defending it because of the success he enjoyed as a young industrialist in the 1860s selling the products of his metal manufacturing business in the old world as well as the new.[60] But the sector in Britain that benefited most from the expanding European market was not the staple industries, metal manufacturing and cotton textiles, but rather the woollens and worsteds industry of Yorkshire. Textiles generally fared better than metal manufacturing under the terms of the 1860 treaty, as Cobden recognised.[61] However the comparative importance of Europe as a market for cotton textiles declined after 1820, while their volume of sales expanded in the warmer climates of Latin America, Asia and Africa. The European market deteriorated also in quality as it began to take more cotton yarn than cloth.[62]

For British woollens, the European market was of crucial importance for a mixture of reasons, some fleeting, some fundamental. Behrens had asserted the interests of West Yorkshire woollens during the negotiations in Paris more effectively than the somewhat negligent spokesmen had done for Lancashire cottons. More generally, the weakening of cottons increased the opportunity for woollens. Woollens profited widely from the dearth and high price of cotton

during the American Civil War. Alderman Mitchell congratulated the Bradford Chamber of Commerce at the beginning of 1862: the minutes reported
him as saying that, 'While in Lancashire, unhappily, we saw great commercial
depression, so that funds had to [be] subscribed in many towns to give relief to
those in distress, yet in Bradford we were passing through a winter in which
the working classes were well employed. During his fourteen years' residence
in Bradford, [Alderman Mitdell] did not know that there had been a winter
when the working classes were so well employed as they had been during the
present, and this was mainly owing to the commercial treaty with France.'[63]
Bradford did even better than other centres of the woollens industry in Yorkshire. Fashion added to its fortune. The particular blend of worsted wear in
which Bradford specialised included warps of cotton, which remained cheaper
than wool, and were used to produce a hard and lustrous cloth which went well
over the crinolines of the day, better than the more expensive all-woollen
worsteds in which the French specialised.[64]

For France, the impact of the tariff-reducing policy that Napoleon III introduced looked different. His ministers had tackled tariffs on two fronts. Unilaterally, they moved in the same direction though not as far as the British,
removing prohibitive import and nearly all export duties and reducing the
duties on imported grain to about 3 per cent *ad valorem*. On the diplomatic
front, the French far outstripped the British in the pace and extent of their
treaty-making. The persistence of the French government was the more
remarkable because the initial economic results of their policy were more upsetting than encouraging. The iron and steel industry reeled under the impact of
competition from Britain, and imports of pig iron and steel increased sharply.[65]
French imports in general rose discouragingly in 1861 while their exports fell.
A bad harvest and the disruption of the American market could be used to
explain these results. They still cast a worrying shadow on what the British
embassy in Paris praised as 'a policy of commercial liberty'.[66] However, in 1863
the French iron and steel industry, braced by foreign competition to increase
its efficiency and decrease the costs of production, began to recover. Foreign
firms were forced 'to give up most of the gains obtained during the two preceding years on the French market'.[67] By the end of 1865 *The Economist* felt
able to congratulate 'our neighbours' on the official French trade figures.[68]

There was something rueful about these congratulations because, even in the
bad year of 1861, France exported much more to than it imported from Britain.
In 1864 those exports totalled 891,000,000 francs as against imports valued at
567,200,000 francs. The staple French exports, unlike the British, were luxury
goods such as the wines of Bordeaux, the silks of Lyons and stylish *articles de
Paris* – jewellery, clocks, furniture and high-fashion clothing. But the French
also replaced the British as suppliers in the construction of their own railway
system. The wry congratulations of *The Economist* reflected a mounting worry

in Britain that the French were not embracing the policy of the freeing of trade, to which Napoleon had introduced them, as warmly as the British had after Sir Robert Peel inaugurated it in the 1840s. The trade figures after 1860 made the benefits of free trade for the French obvious to the British, but not to the French.

This difference in interpretation was to become maddeningly apparent over woollens, especially over the mixed woollens on which Bradford particularly prided itself. Cobden's treaty raised up a rival to Bradford in Roubaix, on the French border with Belgium. According to an official French report of 1867, 'The Roubaix manufacturers who, in 1861, were principally noted for their fancy stuff woven by hand, began a resolute competition with Bradford; borrowed its modes of spinning and weaving; bought its power looms, and imported its finishing machines.'[69] By 1866 the mayor of Roubaix was able to report that over the past five years the town's population had almost doubled, the amount of raw wool that it processed had more than trebled, and its output nearly trebled. The manufacturers and merchants of Bradford would not have begrudged this achievement if the men of Roubaix had not stiffened their protectionism and demanded higher customs duties on Bradford goods. The merchants of Roubaix competed effectively with those of Bradford in foreign markets and even sold their wares in Bradford itself. But why should that success induce Roubaix to improve the terms of access for exports from Bradford into the French market? The talk in Bradford about equity and justice fell on deaf ears in Roubaix.

Though extreme and in some ways distorted, the reaction in Roubaix provided an indication of the ambivalent French response to the policy of commercial liberalism on which Napoleon III had embarked. France had enjoyed remarkable economic growth since 1840, 20 years before the imperial change in policy. The growth had been especially rapid between 1852 and 1857. But in 1860, the year of the Anglo-French treaty, the pace actually slackened, and it remained slower thereafter. Furthermore, the French regarded the growth of industry as a mixed blessing. It accentuated the unequal distribution of wealth among the regions of France, undermining for example the textile industry of the south-east and south-west in the face of competition from the technologically more sophisticated north.[70] Such differing regional fortunes were not unknown in Britain, but there they had been moderated by the emergence of great manufacturing industries in former backwaters of the Midlands and the north. In any case, the French were less willing than the British to sacrifice any sector of their society to foreign industrial competition.[71] They implicitly denied the Ricardian principle, basic to free trade, of comparative advantage, whereby, in the famous example embodied in the Methuen treaty of 1703, Portugal concentrated on the production of wine while England focused on woollens. (That application of the principle ignored the fact that, while England never produced much wine, Portugal had possessed a woollen textile industry which the Methuen treaty destroyed – an outcome the Portuguese bemoan to this day.) The French aversion to the unrestrained workings of comparative advantage prevailed without exposing itself in articulated economic theory. Napoleon's trade policy was still safe at the end of 1865; but it was not secure.

Belgium, on the other hand, had come upon the commercial policy that 'conformed most closely to its interests'.[72] It was a policy of negotiated tariff reduction, as distinct from the British policy of unilateral reduction rarely accompanied by negotiation, and it required an interventionist state. Belgian officials from the King on down regarded the promotion of commerce as among their primary responsibilities. Belgium pursued the art of commercial treaty-making assiduously, as befitted a small but highly industrialised state at the crossroads of Western Europe. The treaty with Britain set the Belgian tariff on textiles, while the treaty with the Zollverein set the tariff on chemicals. The treaty with the Netherlands involved a settlement of the old quarrel over the Scheldt tolls. The Belgians gave Italy the reductions it wanted on preserved fruit, oil seeds, sardines and olive oil. The treaty with Sweden and Norway reduced the tariff on timber. In 1865, once their web of treaties was complete, the Belgians sustained the momentum towards freer trade by revising their general tariff downwards, below the conventional treaty tariff on some items. These included iron which, no longer fearing competition, Belgium marketed in 25 countries. All in all, Belgium rejoiced in this 'période . . . d'apaisement et de détente. On liquida toutes les vieilles querelles. . . . Le libéralisme économique, allié à un de politique contractuelle active, allait nous assurer une ère de prospérité incomparable' ('period . . . of calm and relaxation. The old disputes are settled . . . Economic liberalism, with active political reinforce-ment, assured us of an era of incomparable prosperity).[73]

Switzerland, another small crossroads country with a vigorous economy, shared the Belgian enthusiasm for tariff-reducing diplomacy and profited from it similarly well. But Italy, which shared their faith in the policy, suffered for it.[74] Throughout the 1860s Italy adhered, in general terms though not in detailed practice, to the philosophy of free trade which Cavour had imbibed from the British, and produced one of the most liberal tariffs in Europe. Commercial treaties gave the newly unified kingdom of Italy the political benefit of recognition which Catholic states were otherwise reluctant to confer. But economically, aside from infusions of private investment capital from its treaty partners, from France, Britain and to a lesser extent Belgium and Switzerland, the policy proved costly. It depleted the customs revenue, which the new state needed to set its financial house in order. It impoverished the economically backward south, which was far from the main markets of Europe. The country as a whole could not benefit from the opening of international trade so long as its railway system remained slim.

It was too soon to reach any clear assessment of the economic results of the inclusion of Prussia at the head of the Zollverein in the broader European network initiated by Britain and France. The Prussian treaty with France did not take effect, and the treaty with Britain was not signed, until the spring of 1865. Economically the Prussian objective may have been largely defensive, to regain the French market which the Anglo-French treaty threatened to alienate. The Prussian treaties with France and then Britain boded fair to secure at least that end. The political benefits of these treaties for Prussia were, on the other hand, already quite clear. They constituted a successful extension of the policy that Prussia had pursued to make itself leader of a *Kleindeutschland* excluding Austria. This was a result that neither Cobden nor Napoleon III had envisaged when they initiated the treaty network.

Chapter 4

Dividends in Wartime, 1866–1872

'... it is not an expansion of trade which one wishes to see as the result of [the renewal of the Anglo-French] treaty, but it is ... the putting away from the minds of all individuals connected with the two countries of the idea of war.'

Edward Miall, MP for Bradford, to the
Chamber of Commerce, 24 Jan. 1870

Cobden died in 1865; and the prospects for realisation of his faith that commerce would replace war as the determining force among nations faded with him. He had hoped that the commercial treaty-making that he inaugurated in 1860 would bring peace even more than prosperity. In the event this treaty-making was accompanied by prosperity and war. Within four years of Cobden's death and the completion of the treaty network, two major wars transformed the political map of Europe. To add to the perversity, Europe prospered economically. Its international trade expanded on the whole more rapidly during the period of war and its wake, between 1866 and 1872, than in the more peaceful early 1860s. Commercial diplomacy also served to consolidate the gains of war. Even so, the second of these wars, which broke out during the negotiations for the renewal of Cobden's treaty with France, placed that treaty and with it the entire network in jeopardy.

From the outset, war had provided the context within which the commercial treaty network was created. It was prompted in 1859 by war in northern Italy. Afterwards attention was focused on the European market by the American Civil War. War was commonly regarded as inimical to commercial development and likely to disrupt the market. But that did not always turn out to be the case. For instance, the war that broke out between the Danes and the major German states over Schleswig-Holstein was expected to depress the Easter market at Leipzig in 1864. Yet Crowe reported that 'German customers bought briskly enough; & a fair quantity of goods was taken for Italy, Switzerland, the Netherlands, Sweden and Norway, Russia, the Levant, & North and South America.'[1]

The blessings of peace and the beneficent consequences of the commercial treaty network seemed nonetheless clear from the end of 1865 into the early weeks of 1866. Crowe reported that the Michaelmas fair at Leipzig was 'a good one for many branches of trade, in part because of the cessation of hostilities in the United States, in part, because of the impulse due to the treaty between the Zollverein, France and England, which came into force in July, in part because of the rise in value of cotton & yarns.'[2] There was a rush to take advantage of the reopened American market. The blossoming trade distracted the Prussian business community from the divisiveness of Bismarck's ministry in other regards. 'The people generally,' Crowe reported, 'is content to contemplate the gradual improvement of its welfare, and finds a consolation in the conviction that, whatever may be the evils attendant upon the complication of the political situation, there is something for which it may be grateful in the progress of liberalism in the principles of international trade.'[3]

a. The Austro-Prussian War

Bismarck's machinations soon darkened the sky. Taking advantage of Austria's internal problems, he picked a fight with Prussia's inveterate rival in spite of their recent commercial treaty. The fight threatened to engulf much of Germany, particularly Saxony, which lay across the most direct route from Berlin to Vienna, and turn the member states of the Zollverein against each other. It was also likely to involve Italy, which sought to wrest Venetia from the Austrians. In this and other ways the conflict affected several means and areas by which Napoleon meant to extend the sway of France in Central Europe. The Emperor feared further aggrandisement of Italy, but seemed likely to gain from the division of Germany and the enfeeblement of one or other of its rival powers. The impending war depressed trade and pushed commercial questions aside as of secondary importance. A meeting of the Zollverein, called to deal with, among other things, a dispute in which the British woollens industry was keenly interested about the definition of fulled cloth, had to break up before it could reach any decision. The talks between Austria and Britain, called to work out terms to make their recent treaty effective, had to be suspended.

As military manœuvres commenced, Crowe became involved as representative of a neutral power in the central location of Leipzig. With the approval of the Foreign Office, he accepted responsibility for the regional interests of Austria, whose consul had been incarcerated by the Prussians. He despatched news of the opening hostilities, dealt with the Prussians when they occupied Leipzig and warned of the disaster that awaited the King of Hanover when he invaded from the west. On the eve of the climactic battle of the war, Britain agreed with Austria to postpone their commercial negotiations until three months after the return of peace. Next day, on 3 July 1866, defying widespread predictions, Prussia crushed Austria across the Bohemian border at Königgrätz. Never was the transforming power of battle more clearly demonstrated. For a moment Napoleon III seemed to be 'the all-powerful arbiter of Europe'.[4] But it soon became apparent that the pre-eminence of France was in fact diminished by the aggrandisement of Prussia as it proceeded to form a North German Confederation. Within three months a second power had further clouded the ascendancy of France when Italy won Venetia from the Austrians. Lord Stanley, the new Foreign Secretary in Britain, observed of the French emperor: 'In 1859, he encouraged an Italian war, hoping to establish an Italian confederacy dependent on France. Instead of that he has created a strong united Italy, not even friendly to France. In 1866 he has allowed a German war to begin, hoping various results none of which has been obtained. He has created by the side of France a strong compact German empire fully the equal of France in military power. Was ever man so over-reached twice?'[5]

The erstwhile liberal opponents of Bismarck in Germany rushed to make their peace with him. Their switch in sentiment was intensified by revulsion at the interest Austria displayed, before the outcome of the war was fully apparent, in obtaining assistance from France. Crowe reported that, two weeks after Königgrätz, the liberal nationalists of the Nationalverein resolved that 'A constitution for Germany exclusive of Austria is necessary; in virtue of which Prussia should wield supreme military, diplomatic and commercial command.'[6] Prussia had seized control of the Zollverein even before its military victory. Afterwards it formalised its control by replacing the requirement for unanimous agreement from the members with weighted majority voting. Bismarck's reliance on blood and iron triumphed all the way. The weakness of commercial considerations was underscored by the sad calculations of Saxon traders over what to do after their country chose the losing side and was allowed to retain only vestiges of its former independence. As Crowe reported, 'If Saxony were annexed to Prussia the cost of maintaining the Saxon troops would be doubled, but the expense of maintaining a Court & numerous officials would more than counterbalance that; moreover the interest on the war contribution to Prussia (half a million per annum) would be saved: the thrifty Saxon will soon perceive that he has merely retained independence in the administration of local affairs for an indefinitely short period at the cost of 2,000,000 Thalers per an: & this fact would in time sap the foundations of loyalty.'[7]

But that was not how the balance was weighed or the events of the year interpreted by *The Economist*. In an astonishing affirmation of faith in the supremacy of commerce, it declared in the wake of the war that 'European nations have made real progress in learning to appreciate their relations of inter-independence.' What *The Economist* had in mind were the commercial provisions of the peace treaties that Germany and Italy made with Austria as well as the reorganisation of the Zollverein, and on the British side a strengthening of the commercial division at the Foreign Office. 'The sound of the last cannon has scarcely died away when the diplomatist again appears on the scene, but this time it is not for the purpose of establishing arbitrary principles of dismemberment or capricious distributions of territory, but for the useful purpose of extending the basis of the commercial relations of the different members of the European family.' It found 'every reason to hope that we shall see as the result a large development of commercial intercourse between Austria and Italy, and important modifications in the same relations between Austria and Germany, and between the Zollverein and the other German States'.[8]

There was a stark contrast between this effusion and the report that Crowe submitted on the trade of Leipzig for the year that was coming to an end.[9] There was no light on the horizon for the defeated allies of Austria. An epidemic of cholera and a bad harvest combined with the ravages of war to make 1866 'peculiarly disastrous to Saxony. . . . Yet no year opened under more favorable auspices.' The inflow of raw and semi-manufactured materials, particularly iron and cotton yarn, into the Zollverein, accelerated by the commercial treaties of the previous year, had set Saxon textile mills working overtime to meet anticipated demand,

> when suddenly the prospects of peace gave place to expectations of war. . . . Prices rapidly fell; merchandize was withdrawn & stored, or exported to the United States [which responded by heightening its tariff walls], & orders were countermanded in every direction. . . . A panic took possession of the labouring classes in consequence of the extensive stoppage of works undertaken by private enterprise; there was a run in April upon all the savings banks of the country, and the government offices for the sale of salt were besieged by alarmed housewives. In May the Prussian troops closing in upon the Northern & Western frontier & the Austrians gathering to the South and East increased the alarms of the Saxons whose fertile territory seemed on the eve of becoming a battle field. There was but one cry from the manufacturing & trading towns throughout the land, the cry for peace at any price. . . . Perfect stagnation marked the summer months. . . . The rapid progress of the war which enabled Prussia to dictate terms at Vienna would have produced a more complete change in the condition if [Saxony] had been included in the treaty. . . . The postponement of the separate peace till late in the year kept the mercantile & manufacturing world in painful suspense, & trade did not recover from its languor till 1866 had expired.

The Michaelmas fair at Leipzig was 'one of the poorest of its kind . . . for years'.[10] Cholera continued to rage 'intensely . . . & carried off many victims even amongst the few visitors . . . business was almost nominal'.

The setback to Leipzig and Saxony proved permanent. Military defeat and subjection to Prussia reduced the significance of Saxony and of the Central European fairs at Leipzig, already undermined by improving transcontinental rail transport, while across the Atlantic the victorious North raised the

American tariff and thus kept Saxony out of a market on which it had depended. The British Foreign Office turned its attention towards the coal and iron industries of the Ruhr in western Prussia, site of the major rising challenge to Britain's industrial ascendancy. Britain lacked adequate representation in the Rhineland after withdrawing its mission from Frankfurt, another casualty of the war, which lost its independence and much of its accumulated wealth for siding with Austria. The increasingly perceptive reports Crowe sent in from Leipzig prompted Lord Stanley to ask him for periodic reports on the economy of the Rhineland and Westphalia. Stanley explained that 'the prosperous industry of those Provinces . . . has attracted much attention in this Country' because (to British surprise) it was 'successfully competing with that of the United Kingdom'.[11] How was this possible? What was 'the nature and extent of such progress'? Under what conditions was it being made?

On his first visit of inquiry to the Rhineland, Crowe saw plenty of evidence of the social cost of the war. He came upon 'a considerable stream of emigration . . . flowing from South Germany towards the outports'.[12] Back in Leipzig he found continuing emigration from the Austrian empire, 'Bohemians driven by hunger to abandon their homes'.[13] But the situation in the Rhineland itself was very different. There Crowe discovered an industrial boom that the war had slowed but not stopped. The boom embraced the industries at the heart of the industrial revolution: textiles, coal and iron. The textile-makers of the Rhineland imported their raw material, yarns and machinery from or through Britain but then produced fabrics 'which compete with those of Great Britain if not frequently on our own, certainly on many great neutral markets in Europe & America'.[14] The output of the Ruhr collieries had been rising rapidly over the past ten years. Although it was inferior in quality to the best British steam coals, the coal of the Ruhr was closer and hence cheaper to transport to the major industrial consumers in Belgium and France, where it competed successfully with all rivals, whether British, Belgian or French. 'It is scarcely possible to describe the pleasure & excitement caused in the Ruhr districts by the fact that during 1865 & 1866 [regardless of the war] Westphalian coal was carried with profit to the Belgian coal basins of Charleroi and Mons & even over the frontier into France.' As for the iron industry, though momentarily depressed, it had increased its output over the past decade even more rapidly than the collieries.

In a second report on the textile industry of the Rhineland, Crowe showed how, regardless of the British teaching that tariffs were invariably harmful, the Zollverein tariff was tailored to develop the German economy. The German textile industry, like the British, was divided mainly between cottons and woollens, leaving silks to the French. On the cottons side, the Zollverein tariff had focused on yarn ever since 'England overflowed Germany with that produce & put an end to spinning by hand.'[15] Imports of yarn into the Zollverein had fallen by more than 60 per cent under a tariff which declined from nine shillings in 1845 to six shillings in 1865 as the Germans built up their own productive capacity. The Germans dealt with woollens differently from cottons. Imports of woollen yarns had risen sharply, while those of cotton were falling. During the cotton famine, German manufacturers took a leaf out of Bradford's book and produced fabric of mixed wool and cotton. They found it 'easier . . . to compete with the British in half woollens than in cottons, and also in the higher grades of cloth than in the lower'. They were not yet competitive in cheap woollens, as merchants of West Yorkshire appreciated: hence their concern to hold down the continental tariff on goods of this quality.

The 'extraordinary development of the worsted manufacture in Germany'[16] and the entry of German yarns into England and Scotland kept West Yorkshire anxious for better access to the Austrian market. The Anglo-Austrian treaty of 1865 enabled Britain to benefit from the tariff reductions in Austria's treaties with the Zollverein and France, but the worsted producers of Yorkshire hoped for more; and the Foreign Office assumed that Britain was entitled to better terms in return for the reduction in the duty on bottled wine. The anxiety of the Bradford merchants increased over the summer of 1866 when the Liberal government in Britain was defeated over its Reform Bill. The Chamber of Commerce had come to think better of the Liberals after Russell reorganised the commercial activity of the Foreign Office. Now that Cobden had gone, the merchants of Bradford regarded Gladstone as their best friend in the business of government. They gave the incoming Conservative ministry a cool reception; and they grew more apprehensive at the discovery that Austria had concluded its treaty with France before settling the detailed provisions required to give full effect to the treaty with Britain. Behrens insisted to the Conservative Foreign Secretary, Lord Stanley, that 'our interests and those of France are so dissimilar, that rates of duties which may be easily conceded by the French negotiators, because they are of no real importance to their commerce, may be, and frequently are, highly prejudicial to that of England.'[17] Stanley, who prided himself on his understanding of the needs of the textile industry in Lancashire, moved promptly to finalise the agreement with Austria.

But the Austrians had lost interest in the agreement.[18] They used the clause in their peace treaty with Prussia that required revision of their commercial relations with the Zollverein – the clause that so gratified *The Economist* – to postpone further discussion with Britain. The postwar constitutional transformation of the Austrian empire into Austria-Hungary provided a further pretext for delay. Yet the desire of the Austrians to regroup their forces, which underlay the constitutional change, also revived their interest in a less protective commercial policy, to stimulate and so strengthen their industry through foreign competition. Furthermore, the enhanced position of Hungary with its surplus agricultural production increased the support for lower tariffs. Mercantile concern in Britain focused on the desirability of *ad valorem* duties in the Austrian tariff instead of the current specific duties which kept cheap but heavy British textiles, cottons as well as woollens, out of the Austrian market. Louis Mallet, the British negotiator, devised a package of tariffs that won approval from the Austrian government and came close to the spirit though not to the letter of the 1865 treaty. Lord Stanley was reluctant to agree because it would not be implemented until the protracted Austrian negotiations with the Zollverein were concluded. He was even more concerned because, until that time, news of the package could not be transmitted to the British merchants who were continuing to press him. But he finally assented, and an agreement along Mallet's lines was signed in September 1867.

Economic developments are rarely as dramatic and readily identifiable as political ones. It was not until the end of 1867 that economic analysts sensed a change of tide in the European economy that had begun the previous year, before the outbreak of the German war, and it remained almost impossible to interpret the change in a broader context. The preceding four years seemed in retrospect to be 'a period of rising confidence, brisk markets, and advancing prices'.[19] Prices began to fall after a financial panic in May 1866 precipitated by the collapse of a London bank, Overend Gurney, which reflected a more general unsettledness of the money market in the wake of the American Civil War and rumours of war in Europe.[20] By the end of 1867 prices for cotton were down 70 per cent, for wool 33 per cent, for iron 20 per cent. Wages moved in the same direction, falling in all related trades by some 20 to 30 per cent. Initially these trends looked unwelcome, even disastrous. Yet their impact on import and export trade turned out to be less than was feared. Reduction in the price of British exports was gradually followed by an increase in volume, particularly for cottons but also for iron and woollens. Imports were down in 1867 compared to 1866 (though above those of 1865), but exports of merchandise were generally up. The change in prices since 1866 did not alter the upward trend in the value of British exports, which, aside from cottons, had risen by more than 37 per cent since 1862.[21] Cottons continued to be the exception after, as they had been during, the American Civil War. But Britain had made up in woollens and linens what it had lost in cottons, and in 1868 the value of exports rose as Britain supplied the goods for railway construction overseas. The impact of the American war on British commerce thus looked 'unexpectedly small'. By 1868 the same could be said of the German war and the financial crisis of 1866.[22]

In Germany itself, the commercial outlook turned promising in the wake of the war. In Leipzig Crowe found 'symptoms of recovery in every branch of business. . . . To replace the market of the United States which has become contracted for German manufactures by high duties on cottons & woollens, new markets were opened up in Asia; and money was freely subscribed to facilitate intercourse by railway with European countries & the Levant.'[23] He discovered to the west that 'The collieries of the Ruhr basin worked full time during the whole of 1868, employed their men at higher wages than in previous years, and raised . . . half a million tons more [fuel] than in 1867.'[24] Under the leadership of Delbrück, Bismarck's liberal lieutenant for economic affairs, and urged on by Prussian industrial interests, the Zollverein pursued a policy of reducing tariffs both bilaterally by treaty and unilaterally. In March 1868 the Zollverein reached agreement with Austria. The tariff reductions in that treaty were then generalised by incorporation in the Zollverein tariff, which was lowered further unilaterally for certain cotton goods, linen yarn, pig-iron, some forms of steel, drugs, fine leather goods and some other commodities.[25] The tariff remained discretely protective of vulnerable sectors of the textile industry. But the iron industry in Westphalia and the Ruhr participated well in the widening international economy, importing what it could not yet produce for further processing, and competing effectively with the British and Belgians in exports to other countries. In the spring of 1870, Crowe reported that 'Germany has finally recovered from the depression which marked its trade and industry in past years . . . the Zollverein market has been made to absorb more home made articles, and a larger business has been with South America, the Levant and the ports of the China Seas. Whilst the manufacture of cotton stuffs displayed little or no improvement of note that of woollens exhibited a clear increase.'[26]

For the moment even Austria proved willing to liberalise its tariff, though to a more limited degree than the Zollverein. The conclusion of Austria's treaty with the Zollverein cleared the way for a resumption of the talks with Britain. Beyond the benefits of the Austro-German treaty to which it was immediately admitted, Britain also wanted the terms outlined in the tentative agreement Mallet had reached with the Austrians, particularly on *ad valorem* duties for textiles. But that agreement, and especially its textile clauses, was unacceptable to industrial interests well represented in the Austrian legislature, which was itself strengthened by the reform of the constitution. In the face of this resistance, the Austrian government whittled down the Mallet package until little was left of its provision for textiles. The British dragged their feet throughout the negotiations but ultimately always gave way. The treaty, which was concluded at the end of 1869, did not possess much of substance or significance.[27] It nevertheless involved more than a most-favoured-nation clause, something Britain had not achieved since its treaty with Belgium.

While Germans, particularly the Prussians, spread their wings after 1866, the French began to pull theirs in. Freer international competition had not emboldened them, as the manufacturers and merchants of Bradford were dismayed to discover. Several of the latter went to the Paris Exhibition of 1866 to see the French display, but when they headed north to Roubaix, they met with hostility. One French master told them that he 'considered that the town of

Roubaix was sold, and that the treaty effected by the efforts of Mr. Cobden was inflicting serious and ruinous effects upon the manufacturing industry of France, and especially that of Roubaix.'[28] (The disconcerted Englishmen offered 'To all those gentlemen who . . . did not receive us with the hand of fellowship . . . our pity and forgiveness.') Meanwhile, the failure of the Crédit Foncier, a bank set up at the launching of Napoleon III's imperial enterprise, cast a discrediting light on his entire policy, as did the collapse of the empire he tried to set up in Mexico. The French economy fell into recession in 1867. So did the British. But the two countries reacted to their common recession quite differently, partly because of the different times from which they dated the commencement of their policies of tariff reduction. The British considered theirs to have begun with the repeal of the Corn Laws, an event followed by an era of periodic prosperity. The French, however, dated their change from the Anglo-French treaty, since which time their economy had slowed down. The recession had much to do with the glut of cotton released after the American Civil War; the resulting fall in prices, which extended to all textiles, led to bankruptcies, cutbacks in production and labour unrest. French manufacturers of cottons found themselves 'unable to meet the competition of British Spinners'.[29] France did not find compensation for the troubled cotton side of its textile industry either in woollens, as did the British, or in its already established pre-eminence in silks. The recession in textiles was accompanied by a slowdown in railway construction.

In 1868, a cotton spinner from Rouen, Augustin Pouyer-Quertier, launched a campaign to reverse Napoleon's tariff policy by denouncing the Anglo-French treaty when it was about to fall due for renewal.[30] British cottons had undoubtedly been dumped on the French market in connection with the American Civil War and the cotton famine.[31] The veteran statesman and protectionist, Adolphe Thiers, gave the spinner his backing. Blaming the recession on the emperor's policy, Pouyer-Quertier carried his campaign from the legislature into the country at the elections of 1869. He secured a sufficiently encouraging response from urban industrial workers to prompt some backtracking by the Emperor. Moving towards political at the expense of economic liberalism, Napoleon offered additional powers to the elected legislature, including the right to approve or reject tariff treaties, and a commission (later a legislative committee) of inquiry was set up into the effects of the 1860 treaty and the resulting network. The prospects for free trade hung in the balance; which way it would tip was not at all clear. Napoleon's actions effectively stopped the growth of the commercial treaty network. But the legislature declined to exercise its new powers in a protectionist direction. France could still reduce its existing tariff and advance towards freer trade; alternatively it could reverse that process, seek to raise its tariff as treaties came up for renewal, or renounce its commercial treaties entirely.

The uncertainty in France perplexed the British. Did the French not recognise how well they had done from their commercial treaties? Did they not see that Britain had done even better by getting rid of most tariffs entirely? While since 1860 France had set the pace of tariff reduction by treaty, Britain had continued to set the example of minimising if not eliminating its remaining duties: on hops in 1862, sugar and grain from 1864 to 1869, and timber, its last remaining duty on raw material, in 1866.

When Gladstone became Prime Minister at the end of 1868, he launched what became a national discussion about the course to follow when the Anglo-French treaty came up for renewal in 1870. Gladstone's experience and responsibilities as Chancellor of the Exchequer over the past eight years had dimmed his enthusiasm for Cobden's handiwork in the construction of a web of commercial treaties. Its principal supporter in cabinet was Cobden's closest associate, John Bright, who joined as President of the Board of Trade, but proved ineffective in executive office; moreover, precarious health induced him to retire before discussion of the French treaty was completed. W.E. Forster, the Bradford woollens manufacturer who rose to prominence as an advocate of assertive commercial diplomacy, was brought into the ministry, though not initially into the cabinet, with responsibility for education, a subject closely related to the growing awareness of Britain's deficiency in international economic competition. But Gladstone made Robert Lowe Chancellor of the Exchequer, and thus put the most outspoken critic of commercial treaty-making into a position of decisive importance.

As for Gladstone himself, he was more than ever averse to any loss in the revenue that the Treasury derived from the few remaining customs duties. He had also come to loathe the 'haggling'[32] inevitable in tariff treaty negotiations. Yet he continued to share Cobden's faith in free trade as conducive to peace as well as prosperity. He told the Foreign Office to remind the French government of 'two points': first, that British experience 'has established that great as is the advantage of substituting duties for prohibitions, & moderate duties for high ones . . . sweeping away duty altogether is by far the most beneficial'; and second, that the 1860 treaty had surely produced 'such a revelation to France itself of its own productive energy and power . . . that they will desire to extend the range of an experiment so inviting from its ascertained results.'[33] As for renewing the treaty of 1860, Gladstone hoped that, if the French were not yet ready to follow the British example by getting rid of most of their customs duties, they would at least agree to lower their existing treaty tariff.

That hope faded in face of the demand in France for increased protection. The question for Britain then became one of whether to preserve the existing treaty without improvement or, even, with some worsening of its terms. As the outlook darkened, the British ambassador in Paris persuaded the Foreign Secretary, Clarendon, and through him Gladstone not to do anything that might place the renewal of the 1860 treaty in jeopardy.[34] But there was little the British government could do to maintain the kind of agreement they wanted if the French were determined to amend it. Britain had nothing to offer by way of tariff bargaining; and even if it had, Gladstone would have recoiled from using it. Why offer anything when French goods already enjoyed largely free entry to the British market? No member of Gladstone's ministry would give a moment's countenance to the notion of threatening France with retaliatory tariffs. On the other hand, failure to renew the 1860 treaty in some form would deprive Britain of most-favoured-nation access to the benefits of the French commercial treaty network, which was considerably larger than the British, and hence subject Britain to discriminatory treatment in much of the continental market. In conveying Britain's concern to the French government, Lord Lyons, the British ambassador, reverted to the Cobdenite association between commercial diplomacy and good political relations. 'Could it be supposed that cordial feelings would exist in England towards France, if heavy protective duties were imposed upon English produce, while that of other countries whose treaties could not be put an end to immediately, was admitted at lower rates [?]' And again: 'It would . . . be very grievous if . . . the friendly and cordial feelings which had sprung up between the two nations should be sacrificed to the shortsighted and selfish clamour raised by certain branches of French industry.'[35]

While the British government discussed the subject in private, *The Economist* pressed the discussion in public. It was worried by questions about the renewal of the 1860 treaty that were being raised not just in France but also in England, in the Associated Chambers of Commerce and even in Lancashire, home of the cottons industry and the original heartland of free trade. Depression descended on east Lancashire between 1867 and 1869, bankrupting many manufacturers and reducing the value of the property of those who survived by as much as 60 per cent.[36] To counter questions from the north, *The Economist* turned out a succession of reports in 1869 on the benefits of the treaty. Beginning on the British side, the first report marshalled statistical evidence to show that British imports from France had at least doubled in the eight years since the treaty was concluded, that British exports had more than doubled and that exports of strictly British produce excluding the re-export of goods imported from abroad had likewise doubled.[37] As for British uneasiness that 'the increase of our exports to France – especially the exports of British produce – has not been on the same scale as the increase of our imports from France', *The Economist* put this contrast down to the lower level of industrial development in France as compared to Britain. While iron exports to France had fallen and exports of machinery and cutlery had risen only slowly or uncertainly, the export of coal had risen well. The most encouraging changes were:

in woollen, linen and cotton yarns and manufactures, but most of all in woollens. . . . With regard to woollen manufactures . . . before the treaty we sold very little to France. The highest of the three years before the treaty was 1858, when we sent 3,896,000 yards and 29,733 pieces, besides a small quantity entered only at value – the total being 260,500*l*. In the last three years, however, we have exported as follows: –

	Value	Quantities
1865	£1,685,000	20,864,000 yards
1866	£2,785,000	31,196,000 yards
1867	£3,110,000	27,139,000 yards

Turning to French dismay at the setback that some sectors particularly of their textile industry said they had suffered from their loss of tariff protection against British competition, *The Economist* did not dispute the claim. 'If the adjustment rendered inevitable a good deal of suffering in France, because the things they got cheaper from England had hitherto been supplied by manufacturers of their own, who now went to the wall, the general community in France must nevertheless have gained far more.' But consolation for consumers at the expense of producers did not have the appeal in France that it had in Britain. Aside from that general point, *The Economist* looked more closely at the figures for textiles to show that 'Except for cotton . . . the total French export of textile fabrics to all countries, as well as to the United Kingdom, has increased.' Noting how the French dominated the market in some categories of woollens manufacture, it counselled: 'these they ought to cultivate.'

The debate continued to revolve around textiles. Thiers as the leading protagonist of protection in France argued that the coarse fabrics produced in England not only controlled the lower end of the market but were displacing the more finished French products. Willing here again to concede the point. *The Economist* could only hope that the expansion of international trade would 'increase the number of moderately rich consumers' and thus overcome 'the apparent levelling tendency of free trade in the matter of finish'.[38] The journal used British experience to reassure the French. It drew attention to the return of the British cotton export trade to the level of 1860 and the improvement in the prices that textiles, expecially cottons, had begun to command, along with 'the very considerable increase in the exports of woollen and linen manufactures'.[39] The United States had been raising its tariff since the close of the Civil War, but so far British cottons had found markets elsewhere to offset losses in the American market.

By the end of the year *The Economist* could sigh with relief that the French government had not reversed its commercial policy but simply appointed a commission of inquiry into complaints about the commercial treaties. This had found defenders among the wine and silk producers of Bordeaux and Lyons and the shipping interests of Marseilles to counteract the protectionist textile manufacturers in the north of France. But the encouragement from southern France was offset by a revival of protectionism in the north of England, with political support from some Conservatives. *The Economist* explained this unwelcome phenomenon in Britain as a consequence of the disruption to the cotton trade caused by the American Civil War. The journal also attempted to minimise the importance of Britain's adverse balance of trade by pointing to some components of the nation's highly favourable balance of payments: 'our enormous investments abroad', 'the large commission business which our merchants and bankers transact' and 'the freights which are due to us as the carriers of the world's commerce'.[40]

While *The Economist* mounted its defence of the Anglo-French treaty, the Chamber of Commerce in Bradford pressed for an improvement and extension of the agreement. The prominence of Bradford in this movement had as much to do with the personal capacity of Jacob Behrens for information gathering and analysis as it had with the woollens industry. Though according to Behrens and his colleagues the level of tariffs on the continent was of vital importance to their industry, Lancashire with its cottons was if anything more agitated at the end of the 1860s and the beginning of the 1870s about tariffs than was Yorkshire. Still, by all accounts, woollens had done better than any other sector of British industry through the treaty with France and its surrounding network. Trade with the continent had lifted Bradford and its wares to their pinnacle of achievement, symbolised by the opening of a grand Victorian Gothic Wool Exchange at the heart of the town in 1867. The town's merchants had accumulated a detailed understanding of continental commerce unparalleled elsewhere in England. Some, like Behrens, came from families in business on both sides of the Channel. Between them they could command most of the languages each with its own idiosyncratic terminology, used in the textile industry on the continent; indeed, they asked the Foreign Office for all the information it received on foreign tariffs in the original language rather than in translation.

They favoured British participation in all the burgeoning extensions of European economic integration, including the Latin Monetary Union and the establishment of a uniform system of weights and measures, and pressed the Foreign Office to keep pace with the French in treaty-making. But to no avail. When a deputation to the Chancellor of the Exchequer, Robert Lowe, from the Associated Chambers of Commerce argued in favour of a treaty to open up the highly protected markets of Spain and Portugal, the Chancellor told them that 'negotiating Foreign Treaties of Commerce was mother of the heresy of Reciprocity as against Free Trade. . . . If they were to negotiate with Spain and Portugal, they would in effect be conferring an immense advantage upon them for their illiberality.'[41] The Associated Chambers were as devoted as Lowe to the freedom of trade from governmental interference. The point of disagreement concerned whether bilateral tariff-bargaining would bring about free trade. No Chamber of Commerce thought yet of reinstating tariffs to strengthen Britain's bargaining position.

The leaders of the Associated Chambers continued to look disparagingly at the competence of the Foreign Office when it came to treaty-making. They wanted a greater hand in it themselves. In every other regard they dealt on their own with the business of the European market: for instance, they sent their own delegations to international exhibitions like the one of 1866 in Paris. The delegation from Bradford included the technicians and members of leading firms who were most able to size up the French competition. There was something refreshing about the reports these delegates submitted upon their return home. They showed none of the formalism of the Foreign Office and the Board of Trade, nothing also of the remote theorising of *The Economist*. Though proudly patriotic, they came to France to learn from the competition, looking closely at the woollens and worsteds on display and at the machines that produced them. The French manufacturers put on a better show than their British rivals. It was hard to arrive at a definitive assessment of the French accomplishment because some of their most impressive cloth had been spun and woven specially for the exhibition and they refused to price the goods on display. It was nevertheless clear that, in the finer pure woollens, the merinos and poplins, and also in fine yarns and fabric with twists of gold, silver and silk, French production was unrivalled. But equally, when it came to mixed fabrics, particularly to the cotton warp worsteds known as 'Bradford good',[42] no one could beat the town that had made them famous. Likewise, the Yorkshiremen were impressed with the painstaking skill of French artisans – there were still 200,000 handloom weavers around Roubaix and Rheims – but when it came to tools and machinery Britain reigned supreme, 'enabling us as Englishmen to stand in the envied position of being the best tool-makers in the world'.[43] With regard to dyeing and finishing, each country had its speciality.

The European market in woollens and worsteds was thus highly competitive; Roubaix was catching up with Bradford; and the competition was not restricted to Britain and France. 'The coloured checks and shawls of Austria, Prussia, and Saxony, and the damasks of Austria, show to great advantage. An excellent case is shown from Belgium. . . . The goods shown from Carlsvik in Sweden fully maintain the high position they took in 1862.'[44] Everywhere on the continent the makers of woollens were approaching British standards of production, in part by employing machines brought from Britain.

The delegates from Bradford brought home a warning against complacency: 'every exertion is being made to supersede us altogether; and without some great effort on our part be made, the time is not far distant when such will be the case'.[45] At the same time they took care to point out the bearing of tariffs on what they had seen, noting the backwardness of the highly protected products of Russia and Spain, and crediting the rapid improvement of French production to bracing competition from Britain since 1860. They ended their report with statistical tables

> showing the effect of the French Commercial Treaty in very largely extending the worsted trade of that country, and showing that it has led to a large, though not rapidly increasing, importation of Bradford yarn and goods into France; and at the same time to an increased exportation, the effect being thus a mutual benefit to the manufacturers as well as to the consumers of both France and England. Is it not a fair inference from these facts that it would be a still further benefit to both countries if the remaining 10 per cent. [duty on woollens in the French tariff] were out of their way, and would not the same result follow from a reduction in the prohibitory tariffs of other countries?[46]

The Bradford Chamber drew up detailed reports, first for the Board of Trade and the Foreign Office[47] and then for the French legislative inquiry in Paris,[48] on the operation of the Anglo-French treaty over the past decade in order to substantiate the case for improvement in its terms. These reports provide perhaps the most thorough contemporary analysis of the impact of the treaty on trade between the two countries and the best comparison of production in one sector of industry. The report to the British government was certainly the closest and most comprehensive that it received on the subject of the treaty from any sector of British trade and industry. The report commanded attention because, as its appendix showed, woollens constituted Britain's most valuable export to France (Table 4.1).

But figures to convince the British government of the importance of woollens among exports to France might easily convince the French government that Roubaix was right to protest against the supposed deluge of British woollens on to the French market. The president of the Consultative Chamber at Roubaix inflated the volume of the inflow of woollens from Britain by insisting that they were routinely undervalued by 25 per cent. The Bradford merchants, while rejecting that claim as a slight on their probity, admitted that the book value of their goods as they entered French customs was often higher than the prices actually paid for them after haggling in the market. They stood on firmer ground when they compared the costs of production in the two countries. The merchants of Roubaix claimed that they were routinely undercut because Bradford's costs were lower, but Bradford produced a counterclaim that showed that, while machinery and fuel were cheaper in England, Roubaix enjoyed a decisive advantage in the cost of labour. French wage rates were lower and hours of labour longer, a situation that prompted some manufacturers in

Table 4.1 Exports to France, 1868

Agricultural and natural produce		subtotal	£476,849
Articles for manufacture including			
coal	£872,568		
cotton yarn	£256,366		
iron	£504,053		
linen yarn	£236,579		
machinery	£380,812		
silk	£436,487		
wool	£349,064		
woollen yarn	£893,561		
miscellaneous	£954,595	subtotal	£4,884,085
Manufactured articles including			
arms and ammunition	£156,358		
cottons	£1,105,316		
cutlery	£120,434		
linens	£189,880		
woollen manufactures	£1,908,308		
miscellaneous	£558,221	subtotal	£4,038,517
Beer, ale, and spirits			£26,537
All other articles			£1,226,746
Total exports			£10,652,734

Bradford to warn the government that the alternative to reduced tariffs abroad would have to be lower wages at home. Turning the argument from Roubaix completely around, Bradford contended that the only unfair burden under which the French woollens manufacturers laboured was the tariff imposed by their government on imported yarns, coal and machinery.

Bradford admitted in its report to the British government that the 1860 treaty had forced the manufacturers of Roubaix 'to employ the latest inventions and improvements in machinery, and to seek their remuneration rather in the profits from large returns, than from the exorbitant prices which their former uncontrolled command of the home market allowed them to impose upon the French people'. But the Bradford merchants insisted that their French rivals had risen to the challenge with such 'characteristic intelligence and energy' that their operations now extended beyond France 'to all parts of the world', including Britain. 'Some of the largest establishments at Roubaix state with just pride, that they are almost exclusively working for the English market.' Apart from silks and wine, woollens now constituted the most valuable of all French exports to Britain. Drawing upon information submitted to the Paris exhibition by Cobden's old companion Chevalier, the report from Bradford pointed out that the number of power-looms in Roubaix had risen from 1,000 in 1859 to 15,000 in 1867, 'all of the newest and most improved construction'. The wages that Roubaix makers had to pay were less than half those of Bradford; and while fuel cost more in Roubaix, that was a minor consideration compared to wages. To cap it all, the total value of the woollen worsteds that France exported to Britain was much higher than that of the mixed worsteds Britain exported to France. Added to the other commodities traded between the two countries, the value of all French exports to Britain exceeded by £23,233,592 or 580,839,825 francs the value of all British exports to France.[49]

Having demonstrated the advantage France reaped from the 1860 treaty, the Bradford report then turned to the tariff. At 10 per cent *ad valorem* for woollens and 15 per cent for textiles in which cotton predominated, the French tariff kept British exports, particularly of heavy mixed fabrics, down. 'The great mass of the low and middle classes of French women are thus deprived of a cheap, warm, and most useful material of clothing which is peculiarly adapted to their tastes, and to the climate of France.' And the French tariff bore still more heavily on yarns. The report concluded with a call for abolition of the tariff on yarns and piece goods, failing which 'the duty on all kinds of wool goods, with or without admixture of cotton, [should] be not above 5 per cent. *ad valorem* for a few years longer, as the last step towards entire abolition.'

The discussions that went on in the British cabinet and business community about renewing the Anglo-French treaty came together in the spring of 1870 in the House of Commons. Gladstone provided little indication of the position his ministry would take up on the general issue when he told the House in February that 'we have not entertained any undue aversion from commercial treaties, although we feel we have reduced them to the very narrowest margin'.[50] A debate took place at the beginning of May on a motion from one of the MPs for Manchester, Hugh Birley, proposing the appointment of a select committee to inquire into the operation of the treaty with France and its effects on all branches of British trade.[51] Birley drew attention to the anxiety among the Associated Chambers of Commerce about the terms upon which the treaty would be renewed. While financial, mercantile and shipping interests in Britain had benefited from the treaty, British industry had its doubts, he said. The plate-glass manufacturers for whom Birley spoke faced 'formidable competition' from France, while the silk trade of Coventry had been all but wiped out. Continental countries were building up their industries, often with assistance from British investors, British coal, skilled British labour and British machinery.

Birley backed his motion with solid information and kept within the reigning consensus on the principles of free trade, but the proposal was hijacked by advocates of retaliation and outright protection. Some harked back to the Corn Laws, and there were murmurs of what later became a demand for 'Fair Trade', for a tariff policy that was more assertive and protective of British interests, particularly *vis-à-vis* France. They placed not only the French treaty but the whole policy of free trade in question, thereby damaging the proposal they espoused. Birley was further weakened by opposition from another MP for Manchester, Sir Thomas Bazley, who questioned the basic claim that British trade was depressed. With the motion thus countered, Lowe as Chancellor of the Exchequer had little difficulty repelling it, and it was crushed in the vote. But the questions Birley asked would not go away.

b. The Franco-Prussian War

From the time that the legislative inquiry into the tariff was set up in France, the woollens manufacturers and merchants of West Yorkshire tried to keep abreast of its deliberations. In a display of diplomatic finesse, for 'fear of estranging our best friends the Wine growers of France', the Council of Bradford's Chamber of Commerce declined to forward a recommendation it otherwise favoured, to equalise the treatment of France with that of Spain and Portugal under the British wine duties.[52] When the French inquiry handled Lancashire cottons with hostility, the woollens representatives of Yorkshire intensified their efforts. Behrens left for Paris to be on hand when local interests came up for scrutiny. When the French kept him at bay, Forster moved Lord Clarendon at the Foreign Office and then Lord Lyons at the Paris embassy to give what assistance they could both to Behrens and the agent from Manchester. The Chambers of Commerce in Manchester and Bradford co-ordinated their efforts closely. A small delegation from Yorkshire went out to reinforce Behrens and joined the Manchester delegation before it left Paris. There was some difficulty in selecting delegates from the woollens industry because of suspicion among Bradford merchants that Behrens and the Council there were not sufficiently insistent upon improvement of the terms of the 1860 treaty. When the Manchester delegates finally gained direct access to the French inquiry, they were received cordially: 'it appeared that anybody was allowed to ask questions.'[53] But the French inquiry contrived to complete its investigation of the woollens industry before the delegates from Bradford were informed that it had opened.

This twist of events – and indeed the entire proceedings of the French inquiry – was suddenly and unexpectedly overtaken by the outbreak of war between France and Prussia together with nearly all the German states including Austria. Only days before, a young Liberal backbench MP who was to play a large part in the subsequent history of the Anglo-French treaty, Sir Charles Dilke, had renewed Cobden's praise of international trade for 'creating a community of material interests which is the surest guarantee of peace'.[54] The ensuing war did not entirely discredit that hope, for, though swiftly decisive in military and hence political terms, the Franco-Prussian War had paradoxical economic consequences. These had mainly to do with the financial and territorial penalties imposed by Prussia upon France, which left the economy of the new German empire overwrought while rousing the defeated French to pay the financial penalty with a speed that astonished Europe. The impact of the war on the European commercial treaty network was also surprising. The postwar leadership of France failed in its attempt to use the costs of the war as an excuse for raising the French tariff, while sympathy for France softened Gladstone's response to the demands of its government. Nonetheless, the protracted negotiations between the two countries over the renewal of their 1860 agreement weakened commitment in both to the entire enterprise of commercial treaty-making.

These negotiations were overshadowed by the financial punishment that the victorious Germans imposed upon the defeated French. But before the magnitude of that penalty was known, Bismarck indicated that France would have to pay an even dearer forfeit in territory, ceding to Germany the Rhineland provinces of Alsace and Lorraine. That prospect perplexed and divided the textile manufacturers of the new German empire. The German spinners and calico printers of Lorrach and Offenburg just east of the Rhine were afraid that, without protection from the Zollverein tariff on textiles, they would be driven out of the domestic market by their more extensively developed competitors in Alsace. The Rhinelanders therefore pressed for the exclusion of Alsace and Lorraine from the Zollverein rather than have the Zollverein become coterminous with the new German empire. But further to the east, the textile manufacturers of Saxony felt less threatened by the annexation, believing that the Germans could hold their own because they paid lower wages than the French.

Bismarck took care to sound out the pertinent industrial interests. Though he eventually insisted on the annexation, he took note of the Rhineland warning that in future France would 'take very good care not to enter into commercial treaties with Germany; and, on the contrary, being in a state of prostration superinduced by war, will frame a new tarif [sic] with very high import duties'.[55] Bismarck's desire to preserve the 1862 commercial treaty between France and the Zollverein was strong enough to persuade the postwar French negotiators that it constituted 'the only weapon of any value with which [France] might wring concessions from Germany'. Bismarck declared that 'he would rather begin a shooting war again than to become involved in a tariff war', and he threatened to break off negotiations completely unless France granted German commerce most-favoured-nation treatment on a permanent basis.[56] The French agreed so long as the concession was reciprocal. Instead of adopting an unconditional formulation of the most-favoured-nation clause, Clause II of the Treaty of Frankfurt, the postwar peace settlement between the two states, bound France and Germany to grant each other as favourable a tariff as they granted to six other specified countries: Britain, Belgium, the Netherlands, Switzerland, Austria and Russia.

The terms of the settlement that ended the Franco-Prussian War turned it into the most traumatic defeat in modern French history; they also shifted the centre of gravity in Europe, economically as well as politically, away from the Atlantic seaboard and eastwards across the Rhine. Napoleon III's rule collapsed with his defeat at the battle of Sedan. The so-called Second Empire of the French was replaced as the premier power on the continent by a new German empire formed around Prussia. The territorial and economic provisions of the Treaty of Frankfurt envenomed the peace settlement. The cession of Alsace and Lorraine wrenched the economic relationship of France and Prussian Germany out of its previously co-operative mould, to say nothing of the impact on the historic sense of the identity of France. The financial indemnity of five billion francs that the French were forced to pay shocked them into a great display of national resolve, while the economy of the Germans staggered drunkenly as they devoured their sudden access of wealth. The 'natural effect' of the indemnity was 'to put France about eight years behind in its industrial career';[57] and the borrowing that France undertook to pay it left its economy 'heavily mortgaged'.[58] It was, however, only slowly that the numbing impact of the financial penalty on French enterprise became apparent. The obligation laid by the Treaty of Frankfurt upon France to treat Germany forever afterwards in matters of trade and tariffs as a most-favoured nation gave an immediately bitter twist to French commercial policy.

Adolphe Thiers became chief executive in the republic that emerged out of the ashes of the Second Empire, selecting the even stiffer protectionist Pouyer-Quertier as his finance minister. These two used the need for additional revenue to pay off the war indemnity as justification for the increases they wanted to make in the French tariff when renewing the treaty of 1860 with Britain. Their proposals perplexed the Gladstone ministry. There was no obviously right response to make. Had it not been for the war indemnity, no one in Britain would have hesitated to reject Thiers's demand. To sanction tariff increases would be to reverse what Cobden had worked for. The harmful effects would not be confined to Britain. Thiers made clear that he intended to use Britain's agreement to the increases to pave the way for upward revision of the customs dues authorised in the French treaties with other European states, all of which would come up for renewal over the next few years.

The main countervailing consideration for Britain was the desire to co-operate with France in its effort to pay off what was widely held to be a grotesquely unfair financial penalty. This faded when it became evident that Thiers was playing on this sympathy to increase the tariff protection of French industry, but there were, however, further reasons to accede to his demand. Thiers threatened, if it was rejected, to terminate the treaty of 1860, the hinge on which Britain's access to the lowered tariffs of the European commercial treaty network turned. The loss of most-favoured-nation status would subject British exports to adverse discrimination in continental markets.

While the Foreign Office was still coming to grips with this conundrum, the woollens manufacturers of Bradford reacted with dismay at the prospect of any impairing of the terms of the Anglo-French treaty, something made worse for them by the vagaries of fashion. The French retreat from the terms of the Cobden treaty coincided with a shift in female fashion away from the stiff fabrics, mohairs and alpacas of Bradford which hung well over the bustles of the 1860s and towards pure woollens which clung closer to the female figure: in the making of the finest pure woollens the French were the masters. Bradford was slow to detect and respond to the change. However, the more obvious and immediate threat had to do with the French tariff. The Council of the Bradford Chamber despatched letters to Mallet at the Board of Trade and to Forster, now in the cabinet, to ascertain exactly what was going on. The news that came back hurried the Council into special session. But the oblique way in which the Council expressed its response to the threatened change in the French tariff indicated that its members recognised the dilemma in which Britain found itself. In ringing tones but ambiguous words, the Council announced its 'strong and unanimous feeling that no deviation from the Treaty should be agreed to which should apply to the interval which must elapse before the notice to be given under it can expire'.[59] However strong the feeling, the British were in a weak negotiating position. They lacked the power of tariff retaliation, nor did the government want it. All Behrens could devise was a warning that, if the French imposed higher duties, 'public opinion would be aroused to such a length that our Government would be unable to resist the demand, for retaliation in the shape of a higher duty on French wines and silks'.[60]

By the end of July 1871 it was clear that the French were determined not only to raise their tariff but to target woollens in particular, at least doubling the *ad valorem* duty on them to 20 per cent. That prospect made worsted woollens manufacturers willing to consider 'any proposals' so long as they were given time to fulfil existing contracts.[61] They turned their attention to alternative markets. Behrens developed business with China and Japan, but interest in the Yorkshire woollens industry fell mainly on Spain and Portugal. The Iberian countries had reacted angrily to the customs duty that Britain had reduced on wines with a low alcoholic content as part of its 1860 agreement with France:

for that reduction in effect discriminated against their 'heavier' wines. Portugal had retaliated by imposing a high tariff specifically on British exports. The British Treasury had frustrated efforts to reach a settlement with Portugal. But if France reneged on its undertakings in the 1860 treaty, surely Britain would be free to reduce the duty on heavier wines far enough to secure a reduction in the punitive Portuguese as well as the Spanish tariff on British goods. Yorkshire's interest in this market quickened when Germany concluded a commercial treaty with Portugal that gave German woollens and worsteds much better terms than the British enjoyed.[62]

Still the game with France was not yet up. If Britain would accept the principle of some raising of the French tariff, then the specific details, including the targeting of woollens, might be negotiable. That was the argument presented to the cabinet by the Board of Trade under its new president, Chichester Fortescue, with support from Lord Lyons at the Paris embassy and from Cobden's comrade of yore, John Bright, who had retired from office. Mallet at the Board of Trade kept the officers of interested Chambers of Commerce abreast of the negotiations with France.

The British decision ultimately rested with Gladstone. He found the renewal of the Anglo–French treaty 'one of the most nicely balanced questions'[63] he had ever encountered. He shared with Cobden the British honours of the treaty's parentage. But he admitted to 'great disappointment at finding that the Treaty of 1860, which I looked to as the great instrument of further and more effectual progress, is to be made by the French Government the starting point of a backward movement, of which the present proposals may be only a first manifestation'. If the issue was simply a matter of commercial policy, he felt strongly inclined 'to fall back upon our old basis, namely, that the cause of freedom in commerce will, as a rule, be most effectively advanced by leaving each nation to consider the subject in the light of its own interests'.[64] But on the other side lay a political consideration akin to the one that moved Gladstone as well as Cobden to embrace the original treaty. Though free international commerce might not be the complete antidote to war – the Franco-Prussian War had certainly shattered confidence – it might still foster better international relations. Gladstone furthermore felt 'a great desire to exhibit sympathy'[65] with France in the wake of its devastating war with Germany.

Amidst the anxieties awakened by Thiers's assault on the Cobden treaty, a more promising opportunity in commercial diplomacy from the German side was allowed to slip by.[66] In the summer of 1871, Bismarck looked at the possibility of continuing the tactics of tariff reduction that had served him so well *vis-à-vis* Austria and to which he had adhered in the Treaty of Frankfurt. The network of commercial treaties fettered Thiers's freedom for manœuvre in Europe. Bismarck wanted to keep it that way. In order to strengthen the network's restraining capacity, he inquired whether Britain might be willing to amplify its commercial treaty with the Zollverein. The only reciprocal response he required was a reduction of duty on spirits, which discriminated against all imports in favour of domestic whisky, or so the Germans claimed. The British, however, rejected the allegation. Gladstone recoiled from any loss of revenue to the Treasury from the spirits duty, which was substantially more lucrative than the related duty on wine; and Lowe reinforced his opposition. Bismarck's inquiry was allowed to go virtually unnoticed. With it passed a rare opportunity to lock Germany into the network and reduce Bismarck's freedom to set the German tariff unilaterally, a freedom he was to exploit to Britain's cost at the end of the decade.

Meanwhile the German economy blossomed luxuriantly. Crowe marvelled in the spring of 1871 at 'the wonderful spectacle of a nation engaged in a great and exhausting war, issuing from that war with undiminished credit and comparatively small commercial losses'.[67] He had never seen 'a more buoyant market' than the Leipzig fair that Easter. 'German buyers, Poles, Russians, Danes, Swedes, Italians, and Americans, and a few Southern Frenchmen were amongst the arrivals and the complete collapse of French manufacturing power combined with total absence of French wares gave a marked advantage to holders of German Swiss and English goods.'[68] The boom spread beyond Germany as other European producers rushed to fill the gaps left by the prostration of France. British exports grew in volume and value faster in the early 1870s than at any other time before or since. Such were the dividends of war. Towards the end of 1871 Crowe reported: 'There never was a time when public prosperity was apparently greater than it is at present in Germany. Manufactures are active, and production is only checked by the difficulty of obtaining raw material and coals.'[69]

Still he detected 'much below the surface to suggest anxious contemplation'.[70] The five billion francs taken from the French was too much and came too fast for the good of the German economy. Four million thalers were lavished upon the soldiers and statesmen who had distinguished themselves in the war. 'Money is so abundant,' reported Crowe,

that people seem not to know what to do with it. . . . There is much to suggest unsoundness in the way in which financial speculations are being carried on. Within less than six weeks past, scores of companies have been formed for banking and other purposes throughout Germany, the scrip of which has been issued at high premiums. The redundancy of money, attributable to the chance winning of milliards from France is not like a redundancy of money earned by trade and manufacture. It is a plethora of an essentially unhealthy kind which is not unlikely at no very remote period to lead to a crisis of a disastrous character.[71]

At the close of 1871 Thiers asked the French legislature to denounce the commercial treaties that were due for renewal, the treaty of 1861 with Belgium as well as the 1860 treaty with Britain; and early in the new year the legislature agreed. Britain faced hostile discrimination in the French market and in shipping to French ports unless it agreed to a revised treaty with less favourable terms. Some advisers to the British government suggested that still more was at stake. The ambassador in Berlin, Lord Odo Russell, argued that Britain could use commercial treaties to bring its influence to bear in the councils of Europe without involvement in political alliances or resort to armed force.[72] Thus an able Whig diplomat adapted Cobden's gospel of peace through commerce to the realities of European power politics.

Gladstone's vision no longer extended that far. He preferred the unilateral freeing of trade in the 1840s and 1850s to the frustrating bilateral treaty-making of the 1860s. Moreover, the cotton interests of Lancashire called for dismissal of Thiers's demands even if that meant loss of the 1860 treaty, which had never done much for them.[73] Still, it had done a lot for the woollens of Yorkshire. Reluctantly Gladstone concurred with a majority of his cabinet in approving a succession of attempts to reduce the worsening of the terms of a new agreement with France to tolerable proportions. Representations and expert testimony in London and Paris from the Chambers of Commerce in Yorkshire enabled the British negotiators to bring the increase in the tariff on woollens down to what Yorkshire found bearable.

That achievement was enough to alienate the more extreme French protectionists led by Pouyer-Quertier from Thiers's policy. To maximise income from customs duties in order to pay the indemnity to Germany, Thiers had proposed extending them to raw materials, a plan that alarmed otherwise protectionist industrial interests which had learnt over the previous decade to appreciate freedom from this addition to their costs of production. To win over these interests, Thiers offered to compensate them for the tariff they had to pay on their raw materials by increasing the tariff on manufactured imports that contained the same raw materials. But the resulting total increase in the French tariff exceeded what Britain deemed tolerable. In lowering it to a level that Britain would accept, Thiers forfeited the protectionist backing he needed. Unable to formulate a broadly acceptable plan, he resigned.

The succeeding government, lacking strong convictions on commercial policy, fell back upon the 1860 treaty, assuming that the British would be happy to renew it. Recent experience with Thiers had, however, intensified Gladstone's uneasiness over tariff treaties. There were drawbacks to a renewal. It deprived Britain of the freedom to adjust its wine duties, whether to raise additional revenue in lieu of income tax as Gladstone was inclined to favour, or to reduce the duty on heavy wines and thus overcome the perceived unfairness that closed Spain and Portugal to British exports. Nonetheless, Gladstone agreed to a renewal until 1877, when the rest of France's commercial treaties would come up for reconsideration, as the least bad of the alternatives open to Britain. But he let France know that he would oppose any further extension after that date.[74] He spoke cordially about the original treaty in the House of Commons, but there was a negative undercurrent. Co-operation with France had done more to advance free trade on the continent than Britain could have done alone. France was better able to point the way because, he said, 'the commercial superiority of England was so paramount that other countries could not disabuse from their minds the feeling that any suggestions coming from us must be dictated by selfish motives, and, if adopted, must result in disadvantage to themselves.'[75] The implication was that Britain should leave the leadership of the movement towards free trade on the continent in French hands.

The aversion Gladstone felt towards commercial treaty-making also appeared in his rejection of the repeated demands of the Associated Chambers of Commerce for the appointment of a Minister of Commerce of cabinet rank to overcome the division of responsibility between the Foreign Office and the Board of Trade in commercial diplomacy. Palmerston and Russell had been no more forthcoming, but Gladstone was the first Prime Minister to argue the point with the Associated Chambers. His opposition was the more significant because the Chambers of Commerce had regarded him as their best friend in government.

The institutional arrangements for commercial diplomacy deteriorated in 1872. Prompted by Mallet, the Board of Trade had regularly prodded the Foreign Office to take more initiative and seek out opportunities for further commercial treaty-making. Most recently the Board had pressed for a reduction in the duty on heavier wines in order to open the Spanish and Portuguese market. That encroachment on the needs and prerogatives of the Treasury infuriated Lowe, and he called for the transfer of the Board's responsibilities for fact-gathering on foreign trade to the Foreign Office.[76] Mallet, exasperated by the government's resistance to his advice, seconded Lowe's recommendation in the hope of bringing all responsibility home to the Foreign Office. So the deed was done.

These developments in commercial diplomacy were obscured in business circles by excitement at the temporary removal of French competition and the enrichment of Germany. Trade and industry boomed, not least in Britain, in the wake of the Franco-Prussian War. The flood of money from France enabled Germany to place its currency on the gold standard and hence enhanced the financial importance of London. The centre of economic gravity on the continent shifted within as well as towards Germany. Commerce moved north, to the new imperial capital of Berlin and the Hanseatic ports of Hamburg and Bremen, and west, to the iron and steel producers, coal mines and textile mills of the Rhineland and the Ruhr. The British Foreign Office responded to this shift by transferring Crowe from Leipzig to Düsseldorf.

But France retained its centrality so far as British commercial diplomacy was concerned. The European market had never looked more lucrative. The proportion of total British exports going to Europe soared in the late 1860s and early 1870s from 33 to 40 per cent, double what it was to the next largest continental market, North America.[77] And as *The Economist* observed: 'The commercial relation of France to England is the keystone in the arch of European commerce.'[78]

Chapter 5

The Impact of Depression, 1873–1879

*'The prospect everywhere seems dark to the free traders who fear
that protection will show very strongly at Vienna & in Paris.'*

J.A. Crowe to Lord Odo Russell, 27 Nov. 1876

The Franco-Prussian War, which transformed the political map of Europe, precipitated an equally sharp change in its economic fortunes. In May 1873 the
postwar boom burst. Prices fell steeply, though not the volume of trade. The
rate of increase in international trade also dropped from its all-time high in
the preceding years. At first the recession was interpreted as just another fluc-
tuation in an essentially healthy economy. It did not hit every country equally
hard; for a little while, France seemed comparatively unscathed. But the slump
persisted to the end of the decade. Though there were periods of improvement
thereafter, not till the final years of the century did Europe quite recover from
what it came to call 'the great depression'.

Naturally the depression had a large impact on the commercial policy of the
European states. Though Britain as the most liberal of these states disclaimed
governmental responsibility for the performance of the economy, the electoral
fortunes of British governments rose and fell with fluctuations in the economy.
On the continent the governmental assumption of responsibility was higher.
The determination of statesmen there to build up their nations' industry
was accompanied by willingness to protect it in adversity. In any case, since the
advocates of tariff reduction took credit for the prosperity of the past dozen
years, they could not escape blame for the depression that ensued. And
every state had to concern itself with the revenue it received from customs
duties.

Still, the movement towards tariff protection was not immediate. Nor was it
universal even on the continent. It was mixed up with another, different and
more widespread tendency in trade policy towards unilateralism, in other words
towards the assumption that each state should decide its commercial policy for
itself. That was one principle on which Gladstone and Bismarck agreed. It was
a form of national self-assertion even where, as in its Gladstonian form, it was
accompanied by insistence on economic freedom for the individual and for business from interference by the state. Unilateralism in trade policy boded ill for
the commercial treaty network that Cobden and Napoleon III had originated.
But those two men were followed by an anomalous assortment of successors,

including Conservatives as well as Liberals in Britain and liberal republicans in France, who tried to make use of the network and have it serve the needs of their particular countries.

a. The Onset of Depression

Nowhere did the depression strike more suddenly and with more acute effect than in Germany. Three years earlier, in May 1870, the Zollverein had reduced its tariff, particularly on iron and steel. The war interrupted further extension of this policy, but victory confirmed it. What had German machinery to fear from competition when its engines of war had performed so effectively? The money from the French indemnity fuelled industrial enterprise, expanded trade and eliminated governmental concern about revenue from customs duties. Pride in the shared victory overrode the protectionist impulse in the southern German states which were incorporated in the new empire. Accordingly, in the spring of 1873 liberal ministers led by Delbrück, whom Bismarck kept in charge of economic policy, proposed steep reductions in the iron and steel tariff, bringing Germany close to fully free trade in this sector. The iron industry in alliance with still protectionist southern Germans managed to confine the elimination of duties to pig iron, raw steel and ships, deferring abolition of the remaining tariff on all other sorts of iron, machinery and engines till the end of 1876.[1] The cheaper costs of the basic inputs of the industry increased the value of the protection remaining for its more highly finished products. The compromise won quick acceptance. Germany acted once again unilaterally; but that only pleased free traders.

Immediately, however, the outlook changed. No sooner had the spoils of military victory persuaded Germany to take this further step towards free trade than the nearby Viennese stock market crashed, fevered by the overflow of loot from France. This panic in May 1873 was followed in June by a rapid depreciation of securities at Berlin. Meanwhile the money market in the United States which had financed the construction of new railways broke down, depriving the heavy side of the British iron and steel industry of its largest single market.[2] The circumstances that encouraged continued tariff reduction were reversed. Prices and wages fell, slashing profit margins and consumer buying-power. The rapid expansion of industrial plant in the past couple of years gave rise to the problems of overproduction. The iron industry in annexed Alsace and Lorraine now looked like an addition to the causes of depression rather than to the industrial capacity of Germany. Unable to shut their furnaces down without permanent loss, and confronted with a falling domestic market, German iron manufacturers concentrated on exports. By selling their goods in foreign markets at virtually cost price, they contrived in the depths of the depression to build up a favourable balance of trade and turn their industry for the first time into 'a serious international competitor'.[3] But in order to do so, they sought to raise their domestic prices, whether through price-fixing cartels or by raising the tariff against foreign competition. Until it went up, Britain remained able, through transport by sea which was cheaper than rail, to penetrate the German market close to the Baltic ports.

Though it was less immediately apparent, 1873 proved to be a turning point for Britain as for Germany. The financial centrality of London was enhanced that year when Germany felt able, with the wealth it had extracted from France, to place itself on the gold standard, which the City of London in effect administered. Thus increasing financial ascendancy diverted attention from, and was regarded as compensating for, Britain's gradual loss of industrial pre-eminence during the ensuing depression. No longer able to boast of itself as 'the workshop of the world', Britain was becoming more of a *rentier* economy, dependent on the income from its foreign investments to offset its deficit in trade and business services.[4] That loss was to some extent inevitable as other parts of Europe – the Ruhr, the Berlin area, Upper Silesia, Saxony, Alsace-Lorraine (now in Germany), Belgium, the Paris basin and Lyons in France – caught up with the level of industrialisation achieved in Britain.[5] Even so, this competition did little to stimulate industrial enterprise. Britain was also slow to recognise the abnormality of the boom that it enjoyed in the European market during and in the wake of the Franco-Prussian War. Nor did British manufacturers understand the protectionist accusations of 'dumping' which greeted their subsequent attempt to sell their textiles and iron and steel in the continental market at close to cost price,[6] as the Germans were doing in their export market. Certainly 'dumping' was unexceptionable if it simply meant taking advantage of the reduction in average production costs by making more intense use of plant.[7] The volume of British exports, especially of textiles to the continent, grew at a faster pace from 1871 to 1876 than in any other five years in the nineteenth century.[8] But this export expansion, spurred by depression, not only exacerbated the fall in prices but raised a cry on the continent for protective tariffs to stem the British flood.

To widespread amazement, France temporarily escaped the worst of these vicissitudes and congratulated itself on its avoidance of the turn of fortune that had afflicted its recent conqueror. Ministers pointed with delight to the favourable balance of trade that France enjoyed in 1873, better than any it had had in the reign of Napoleon III. The apparent boom strengthened the advocates of a return to Napoleon's liberal trade policy and thus revived the fortunes of the commercial treaty network. Between 1873 and 1877, sympathisers with free trade occupied at least one of the offices of state responsible for trade policy: the ministries of finance, commerce and agriculture. Their aim was to renew the many commercial treaties due to expire in 1877 and to turn the so-called conventional tariff as laid down in these treaties into the general French tariff applicable to all countries.

The British did not draw encouragement from the French boom, despite its strengthening of the forces for free trade. *The Economist* belittled the growth, pointing out that the branches of trade in which France was doing well – silks, woollens, leather goods and metal work – were its usual areas of strength. As for the favourable French balance of exports over imports, it observed that the loss of Alsace-Lorraine turned what had been a home trade into an export trade, and that French exports were down because the need to pay the war indemnity to Germany had diminished French purchasing power.[9] Of greater concern was early evidence that the downturn in the rest of the continental economy was confronting Britain with stiff competition from Belgium in iron and steel and, still more seriously, from Germany in many lines of industrial production – not only in the continental European market but at home in Britain and overseas, particularly in South America, where Britain had not experienced rivalry before. The Belgian iron manufacturers slashed their prices early because they were among the first to feel the force of the depression.[10] But the first outcry in Britain was against German competition, and protest was extended to apply to 'German partnerships in English houses'.[11] Sensitivity was heightened by a new awareness of the importance of continental European trade. Hitherto the United States had attracted attention as the largest single national market for Britain's foreign commerce. The magnitude of the trade with Germany had been disguised by the latter's political divisions; statistics had been collected separately for each state. But the customs report for 1873[12] showed that the value of goods that Britain imported from and exported to France and Germany totalled more than its trade with the United States. If the Netherlands and Belgium were included, British trade with continental Europe (excluding Russia) was far greater than it was with the United States.

The depression would not have been so deep and protracted anywhere in Europe if it had been confined to manufacturing and the products of industry. But the downturn was extended to agriculture by a set of changes begun earlier, after the American Civil War, but that did not become evident until the mid-1870s and needed another decade to take full effect. European farmers saw the price they could command for their produce fall, their domestic market flooded and their export market destroyed by a massive influx, particularly of wheat, from the United States, now that it had repressed its divisions, and from Russia in the wake of the emancipation of the serfs. Technological improvements such as the reaper, sower, fertilisers, drainage tiles and new strains of wheat increased agricultural output.[13] The transportation of foodstuffs was also improved and made cheaper by rail and, much more, by water transport with the growth of steam power and facilities for refrigeration.

The ingredients of bread had always stood at the heart of European controversy over tariffs. That was true of Britain from the fight over the Corn Laws in the 1840s to the fight over tariff reform and food taxes at the beginning of the next century. It was even more the case on the continent, where agriculture accounted for a far larger proportion of the economy. When Britain repealed the Corn Laws, about 22 per cent of its active population worked on farms and about 37 per cent in manufacturing industry. The proportions in continental Europe as a whole in the early 1860s were 63 per cent in agriculture and 18 to 20 per cent in manufacturing industry. Even in some of the more industrialised countries on the continent – Germany, Belgium, Sweden and Switzerland – over half of the active population was employed in agriculture and only around 20 per cent in manufacturing.[14] Continental countries were therefore less able than Britain to offset agricultural losses with industrial gains. The United States made matters worse after the Civil War by heightening the tariff protection it gave to its industry, thus preventing the Europeans from paying for their soaring agricultural imports with industrial exports. The temptation for Europeans to follow suit and retaliate against agricultural imports from the United States was strong if not irresistible.

Europe enjoyed close to free trade in foodstuffs after the commercial treaty-making of the 1860s. In Germany free trade had found its most ardent advocates among the land-owning Junkers of eastern Prussia. They wanted unimpeded access to export markets, particularly Britain, and they opposed any increase through tariffs in the price they paid for the metal manufactures, the implements and machinery they required from the Ruhr. But now continental landlords and farmers sought to protect their prices in ways that the free market did not allow. Britain associated free trade with the prosperity it enjoyed for a whole generation after the repeal of the Corn Laws. But continental farmers now learnt to equate free trade with depression. They were arguably wise to do so. Without tariff protection against the foreign flood, agricultural prices were driven down even when poor harvests reduced European production. Increases in price and hence in farm income which tariffs allowed would have raised the industrial buying-power of the farming community and thus helped to counteract rather than compound the depression in industry.[15]

The depression in agriculture became apparent more slowly than it did in industry, particularly in Britain, where the farmers found a satisfactory market for their harvests through till 1875, even at lowered prices. In other regards also the economic news was not uniformly depressing. Imports into Britain fell initially even more steeply than exports; and while the value of trade in textiles diminished, the volume of the trade went up. It was falling prices that made industry anxious.

The financial community remained complacent. *The Economist* took heart from a comparison of the population figures for the major countries of Europe since the wars that opened the century. It had taken the concerted forces of Britain, Russia, Prussia and Austria to defeat the pretensions of France under the great Napoleon. Since then, thanks to different rates in the growth of population, which had been accentuated by the unification of Germany, the journal found that Europe had become 'inherently more stable' (Table 5.1).[16]

Table 5.1 The Population of the European Great Powers

	Numbers	Percentage of Total	Numbers	Percentage of Total
	1811		1871–75	
Great Britain	12 million	8.7	27.5 million	12.8
France	29 million	20.8	36 million	16.8
	1816			
Germany	21 million	14.8	41 million	19
Austria	28 million est.	20	36 million	16.8
Russia in Europe	48 million	35.7	71 million	34.6
Total	138 million		211.5 million	

What impressed *The Economist* about these figures was the comparative growth of Britain and 'the great increase of Germany, which now dwarfs both France and Austria. . . . Now France is only one of several great States, one of which – England – is, for the first time for centuries, nearly equal in numbers and enormously superior in resources; and another, Germany, is greater in population, and in immediately developed warlike power, although, perhaps, not in undeveloped resources.' Its contentment at this sort of balance of power in Europe was enhanced when it thought again about 'the financial prosperity of France, as compared with the poverty of Germany',[17] proven by the 'astonishing ease' with which France was paying off the war indemnity imposed by Bismarck.

b. The First Governmental Responses

Reports from the continent and closer to home ruffled the confidence of Lord Derby, Foreign Secretary in the Conservative ministry that came to power in Britain in 1874. Joseph Crowe reported to him from Düsseldorf at the beginning of the next year that continuing layoffs in the iron industry were 'preparatory to an agitation' to postpone the final abolition of the iron duties,[18] due to take place in 1877. He assured Derby that the German government would not give in to such a demand, but Crowe's confidence emanated from a British perspective: 'the iron trade is not suffering more in Germany than in Scotland or Yorkshire, & prices of pig iron on the Rhine are still regulated by those of Glasgow. Germany,' he intoned, 'requires not protection but free trade for the expansion of her manufacturing power.' While he noted protectionist talk also among the woollens manufacturers of Saxony, he reported happily on the increasing penetration of British woollens into the German market without noting that this success might spark the Saxon protectionism. Within six months Crowe's confidence began to ebb: 'protectionism,' he reported, 'is gaining ground in proportion as the state of trade gets worse.'[19] Towards the end of the year the outlook improved. Crowe was assured by the leader of the agricultural interest in the Reichstag that it was 'firm in the wish to free the import of iron from every sort of duty'.[20] Even so, Britain could no longer take the European tariff reductions of the last 15 years for granted. Belying British faith, some continental states were obviously tempted to reverse rather than continue their advance towards free trade.

Lord Derby was impressed by Crowe's reports.[21] His warnings about rising protectionism in Germany coincided with agitation in Yorkshire over plans for protectionist revision of the treaty tariffs in Italy and Austria. Italy had already given notice of its determination to revise its tariff upwards, a revision that would afford protection particularly to the textile industry.[22] Austria was moving in the same direction according to a report Jacob Behrens received. Though the Italian tariff eventually gave its greatest protection to Italian cottons, the cry of alarm in Britain was raised by the woollens industry of Yorkshire rather than by the cotton masters of Lancashire, who were more concerned about the prospects in India. Early in 1875 W.E. Forster, who was by now a leader of the Liberal opposition in the House of Commons, was asked by the Chamber of Commerce in his constituency 'to see Lord Derby for the purpose of urging upon him the necessity of Government being doubly vigilant in the matter of the renewal of all Commercial Treaties'.[23] Behrens wrote to Derby to explain that 'our trade with the Continent has obtained such a development that any interference with it would be a calamity of the gravest importance . . . the pressure of foreign competition is already so severely felt, that the slightest additional impediment may prove fatal'.[24]

A man of meticulous business habits, Derby took pride in his rapport with the commercial and industrial interests, particularly of Liverpool and Lancashire. Working through the staff at the Foreign Office, he entered into a correspondence with Behrens that had a lasting impact on the process of commercial treaty-making in Britain. Behrens secured encouragement from Derby to broaden his base of representation beyond Bradford to include the main centres of woollens manufacturing in England. Hence he established a Joint Committee of the Yorkshire Chambers of Commerce and included representation from the woollens industry at Rochdale in Lancashire and at Kendal in Westmorland. For Derby's consumption, Behrens also developed a compelling explanation of the need for special treatment of worsted woollens. Derby, for his part, incorporated the merchants into the negotiating process more fully than had been the case since Cobden's day.

While Behrens was putting his Joint Committee together, the need for closer co-operation between business and government in commercial diplomacy was pressed upon the House of Commons. The Foreign Office was now fully responsible for assembling the information pertinent to commercial treaties as well as for negotiating them. The man placed in charge of the consolidated commercial department at the Foreign Office, C.M. Kennedy, had distinguished himself as an undergraduate in the study of political economy. He made a favourable impression on the British mercantile community during his first overseas assignment, in the 1872 negotiations between Britain and France in Paris. He persuaded the British merchants resident there to create a Chamber of Commerce for themselves. However, Kennedy was merely a departmental administrator. He lacked the interdepartmental weight as well as the experience that Louis Mallet (removed by promotion to the less politically contentious India Office) had brought to commercial treaty-making from the Board of Trade. Kennedy was thus even further than Mallet from what the Chambers of Commerce thought indispensable if their needs were to be adequately addressed. They wanted representation at the highest level of government, in the cabinet.

To widen the base for their demand, the Associated Chambers of Commerce secured support from the Central Chamber of Agriculture to move in the Commons for the creation of a cabinet-level Ministry of Commerce and Agriculture. Their model came from France, the pace-setter in European commercial diplomacy. At the beginning of April the commercially liberal French Minister of Agriculture and Commerce, the Viscomte de Meaux, launched an effort to turn the conventional tariff of Europe into the general tariff of France and to proceed on that foundation to liberalise the European conventional tariff further. He began by seeking advice from the French Chambers of Commerce.[25] If only the British government would follow that example!

The motion of the combined British Chambers was presented to the House of Commons by Sampson Lloyd, banker from metal-manufacturing Birmingham and Conservative MP for Plymouth, who was president of the Associated Chambers of Commerce. Displaying the protectionist leanings that would later make him a leader of the campaign for 'fair trade', Lloyd insisted: 'Our position as a commercial nation . . . could be maintained only on condition that the Government appreciated and, as far as possible, removed the impediments which beset our commerce on all sides, and gave it that new and legitimate help and protection which consisted . . . in securing to British capital and enterprize [*sic*] a fair field abroad.'[26] Using evidence supplied to him from Bradford, he described the inefficient dispersion of commercial concerns among half a dozen departments of state. Merchants with inquiries found themselves shuttled from one department to another, each disclaiming final responsibility. The spokesman for the Chamber of Agriculture described similar ineptitude in the handling of foot-and-mouth disease.

The rest of the debate concentrated on commercial treaty-making and exposed the drawbacks of leaving commercial diplomacy to the Foreign Office. Speaking for the government in lieu of Derby who sat in the Lords, the Chancellor of the Exchequer, Sir Stafford Northcote, argued that since Britain refused on principle to engage in bilateral bargaining on tariffs, there was little need for tariff treaties. Disraeli as Prime Minister put in a better performance when defending the existing departmental structure. The Chambers of Commerce were unlikely to take serious issue with his contention that 'In 99 out of 100 commercial interests which call for . . . the attention of the Government – the intervention of the Foreign Office is required.'[27] The motion was ultimately withdrawn, but not before an irritated Liberal MP, John Whitwell, representing the woollens industry in Kendal, reminded the government that 'many of their foreign Commercial Treaties would within the next two years have to be re-arranged'.[28]

By midsummer, when nothing more seemed to be happening, Behrens badgered the Foreign Office for information, stressing how important it was that British mercantile interests be actively represented in the tariff discussions on the continent. His concern was shared by Mallet, who had been shunted by the previous government away from commercial diplomacy into the India Office. At a special banquet of the Cobden Club, to which continental sympathisers with free trade had been invited, Mallet called anxiously for British participation in the impending reconstruction of the European network of commercial treaties. The speeches on that occasion were rushed into print with a preface by Mallet in which he attempted to drive home the benefits Britain had reaped from the lowering of European tariffs over the past 15 years. He claimed that since 1860, through 50 or 60 treaties, tariffs in Europe had been reduced by some 50 per cent. According to his calculations, the annual value of the trade in British exports to the European countries with which treaties had been concluded had more than doubled, from £32,489,000 in 1859 to £81,297,000 in 1874.[29]

There were signs before parliament rose in August that the government was responding to this campaign. The Foreign Office assured the most actively concerned MPs – Ripley of Bradford, Whitwell of Kendal and Sampson Lloyd – that Lord Derby would 'do all in his power' to see that the Chambers of Commerce received the information they wanted from the continent,[30] including copies of existing tariffs and the statistical tables on trade issued by foreign governments. The information began to arrive before the end of the month.

Kennedy, who collected the information at the Foreign Office, relayed it in a memorandum to Lord Derby.[31] His tables of statistics on trade amplified Mallet's summary, constituing the fullest analysis to date of European trade from a British perspective, though they were still neither extensive nor closely detailed. Kennedy interpreted them as supporting Mallet's advocacy of commercial treaties. But the argument was not entirely borne out by the accompanying figures.

Kennedy compared the figures for Britian's trade with its treaty partners before and since they reached their agreements. Using 1873 as the most recent year for which the figures were complete, he showed that the total of British imports and exports had increased

with France by 178 per cent, from £26,431,000 in 1859 to £73,535,000;
with Belgium by 212 per cent, from £8,731,000 in 1861 to £27,305,000;
with Italy by 41 per cent, from £8,785,000 in 1862 to £12,402,000;
with Germany by 26.5 per cent, from £44,764,000 in 1865 to £56,635,000;
with Austria by 74.5 per cent, from £1,538,000 in 1865 to £2,684,000.

The increases here with France and Belgium, Britain's original treaty partners, were particularly impressive. Kennedy made similar comparisons for Britain's trade with the four leading states with which France had made agreements but Britain had not, and also for Russia, with which France as well as Britain had failed to conclude a commercial treaty. Between 1865 and 1873, British trade had increased

with Holland by 38 per cent, from £27,373,000 to £37,850,000;
with Russia by 19 per cent, from £27,563,000 to £32,734,000;
with Sweden by 112 per cent, from £5,829,000 to £12,343,000;
with Spain almost 100 per cent, from £7,784,000 to £15,500,000;
with Portugal by 52 per cent, from £5,021,000 to £7,667,000.

Cumulatively, these figures indicated that British trade had done well under the European commercial treaty regime, but they did not indicate how much of the credit for that improvement should go to the treaties. Trade with Germany, for example, came out poorly if ranked by percentage (a calculation Kennedy did not make), yet the value of that trade to Britain was second only to that with France. British trade with Spain stood comparatively well by a percentage ranking, yet the Spanish tariff discriminated against exports from Britain. The total value of British trade with foreign countries exclusive of British possessions had more than doubled, from £245,750,000 in 1859 to £530,134,000 in

1873. Within these totals and between those years, British exports to European countries as a proportion of Britain's total foreign trade remained close to 20 per cent.

There was further encouragement to be drawn from the simple division Kennedy made between the less and the more highly finished exports, particularly for woollens (Table 5.2). Industrialisation on the continent was not yet driving British exports out of the more highly finished lines of production.

Table 5.2 Value in Pounds Sterling of Produce of the United Kingdom Exported to European Countries (exports of woollen yarn and woollen cloth)

	France		Belgium		Italy	
	yarn	cloth	yarn	cloth	yarn	cloth
1859	176,118	243,286	143,317	233,021	15,507	501,761
1873	357,454	3,531,053	49,637	610,005	7,000	723,798

	Germany		Austria		Spain	
	yarn	cloth	yarn	cloth	yarn	cloth
1859	1,789,660	1,304,947	. . .	46,906	6,484	106,536
1873	2,593,907	4,288,662	. . .	67,064	. . .	101,865

	Portugal		Total	
	yarn	cloth	yarn	cloth
1859	. . .	112,800	2,131,086	2,549,257
1873	. . .	165,838	3,007,998	9,488,285

Even so, sensing that the implications of the statistical evidence were not as obvious as the advocates of commercial treaty-making would have it, Kennedy lowered the pitch of his argument. 'Commerce,' he told Derby, 'is more complex in its nature now that it was in 1860: competition is much more keen. Now less than ever can England afford to disregard the commercial policy of other countries.' At the same time Kennedy faced up more candidly than anyone had yet dared to the need for Britain to reduce its expectations in the next round of European treaty-making. Cobden had hoped to ignite a bonfire of tariffs on the continent, leaving behind only revenue-producing duties, as in

Gladstone's budget for 1860. That expectation had faded; but everyone in Britain who had any interest in the subject, merchant and diplomat alike, continued to assume that commercial treaty-making would be worse than useless unless it involved tariff reductions. Kennedy now warned that continental tariffs were likely to rise. To make such a probability look less outrageous, he suggested that changes in the costs of production might justify the increase, particularly for metal manufacturing and perhaps also for woollens. Britain might be able only to restrain the amount of the increase.

His argument moved out of line with his statistics when he pointed to wine duties as Britain's best bargaining tool. He adopted Mallet's proposal that Britain should seek better terms with Austria, Italy, Spain and Portugal by adjusting its wine duties as they desired. This advice was reinforced by pleas from Britain's representatives in Germany for reduction in the related spirit duties as a gesture that would strengthen the advocates of free trade there. But the trade figures undermined this proposal by revealing that Britain's trade had grown with Spain and Portugal, with whom over the past decade Britain had conspicuously failed to reach commercial treaties, even more rapidly than with some of Britain's treaty partners. Since 1860, when Britain lowered its duty on light wines in favour of France, British imports of Portuguese wine had more than doubled and of Spanish wine had nearly trebled.[32] Why, then, should Britain accede to the Spanish and Portuguese demand for an adjustment in the wine duties, depriving the British Treasury of revenue on which it relied?

Kennedy moved on to firmer ground when he turned from rates of duty to classification of goods. This subject was of acute concern to metal manufacturing and still more to the textile industry where the composition and the treatment of fabric were ceaselessly changing. British merchants were sure that continental states exploited this complexity by framing bilateral tariff treaties in terms designed to foster trade with each other while damaging distinctively British lines of production.

Kennedy closed his memorandum with a succinct summary of the policy he wished Derby to pursue:

> It will not be possible to refuse assent, either formal or tacit, to some increase of foreign customs duties, but the main object in view should be to uphold the principle that these duties are to be moderate in amount and to be levied for fiscal purposes; to reduce to a minimum any increase of a possible protective character; and, unless in most exceptional circumstances, not to admit any differential treatment.

Kennedy's advice met with stiff resistance from the upper echelons at the Foreign Office but won support from Sir Stafford Northcote. Both the permanent undersecretary at the Foreign Office, Lord Tenterden, and the assistant undersecretary, Villiers Lister, recoiled from the thought of bargaining with continental states over tariffs – Tenterden called it 'haggling and higgling'.[33] They regarded it as a violation of the principles of free trade and as demeaning to British dignity. Britain should always demonstrate by its behaviour that the state that lowered its tariffs benefited itself as well as its trading partners. Villiers Lister was willing to see Britain reduce its wine duties, but he insisted that it should do so unilaterally, hoping but not bargaining for tariff reductions from wine-producing countries; and he expected the Treasury to reject this course of action, as it duly did, because of the loss of revenue.

Northcote as Chancellor of the Exchequer did not challenge that decision. Yet, beneath his meek exterior, Northcote possessed a degree of imagination, at least on matters of international trade, that was unusual among British statesmen. He knew something of international commerce and commercial diplomacy from his experience with the Board of Trade in the 1840s and again as its president in 1866–67, when he had worked with Mallet. In both periods Northcote had envisaged the possibility of convening a congress of the states of Europe to stabilise if not to reduce the tariffs that divided them. Kennedy's memorandum brought this notion back to Northcote's mind when he realised that the continental states in the commercial treaty network were on the verge of 'modifying and recasting their tariffs with one another behind our backs . . . quietly injuring our interests'.[34]

Even before the Treasury ruled out alteration of the wine duties, Northcote appreciated the weakness of Britain's position, having few if any tariffs of its own to bargain with in the impending negotiations on the continent. Yet Britain remained the world's greatest economic power, and it enjoyed a recognised political position in the Concert of Europe. These assets could be brought to bear if the forthcoming revision of the European treaty tariff took place in a multilateral conference or congress. In such a forum the common interests of the participating states might induce them to lay down liberal guidelines for the revision. Such principles need not be rigidly applied. Northcote envisaged leaving the various states free within the agreed principles to set their own tariffs in accordance with their particular financial needs.[35] He thus allowed for upward adjustment. But he hoped that, when assembled together, the states of Europe would see the folly of protecting their economic interests against each other and would appreciate instead the enriching wisdom of unimpeded mutual trade. He was well aware that the congress might fail. Still, by attempting to convene one, Britain would at least demonstrate the liveliness of its interest in the development of European trade.

Derby did not respond to Northcote's initiative directly or quickly. But in his own methodical way Derby strengthened his understanding of the situation. Through the correspondence of the Foreign Office with the Italian authorities as well as his own with Behrens, he saw that, as least for woollens, the classification of goods for customs purposes might be more important than the rate at which the duty was imposed. Here, in the classification of goods, was an issue that Britain might address effectively despite its lack of tariffs. The Foreign Office accordingly asked the Chamber of Commerce in Bradford for confirmation of Behrens's argument.

Behrens replied with a careful explanation of why classification was so important. Drawing upon 'a very elaborate Table of values in relation to weights' recently given to the Austrian authorities for protectionist purposes by one of their Chambers of Commerce,[36] Behrens showed how the Austrian classification of woollen textiles worked against the cheap but heavy mixed cloths of Yorkshire. He was content to leave pure woollens subject to valuation by weight. But mixed woollens required a different basis of valuation, one that recognised that heavy might mean cheap and light expensive. Bradford was anxious to shore up its business in heavy fabric cheapened by the incorporation of warps made of shredded old woollen cloth or 'shoddy'. Behrens's concern with regard to Italy was intensified by the secretiveness of its tariff talks and by the involvement of Switzerland, Austria and the prospective involvement of France. If the system of classification worked out by Italy and Austria were to be extended through the treaty network, 'the mere granting of a most-favoured-nation clause would . . . impose extravagant and prohibitive duties upon the tissues' that Yorkshire exported to the continent. Britain, lacking tariffs to bargain with, had relied upon the most-favoured-nation clause for participation in the benefits of the European treaty tariff. Behrens argued that, far from being a blessing, the application of the most-favoured-nation clause to Britain 'could not be considered otherwise than an unfriendly act' unless the Austro-Italian system of classification were revised.

Prompted by Behrens's warning, Derby asked Italy's roving commercial emissary, Luigi Luzzatti, to add London to his itinerary, and invited spokesmen for the Yorkshire worsted makers to meet him.[37] Here at last was a Foreign Secretary involving manufacturers and merchants in the negotiating process as Cobden had done. Derby confirmed the good impression his letter made when he received a deputation from the Yorkshire Chambers of Commerce. With reporters from the press in attendance, he repeated the familiar assertion that Britain had no tariffs to bargain with. But he showed how he understood that 'more important than the actual amount of the duty . . . [was] that . . . the duties . . . should not be levied in a manner to press unfavourably and unfairly upon the cheaper and heavier and coarser class of manufactured goods.' He also understood that, 'in consequence of the mode of classification adopted', the most-favoured-nation clause could turn out 'very far from being an equality in reality'.[38] He put the Yorkshire merchants in touch with the Foreign Office emissaries who were to handle the negotiations in Italy; and these visited

Yorkshire before leaving for Rome. In London, Behrens and his colleagues met Luzzatti, who seemed persuaded by their argument and asked for samples to show the Italian customs authorities.

In the midst of these increasingly amicable dealings with Yorkshire, Derby received an overture from France that enabled him to act on Northcote's suggestion. Encouraged by the response of the French Chambers of Commerce[39] to its springtime inquiry about the conventional tariff, the French government approached the British about opening negotiations on the renewal of Cobden's treaty before its expiry in 1877. Support for renewal had strengthened in the silk industry, where France was dominant, and remained firm in the maritime ports and the wine-producing regions, where good harvests counteracted the onset of a vine-destroying disease, phylloxera. The French iron industry had recovered from the flood of imports from Britain after 1860 far enough to command the domestic market and to concern itself instead with the export market. French producers of cotton textiles remained fearfully protectionist, as did the producers of pure woollens; but opinion was mixed elsewhere in the woollens and worsteds sector. There was a widespread desire in France for specific in place of the existing *ad valorem* duties, a change that would impede imports ever more effectively in a time of falling prices. The most-favoured-nation clause was falling out of favour in France partly because, under the Treaty of Frankfurt, Germany would always benefit from it. Even so, the French commercial community was sufficiently content with the existing conventional tariff to favour basing the country's general tariff upon it. Most of the Chambers of Commerce also favoured negotiating a renewal of the treaties with the country's trading partners.

Lord Derby not only welcomed the French overture, he proposed to expand it, in line with Northcote's suggestion, to involve other states with whom trade negotiations were due to begin, particularly Austria and Italy, the Netherlands and Germany.[40] Derby's interest in multilateral negotiations was fortified by a report from Crowe in Düsseldorf on the desire of German free traders for some indication that Britain wished to renew its trade agreements.[41] The French government, which was already involved in negotiations with Italy, welcomed Derby's proposal. In this way France and Britain as the original treaty partners would initiate the collective updating of the network. Both countries had reason to fear damage to their interests from piecemeal bilateral renegotiation of the component treaties such as the talks between Austria and Italy.

Thus the year 1875 ended hopefully, all the more so when the Reichstag reconfirmed the liberal commercial policy of Germany. Britain and France were preparing to renegotiate Europe's interlocked tariff treaties early in the hope of reducing the barriers to trade within the European market. Germany was moving unilaterally in the same direction, counteracting the contrary movement in the lesser economies of Austria and Italy. Within Britain, for the first time since 1860, the most anxious merchants in the Yorkshire woollens industry were co-operating harmoniously with the government.

c. The Renegotiations of 1877

The year-end hopes of 1875 were to be disappointed but not quite dashed over the next two years as, one after another, the European commercial treaties and national tariffs came up for revision. The outlook was darkened by the depression, which not only persisted longer than experienced observers expected but even intensified. The prosperity that France had enjoyed since her military defeat came to an end.[42] Wheat from the United States flooded into the German market, driving the domestic price down and thus undermining the livelihood of the east Prussian Junkers and their hostility to protective tariffs.[43] Imports especially of foodstuffs rose also in Britain. As for British exports, the prices they could command fell faster than their quantity could rise, worsening the balance of trade. The export deterioration in Britain was particularly acute for the worsted stuffs of Yorkshire, where the quantity of exports decreased while going up in most other sectors.[44]

The remarkable fact was, however, that this depression did not bring about a change in commercial policy more quickly and decisively. The enormous expansion of European trade and industrial capacity over the past 15 years had convinced the ministers in charge of commercial policy in the major economic powers of Europe that tariff reduction was mutually advantageous. Even the industries that protested most loudly at any loss in tariff protection had learnt to compete with their foreign rivals and to extend their productive capacity from the domestic market into exports. The new-found faith of continental governments in tariff reduction was upset by the depression of the mid-1870s. Even so, the governments of Europe would not be persuaded to abandon their liberal commercial policies by directly economic considerations. Their course would be dictated by political concerns, whether about electoral support, governmental income or national rivalries and security, though all of these factors naturally had some economic determinants. Reinforced by developments in thought and popular mobilisation, these concerns modified the commercial policy of every European government, including the British, and all in different ways.

All of these economic and political developments put a strain on the commercial treaty network. Resentment mounted in each of its member states over the fetters that the network imposed on their freedom of action, especially the most-favoured-nation clause which obliged them to give every participating state the trading concessions designed for particular partners. The network increased the economic interdependency of the signatory states and promoted the growth of their exports, but it also interfered with the development of their domestic markets and their attempts to alleviate the social as well as economic suffering inflicted by the common depression. The interconnections of trade as well as the bonds of the network ensured that the tariff revisions, whether national or by treaty, which were scheduled for completion in 1877 remained firmly interlocked. No country retreated entirely into its own economic shell, however strongly the depression nourished the appeal of economic nationalism. Even the Austrians, whose conversion to commercial liberalism had been slow and shallow and whose return to protection was swift, remained anxious to strengthen their hold on their multinational empire through commercial treaties. But neither was any European government willing to subordinate its individual interests to those of the European market as a whole. Even the most liberally inclined, Switzerland, for example, as well as Britain, gave revenue considerations, aggravated by the depression in trade, a higher priority than tariff reductions that might eventually expand European trade.

The tariffs and tariff treaties in a host of countries were up for revision: Italy, Austria and Switzerland, as well as the pivotal three, France, Britain and Germany. This opening encouraged other countries not yet fully part of the network, particularly Spain and Portugal, to push themselves in. There was an opportunity, then, for expansion of the network and hence of European commerce as well as a risk of defections.

Though every set of trade talks had wide ramifications, the fate of the network depended ultimately on Britain, France and Germany. But they could not agree on the forum at which they would set their tariffs, whether a multilateral congress of the members of the network, or bilateral talks within each pair of treaty partners, or unilateral action by the individual state. Britain preferred multilateral action, France bilateral and Germany unilateral. The tariff of Germany was set largely by its legislature, hence the crucial battles there were fought internally. What the forces of commercial liberalism in Germany sought from Britain was encouragement. They no longer needed a further commercial treaty with France because of the perpetual most-favoured-nation provisions in the peace settlement at Frankfurt. The only commercial treaty negotiations that seriously affected the German tariff were those with Austria. The government of France, on the other hand, backing away with the onset of depression from the multilateral forum it had recently favoured, preferred to forward its interests in bilateral negotiations with its trading partners. This strategy enabled France to tailor each treaty to the advantage of its own industries that were particularly involved in the trade with the country at issue, without concern for and even to the detriment of its other treaty partners. Tutored by Jacob Behrens, Lord Derby understood how the French strategy could endanger British commerce. He favoured multilateral action as a way for Britain to avoid damaging agreements among its treaty partners and, more generally, the bargaining that appeared inevitable in bilateral negotiations. Britain hoped that a congress on the conventional or treaty-made tariff of Europe would draw forth the common interest of every state in the expansion of trade and thus weaken protectionist interests in the individual countries.

The depression made the Conservative government even more reluctant than its predecessor to use its best bargaining lever, the wine and spirits duties, for fear of the loss to the Treasury. Revenue fell, while the outbreak of war in the Middle East threatened to increase the demands on governmental resources. Yet the wine and spirit duties might have done as much for Britain in the tariff renegotiations of 1877 as they had for Cobden in 1860. Nearly all the countries involved in the tariff talks of 1876–77 – Italy and Spain, Germany and France – pressed Britain for concessions on these items, and they were willing to pay handsomely for them.[45] Their argument was strong, and it struck at British pretensions on free trade. The wine and spirit duties were punitive, preferential and protective. Though reduced in 1860, the duty on cheap light French wines still often doubled and in extreme cases quadrupled their retail price.[46] This was worse than anything in the French tariff on British goods, and it discredited Britain's application of the doctrine of comparative advantage, a basic assumption of free trade. Louis Mallet drove the point home: 'That any fiscal legislation should interpose such obstacles to the natural exchange between two countries so eminently fitted to supply each other's wants as France and England, is a state of things which no Free Trade Power can, consistently with its principles, quietly accept.'[47] Because Britain levied its wine duties at a specific rate rather than *ad valorem*, they proved ever more oppressive at a time of falling prices and also discredited the insistence on *ad valorem* duties for British woollens. The British duties discriminated against the heavy wines of Sicily and the Iberian Peninsula in favour of the French. Moreover, despite British protestations to the contrary, the high wine and spirit duties protected domestic breweries and Scottish distillers against cheap continental wines and German spirits. (There was as yet little direct international trade in beer, at least so far as Britain was concerned.) Even so orthodox a journal as *The Economist* admitted that the main continental complaints were valid.

The demand from British exporters for the opening of the Mediterranean markets through concessions on the wine duties remained firm, while resistance weakened inside the civil service. Spokesmen for the customs authority devised schemes to minimise the loss to the Treasury. Though customs officials questioned the benefit to Britain's continental trade, the Inland Revenue Department declared its willingness to accept a reduced scale of duties 'if, by its adoption, our commercial negotiations upon other points could be more successfully carried on'.[48] Villiers Lister at the Foreign Office was willing to extend the reduction to the light wines of France as well as to the heavy wines of the

Mediterranean because of the intense rivalry between the two sides and their suspicion of anything that tended to favour the other.

Yet Derby and Northcote did not try to overturn the routine rejection of this demand by the Customs and Inland Revenue officials. The prospective longer-term gain to the Treasury from increased imports of wine and generally expanded trade with the continent could not compensate for an immediate loss of revenue in a period of depression. In accepting the Inland Revenue ruling, British governments of both parties, Conservative now as well as Liberal, aban-doned the strategy through which Cobden had inaugurated this liberal era in European commercial policy. In doing so, they destroyed any prospect of further liberal improvement in European tariffs.

Britain's refusal to consider reducing the spirit duty in 1876 disheartened German free traders early in their struggle against resurgent protectionism. The Foreign Office was aware of the problem, though it responded helplessly. Crowe relayed four reports from inquiries commissioned by the Handelstag, or Chamber of Commerce, in Berlin on the tariff question. There was a chorus of complaint in Germany, whether from textile manufacturers or the iron and steel industry, about Britain exploiting the low German tariff to flood the market. The Handelstag inquiries focused on comparative production costs. The British liked to dwell on the advantage their continental competitors reaped from cheap labour. But the Germans, like the French, emphasised the advantages Britain enjoyed from cheap transport by sea and inland waterways, from closeness to the main ports of entry for raw materials, from cheap and good coal and machinery, from low interest rates or from the skill of British labour. Amid the depression from which all countries were suffering, the British were dumping their goods at scarcely cost price on whichever continental market had the lowest tariff: '& this,' cried the Handelstag, 'is Germany.'[49] Crowe accepted this accusation while attempting to refute its protectionist application. 'If England pours in & stores in Germany, it does so at periods of crisis only, & when the overplus of production must be got rid of at any price! No tarif [sic[50]], be it ever so high can deal with a crisis of this kind.'[51] The ire of German iron and steel makers was so concentrated upon Britain that, while they wanted most-favoured-nation relations with other continental states, they wondered 'whether such a clause conceded to England would not give Great Britain too much influence over Germany'.[52] Representatives of the iron and steel, cotton, chemicals, sugar, linen and leather industries formed a Central Union of German Manufacturers in 1876 to press for tariff protection. Germany did not, however, rush into protectionism. Liberal views remained strong in much of the mercantile community. At the end of the year Crowe could report, somewhat optimistically, that the Reichstag 'finally settled all commercial questions of the time in the sense of free trade'.[53]

In the spring of 1877 the government of France attempted to open the renegotiation of its many commercial treaties through an agreement with Britain. But French talk of tariff increases and British aversion to reducing the wine duties brought about an early suspension of these talks. The *seize mai* (16 May) crisis, when the President of France threw out a republican ministry in favour of a monarchist one, then overshadowed the trade talks. They were set back further when the new ministry revealed the extent of the tariff reductions that it was willing to make in return for reduction in the British wine duties. With commercial liberals still in charge of trade policy, France sought a 50 per cent reduction in the British wine duties in return for a 25 per cent reduction in the French duty on iron, steel and coal and a 10 per cent reduction on textiles. These figures were doubled in the French press.[54] The reports roused the protectionists under Pouyer-Quertier to mobilise their forces throughout the country, and they made considerable headway in the legislative elections of October.[55] The commercial liberals in the French executive never thereafter regained the initiative they had enjoyed since the fall of Thiers.

The immobility of the great powers allowed the lesser economies of Italy, Austria and Spain to set the direction of European commercial policy. Italy and Spain used treaty negotiations with other countries to put pressure on Britain to reduce its wine duties.[56] Italy signed an agreement with France that increased the French advantage over the British in the Italian market[57] and replaced *ad valorem* with specific duties on textiles, to the detriment of heavy British textiles, which the Italians were learning to produce for themselves. Spain reached an agreement with Germany that discriminated against the goods of Britain and France in order to gain access to their market for wine; France soon escaped discrimination by reaching its own agreement with Spain.

Austria engaged in two forms of tariff revision in 1877, both designed to release it from the treaty network of the 1860s. Austria had already given notice of its wish to terminate its treaty agreements when they expired, as its treaty with Britain did at the beginning of the year. Britain did not lose because it had not gained much from this treaty and supplemental convention with Austria. But commercial liberals generally, including the British, were shocked by the level to which Austria proceeded to raise its autonomous tariff. The only treaty agreements that Austria showed any interest in renewing were with its neighbours. They included Italy and Romania but above all Germany from which Austria could not readily detach itself. The autonomous Austrian tariff of 1877 later came to be regarded as marking the point at which continental Europe turned away from a liberal towards a protective tariff policy. But at the time attention focused not on the autonomous tariff but on the Austro-German negotiations to revise the commercial treaty between them, for it would set the terms of most-favoured-nation access to the trade of both countries.

Derby did what he could to involve Britain in these continental negotiations. He put British Chambers of Commerce in direct touch with the commercial emissaries of the French and Italian governments. He ensured that Crowe was called from Düsseldorf to Berlin whenever the Austro-German talks convened there. Crowe was instructed to make sure that British interests, particularly in the cheaper lines of production, were not overlooked or damaged.[58] But though he was accorded official observer status in Berlin, the proceedings were conducted in secret. Austria rejected any British presence as incompatible with its rightful independence and refused to receive Crowe in Vienna when the talks moved there.

Even so, the long-anticipated year of 1877, when so many of the European conventional and autonomous tariffs came up for revision, ended less anxiously for the British than it had begun. The protective or discriminatory turn that many of the talks had taken was still tentative, except in the case of Spain. The Franco-Italian agreement awaited legislative confirmation. The Austro-German talks proved difficult, with Austria insisting on a much higher tariff than Germany would tolerate. Towards the end of the year, with no conclusion in sight, Austria prolonged its existing treaties, including the treaty with Britain, for another six months. The suspension of the talks between Britain and France was obscured by the governmental crisis in France and the war between Russia and Turkey.

The British mercantile community found Derby's involvement in the tariff-making on the continent reassuring. Yet the warning signals from abroad did nothing to reduce its demands, least of all those from West Yorkshire. They were raised, on the contrary, by the depression, which fell even harder on Yorkshire than elsewhere. Bradford riveted its attention on the tariff talks. The prosperity of the town reached its peak in 1875;[59] and though that was not immediately apparent and would not be accepted by its business community for a long time, its leaders fought for lower continental tariffs in the knowledge that their welfare was at stake. The Chamber of Commerce co-operated with an investigation in 1876 commissioned by the French government to compare the costs of production in the woollens industries of the two countries. The government and centres of woollens production in France, with the exception of Roubaix, welcomed a return investigation sent over by Bradford. But the two investigations led to opposite conclusions. While the investigators from Bradford reported with admiration on the skill of their French rivals and with envy on their cheap labour, the French industry expanded on the competitive advantages enjoyed by the English and demanded heightened tariff protection against the cheap mixed fabrics of Yorkshire.[60]

Outraged, Bradford hardened its insistence that the Foreign Office refuse to consider any such increase. When the Anglo-French negotiations opened in March 1877, the Chamber of Commerce demanded that the French duty on the woollen cloth of Bradford be eliminated, that the duty on yarns be reduced to a nominal level and that the duty on cotton warp goods be halved to 5 per cent, decreasing by 1 per cent every two years so as to vanish entirely in a decade.[61] If France did not meet these demands, the merchants of Bradford indicated that they might press for a complete British withdrawal from the treaty network. Thus the same economic distress that pushed continental economies towards higher protection induced British industry to demand cuts in continental tariffs. On all sides there were signs of retreat from the network of treaties towards national independence in commercial policy.

d. The Departure of Germany

'Germany [is] preparing to separate herself from the economic union,' Luzzatti of Italy wrote with regret at the end of 1878.[62] He placed much of the blame on Britain, tracing the continental retreat from liberal policies back to Britain's refusal to bring its wine duties to bear in the network negotiations. 'England, whose endeavour it has been to make the principles of Free Trade triumph in the Treaties of Commerce [is] gradually losing her influence, partly from a lack of the ability so eminently displayed in 1860.'

Whatever the effect of the Disraeli government's reluctance to continue bargaining over the wine duties as Cobden had done, Britain's weakness had still more to do with the setback to its economy in the depression. It was particularly hard on the sectors of British industry most dependent on the European market, especially woollens. Exports generally continued to fall. In most sectors the drop was in price rather than volume, where there was often a substantial increase. But the export of woollen fabric fell even more in volume than price.[63] Even more serious was Britain's loss of its technological advantage over its continental competitors. *The Economist* reported that the French textiles displayed in the Paris exhibition of 1878 surpassed those of Britain,

> not simply in those fancy fabrics for which the French had long had a reputation, but in the higher class of fine broad cloths, in which the products of Saxony and the West of England used to stand pre-eminent. . . . The technical power which the French designer and weaver has obtained over [the various materials in woollen worsteds, including silk and mohair], and the perfection to which the dye and finish has for years past been brought is a lesson which the English manufacturer of mixed fabrics appears only now to have taken to heart.

Even the productions of Austria displayed excellence 'in the very points on which English manufacturers have hitherto congratulated themselves, – fineness and evenness of texture and perfection of finish'.[64] There was evidence by the end of 1878 that in metal as well as textile manufacturing Britain was losing ground in the upper, more highly finished lines of production.[65] The best solution to these questions that *The Economist* could find lay in 'opening up new markets and raising up new nations of consumers'.[66] Did that mean in effect abandoning Europe?

Yet it was the continuing strength rather than the emerging weaknesses in the British economy that alienated continental Europe from commercial liberalism during the great depression. The cry went up amid the falling prices that Britain was dumping goods on the continental market when it could no longer sell them further afield. The French were concerned mainly about textiles, the Germans about iron and steel. It did British respondents no good to point out that the trade figures belied these accusations, that the French textiles industry was faring better than the British, or that German iron and steel producers suffered no more than British. Having spent the previous generation struggling to establish themselves against superior British competition, continental industrialists felt themselves undercut once again by Britain with the aid of Cobden's treaties. The iron masters of the Ruhr, like the worsted manufacturers of Roubaix, blamed Cobden's creed of minimal tariffs for rendering them defenceless.

Continental adherence to commercial liberalism did not crumble quickly. Even protectionists in France appreciated the benefit to business of the reliability that treaty commitment gave to tariff levels. Protectionists criticised the most-favoured-nation clause because it diminished this dependability by making the tariff, say of France, subject to change whenever one of its most-favoured treaty partners reached an agreement with yet another country. The German government clothed its changing commercial policy in the language of liberalism. But as in the emerging movement for 'Fair Trade' in Britain, Germans turned back to the bilateral terminology of an earlier commercial liberalism and cried for the reciprocity that Britain had abandoned in the 1840s.[67] 'Our policy,' the German government declared,

> is a free-trade policy in the broadest sense of the word, the advantages of which are not to be denied so long as we have reciprocity. Without reciprocity free-trade does absolute harm to the state which 'generously' sacrifices every thing to its principles. . . . France . . . in spite of all her revolutions has become the richest country of the European continent because in commercial matters it only takes cognizance of its national views and interests.[68]

The key word was reciprocity. To the British it meant bargaining and hence repelled respectable free traders. Everywhere else it meant simply mutual exchange of advantages as a basis for international commercial relations. Was not reciprocity the basis of relationships in every market? But the market, as advocates of reciprocity conceived of it, was between producing nations, whereas the prevalent view in Britain was of a market between individual economic actors in which the interests of the consumer should reign supreme. The British thought of their viewpoint as universally valid and altruistic, though they were not, of course, disconcerted by the fact that it had served their national interests supremely well for 30 years.

The friends and representatives of Britain and commercial liberalism on the continent urged the British government to reconsider its passive policy. They wanted Disraeli's government to assert national interests in the commerce as robustly as it did in the politics of Europe. French and German free traders argued, according to Crowe's report, that Britain should abandon its insistence on free trade as

> a fixed and unalterable principle . . . 'You cannot, they say, beat down protectionism abroad unless you [England] make up your mind to say to foreign powers, that if they proceed on the lines they have lately taken it is time for Great Britain to consider whether it may not be advisable to initiate measures of reprisal. You have beaten Russia [in its conflict with Turkey], they add, by showing that you are prepared to fight, you will beat the protectionists by doing the same thing; & in the end free trade will conquer.'[49]

The new British Foreign Secretary, Lord Salisbury, took note. Disraeli had moved him from the India to the Foreign Office when Derby would not stand up to the demands of Russia after its military victory over Turkey. Salisbury immediately impressed the chancelleries of Europe by issuing a masterful statement of Britain's position in the Middle East. In a similar spirit, right from his first months as Foreign Secretary he took an active interest in the European tariff discussions, with which Louis Mallet had familiarised him when they were both at the India Office.

With an eye to finding crucial leverage in these discussions, Salisbury turned to the wine duties. He read the memoranda that had been exchanged within the government on these duties over the past year and found enough encouragement to reverse the decision against reduction. With Northcote's acquiescence, Salisbury made a circumscribed offer to Spain. Any significant reduction in the higher rate of duty on the heavier wines in which Spain was interested would cost the Treasury at least £400,000 in the first year,[70] an amount that Salisbury recognised as more than could be tolerated at a time of depression. He therefore offered to reconsider the details though not the basic scale of the duty if the Spanish thought that it pressed unfairly upon them. The proposal left the Spanish unimpressed.

The best time for an offer to wine-producing countries had in any case passed. France was no longer interested, preoccupied as it had become with internal controversy. Under protectionist pressure from the legislature, the

French government initiated a basic change in its commercial strategy, though it remained liberal in ultimate intent. Instead of turning the treaty tariff into the general tariff of France and then offering further reductions in renegotiating its treaties, the government proposed increases in the general tariff, increases that could be removed in negotiation with its treaty partners.[71] The French legislature kept up its pressure on the executive by rejecting the agreement it had reached in 1877 with Italy.

The focus of attention moved away from the Atlantic seaboard to Central Europe, where Germany was re-examining its autonomous tariff and revising its treaty tariff in negotiations with Austria. Though both sets of discussions were veiled in secrecy, the signs did not bode well for free trade. There was evidence in March of a rapprochement between the hitherto free-trading landowners of eastern Prussia, whose market for grain was depressed by cheap imports from Russia and the United States, and the arch-protectionist iron and steel producers of the Ruhr. A breach developed at the same time between Bismarck and the free-trading National Liberals on whom he had previously relied for legislative support. Meanwhile the emphatically protectionist Austrians were proving less interested than the Germans in reaching a compromise agreement.

As usual, the effective decision-maker in Germany was Bismarck and the decisive considerations were political. The change in tariff policy was only the most obvious manifestation of an extensive recasting in Bismarck's political alignment. Even within the confines of commercial policy, Bismarck was more anxious to raise revenue for the imperial government than to gratify the iron masters of the Ruhr. Veiled in the depths of summer and far from Berlin in Heidelberg, a conference of finance ministers from the member states of the German empire was convened to consider ways to replenish the imperial coffers. The agenda, which an informant enabled Crowe to transmit to Salisbury,[72] contained a whole range of possible excise and customs duties on, among other things, tobacco, beer and spirits, petroleum, sugar, coffee, tea and dried fruit. But it became clear that duties on these goods could not generate the amount needed by the imperial treasury unless the German tariff was raised generally. That evidently was Bismarck's intent.

The reconstruction of the German tariff was suspended, pending the outcome of the negotiations with Austria. Only in November, when they seemed likely to fail, did the German government resume work on its tariff legislation for the coming year. Bismarck heralded the change with a public statement.[73] After explaining that an increase in imperial income had become necessary, Bismarck added:

> The present depression of German manufactures and the tendency apparent in America and in great neighbouring states, after the lapse of

commercial treaties to give increased protection to home production, demand that we should ascertain whether it may not be desirable to give to our national manufactures a larger control of the home market, at the same time that we bring together such matter as may enable us by treaty to break down the barriers impeding the expansion of our exports.

Austria dashed any lingering hopes for further reduction in the tariff barriers between the two countries by refusing to prolong its existing treaty with Germany 'even for a day'[74] beyond the end of the year, when it was due to expire. That refusal exposed Germany to the full rigours of the high general tariff that Austria had meanwhile devised. It would fall not only on Germany but on every other state, including Britain, that relied on its commercial treaty with Germany for favoured-nation access to the Austrian market. Bismarck, who wished to preserve good political relations with Austria despite their commercial disagreement, secured a minimal commercial treaty guaranteeing only Germany most-favoured-nation status in the Austrian market and continued co-operation in their cross-border commerce.

Britain was left helpless in face of the Austrian return to protection and the recasting of the German general tariff. Salisbury asked his ambassador in Berlin, Lord Odo Russell, whether there might be any way for British business interests to make representations to the German government on its tariff revision as they had when Italy and France were attempting to revise their treaty tariffs with Britain. 'I greatly doubt,' replied Russell, 'whether the German government in its present illiberal frame of mind . . . would consent to preliminary or special "pourparlers".'[75] Russell still inquired whether, instead of receiving a British representative, Bismarck would appoint his own agent to receive British representations, perhaps at the German embassy in London; but the request was turned down. All that Russell could do, with Salisbury's blessing, was to bring Crowe to Berlin while the German tariff was under consideration. Through his contacts in the German business community and the government's commercial bureaucracy, Crowe could find out better than anyone what was going on and what it might mean for British trade.

The British government was taken aback by the popularity of Bismarck's change of policy and also by its anti-British direction. British commentators had assumed that, though the French conversion to free trade might be dubious, the Germans were genuine believers. But Russell began the new year with a report on 'the steadily growing agitation, not only in favour of reimposing import duties on iron generally, but also of taking measures as may tend in particular to exclude English competition altogether from Germany'.[76] There was no mistaking the movement towards protectionism in Germany. It was apparent even among the National Liberals, the previously staunch supporters of liberal commercial policies whose cohesion broke before the contrary tide.

According to Crowe's estimate, one-fifth of the National Liberals now proclaimed themselves 'protectionists of the strongest type & ⅕ᵗʰ more will be dubiously on the same side'.[77]

This rapid apostasy was not peculiar to Germany. It occurred in Britain, in the Associated Chambers of Commerce, and won some of its strongest advocates in Bradford. Article after article appeared in the leading periodicals either making or refuting the case for reciprocity.[78] The movement in continental Europe towards protectionism confirmed the most insistent British free traders in their belief that the commercial treaty-making of the 1860s had been a dire mistake.[79] But others found the root of the problem in the earlier British abandonment of reciprocity. Sampson Lloyd, chairman of the Associated Chambers and an early advocate of what came to be known as 'Fair Trade', talked of reciprocity when he petitioned Lord Derby against 'signing treaties of commerce with those foreign nations which have imposed, or intend to impose, higher import duties upon English manufactures'.[80]

The president of Bradford's Chamber of Commerce, Henry Mitchell, opened its annual meeting with a declaration in favour of retaliatory duties on imported luxuries to offset the damage foreign tariffs did to English commerce.[81] Forster replied with a lengthy defence of free trade. He insisted that retaliatory duties on luxuries would do nothing except dishearten foreign free traders who expected Britain to set a good example. He damned reciprocity as 'retaliatory protection'.[82] But Mitchell received support from other prominent members of the Chamber: Ripley, who had joined Forster in the parliamentary representation of Bradford but as a Conservative; and Lister, by now the greatest of Bradford's manufacturers. Lister had built up his wealth by developing ways to reduce the cost of incorporating silk into mixed fabrics. Silks were the one sector of the British textile industry that by all accounts had been ruined by the loss of tariff protection under the terms of Cobden's treaty. Sensitivity to the costs of Cobden's general policy made Lister a forthright protectionist. The debate in Bradford revolved naturally around textiles, and hence had more to do with the French treaty than with the autonomous German tariff. The Bradford Chamber of Commerce paid no attention to the developments in Germany until their focus turned from iron and steel to textiles.

Behrens sat silent through the debate. The depression that produced a protectionist consensus in much of Europe destroyed the consensus in Britain in favour of free trade but failed to produce any widely acceptable alternative. Nowhere was this clearer than in Bradford. The makers and merchants of woollens and worsteds turned angrily on each other over what to do about the declining fortunes of their industry as it was pushed out of the continental European market. They all knew what they wanted: open access to that market. But they fell to quarrelling about how to obtain it. The reimposition of tariffs, even strictly for bargaining purposes, might well make tariff barriers a permanent feature of the European commercial landscape. Uncertain what to do as his associates quarrelled, Behrens said nothing beyond seconding the nomination of Mitchell for another year as president.

The debate in Bradford was repeated elsewhere, on a broader scale and at higher levels, including the next annual meeting of the Associated Chambers of Commerce and in the House of Lords. The Associated Chambers of Commerce displayed the same acute concern about, and the same inability to agree on, an alternative to the country's current commercial policy.[83] The resolutions that Lord Bateman presented to the House of Lords in favour of reciprocity elicited another of Disraeli, now Lord Beaconsfield's paradoxically negative defences of free trade. He told the Lords that, 'practically speaking, Reciprocity, whatever its merits, is dead. You cannot, if you would, build up a reciprocal system of Commercial Treaties. You have lost the power.'[84]

Uncertainty about how to deal with the developments in Germany muted the response of the British iron and steel industry. It was not until April that Salisbury received anything from the British Iron Trade Association to pass on to the embassy in Berlin. Even then the association simply wished to know what the terms 'raw iron' and 'manufactured iron' as translated from the German bill actually covered.[85] The Germans were not threatening British iron and steel in 1879 with tariff levels worse than the British had welcomed as a historic concession from the French in 1860. When Crowe looked closely at the initial proposals of the German government, he dismissed the fear that they would close 'the German market altogether to the British Iron Trade', for he was confident that the German manufacturers could not do without British pig iron.[86] Bismarck reduced British alarm with periodic assurances that he intended to put trade back on a treaty basis as soon as the general tariff was in place.

But at the same time the Chancellor prompted the Reichstag to push the tariff higher than the government had originally proposed. Protectionist industrial interests needed no such encouragement, but Bismarck gave the converts to protective tariffs among his fellow Junkers the courage of their new-found convictions. As the debates in the Reichstag reached their conclusion, Crowe warned Salisbury 'how strongly the current has set in against free trade in Germany . . . the anti-protectionist party has been almost silent, and members who ventured to plead for lower duties on half manufactured produce have carefully guarded themselves against being considered free traders.'[87] He increased his estimate of the adverse impact on British trade, particularly for heavy textiles, on which the Reichstag pushed the tariff to 30 per cent, double the French level of 1860. Though not inclined to despair, Crowe knew that British exporters would have to fight harder for a share of the German market. In the first of several reports on the probable impact of the German general tariff upon particular industries, he warned cotton manufacturers that 'the English market in Germany will to some extent be curtailed unless we can by reducing prices, freight and commission neutralize German legislation; and with help of the name, which England is acknowledged to possess and which alone has been described as worth 10 p. cent for some classes of thread, continue to supply Germany now as we supplied her before.'[88]

Salisbury learnt from his experience alongside the British commercial community. In May, as soon as the Bradford Chamber of Commerce noticed and began to protest at the German tariff proposals on mixed woollens, he transmitted their objections to Lord Odo Russell for presentation to the German authorities in Berlin. Russell did as instructed, but he confessed to Salisbury that he did not pass on the statement 'that the imposition of the proposed heavy duties would certainly result in the entire cessation of exports of woollens to Germany'. He explained that, 'in the present state of feeling in the German Commercial World as regards the taxation of foreign industry, which feeling is more especially directed against England . . . the argument of the Yorkshire Chambers of Commerce . . . would be received with undisguised satisfaction.'[89] Russell repeated his comment when Salisbury relayed a protest from the jute industry at Dundee which declared that it would be prevented under the new tariff from exporting – the Germans said flooding[90] – its goods into the German market. When Salisbury insisted on transmitting the protest, the German legislature responded by increasing its tariff on jute.[91] German reaction was intensified by the British exporters who hurried great quantities of metal and textile manufactures to Germany before the tariff was due to rise. The usual level of exports doubled for cottons and pig iron, trebled for linens and scrap iron, and for some woollens quadrupled.[92] When Bismarck learnt what was happening, he subjected the British goods stacked up in German warehouses to the new tariff even before it was technically in force. His abrupt action struck British exporters as outrageous. Salisbury began to wonder whether Britain might respond with something more effective than indignation.

Chapter 6

Disengagement between Britain and France, 1879–1882

> 'The French ambassador said "that he was no doubt a free-trader, a 'libre-échangiste,' but that he was a 'libre-échangiste Français,' that he recognized the necessity of paying due consideration to the interests of national industries.
>
> 'In that case, I said, I must venture to doubt whether a 'libre-échangiste Français,' in his Excellency's acceptation of the term, was not what in English we called a protectionist."'
>
> Lord Granville to the Secretary of the British embassy in Paris, 10 Aug. 1881

However important the change in Bismarck's trade policy may have been in the return to protectionism, it did not fundamentally upset the network of commercial treaties. Germany extricated itself, in connection with the enactment of the general tariff, from all of its commercial treaties except for two. Both were most-favoured-nation commitments, one desired, the other regretted. Bismarck had taken care to preserve the most-favoured-nation relationship with Austria, the beaten rival he now wished to draw close against France. He had come to regret that, in the Treaty of Frankfurt, he had bound France and Germany to most-favoured commercial treatment of each other. That obligation intensified his aversion to the whole network of treaties.

The departure of Germany cut away a portion of the network, but not its centre. The network had been woven around the Anglo-French treaty of 1860 and still bore the marks of its origin. That treaty, framed in the interests of Britain and France, set the terms on which the ensuing treaties were built. Kennedy at the commercial department in the Foreign Office reminded Lord Salisbury of the continuing value of this framework as he prepared for talks with France to renew their treaty.[1] Even though Britain's treaty partners sometimes reached agreements among themselves that did not serve Britain's particular interests, those provisions were neither consistent with the spirit nor promoted by the terms of the original agreement. A Belgian analyst of the network[2] admitted that 10 per cent of the conventional European tariff was meant to protect continental producers against Britain's industrial superiority. Cobden had tacitly accepted such discrimination in 1860 as temporarily unavoidable. The British mercantile community hoped to get rid of all such barriers and had welcomed the 1860 treaty as the first step towards that end. They expected the commercial diplomacy of Europe to keep moving in that direction. That was the British objective – if only it could be obtained – when Cobden's treaty came up for renewal: another lowering of the tariff walls that impeded the flow of trade among the states of Europe.

That, or something close to it, was also the goal of the ministers in charge of the discussions on the French side. And they proved able, after a long and stiff fight with the forces of protectionism, to secure legislative approval for a general tariff suitable for ministerial purposes in the ensuing treaty negotiations. Lesser states in the network hovered around the Anglo-French discussions to promote a successful outcome.

Yet, in talks that stretched on till 1882, Britain and France failed to reach agreement. It was certainly not for lack of trying or even of a broad measure of concensus. The leaders on both sides espoused liberal commercial principles and spoke the language of free trade, even if they did not mean quite the same thing by it. There were still complementary as well as competitive elements in their two economies, pre-eminently the French export and the British import of wine.

But both governments were subject to electoral, industrial and to a lesser extent fiscal pressures that restricted their freedom to make concessions crucial to each other. The treasuries of both Britain and France found themselves in improved balance by 1880. Yet the same consideration for revenue that made the British Treasury hostile to reduction of the wine duties led the French finance ministry to advocate replacing *ad valorem* with specific duties, which were so much more lucrative at a time of falling prices. A demand for 'Fair Trade' burgeoned among the British electorate; this was weaker than French protectionism but focused particularly on the treaty with France. In terms of the economic sector, the talks broke down over cheap and heavy textiles, with France insistent on a higher tariff, which Britain absolutely refused.

The failure of the two originating powers to renew their agreement did not, however, precipitate the collapse of the treaty network. Reluctantly the other treaty partners of France agreed to renegotiate their agreements. The revised French treaties were likely to do British interests more damage than their predecessors had, all the more so because of worsening political relations between Britain and France over Egypt. Cobden's belief in the beneficent relationship between low tariffs and peace was mirrored in reverse by the deteriorating political as well as economic relationship between the two countries after their trade talks broke down. Even so, Britain did not abandon commercial treaty-making or return to the bargain-free purity of unilateral free trade. Instead it pressed its commercial diplomacy into corners of Europe that had not been integrated into the network of the 1860s.

a. Lord Salisbury's Discontent

In the spring of 1879, three would-be activists on commercial policy mulled over the alternatives Britain might pursue. During a pause in the debates on the general tariff in Berlin, Crowe came to London for consultations. He was impressed by the weakening of commercial liberalism in France as well as Germany. He aired his ideas first with Lord Salisbury, and then at the India Office with Mallet who carried Cobden's torch. The rivalry among the states of Europe through which Salisbury had navigated so ably over the Russo-Turkish war shaped Crowe's thinking on commercial matters. His attitude was confirmed in the clubs of London where he 'met numbers of men of the liberal & free trade party who talk of reciprocity – meaning reprisals – as a thing that might at a pinch be advocated whilst among conservatives [he] found men who argued that reprisals are the true policy of this country'.[3] Thus encouraged, he harked back to possibilities that Britain had missed over the previous year. He wanted it to throw its weight around, taking advantage of the freedom of manœuvre regained when Austria, Germany and France denounced their treaties. As he put it to his chief in Berlin, 'my policy in commercial matters was to pit France ag[ains]t Germany. Get a treaty from France, & then concede or withhold our concessions to France to or from Germany according as Germany was stiff or inclined to yield a point to us.'[4]

The wine duties were crucial to any hope Britain might have of escape from the impasse in which it found itself. The still-deepening depression ruled out a reduction in 1879, though Northcote as Chancellor encouraged brighter hopes for the following year.[5] British exports continued their fall, and the deterioration grew even more acute in cotton textiles than in woollens. Crowe considered increasing as well as reducing the wine duties, though on balance he expected more from the latter. He thought of threatening France with an increase

in order to obtain equivalents, or to go a step further by reducing the wine duties in return for larger French concessions. What France might grant we could refuse to Germany if we denounced the most favoured nation clause treaty. Further we could threaten Germany with a return to higher wine duties & an increase especially to the duty on wine in bottles respecting which we had hitherto been bound by treaty with Austria.

By working this seesaw we could hope to get concessions from Germany.

There was more to be got however both from France & from Germany, something too at the same time from Portugal & Spain by reforming our wine duties by reduction, than by menacing those countries with reprisals in the shape of higher duties.[6]

Between them, however, Salisbury and Mallet eliminated both alternatives. Salisbury ruled out reduction because of the loss of revenue. He had already shocked the French ambassador by suggesting that, if France raised its duty on textiles, the British public might demand 'a corresponding increase in the Wine Duties'[7] which would help to meet the Treasury's need for revenue. But such retaliation was anathema to all orthodox free traders. Mallet warned that, 'if Lord Salisbury means to raise the wine duties, he will be inaugurating protection.'[8] Mallet was willing to challenge some preconceptions common among British free traders. In an open letter on reciprocity to the chairman of the Cobden Club, he pointed out that Britain drew 'a larger revenue from customs than any country in the world, except the United States'.[9] He dismissed the boast that the British tariff was only for revenue purposes by pointing out that tariffs of any sort were an impediment to trade. Turning his guns on the emerging Fair Traders, he deplored their concentration on the treaty with France and pointed out how unfair it would be to retaliate against France, 'which as a rule taxes our imports about 20 per cent. or less, while we leave untouched a country like the United States, which taxes them double'.[10] He could have pointed out also that, while British exports to Germany had fallen by over 30 per cent and to Italy by over 40 per cent since 1872, the fall to France had been less than 10 per cent.[11] But Mallet's purpose was not to make the case for France. He was willing, as Cobden had been, to bargain vigorously with continental states. Still, again as with Cobden, his bargaining chips would consist only of proffered tariff reductions. Mallet was happy, indeed anxious, to offer a reduction in the British wine duties in exchange for a reduction in the foreign customs dues. But he refused to countenance any raising of British duties even as a threat to bring about multilateral reductions. Such a threat would, he feared, take Europe back to the days of retaliatory tariffs and protection.

The failure to agree on an active alternative left British commercial policy in its usual paralysis. The initiative passed once again to France. For the past two years the debate in France, as in Germany, had revolved around its own general tariff. To clear the way for that discussion, at the end of 1878 France denounced its treaty with Britain. Even so, the debate in France continued, more than in Germany, to be shaped by the network of treaties. The French framed their general tariff to serve as the basis for the talks that would ensue with their treaty partners.

There were basically three options for France. The first, and most liberal, was to bring the general tariff down into line with the current conventional tariff and then seek to reduce the conventional tariff in negotiation with treaty partners. This course of action would have come closest to British desires, but it looked increasingly unlikely after the *seize mai* crisis of 1877 and the rise of protectionist sentiment in the French legislature. The remaining two paths both involved raising the general tariff. One required an increase to frighten treaty partners into making concessions in return for which France would bring the conventional tariff back close to current levels. The liberals in charge of the foreign and commerce ministries chose this option since they thought it likely to pass through the legislature. Protectionists, who won control of the tariff committees set up by the legislature, pursued the third option. They sought a substantial increase in the general tariff, large enough to give French industry all the protection it desired, regardless of the wishes of the country's current treaty partners. If the latter then chose to break off negotiations with France and the network of treaties collapsed, so much the better.

The French burdened the renegotiation of their commercial treaties with another constraint. Talks could not begin until the general tariff was enacted, but they would then have to be completed and legislative approval of the treaties secured within six months. This time limit was meant to underscore the threat to treaty partners of the high general tariff if they did not renew their agreements. The French ministry accepted this fresh condition to allay suspicions in the legislature about commercial treaties. The additional pressure vexed the negotiating process even before it had begun.

For more than two years, throughout the legislative debate on the general tariff and the ensuing negotiations with Britain, the government of France was led from the centre left by ministers who wished to preserve the liberal commercial policy of Napoleon III, including the maintenance of good relations with the British. Occasional ministerial reconstructions did not alter that policy, partly because for most of the time Pierre-Emmanuel Tirard remained in charge as Minister of Commerce. Tirard had imbibed his commercial liberalism from early involvement in the gold and jewellery export business, where he found governmental interference exasperating.[12] The dexterity he developed as a legislative tactician increased his ability to implement his views. But the leading spirit in the ministries of the early 1880s, though not in office himself until the closing weeks in the negotiations, was Léon Gambetta. It was Gambetta who spoke to the British ambassador once the tide of debate in the legislature turned in the direction of the government, emphasising 'the great importance which he attached, with a view to political as well as economical relations, to establishing a satisfactory Commercial Treaty with Great Britain'.[13]

The best that Gambetta could propose, however, was not enough for the British and too much for Tirard. The British hoped for further tariff reduction on the French side, but even before the negotiations got underway all that Gambetta thought feasible was prolongation of the existing treaties. Tirard hoped to approximate that objective, but with some modifications to increase governmental revenue as well as protection for the most sensitive French industries. Though he persuaded the legislature to raise the general tariff by 24 per cent, he intended to bargain that increase away in renegotiating the commercial treaties. But he was determined to change the current *ad valorem* duties on textiles into specific duties based on weight, the change most dreaded by the British textile producers whose best market lay in cheap and heavy fabrics. By setting the specific duties at rates above the current *ad valorem* percentages, the French authorities made sure that the new rates would have the intended revenue-producing and protective effects.

The change was welcomed not only by French protectionists but also by the most eminent liberal in French politics at the time, Léon Say, Minister of Finance in many governments of the 1870s. Son of Adam Smith's leading French disciple and himself a political economist of almost Gladstonian severity, Say nonetheless embraced specific duties for their revenue-producing capacity, particularly at a time of falling prices – the same consideration that attached the Inland Revenue and the Treasury in Britain to their own specific wine duties. The impending change from *ad valorem* to specific duties in France led the British ambassador to warn Lord Salisbury that Britain was unlikely to obtain terms as good as those of 1860, let alone better. 'I watch the progress of the [general tariff] Bill,' he wrote, 'with painful anxiety . . . remonstrances on the part of foreign nations during its passage through the Legislature would, in the present state of feeling in the Chambers and the country, simply supply the protectionists with effective weapons.'[14]

Despite this warning, Salisbury responded to Gambetta's overture as rigidly as any Liberal Foreign Secretary might have done. He gave no hint of his heretical ideas about playing with the wine duties. Instead he adopted a line on specific duties for textiles that was all that Behrens of Bradford could have wished, pointing out the unfairness of the burden that such duties at the proposed French rate would impose on clothing designed for 'the labouring classes'.[15] Gambetta's pacific interpretation of French policy only stiffened Salisbury's response. He warned that the French tariff proposals would not only 'diminish trade generally between the two countries, and in several classes of goods . . . put an end to commercial intercourse', but would also damage 'the general relations between Great Britain and France'.[16] Still, if nothing better was available, Salisbury was willing to accept Gambetta's suggestion of renewing the existing commercial treaties between the two countries. He thus did not deviate from the basic lines of policy that had been pursued by successive Foreign Secretaries since 1860. An impending loss of power may have increased Salisbury's rigidity. By the time the message from Gambetta reached the Foreign Office, the British Conservatives were facing defeat in a general election.

That prospect nevertheless hastened Salisbury's effort to make a precedent-setting appointment in the diplomatic establishment. Periodically since becoming Foreign Secretary he had been urged by Odo Russell at the Berlin embassy to institute a new type of appointment, that of commercial attaché, and to begin with Crowe. Crowe was of great assistance to Russell and, through him, to the

Foreign Office during the Austro-German commercial treaty talks and the Reichstag debates on the German tariff. But Russell had to bring Crowe from Düsseldorf to Berlin whenever those discussions took place. Between times Crowe was expected to limit his activities to his consular district; although he established some unusually revealing connections within those confines, he could not maintain regular contact with the central discussion in Berlin. Whenever he was brought to Berlin on special assignment, Russell had to seek recognition of Crowe's diplomatic status from the German Foreign Office. Despite these limitations, Crowe had demonstrated a quality of commercial service rarely provided by the regular consular and embassy staff. Consuls were expected to concentrate on industry and commerce within their assigned districts.[17] Secretaries of embassy had to submit annual reports on the trade and commerce of the states to which they were accredited; and their ability to do so improved with experience and encouragement. But commerce was not their primary interest, even if they overcame the social prejudice against it; and they certainly did not have the frequent contact with businessmen that Crowe enjoyed. His reports on the fluctuating cast of thought on commercial policy among bureaucrats as well as businessmen showed that he had his finger on the pulse of foreign opinion in this regard better than the existing staff in embassies and in the commercial department of the Foreign Office.

That was not something that Foreign Office regulars were happy to admit. When Salisbury proposed the novel appointment for Crowe, it met with opposition not just from those who were disdainful of commerce but from Kennedy as head of the commercial department. He criticised Crowe's skills as a translator, though no one matched Crowe's ability to make his way among Germans in conversation. Kennedy argued that he added little to what could be learnt from the secretaries of embassy. Because Crowe was best known to the public as a writer of books on Renaissance art, Kennedy dismissed him as 'a man of literary habits'.[18] Kennedy may have been alluding to the dislike in Chamber of Commerce circles for consuls who lacked commercial experience. But by now Crowe was well known among those engaged in trade with the continent for his commercial reporting. Furthermore, his expertise as an art connoisseur saved him in political circles from a reputation for fanaticism on commercial matters such as Mallet suffered from. Nonetheless, the senior staff at the Foreign Office shared Kennedy's hostility to the proposed appointment. 'What would be the position of a commercial attaché?' sniffed Lister, the assistant undersecretary, unaware that continental states like Russia already made comparable appointments: 'How would foreign Governments and exclusive foreign society receive a bagman disguised in a uniform?'[19] 'Lister is severely orthodox,' Salisbury countered, 'and rather looks upon all traders as an old maid looks upon all men – as being in a conspiracy to surprise him into the grant of some illicit favour.'[20]

Salisbury pressed ahead with the appointment all the more urgently as the moment of his loss of power drew close. Because members of the House of Lords were expected to keep their distance from elections to the House of Commons, he went to Biarritz for the weeks of voting. But fearful that the resulting delay in his communication with the Foreign Office might prevent Crowe's appointment from receiving royal approval before the change of government, Salisbury drew up Crowe's new commission in his own hand for immediate submission to the Queen. Crowe, sent to London to expedite things, met with a brusque reception from Kennedy and learnt afterwards that Kennedy and Lister had denounced the appointment as 'a gross job'.[21] Salisbury completed it in time. It was his last act as Foreign Secretary this term.

The appointment made Crowe commercial attaché to the embassy in Vienna as well as Berlin, though he was expected normally to reside at the latter. Salisbury noted in Crowe's commission:

> Specially at a moment when extensive experiments in fiscal legislation are in progress, & when ever larger changes are supposed to be in contemplation, it is important that their commercial results should be studied by a diplomatic officer specially devoted to that duty . . . he should be . . . at liberty to take up his residence from time to time in whatever place may seem advantageous for the performance of his duties. . . . Great latitude should be left to him especially at first, with respect to the subject matter of his observations. But his attention should be directed not only to the material progress or decay of the chief branches of manufacture & trade . . . but also to the condition of public opinion upon fiscal & commercial questions at the principal centres of industry. Especially he should be in a position to warn H.M.G. of political movements tending towards legislation by which the interests of British commerce are likely to be affected.[22]

The appointment reflected the heightened concern in Britain about European commercial policy, a concern that the succeeding government was quick to share.

b. Say's Mission and Gladstone's Budget

Before Salisbury left office, he received news of another, more significant appointment in the commercial diplomacy of Europe. The French government sent word that Léon Say was coming to London as a special ambassador, even before the general tariff was fully enacted, to explore the prospects for agreement with Britain and, when the time came, to negotiate the renewal of their treaty.[23] Say thought of his mission as being 'like Cobden's to Paris in 1860'.[24]

Salisbury responded cautiously, leaving the prospective Liberal government to find out what he might propose. His appointment augured well for the talks because Say commanded a great deal of respect in France, across the political spectrum and in both legislative chambers, while his presence in London would distance the talks from scrutiny by protectionists in Paris.

The commercial relationship with France was among the first issues to come before the Liberal ministry put together by Gladstone. He and his Foreign Secretary, Lord Granville, addressed the subject during their first week back in office. The importance of the stance Gladstone adopted on the issue was accentuated by his assumption of the post of Chancellor of the Exchequer as well as that of Prime Minister. He dealt with the delicate relationship between the Foreign Office and the Board of Trade on commercial matters by sending Sir Charles Dilke, a close friend of the new president of the Board of Trade Joseph Chamberlain, to the Foreign Office as undersecretary to take charge of tariff treaty negotiations.

Lister greeted the new ministry on behalf of the permanent officials at the Foreign Office with a memorandum on the wine duties around which the impending commercial discussions were bound to revolve.[25] He drew attention to the preferential effects of the revised duties that Gladstone and Cobden had conceded to the French in 1860, and to which the other wine-producing states of Europe strongly objected. In 1880 as in 1860, the main concession the French negotiators sought from the British was a reduction in the duty on light wines. Such an alteration would deepen the offence to Portugal, Spain and Italy, whose heavier wines would suffer. These countries wanted Britain either to raise the alcohol level in its classification of light wines or to lower the duty on heavy wines. But France would deplore any such change as diminishing the advantage it enjoyed under the current scale. Lister weighed the costs and benefits for Britain. Reduction of the duty on heavy wines would probably bring about a substantial increase in the export of Portuguese and Spanish wine to Britain, but the market in those countries for British goods was not large. The retaliatory tariff that Spain had enacted to induce Britain to treat its wines more fairly had produced a contrary reaction. As for Italy, Lister dismissed it as poor, heavily taxed and protectionist, and its wines as rarely cheap and often nasty. The French market was still the greatest, and Lister concluded that its expansion was worth paying for. But he warned that the French would not be attracted by a balanced reduction of the wine duties at both ends of the alcoholic scale.

The remarks that Gladstone made on this subject in private did not make agreement with France look likely. 'I do not like bargaining away revenues for Treaties,' he told Granville, 'or buying over again from France what has been bought already, if the matter is to be considered as founded on this basis at all.'[26] To Dilke, Gladstone confessed, 'I do not desire to shut the door against "negotiation" but I have little faith in it.'[27] Yet Lister's memorandum reminded Gladstone of his handiwork in 1860. He had not recoiled then from the bargain over the wine duties implicit in the treaty with France. On the contrary, through his budget that year he had turned Cobden's treaty into a milestone in the history of free trade. Gladstone was also disturbed by Lister's testimony that, whatever Cobden and Gladstone may have intended, the 1860 revision had discriminated against the wines of Spain and Portugal and thus violated the non-discriminatory principles and pretensions of free trade. Towards the end of May the Foreign Office alerted its representatives in the wine-producing countries of Europe to the possibility of a comprehensive revision of the wine duties dependent upon the securing of 'equivalent advantage to British Commerce'.[28] Gladstone discussed the Spanish case sympathetically with Dilke;[29] and Dilke raised the Austrian case with the ambassador in Vienna.[30]

The offer that Léon Say developed[31] in discussion with Dilke, while still tentative and vague, turned out to be better than Gambetta had led the previous British government to expect. Say asked the British to concede some reduction, as yet unspecified, of the wine duties; to exclude cattle and other farm produce from the treaty, leaving them under the French general tariff; and to find ways to prevent fraud in the customs declarations by British exporters. The French maintained that fraud was likely so long as customs duties were levied on an *ad valorem* basis: hence their demand for specific duties regardless of declared valuation. This line of argument disguised a revenue-producing and protectionist motivation, though Say told Dilke that 'the French manufacturers . . . would sooner, in many cases, have lower duties and changes of classification in a similar direction than retain [*ad valorem*] duties.'[32] In return, he offered the British not just maintenance but 'amelioration' of the existing French tariff in order to 'develop commercial relations' between the two countries. Briefly dropping the cloak of secrecy in which his mission had been wrapped, Say announced at the Lord Mayor's banquet in London on 1 June 1880 that such a renewal and liberal improvement of the 1860 treaty was in sight.[33]

After a great deal of hesitation, so Say reported to Gambetta,[34] Gladstone's cabinet accepted these terms for negotiation provided amelioration was 'understood as meaning a reduction of duties on the principal products of English industry, though not necessarily a general reduction of duty on all such products'.[35] Say assured the British ministers that the French government was 'sincerely desirous to reduce the duties on . . . iron & cottons',[36] but said nothing about woollens.

The French ministry would not, however, authorise an exchange of written commitments between the two governments. A battle of tactics was being fought between the executive and legislative branches of the French government. After losing the debate on the general tariff in the Chamber of Deputies, the protectionists took their struggle to the Senate, where they were stronger. They hoped to protract the debate there until the lifetime of the legislature expired and general elections were called, when they expected to increase their forces in the Chamber of Deputies. The ministry parried these tactics by moving out of the legislative into the diplomatic arena. They thought it 'necessary to tell the French Senate there was no negotiation' with Britain, yet wanted Say to prepare the way in 'confidential conversations' with a view to the announcement of a treaty by mid-August, when the legislature was in recess.[37] The treaty might then be passed 'even by an unwilling Senate' when it reconvened in November. This plan was interrupted by another stratagem of the ministerial liberals in the Senate. They induced Say, a senator, to stand for election to the presidency in mid-May, even before he had reached preliminary agreement with Dilke. Say's bid was successful; and though he returned to London to complete the initial negotiations, he could not stay on to turn the results into a treaty.

In contrast to the French ministers, Gladstone found the legislative arena highly congenial, and never more so than at this time and on this issue. He stood at the head of a large majority in a newly elected parliament, and he liked presenting commercial policy in the House of Commons. There he acted or at least seemed to act unilaterally, avoiding the appearance of bargaining. He preferred open parliamentary debate to the private manœuvring of diplomacy. He enjoyed debate in the House of Commons as much as Cobden had enjoyed his discussions with businessmen; in turn the Commons brought out the best in Gladstone.

He was in top form when he rose to seek preliminary approval from the House for revision of the wine duties. The request formed part of the supplementary budget he presented as the newly returned Chancellor of the Exchequer,[38] a performance that was reminiscent in substance as well as style of the budget he had presented in 1860 in connection with Cobden's original treaty with France. Now, 20 years later, though Gladstone had reached the age of 70, his powers were undimmed. Even opposition Conservative MPs who could remember the earlier performance were impressed by his continuing prowess.

Gladstone did not merely tinker with the wine duties, he revised them from top to bottom as part of a comprehensive recasting of the taxes on alcoholic beverages, which by his reckoning provided a third of the government's revenue. He intended in doing so to cut the ground from under the Fair Trade movement that was sprouting across the kingdom. It found lively support in manufacturing centres such as Birmingham and Bradford, where exports were suffering, and as yet latent approval in farming districts that were suffering from a run of poor harvests as well as competition from cheap American imports. Gladstone's proposed revision of the wine duties addressed the industrial discontent in Britain that focused on the rising continental tariffs. Bold though this side of his agenda was, it was overshadowed by his response to the depression in agriculture. To that quarter he now offered the abolition of the malt tax, long advocated but never enacted by the Conservatives. By stealing their proposal and placing the taxation of beer, for which the malt tax had functioned, on a more direct basis and at a lowered rate, Gladstone delighted the farmers, bowled over the parliamentary opposition and protected British brewers from competition from imported wine which would be made cheaper by the reduced duty. He was able to do all this because, in spite of the heavy, not yet fully paid costs of military adventures in South Africa and Afghanistan for which the defeated Conservative government had assumed responsibility, the Treasury was for the moment without a deficit. Even so, Gladstone had to add a penny to the income tax to offset the loss of revenue from the malt tax and wine duties. But the House of Commons overlooked that increase in its amazement at his budgetary coup.

Though less astonished, the House was as pleased by Gladstone's proposals for wine as it was by those for beer. He disposed of the charge of partiality in the existing wine duties and at the same time attempted to open up all the continental wine-producing markets to British trade by lowering both ends of the scale. He offered to cut the duty on light wines in half, as the French requested, and proposed to graduate the duty on the heavier wines according to their alcoholic strength up to the point at which they could be classified as spirits, where the duty was more substantially increased. In a remarkable departure from customary practice, he made his proposals for the wine duties provisional, dependent on the conclusion of commercial agreements with interested continental countries. To increase British negotiating flexibility, he allowed his plans for light and heavy wines to be implemented separately from each other. But he also played the game of time limitation that had been initiated by the French. His proposals would hold good only until mid-August, time enough in his estimation to find out whether an agreement could be reached with any of the wine-producing countries.

What delighted the British legislature, however, displeased the continental Europeans. What the wine-producing states sought was special, not even-handed treatment. The value of the concession on light wines was diminished in the eyes of the French by the concession on the heavier wines to their Iberian competitors, and also by the reduced taxation of British beer. The Spanish and Portuguese were similarly disappointed by Gladstone's proposals; the Austrians did not even respond. Furthermore, the openness of Gladstone's action disconcerted the French. Protectionists in the Senate accused the government of failing to honour its pledge not to negotiate commercial treaties until the general tariff was enacted. Léon Say strove, as he left London to take up the presidency, to preserve the understanding he had reached with the government, but the French ministry felt obliged to reaffirm its commitment to the legislature and backed away from the British. Two weeks after Gladstone presented his budget to the House of Commons, the British ambassador in Paris was informed that, though negotiations might begin again in August, no treaty could be signed till the end of the year, nor could it be ratified before the following March.[39] When Gladstone realised that the French would not meet his timetable, he withdrew his proposals for the wine duties. The French Senate nailed the coffin shut on Say's mission by recessing in mid-July without debating the committee report it had received on the general tariff.

c. The Dilke–Tirard Discussions

Though neither government was thus able to press the negotiations forward as quickly as it had desired, both resumed their efforts to reach an agreement. This time the British were more eager than the French. Dilke, who took charge on the British side, tried to advance things with a clarification of the British position.[40] He also stiffened British tactics. Though the Liberals would not countenance retaliation, Dilke threatened the French with independent action, turning Gladstone's preferred mode of conduct into a menace. He warned that Britain had opened discussions with Spain, Portugal and Italy, offering them reduction of the duty on heavier wines in return for their lowering barriers to imports from Britain. He threatened to reduce the duty for heavy wines without touching the duty for light, to the detriment of French exports.[41] But he did not receive a response from Tirard, who took charge on the French side, until October.

The situation had changed from the French perspective. Not only had the Senate outmanœuvred the French ministry, phylloxera, a disease that attacks the roots of grapevines, had transformed France from an exporter into an importer of wines, mainly from its former Spanish and Italian competitors. This turnabout reduced Tirard's interest in the British wine duties. Furthermore, he no longer hoped for anything better than a continuation in the existing commercial relationship between France and Britain – as Gambetta had predicted before Say went to London.

Exchanges between Dilke and Tirard soon brought out the crucial differences in their standpoints. Dilke continued to work along the lines of Léon Say's offer and Gladstone's budgetary response. He remained willing to contemplate reduction in the duty on light wines so long, but only so long, as the French lowered their tariff on the main British exports, particularly, as he told the new French ambassador, on textiles.[42] Dilke sought to encourage the French by reiterating the contention of British manufacturers that Cobden's treaty had proved even more beneficial to France than to Britain.

Britain absorbed a larger proportion of French exports than it had done before 1860. In no sector was the great expansion of French exports to Britain so apparent as in textiles, above all woollens.[43] While French exports to Britain of woollen cloth had risen steadily in value and of woollen yarns had increased fivefold since 1874, British exports to France under these headings had continued to fall. In that short time France and Britain had reversed their positions in this branch of industry: France now selling more to Britain than Britain sold to France.

Tirard replied, tardily,[44] by replacing Dilke's interpretation of the experience of the two countries since 1860 with an account favourable to French purposes. The British liked to think of the agreement of 1860 as an act of much greater generosity on their part than on the French side. Tirard outlined a different story. France, as he told it, through reciprocal agreements tailored to the needs of each country, had spun the web of commercial treaties from which Britain so greatly benefited. But Gladstone, in his budget for 1860, had turned the treaty between Cobden and Napoleon III into part of the general British tariff, without any special benefit to France. While French goods were therefore obliged to compete, for example, with American ones, in the open British market, British goods enjoyed special protection under the 1860 treaty from third-party competition in the French market. Britain benefited further under the most-favoured-nation clause from the reciprocal agreements France had negotiated with other European countries. Gallingly, after the Franco–Prussian War, under the terms of the Treaty of Frankfurt, France was prevented from pursuing its reciprocal strategy with Germany. Tirard pleaded with the British to bargain with Germany on behalf of France. Otherwise, he explained, 'the Protectionist party in France would say that French interests were sacrificed if concessions were made to English trade, of which Germany, under the most-favoured-nation treatment guaranteed by the Treaty of Frankfort [sic], would reap the benefit.'[45] The French concern here was as much economic as sentimental. Since the war, Germany had emerged as its most worrisome commercial competitor in trade, and France had slid from a substantial surplus to a deep deficit in its balance of trade with Germany.[46] Turning to the recent depression, Tirard, like all continental European analysts, pointed out that prices were being driven down by British competition: hence the demand of French producers for higher tariffs.

The lack of progress in these discussions quickened the debate about Fair Trade among British exporters. While Fair Trade found greatest support in Birmingham and Sheffield, nowhere was the debate more bitter than in Bradford. There its sympathisers turned on Jacob Behrens, who had grown old in the struggle to advance the interests of the West Yorkshire worsted industry in the commercial diplomacy of Europe. Yet he still seemed more German than Yorkshireman, and he made too much of his 'private' correspondence with the

Foreign Office, mistaking the English usage of 'private' to mean personal when it meant merely not for publication.

At root what infuriated the merchants of Bradford was the selling of French yarns on the streets of their own town. Though the lower costs of labour in France had something to do with this, the merchants admitted that it had more to do with the technological superiority of the spinning machinery the French had developed.[47] The spinners of Bradford resolved to catch up,[48] but in the meantime it was surely unfair for French producers to retain, let alone to increase, their existing levels of tariff protection. French producers, on the other hand, were angry about the diversion of British woollens exports from Germany, as a result of the heightening of its tariff, to France.[49] The sticking point for Bradford was the replacement of *ad valorem* with specific duties. Specific duties simply could not accommodate the ever-changing variety of textile production, and they were bound to penalise the heavy but cheap fabrics in which British producers outdid their continental competitors.

Gladstone's proposals for reform of the wine duties had delighted the Yorkshire woollens industry with the prospect of opening the Spanish as well as widening the French market.[50] Dilke hoped to use the possibility of a Spanish treaty in return for a reduction of the duty on the heavier wines as a threat to bring the French to the bargaining table for a further reduction on their light wines.[51] But the disappointment in July when Gladstone withdrew his proposals because of the tardiness of the French response deepened in October with the news that the Spanish insisted on specific duties for exports from Britain.

In Bradford frustration erupted in a personal argument between Behrens and his long-time colleague in the Chamber of Commerce Henry Mitchell, the current president.[52] Though their disagreement focused on commercial treaties, it was not easy to see where the two men differed. There was more heat than clarity to the quarrel, as was true of the argument between free and fair trade generally. S.C. Lister was alone among the Bradford manufacturers in advocating reciprocal bargaining and, if that failed, retaliation. The other members of the Bradford Chamber were fully agreed among themselves that no treaty with France would be acceptable unless it improved upon the existing one and rated textiles for duty on an *ad valorem* rather than a specific basis. They also agreed, so far as Spain was concerned, that a simple most-favoured-nation treaty would not be acceptable, that it would have to contain tariff provisions tailored to the needs of British producers. With so much agreement, Behrens and Mitchell seemed to be fighting merely about the intensity of their opposition to specific duties. But the obscurity of the issue did not lessen the emotion. And this reaction in Yorkshire reduced what little remained of Dilke's room for manœuvre, particularly over the substitution of specific for *ad valorem* duties on which the French seemed determined.

d. Waiting for Gambetta

The British and French negotiators fell silent during the winter of 1880–81 while the bill to establish a new general tariff worked its way through the French Senate. Dominated by protectionists, the Senate systematically raised the rates approved in the Chamber of Deputies. Still the Chamber was the more powerful branch of the French legislature. Since it had approved the ministerial proposals for an increase to be bargained away in renegotiating commercial treaties, Dilke had grounds to hope for a successful outcome. The degree to which France had benefited from Cobden's treaty seemed so obvious to British analysts[53] that they could not credit that the French would fail at least to renew if not to improve it. While every country in Europe suffered from the depression, France continued to fare better than most and certainly better than Britain, though the aggregate economy of Britain remained much larger than the French. During 1880 French imports and exports both went up, though the French worried because imports increased substantially more than exports. French imports of woollen tissues increased more than for any commodity except iron ships; yet woollen tissues emerged as much the most valuable French export, particularly now that phylloxera had devastated the vineyards of France. However, the collapse of French interest in the export of wine deprived Britain of its only bargaining chip, as Tirard made brutally clear.

He made use of the procrastination in the Senate to tighten the timetable for treaty negotiations. The treaty with Britain was by all accounts pivotal. It would settle the main terms of the treaties that the lesser members of the network would then try to refine in their particular interests. Accordingly, Tirard put off serious discussions with the British until both chambers of the French legislature had completed their deliberations on the general tariff. He insisted that the diplomatic negotiations would then have to be completed rapidly to allow the French legislature time for ratification.

He would not open even preliminary discussions with the British until an end to the Senate's deliberations on the general tariff was in sight. Then he outlined a simple but inflexible offer of the general tariff as accepted by the Chamber of Deputies without 'the increase of 24 per cent, which had been made for the purpose of affording a means of negotiation'.[54] It need not take long to reach such an agreement, he contended, 'if the English were reasonable'.[55] When the British ambassador objected to this take-it-or-leave-it approach, Tirard explained that 'the temper of the French Chambers left the Government very little latitude, and on the other hand, France had little or nothing to ask for from England, and thus there was . . . not much room for negotiation.'[56] The crucial omission from Tirard's proposals was any reference to the 'amelioration' that Léon Say had led the British to expect. Kennedy at the Foreign Office warned that the 'Chambers of Commerce and merchants trading with France' would be acutely disappointed, and that 'the reciprocity views which are beginning to be put forward in this country will be strengthened.'[57] He pointed out that the tariff as passed by the Chamber of Deputies had increased the duty on some products, pre-eminently textiles, by more than 24 per cent.

His warning prompted Dilke to alert interested Chambers of Commerce in Britain to the character of the French proposals. Dilke wanted to carry the industrial community in Britain with him as he negotiated with the French. He was as open with the Chambers of Commerce as Gladstone had been with the House of Commons; he was still more candid with well-informed individuals such as Behrens. Yet Dilke could not overcome, and indeed initially exacerbated, the general lack of confidence among businessmen involved in international trade in the way men in government handled their interests. Individuals like Behrens who entered the charmed circle fell under suspicion among their fellow businessmen.

Thus, despite his good intentions, Dilke vexed the reaction in Bradford. The Chamber of Commerce greeted his news with consternation and fired off a telegram that epitomised its response: 'urge immediate action to prevent ad valorem duties being abandoned . . . & on no account commit us to higher duties in a new treaty than are at present imposed.'[58] Dilke's private warning to Behrens that there was 'not the slightest chance of getting a Treaty at all if we insist on *ad valorem* duties'[59] would only have inflamed the response if Behrens had transmitted it to his colleagues. As it was, tempers flared and the gulf widened between those led by Behrens who hoped for at least modest improvement in the Anglo-French treaty relationship and the Fair Traders led by the present and past presidents of the Chamber, Mitchell and Shepherd. Shepherd 'was of opinion that all commercial treaties would be better done away with altogether'.[60] Mitchell still wanted a treaty and believed that 'France would give way if England were in earnest.'[61] But as one of his supporters put it: 'They had been trying to convince [French] people for thirty or forty years by pamphlets and speeches, and had made no impression. They could get at them [only] through their pockets and self-interest.'[62] Mitchell wanted to threaten France with a retaliatory increase in the wine duties unless it conceded the amelioration in the current treaty tariff that Léon Say had promised. Otherwise, "[h]aving regard to the distinctly protective nature of this new general tariff, and to the little value which the French Government evidently place upon friendly commercial relations with Great Britain', Mitchell convinced a large majority in the Chamber to demand 'the total and immediate abandonment of all treaty negotiations'.[63] Behrens scoffed at this resolution as 'foolish, ridiculous, and impracticable'.[64]

The Fair Traders of Bradford were not as ignorant of economic and political realities as the advocates of continued commercial diplomacy suggested.

Mitchell learnt that Gambetta advised Britain to 'stand firm' and refuse to put up with any worsening in the old treaty, predicting that France would give way.[65] He relayed this news at a meeting of the Chamber of Commerce which the Fair Traders had irregularly convened to promote their views. When Behrens and other eminent members of the Chamber left the meeting in protest at its irregularity, they met with 'loud hooting and hisses'. The outburst of feeling in Bradford took institutional shape at the national level a week later with the formal establishment of the National Fair Trade League.

Nevertheless the treatment Behrens had received shocked both sides in Bradford. Within a week Mitchell and Behrens sought to mend the breach. At a meeting of the Joint Tariff Committee of the Yorkshire Chambers of Commerce, Behrens confessed his dismay at the apparent willingness of the Foreign Office to settle for a mere continuation of the existing treaty relationship without improvement, while Mitchell urged the members to speak with a united voice.[66] Still, the hostility in Bradford to any agreement that failed to improve upon the existing treaty relationship with France was unmistakable. As Mitchell explained, the worsted woollens districts around Bradford 'were the largest exporters to France, and the action taken [by France] with regard to this treaty was a serious and deliberate blow at their chief industry'.[67] Kennedy amplified Mitchell's argument, pointing out to the Foreign Office that 'The French trade . . . now possessed, for Yorkshire more especially, particular importance, because the recent alterations of Tariff in Germany and Italy, following the adoption of a protectionist Tariff in the United States, have caused great loss of foreign trade.'[68] Germany had taken care in 1879 'to select for the heaviest duties precisely such stuffs as have hitherto been imported from England',[69] and in 1881 further raised the duty of low-priced British cheviots and tweeds.[70]

The mixed woollens of West Yorkshire assumed ever greater significance in the Anglo–French discussions and exposed the differences in commercial policy that drove the two countries apart. Behrens reasoned as a businessman with a thorough understanding of his particular industry. He bombarded the Foreign Office with a series of memoranda, pointing out how the current 10 per cent *ad valorem* duty on woollens in the French conventional tariff had 'closed the French market against a great number of middle and fine class tissues, and confines our exports, in a great measure and in ever increasing proportions, to low-priced heavy goods'.[71] He was ready to admit that Roubaix and Rheims had beaten Bradford in the better fabrics.[72] But the industry in West Yorkshire had adapted itself to this situation by developing a comparatively new line of production to make the most of its advantage in low-priced goods. The Yorkshiremen scoured Europe for woollen rags which they reduced by mechanical or chemical means to a material the English called 'shoddy' – the more flattering French term was 'renaissance'. They used this as a substitute for the expensive pure woollen fibres that gave weight to their cloth. The resulting fabric found its best market among the French working class. 'France,' wrote Behrens, 'is our largest and most constant customer.'[73] Moreover, taking advantage of the *ad valorem* French duty, Yorkshire was able to export its shoddy stuffs through France to Italy, Switzerland and Spain, bypassing the specific or weight duties levied by these countries.

The new general tariff of France was designed to stop this trade. Not content with the achievement of Rheims and Roubaix, the French Senate complained 'of the falling-off of the trade of Elbeuf, Sedan, and other places' where 'old-fashioned Machinery and hand-weaving [was] still in use'.[74] This was protection pure and simple. The French were demanding protection for their weakest industries, whereas the British simply wanted the largest industry in their export trade with France to go on selling the particular product line that they made best and cheapest. The case as Behrens presented it was clear. Displaying a businessman's version of the liberal faith in rational and informed argument, he was sure that the French would find his argument persuasive, as they had done consistently since 1860 whenever presented with 'fair discussion and indisputable proofs'. Behrens could not believe that 'the French . . . really intend to act unfairly towards their country's best customer and most faithful ally.'[75]

As soon as the French legislature completed its work on the general tariff, Kennedy was sent north to the centres of the woollens industry in Yorkshire and then to Middlesbrough to meet representatives of the iron and steel industry. He found the tide of opinion in Yorkshire flowing away from tariff treaties that laid down particular rates of duty towards simple most-favoured-nation agreements that would save British exports from the most blatant forms of adverse discrimination and the full terrors of a general tariff. He received a similar message at Middlesbrough. It was reinforced by the Chambers of Commerce in Glasgow and the Black Country in Wolverhampton.[76] Elsewhere, as from the Potteries, came further pleas for the simplest most-favoured-nation agreement[77] or nothing that would bind Britain for longer than a year or two.[78]

Upon completion of his mission, Kennedy went to Paris for preliminary talks with permanent officials at the Ministry of Commerce. They proved even more rigid than their political masters and informed Kennedy that 24 per cent would be the maximum and not the invariable deduction that Britain could expect from the general tariff.[79] Kennedy replied by drawing attention to the agitation in Yorkshire. He warned that Britain would prefer no treaty at all to a retrograde one and that, once rid of the treaty obligation, Britain would be free to raise its duty on wines.[80] In hinting at retaliation, Kennedy was not misrepresenting the tolerance of the British cabinet, Liberal though it was. Chamberlain at the Board of Trade and Forster, now Chief Secretary for Ireland, suggested warning the French of the possibility of British retaliation, if not by the current ministry then by a subsequent one;[81] and Granville accepted the advice.

The French general tariff was published officially on 8 May, to come into effect on 8 November except where new treaties had been negotiated. Yet the French ministry continued to resist prodding from the British to initiate negotiations by proposing terms for a treaty. Discussion was vexed by differing definitions of the existing tariff relationship between the two sides. The British kept referring to the status quo, in which they included the reductions in the French conventional tariff brought about not only through Cobden's treaty but also through the subsequent treaties with other treaty partners from which Britain benefited under the most-favoured-nation clause. Anything less would be retrograde in the British estimation. But the French insisted on going back to Cobden's treaty as their yardstick. However, no one disagreed in identifying the most contentious issue. As *The Economist* noted, 'It is on the proposed duties on textiles that the new [French] tariff is most anomalous and oppressive.'[82]

Dilke kept the emphasis on textiles and particulary on woollens in an attempt to demonstrate the government's concern and thus head off a hostile resolution that was presented in the House of Commons. The resolution was all the more serious because it was introduced, not by the usual spokesmen for Fair Trade, but by the president of the Associated Chambers of Commerce, Charles Monk. And the most vigorous speech in its support came from the president of the Manchester Chamber, John Slagg, a Liberal. Slagg insisted that the British negotiators 'must ask not only for a reduction, but a very substantial reduction, of the present Tariff duties; and if we failed to obtain that, the Government had only one course to pursue – namely to throw up the Treaty altogether, leaving the French to learn by bitter experience the value of what they would thus lose.' He stated flatly that, 'rather than make a sham Treaty, imposing duties which were wholly unnecessary in the present situation, he would abandon the Treaty system altogether'.[83] When the motion was carried against the government by a majority that included Liberals as well as Conservatives, Dilke was driven to doubt that a treaty with France was any longer possible from the British standpoint.[84]

But the tardiness of the French in commencing negotiations did not reflect a lack of desire on their side for a successful outcome. The French government regarded the talks with Britain as the crucial first step towards a reconstruction of the entire European network of commercial treaties. Tirard was attempting to reconcile protectionist sentiment in the legislature with his continuing belief in the benefits of a liberal policy by securing higher tariffs for the most vocal sectors of French industry while maintaining the treaty network with France at its centre. He hoped to establish those higher tariffs in his negotiations with the British and then induce the continental partners of France to fall into line.

But that was precisely the danger about which British free traders warned. They had counted on the continent to follow the British example, but always towards, never away from free trade. When Tirard found that the British negotiators would not comply with his wishes, he turned to the continental states, seeking to use negotiations with them to put pressure on the British. Dilke had done the same thing the previous summer when he opened discussions with other wine-producing states in order to put pressure on the French.

The continental states fully understood Tirard's change in tactics, as did the British. Anxious to parry Tirard's thrust, the lesser states clustered around the British negotiators when talks with the French finally got under way in June. The first to move were Belgium and Switzerland. The Swiss minister in Paris gave the British ambassador the volume of briefing documents prepared for the Swiss negotiators, begging only 'that it might be considered as strictly confidential; that its existence should not be allowed to become known to the French negotiators, and that it should not be brought into the Conference room, where it might catch their eye'.[85] In return the British gave the Swiss the shorthand reports of evidence from British industries concerned about the French tariff. Germany watched from a distance, anxious to be saved from the French general tariff by the efforts of other states from which it could benefit under the terms of the Treaty of Frankfurt. That entitlement embittered Tirard and reduced his willingness to make concessions in any direction.

Dilke brought Austria and Italy into the discussions and fed them information about the French proposals. Eventually the talks involved the Netherlands, Sweden and Spain – all countries to which France was making overtures by the end of June. The bargaining tool to which all turned was their wine duties. The industry of greatest concern to most was textiles. They looked to Britain to set the basic tariff here, as they did to Italy to set the basic tariff on agricultural produce. But they differed from the British in several regards. Their economies were smaller than the French one. France was also geographically central for them. The continental states were therefore willing to put up with some raising of the French tariff and only wished to ensure that it did not damage the most important sectors of their trade with France. Most of them also let it be known that (unlike the British) they would retaliate if France refused to concede their minimum demands. The only exception was the Netherlands, which went as far as Britain in its commitment to free trade.

Throughout the summer of 1881 Tirard made competitive use of his negotiating timetable to push the various treaty partners into line. He strove to secure, if not completed treaties, at least concrete assurances of agreement before the current conventional tariff expired and the new general tariff came into effect on 8 November. For all those states that reached agreement with France within that period the conventional tariff would remain in effect for another three months, until 8 February 1882, when the new conventional tariff as constituted by the revised treaties would take effect. The British government parried these tactics because it could not be sure of obtaining acceptable terms from France, particularly on textiles. The French improved their offer on some of the less important sectors of trade and on iron and steel, where the British retained technological superiority and the chief competition came from Germany. France's terms on iron and steel were attractive enough to make the British government sorry to turn them down. But the iron and steel industry was neither as involved in trade with France nor as affected by French competition as was the textiles industry, particularly woollens.

In the midst of these negotiations, the House of Commons again intervened. This was not as embarrassing for the government as on the earlier occasion because the attack was now led by the Conservative opposition in the accents of Fair Trade rather than by the Chambers of Commerce. C.T. Ritchie, the Conservative merchant whose motion precipitated a debate, came from the jute trade of Dundee which was suffering, like all branches of textiles, from the rising tariff barriers on the continent. Ritchie pointed out that France absorbed nearly a third of all British exports. What he 'wanted was not Protection, but entrance for their manufactures into foreign markets'[86] – and he was willing to resort to retaliation to get it. Chamberlain replied for the government by playing down the severity of the economic depression. He recognised, as historians have since stressed, that the depression was in prices but not in the quantity of export production. Britain's deficit in the balance of trade was undoubtedly growing, but so, even more so, was 'the indebtedness of other nations to this country'.[87] Prices had also fallen faster than wages, with the result that 'the consumption of every important article of necessity or luxury by the working classes has shown a remarkable increase.'[88] But Chamberlain, with his background in metal manufacturing, displayed little understanding of the nature of the depression in sectors of the economy with which he was not personally familiar. He put the depression in agriculture down to bad harvests, ignoring the deluge of cheap grain from the United States and Russia – a blindness to which, it must be said, aristocratic leaders of this industry were also prone. Chamberlain ascribed the plight of Bradford 'almost entirely to a change in fashion',[89] ignoring the attempt by France to drive the shoddy cloth of West Yorkshire out of the French market.

The whole set of commercial treaty negotiations moved fitfully towards the French deadline of 8 November. Gladstone neither helped nor greatly hindered matters when he delivered a speech in early October that reaffirmed his government's opposition to any departure from free trade, including retaliation. The main material interest of the French in a treaty with Britain, despite the ravages of phylloxera, still had to do with the wine duties rather than with the danger of more general British retaliation. Regardless of Gladstone's words, the British negotiators continued to allude to the implicitly retaliatory possibility of dealing with Spain and Portugal on the wine duties if no agreement could be reached with France.

Meanwhile, whether on or off, promising or disheartening, the talks established Tirard in French politics as the man who best understood the limits of the legislature's tolerance for commercial liberalism. The early elections that had to be called in the summer of 1881 drew further attention to him. Even so, the results of the election made it virtually certain that Gambetta would take office before the year was out. That prospect quickened activity in the trade talks. Dilke wanted to wait for Gambetta, with his avowed anxiety to reach agreement with Britain, to take office. Italy shared Dilke's interest in holding out for a more amenable French ministry.[90] But Tirard was determined to have at least a few completed treaties to his credit before he left office. He was annoyed to find the lesser continental states queuing up behind Britain. Aware that Britain had cultivated that co-operation and suspicious of Dilke's intentions, Tirard abruptly demanded a reduction of the British wine duties in return for an assortment of concessions that Dilke had already dismissed as inadequate. Dilke found himself in the awkward position of negotiating with the person most likely, once out of power, to move the rejection of the agreement he was now attempting to reach.[91]

At the end of October, within days of the implementation of the general tariff, Tirard broke through the logjam by concluding a treaty with Belgium. It crowned his achievement as Minister of Commerce. Belgium's trade with France, mainly in textiles, machinery, metals and coal, came close to duplicating on a small scale the trade between Britain and France.[92] Accordingly, in default of a treaty with Britain, the Belgian treaty served to establish the new French conventional tariff for industrial goods, and thus to perpetuate the commercial policy of 1860 with the revisions that Tirard judged necessary to win legislative approval. In reaching the agreement, he proved his adversaries on both sides wrong, the protectionists who insisted that a treaty compatible with French commercial interests could not be devised, and the British who insisted that his demands did not do basic justice to France's main trading partners.

The agreement allowed Belgium to preserve the current conventional tariff for more than three-quarters of its exports to France and to gain improved access to the French market for another 5 per cent. In return Belgium had to make three concessions. It had to accept specific in place of *ad valorem* duties; to allow France to increase its tariff on more than a tenth of the goods imported from Belgium including coarse textiles; and to reduce its tariff on French wines, silks and luxury goods. 'Not bad' was the Belgian verdict.[93] It was not the improvement on the status quo that Britain demanded, but Belgium was too dependent on the French market to refuse to reach an agreement and thus fall under the general tariff.

The Franco–Belgian agreement was a setback for Britain. It lost Belgian support in its own negotiations with France, and Belgian goods might replace British ones in the French market once the British fell under the general French tariff. Still, there was a silver lining. The British need not suffer the full force of the general tariff if they could secure a most-favoured-nation agreement from France, for that would give them the benefit of the tariff concessions made to Belgium.

e. *Impasse*

Dilke consoled himself with that fallback position only after he had failed to reach the improved agreement he still hoped for from the French. He was looking forward to the arrival of Gambetta, with whom he was already friends. Both were assertive radicals in domestic politics, and both enjoyed the fast company of the Prince of Wales, who joined them at the Moulin Rouge.[94] Dilke was prepared to speed up the chances for agreement by abandoning the British insistence on *ad valorem* duties, having hammered out terms for specific duties that Bradford could reluctantly put up with.[95] The French had converted their *ad valorem* into specific duties at a level markedly above the current conventional rates. But if in amicable negotiation Dilke could whittle these specific duties back to the level of the status quo, the British government would accept that and not insist on amelioration. Still, without the latter there could be no question of reducing the wine duties.

During the change of government in France, Gladstone read the *Balance-Sheet of the World*[96] an experience that fortified his faith in free trade. He concluded from his reading that 'we are so strong in our command of the general market of the world – although we sometimes get a little frightened about it – as to be independent of all huckstering, a matter much more suitable for those who have not yet extricated themselves from the arid labyrinths of Protection.'[97] Drawn up by an English analyst, Michael Mulhall, the *Balance-Sheet* measured the growth from 1870 to 1880 of the major economies of 'Christendom': Great Britain, France, Germany, Europe as a whole, the United States, and the rest of the world, by which Mulhall meant the British colonies. He concluded that, though the figures for the United States indicated that 'this is probably the last time that Great Britain will occupy the highest rank in the industrial nations of mankind, there is no symptom of decline, no diminution of force or energy to cause us any anxiety. On the contrary, the productive labour of our people shows every year a higher ratio per inhabitant, and as compared with other European nations Great Britain is leaving them farther behind.'[98] A pair of graphs showed Britain and the United States towering like alpine peaks above the lesser mountains of France, Germany, Russia and Austria, beneath which

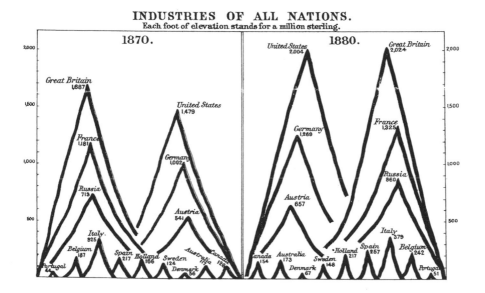

INDUSTRIES OF ALL NATIONS.
Each foot of elevation stands for a million sterling.

lay the foothills of Italy, Spain, Belgium, Holland, Canada and Australia, Sweden, Denmark and Portugal. Commerce admittedly had 'not risen as much as in the previous decade', and manufacturing had 'grown less than any other branch of industry', but banking and shipping exhibited 'an enormous development, as if the finances of mankind were concentrating themselves in London, and the carrying-trade of the seas passing into our hands'. Mulhall turned Britain's deteriorating balance of trade into 'an indication of prosperity' by arguing that Russia and Spain had a favourable balance of trade yet were 'steeped in poverty'. The comparisons he drew with continental Europe invariably flattered Britain. 'Not only is the net income per inhabitant [of Britain] 10 per cent higher than it was ten years ago, but it far exceeds that of any other nation in the world, being more than double the European average and 16 per cent greater than in the United States.'[99] The underestimate that Mulhall arrived at particularly of per capita income in the United States throws his other calculations into question nowadays, but Gladstone found them reassuring.

However, the economic ascendancy of Britain only made the French apprehensive of British competition. Tirard's policy of very moderate protectionism triumphed during his absence from office. Dilke had to wait until Christmas time before hearing from the man whom Gambetta made Minister of Commerce, Maurice Rouvier. Rouvier's background was in banking and he represented a Marseilles constituency, both strong sources of support for commercial liberalism; he also belonged to the Free Trade Association. But he was a neophyte in commercial diplomacy. He learnt quickly at the Ministry of Commerce to respect Tirard's judgement, 'and was perpetually referring to that gentleman,' as the Swiss reported;[100] 'Far from carrying his convictions into effect with a high hand, he was manifestly swayed by the forces which had told upon his predecessor in office.' Initially Dilke was patient. After all, his friend Gambetta would have a lot to deal with in his first few weeks in power. Yet it was disconcerting to see that the new government, while ignoring Britain, was concluding commercial treaties with its other treaty partners: Italy, the Netherlands, Austria, Sweden and Portugal.

When the British ambassador finally raised the subject, Gambetta and Rouvier hastened to arrange a meeting with the British negotiators led by Dilke. But the improvements the French ministers offered to make in their tariff did not move much beyond the lines already marked out by Tirard. The reductions on textiles dealt mainly with the finer yarns. When the French came to grips with woollens using shoddy, the furthest they would go was still double what Dilke and his colleagues estimated to be the current rates of duty under the status quo. Dilke closed the year by suspending the talks, telling the French that 'it would be impossible to conclude a Treaty upon the proposals before us.'[101] The further reductions Rouvier hurriedly suggested to keep the talks going did not change the heart of the issue between the two countries. When Dilke relayed the French offer on shoddy woollens to Bradford to see whether his calculations were correct, Behrens exclaimed, 'if that is a sample of French concessions, I am afraid the Commission might as well have saved the trouble of meeting again.'[102]

Dilke left Crowe, who had been appointed to the British negotiating team, behind in Paris to take a closer look at the calculation of specific equivalents for the current *ad valorem* duties and generally to keep communications open with Rouvier. Their informal talks revolved around cottons and wine. Rouvier focused (as Tirard had) on cottons, where there was room for manœuvre, rather than on the intractable subject of woollens. Crowe encouraged Rouvier with an assurance that Britain would be willing to reconsider its wine duties if only the French government would offer some overall improvement, even if modest, on the status quo.

The suspension meanwhile of full discussions brought the possibility of a simple most-favoured-nation treaty to the fore. The wine duties had a bearing here too, at least according to the French negotiators. They thought that, in return for admission to the benefits of the treaties that France was concluding with its other partners, Britain should agree at least to preserve its wine duties from any alteration that would be to the detriment of French produce. The British were willing only on condition that the new French conventional tariff, that is to say the tariff as shaped by the new treaties, preserved or improved upon the status quo. The crucial component in this tariff so far as Britain was concerned was the French treaty with Belgium. The British government was all the more interested in the Belgian treaty because the Belgian legislature was giving it a rough ride, the kind of reception the House of Commons was sure to give a British treaty if it involved any worsening in the existing tariff. The Foreign Office instructed Crowe and A.E. Bateman from the Board of Trade to draw up an assessment of the Belgian treaty from the British perspective.

Bateman made the case for rejection of a Belgian-style treaty. He emphasised the similarity between Belgian objections to the treaty they were offered and British objections to the French proposals they received: 'there is want of reciprocity in the arrangement to increase French duties while Belgian duties remain at the old rate, and, in particular . . . many so-called conversions of *ad valorem* duties are really large increases.'[103] Why, then, were the Belgians inclined to put up with the new treaty? Bateman's answer brought out crucial differences between the French offer to Belgium and the French proposals to Britain. The principal sectors of Belgian trade with France would fare better under the new treaty than under the existing conventional tariff, whereas the heavy textiles that bulked large among British exports to France would fare worse under the French proposals. Moreover, because 'Belgian exports to France [were] chiefly articles of high value in their respective classes', they were 'lightly taxed by the substitution of specific duties for *ad valorem*', whereas the reverse was true for the heavy textiles of Britain. Even so, the Belgians were counting on additional most-favoured-nation benefits from the treaty that they still expected the British to reach with the French to make their own treaty tolerable.

Crowe reached a more positive assessment of the benefits of an Anglo-French agreement. He claimed that the French offer on the articles in which Britain was most interested, including heavier textiles, was 'much better' than the provision in the Belgian treaty. On the other hand, he listed the substantial benefits Britain might enjoy from most-favoured-nation access to the Belgian treaty, benefits that involved iron and steel, linen yarns, some woollen yarns, most linens, most cottons aside from the heavier kinds, and pure woollens. 'But we shall lose . . . all that the French have offered us in alleviation of the charges on mixed woollens and shoddy goods.'[104] Under any set of terms on offer from the French, the heavy British textiles at the centre of their dispute would face a higher customs barrier than under the current conventional tariff. Crowe made no attempt to disguise that fact, the fatal flaw in the French proposals. Unless France offered some improvement, however modest, to the status quo in this section of its tariff, the British government would not agree to a detailed tariff treaty as distinct from a simple most-favoured-nation agreement, for which they remained willing to settle. There was virtually no disagreement in Britain on this stand. Dilke's account of the reasons for the suspension in the talks to interested Chambers of Commerce won their cordial approval.

The Economist offered the best explanation of the British position. 'The unanimous feeling throughout the country is that we would be far better without any treaty than with one which would increase the already excessive duties levied by France upon our products, and tend to perpetuate a vicious system.'[105] France was reversing the objective of the 1860s treaties and raising rather than continuing to lower the barriers to European trade. Moreover, it was doing so by haggling over the details of the tariff – 'huckstering' *The Economist*, like Gladstone, called it – instead of agreeing to the broad principle of amelioration and proceeding on that basis, as Léon Say had led the British to expect. So were the British sticking to high-minded principle regardless of how the increased French tariff would damage their access to the continental market? No, said *The Economist*: 'this injury we are persuaded will not be permanent. We are confident in our ability to open up new markets for the products which France may exclude, more especially as alteration of her tariff will tend to divert trade into new routes, and at the same time, by increasing the cost of production in France, will make her less able to compete with us abroad.' In other words, as *The Times* had been predicting since the beginning of this set of Anglo–French talks,[106] British merchants would compensate for the diminished market on the continent by expanding their commercial empire overseas.

The trade talks between France and its treaty partners entered a hectic phase at the end of January 1882. The pace was quickened by the prospect of the general tariff falling upon all countries that failed to reach new agreements with France by 8 February. What made the negotiations almost frantic was the simultaneous disintegration of the Gambetta ministry, which had lost the confidence of the Chamber of Deputies by attempting to reform the constitution. Anxious to achieve all he could in the time at his disposal, Gambetta scrambled for an agreement with the British. He was, according to the British ambassador, 'very anxious' for the talks with Britain 'to succeed'. He also argued that the maintenance of 'good feeling towards England in France' depended on renewal of the commercial treaty: 'failure . . . would oblige him to seek for his Foreign Policy some other basis than Union with England.'[107] Pressing further than Tirard and Rouvier had dared, Gambetta offered concessions he felt sure Britain would accept. He offered further reductions on fine cottons and a scattering of other products involving, as he put it, 'les principaux articles visés par la demande des Commissaires Anglais' 'the principal items covered in the demands of the English Commissioners',[108] including selected heavy textiles. But even Crowe had to admit that Gambetta's terms were 'such as we could not accept'.[109] Once again it was the reduction on heavy cottons and woollens that was 'altogether insufficient'.[110]

The unwillingness of the British government to conclude a treaty on the terms offered by Gambetta, the French minister most anxious for agreement, indicated how far the partners of 1860 had drifted apart. The best that Gambetta could offer never amounted to the kind of amelioration of the status quo upon which Britain insisted. So far as heavy textiles were concerned, the maximum French offer did not even match the terms of 1860. On the other hand, as the head of the new French ministry put it, the minimum British demands were 'incompatible with the dispositions of the Chambers and with public feelings in France'.[111] Tirard's return to the Ministry of Commerce after the fall of Gambetta made the British negotiators doubt that France would reach agreement with any of its partners, thus rendering even most-favoured-nation treaties useless. But in fact the incoming ministry, which brought Léon Say back to the Ministry of Finance, wanted agreements with all its treaty partners including Britain. Overcoming resistance from Tirard, the ministry made slight improvements on Gambetta's offer. They still fell short of British requirements.

The divergence between the two countries was accentuated by the eventual acceptance by other treaty partners of the terms that France offered them. At the end of January, after searching debate, the Chamber of Deputies in Belgium approved its treaty with France, as did the lower house in Portugal. At one point the second chamber in the Netherlands rejected its treaty; and for a long time the prospects for a French agreement with Switzerland looked as bleak as they did for Britain. But eventually all save Britain fell into line, and the French extended their string of treaties to include Spain.

Recognising that no better terms would be forthcoming from the French, the Foreign Office abandoned the effort to reach agreement on the tariff and opened negotiations for a most-favoured-nation treaty. Even this proved elusive. The French protested that a most-favoured-nation treaty would leave them tied to the conventional tariff as defined by the agreements they were concluding with their other treaty partners while Britain would remain free to alter its tariff in any way it saw fit. The French ministry therefore demanded that Britain agree to freeze its tariff in return for most-favoured-nation access to the French market. That demand, with its implications for one of the main sources of governmental revenue, struck the British as outrageous. Thinking of the most-favoured-nation status Germany would always enjoy under the Treaty of Frankfurt, Crowe remarked: 'The French will be conceding to the nation they think their worst enemy the privileges which they refused to the nation which they affected till now to consider their best friend.'[112] The French ministry had no intention of bringing about this result. Their demand simply reflected the fear that Britain, having failed to conclude a tariff treaty with France, would woo Spain and Portugal to the detriment of France by offering to equalise the duty on light and strong wines. Dilke had played on this fear in his earlier negotiations with France, and the Foreign Office did not allay it now. At Tirard's prompting, the French ministry secured its demand unilaterally by using a short piece of French legislation to extend most-favoured-nation treatment to Britain. The measure received unanimous assent in both houses of the French legislature. They could withdraw the privilege as readily as parliament could alter the British customs duties.

This action terminated the commercial treaty relationship between Britain and France which Napoleon III and Cobden had inaugurated in 1860. But it did not destroy the network of treaties with other trading partners that had grown up around that agreement. The continuing network preserved much of the conventional tariff that opened the European market to states with most-favoured-nation agreements. Still, the breakdown in the bilateral treaty relationship between France and Britain produced a reaction on both sides of the Channel. Initial responses ranged from disbelief through complacent acceptance to gratification. In France, the failure to renew the British treaty heartened protectionists and dismayed the *libres-échangistes*. Léon Say confessed to the British ambassador 'that he could never have believed it possible that under a Ministry, of which he was a member, an end would be put to the commercial stipulations which had proved so beneficial to our two countries'. But the 'Protectionist spirit had . . . been raised during the last few years to a white heat, and time must be allowed for it to cool.' He accepted the arrangement at which the two countries had arrived because 'commercial discussions should be set at rest . . . If possible, matters should . . . be so settled that nothing should be heard of Commercial Treaties for some time to come.'[113] To such a level had the expectations of the leading economic liberal in France been reduced.

In Britain Behrens reacted with dismay to the abrupt unilateralism of the French regarding most-favoured-nation treatment. Dilke had to remind him that 'Our failure in concluding a Treaty Tariff . . . has chiefly been occasioned by difficulties connected with Yorkshire trade.'[114] Later Kennedy would blame the 'representatives of British trades' who had 'overstated their case' for the failure in 1882.[115] On balance the wool merchants of Yorkshire accepted the outcome with equanimity, though they were disconcerted to discover that at one point the British negotiators had been willing to concede a higher French tariff on some wool tissues than the Bradford Chamber had agreed to.[116] Behrens was rewarded for his latest service to the cause of commercial treaties with a knighthood.

The collapse of the Anglo–French negotiations came as a relief to Gladstone. His general aversion to 'huckstering' was compounded by his embarrassment at the willingness even in the purest free-trade circles to admit that his revision of the wine duties in 1860 had discriminated in favour of the French.[117] He told the House of Commons that, in 'escaping from the meshes of the Tariff Treaty, we have emerged from a murky into a clear atmosphere, and . . . those principles of Free Trade on which we stand in our fiscal legislation are no longer disparaged.'[118]

The commentary in *The Economist* brought out the discomfort peculiar to British free traders about applying market motives to commercial diplomacy. Classical economic theory assured *The Economist* that, 'for such of our products as France may exclude we shall, doubtless, soon find other markets. . . . If France rejects them, we shall get others to take them, and to these others we will at the same time transfer, as far as possible, our demand for products we now obtain from France . . . simply because as trade consists essentially of barter, our commerce must be with those who are ready to exchange with us.' Yet the bartering that invigorated trade was discreditable in commercial diplomacy. While encouraging the British government to open the Spanish market by amending the wine duties, *The Economist* hoped that it would not be necessary to 'enter into any formal engagement. Indeed, after our experience of the French Treaty, the general opinion here will be that the more clear we can keep ourselves of treaties which give to our Free-trade policy the appearance of a bartering of concessions, the better.'[119]

Chapter 7

The Quandary over Commercial Policy, 1883–1888

'The total result . . . of our inquiry into the effects of Free Trade on the development of English commerce during the period from 1860 to 1890, leads to no positive conclusion.'

C.J. Fuchs, *The Trade Policy of Great Britain and her Colonies since 1860* (1893)

The policy of the Gladstone ministry may have been paradoxical. It was certainly scorned as a model for foreign consumption. Yet the reluctance of the ministry to use the tariff for bargaining purposes received resounding endorsement at home. Even Fair Traders respected the refusal of the British government to play the French game. Dilke and the Foreign Office had taken pains to keep the most interested manufacturers and merchants in touch with and in support of the British commissioners throughout the negotiations. Any disposition among British exporters to bemoan the outcome was offset when those who were most threatened by the French tariff found that they could still do well in the French market.

But this consensus did not last long. The failure to renew Cobden's treaty left British commercial policy in more uncertainty than Gladstone cared to recognise. If, as he claimed, 'those principles of Free Trade on which we stand in our fiscal legislation [were] no longer disparaged',[1] neither were they vindicated. Investigations over the next few years only made the situation more perplexing.

For the first time since 1860 Britain was free of specific tariff commitments by treaty to its commercial partners in Europe. The failure to reach agreement with France left the British Treasury free to regulate the wine duties as it saw fit. Britain's remaining commercial treaties with continental countries consisted of little more than the most-favoured-nation clause. It gave Britain access to the conventional tariff of Europe, but that tariff was no longer shaped with regard for the special interests of British industry.

Most continental countries, including the major economies of France and Germany, had adopted some degree of tariff protection. In doing so, they challenged two assumptions of free trade. The first, that experience and rational economic thinking were bound to lead countries everywhere to British-style free trade was proven invalid, at least for this generation. The second, that protective tariffs would damage the economies that embraced them, was about to be tested by the experience particularly of Germany. The first results were not yet in when the Anglo-French treaty talks broke down. There was a further, related assumption. Free traders and their foes alike believed that, in practice though not perhaps strictly according to theory, access to the European market was dependent on tariffs. That conviction too would be tested when the Anglo-French treaty of 1860 lapsed. It is important to remember that the British debate after 1882 on free trade and protection was based on contemporary perceptions of the state of the economy on the two sides of the Channel. Such views rarely correspond to the best reassessments a century later,[2] and in any case were based on much shorter intervals of time, yearly or in triennial or quinquennial grouping, than present-day analysis insists upon.

The impact of protectionism on the continent was not the only subject of uncertainty with an important bearing on economic principle and commercial policy. The nature of the depression at home in Britain was equally puzzling. In many ways, as Chamberlain had shown in defending government policy in 1881, the British economy was faring quite well, particularly in volume of trade and the standard of living of the employed working classes. Yet the businessmen whose profits were squeezed by falling prices felt the impact of the depression. Their feeling fuelled the demand for Fair Trade and, towards that end, for an inquiry into the causes of the depression, the reality of which the government continued to question.

On all sides the premises of the discussion about commercial policy were undermined during the five years following the failure to renew the Anglo-French treaty. The debate took on a partisan character for the first time since 1860, with the Conservatives under Lord Salisbury criticising the inflexibility of Liberal policy. But debate took place also within the Conservative Party as well as between it and the Liberals; the Liberal ministry that Gladstone put together in 1880 remained as divided on commercial policy as the one he had formed in 1868; and the exporting business community was as divided as were the politicians. The injection of a partisan element neither clarified the debate nor pushed it towards a resolution. Nor was there any clear connection between industrial interests and commercial policy. While criticism of free trade spread widely among businessmen in the 1880s, it invariably split individual Chambers of Commerce as well as their national association, and it produced little agreement among the critics about the alternative.[3] The only point to win wider acceptance was the value of most-favoured-nation treatment, and even that continued to be contested. The inconclusive outcome of all this debate, along with developments in the domestic politics of the United Kingdom, eventually forced Salisbury to reaffirm the non-partisan commercial policy that had prevailed before 1882. The only difference he could hope to make was through resourceful but still essentially traditional participation in the commercial diplomacy of Europe.

a. The European Market after 1882

In combination with the protectionist tariff of Germany, the loss of the treaty with France threatened to expel British exporters from the continental market. Yet, contrary to expectation, they continued to do quite well; and their success sustained confidence in free trade. Exporters kept up their sales initially by hurrying goods into France before the duties rose, by cutting prices (though doing so also cut profits) and by taking what advantage they could of the duty on yarns and machinery which the Ministry of Commerce had kept low to encourage French industry.[4] In spite of these efforts, the export of cotton yarn to France fell drastically, as it did to Italy after it raised its tariff in 1882 and again in 1887, and to Russia. Yet cotton yarn exports found compensation elsewhere on the continent, particularly in Germany and the Netherlands. For exports of cotton cloth, the European market held up well in volume though not as a proportion of the total export; and the value of the European market was enhanced by its consumption of the finest qualities of cloth. There was little penetration of the British home market by cottons produced abroad.[5] Exports of textile-making machinery also improved. On the other hand, the heavy mixed textiles of Bradford did as badly as forecast. So did the cutlery of Sheffield, and wrought iron. The renewed French navigation laws also halved the British carrying trade along the French coast. The French tariff began to bite more seriously into British exports the year after it was introduced, though the deterioration owed as much to the stagnation of the French economy as to the tariff. In 1883, after two years of improvement in prices, they resumed their fall, worsening the impact of the specific customs duties that had replaced *ad valorem* rates throughout the continental treaty system.

While British analysts like Crowe, who was now based in Paris, were gratified by the early maintenance of exports to France, they were slow to recognise the diminishing stature of France in the continental economy. The *Balance-Sheet of the World*, which so impressed Gladstone in 1881, had ranked France second only to Britain among the economies of Europe and had pointed out that the French per capita wealth increased during the 1870s at a faster rate than the British.[6] Crowe reiterated this assessment in 1883. 'French commerce will bear comparison with that of any other country except Great Britain,' he reported: 'Her trade greatly exceeds that of Germany.'[7] But the French economy already displayed worrisome features. Alone among the countries of Europe, the population of France was barely increasing in size, thus depressing the domestic market. Phylloxera reduced wine production by some 75 per cent from the mid-1870s to the mid-1880s, assailing one of the mainstays of the French economy. Meanwhile the proportion of manufactured goods in French exports to the rest of Europe diminished, turning France, 'especially in relation to Germany . . . into a supplier of agricultural products, raw materials, and semifinished commodities'.[8] The deterioration in manufactured exports was particularly evident in chemicals, woollens and machinery.[9] To add urgency to the situation, the French stock market suffered a fall at the height of the tariff controversy in 1882, producing a serious financial crisis that brought Léon Say and later Tirard to the Ministry of Finance.

The accumulating bad news tipped the balance of French opinion, especially among the peasantry,[10] further towards protection. Wheat from the United States flooded the country, carried by the expanded French network of railways. Though Tirard seemed protectionist to the British, he had struggled to keep the French tariff as liberal as the legislature would allow. The tariff he left France with was more moderate that Bismarck's in Germany. Moreover, he enlarged the French network of commercial treaties, the only loss being the one with Britain. There was some reduction over the following two years in the French tariff, particularly on yarns to aid the ailing cotton industry, now faring worse than woollens. But the general drift of French commercial policy was in the opposite direction. In the summer of 1882 a resolute protectionist, Pierre Legrand of Lille, broke the grip of commercial liberals on the Ministry of Commerce. The following year the arch-protectionist Méline took over the Ministry of Agriculture. For the moment, furthermore, the hostility of the French in commercial matters was directed more against the British than the Germans. Crowe reported from Paris: 'There is so much dislike to England & Englishmen that the worst motives may be assigned to them with applause.'[11] The falling out of France and England over Egypt added political fuel to the commercial flames. When cholera spread from India through Egyptian ports to Europe, the French accused the British authorities in Egypt of allowing 'their merchants to sacrifice the public health to the rapid transaction of British commercial business'.[12]

Distracted by France and by the depression that affected every country, the British were slow to recognise the rising competitive threat from Germany and the contribution made to it by Bismarck's tariff. The growth of German industry made the British as well as the French economy look stagnant. But that was not apparent to the British until the mid-1880s. At the beginning of the decade the *Balance-Sheet of the World* pointed out that German industry was growing faster than British industry and more than twice as fast as French industry.[13] But the significance of this increase was disguised for the *Balance-Sheet* by the 'enormous increase' in the population of Germany and by its seizure of the industrial provinces of Alsace and Lorraine from France. In contrast to the French and British pattern, German exports grew faster than imports, enough to reduce though not to eliminate the adverse balance of trade. But the productive capacity of Germany was obscured by its still low standard of living, kept down by population growth and taxation. During the 1870s, in an ironic contrast between vanquished and victor, 'while the Frenchman's net income [had] risen 6 per cent, the German's [had] fallen $2\frac{1}{2}$ per cent.'

Failing to appreciate the pace of German growth, British free traders were easily convinced that Bismarck's tariff harmed the German economy. In 1882, the British Board of Trade seized upon a report from German Chambers of Commerce on the first year of their new tariff to point out its baleful effects. The Board prefaced the translation of the report with an exaggerated summary of its findings: 'With a very few exceptions . . . all the districts, whether mining or manufacturing, in the interior or on the sea coast, report an obstinate stagnation in all branches of trade; and a large majority openly charge the new protective policy with disastrous results.'[14]

The Germans themselves responded to the new tariff quite differently. To their gratification, it produced a 'sharp drop in the value of imports'.[15] There was admittedly no return to the boom years of the early 1870s, but the 'acute recessions in the United States and France' from 1882 to 1887 could be blamed for that disappointment. German agriculture did not benefit appreciably from the tariff protection extended to it in 1879. But production in the iron and steel industry posted a steady increase. The tariff could not claim all the credit. The application in the 1880s of the Thomas-Gilchrist process to the phosphoric ores of Germany, particularly in annexed Lorraine, greatly increased the competitive capacity of the iron and steel industry. The practical contribution of the tariff to the improvement, in keeping domestic prices up while reducing imports, may have been 'slight', but the psychological impact was substantial. The tariff 'increased the confidence of the iron manufacturers in their market and of the consumers in the iron industry; the iron masters were thus encouraged to make improvements and the public to invest in them.' Recent research confirms this classic assessment by Ivo Lambi. Ulrich Wengenroth demonstrates that the strength of German exports lay less in advanced technology than in 'their large internal market, hedged about by tariff'.[16] The rest of the story became all too familiar to the British after the mid-1880s. German iron and steel exports increased more rapidly than British ones and eventually surpassed them. This success did not, however, extend to textiles. Though the German export of cottons doubled in value from £5,000,000 to £10,000,000 between 1880 and 1895 while the value of British exports of cottons declined by almost the same amount, Britain still stood far above at the top of this industry, with exports valued at £69,000,000.

The German achievement galled the French as it did the British, and deprived them both of centrality in the European economy. As 'the share of finished goods among German exports grew while the percentage of manufactures in the French export trade in Europe declined',[17] Germany usurped the place France had enjoyed under Napoleon III as the pivotal economy on the continent.

b. The Stalemate over Spain and the Depression

The consensus of approval in Britain that greeted the collapse of the talks with France was eroded during the protracted attempt to reach agreement with Spain. The difficulties in coming to terms renewed debate within the Liberal ministry about the worth of commercial treaties. At the same time Salisbury, in uneasy association with the Fair Traders, sought to broaden the argument about the bearing of tariffs on the depression. The Liberals, however, refused to discuss that issue, and expert reports failed to resolve it.

For more than a decade, Chambers of Commerce in Britain had been pressing the government to open up the protected markets of Portugal and Spain by adjusting the wine duties to accommodate their strong wines. Dilke had used the threat of doing so to press Tirard to improve his offers. He and other commercial activists in the government service such as Sir Robert Morier, the ambassador in Portugal and then Spain, turned to the Iberian Peninsula when the talks with France failed. Morier reached a most-favoured-nation agreement with Portugal in May 1882 to give Britain access to the benefits of the tariff treaty recently concluded between Portugal and France. Hopes rose for a more significant agreement with Spain to open its large market to British goods.

But the treaty that Spain reached with France produced an angry start to the Anglo–Spanish discussions. The Spanish tariff legislation that accompanied the treaty increased the discrimination that Spain had introduced in 1877 against British exports. If the Spanish government meant in this way to force Britain to the bargaining table, the tactic backfired. Chamberlain at the Board of Trade shocked a good many of his cabinet colleagues and the inner circle in the civil service by proposing that Britain retaliate. He told Lord Granville that, 'if retaliation had ever been justified at all, there will never be a stronger case for such action.'[18] Chamberlain wanted 'to increase largely the differential duties on Spanish wines as compared with those of France, Italy and Germany – and to do so to such an extent as may seriously affect their exports to this country'. That was a more robust reaction than Chamberlain's free-trading cabinet colleagues could condone.

But *The Economist* found Gladstone's response to the Spanish move almost as shocking. Displaying more casuistry than courage, Gladstone manipulated the statistics to argue that the export of Spanish wines to Britain had soared under the duties by some 260 per cent. While *The Economist* shared Gladstone's anxiety to avoid any appearance of bargaining for tariff reductions, it insisted as a matter of simple justice that Britain ought to reduce its duty on strong wines, leaving Spain free to deal with its tariff as it saw fit. It accused Gladstone of hiding the injustice by selecting years for comparing the volume of Spanish wine exports to convey an impression of growth when the overall movement had been a steep decline. His presentation, said *The Economist*, was a 'complete burlesque of facts and figures . . . and even if it be the case that [the wine duties'] readjustment would entail a loss of revenue of one or two hundreds of thousands of pounds, we are surely not so poor that this need stand in the way of our doing right . . . especially as by fair dealing on both sides our mutual trade would probably be largely increased.'[19]

The Chambers of Commerce found Gladstone's argument equally unconvincing, and they redoubled their pleas for the government to prise the Spanish market open. Behrens used this reaction to gain a reaffirmation from Bradford of the value of commercial treaties for trade purposes.[20] But before he could transmit the resolution to the government, he ran into resistance from local Fair Traders.[21] A similar debate continued within Gladstone's cabinet. Chamberlain and Dilke adhered to a position similar to that of Behrens in support of commercial treaty-making, while Gladstone and Granville preferred the detached stance of the Fair Traders, though not of course their rationale for it. The Prime Minister and Foreign Secretary pressed the cabinet in the spring of 1883 for a 'general or abstract declaration' against commercial treaties.[22] But Dilke managed to hold them at bay.

Salisbury was alert to the break down of the consensus in the country and sought to exploit it. But he failed to gauge the dimensions of the reviving argument accurately. Though he tried to approach the issue by means of an inquiry, he went too far in setting its terms. Speaking in Birmingham, a hotbed of Fair Trade, he raised questions about free trade. He knew that to speak of free trade without reverence was to touch the Ark of the Covenant, yet he wanted to deflate the quasi-religious pretensions that inhibited discussion. 'I am a free trader,' he protested, '. . . I perfectly believe that as a general rule it is the wisest policy for the country to pursue, yet I acknowledge it as a measure of expediency; I do not acknowledge it as a revelation.'[23] To move the discussion out of the realm of abstraction, he looked at free trade as a matter of historical experience and international practice. He pointed out that Britain had been persuaded to adopt it by men who believed that it 'would be speedily adopted by almost all the other nations of the globe'. Contrary to those expectations, the leading countries on the continent and even Britain's own colonies were now moving towards protection. The fault that Salisbury found in British commercial policy lay, accordingly, not in the underlying principle of free trade but in the way it had been pursued. He charged that 'sufficient precaution was not taken by due treaty and agreement first to secure that other nations should tread in the same path as we did.' This accusation located the root of the problem in the world that Salisbury knew best, the world of diplomacy.

Inside the Foreign Office, prompted by the cabinet debate, Kennedy prepared a memorandum about the bearing of the European treaties of commerce on British trade.[24] With the lapse of the Anglo–French agreement, Britain lost its formative position in the network of treaties. Belgium took Britain's place; and the Belgian treaty with France laid the basis of the European conventional tariff for the products of industry. While still connected to the network through most-favoured-nation agreements, Britain lost the benefit of tariff stipulations adjusted to the needs of its own industry. Kennedy drew up a table to show how Britain had benefited from the commercial regime established in the 1860s and how it was losing from the recent erosion of those benefits (Table 7.1).

Table 7.1 Value of the Exports of the Produce and Manufactures of the United Kingdom (to Selected European Countries) (in thousands of £)

Year	France	Germ'y	Russia	Neths.	Belg.	Italy	Spain	Port'l	Sweden	Austria	Year
1881	16,970	17,431	6,164	8,899	7,075	6,630	3,654	2,092	2,081	693	1881
5-year average											5-year average
1880–1876	15,145	18,943	6,273	9,858	5,521	5,737	3,400	2,121	1,999	796	1880–1876
1875–1871	16,904	26,881	6,146	14,921	6,305	6,686	3,597	2,452	2,486	1,301	1875–1871
1870–1866	11,511	20,468	4,197	10,159	3,612	5,433	2,251	1,789	764	1,202	1870–1866
1865–1861	8,805	14,554	2,716	6,765	2,219	6,391	2,910	1,980	690	882	1865–1861
1860–1856	5,542	12,665	3,021	5,815	1,664	3,977	2,046	1,470	542	1,032	1860–1856
Year											Year
1855	6,012	10,977	. . .	4,558	1,707	2,541	1,158	1,350	545	717	1855
1854	3,175	8,521	53	4,573	1,406	2,273	1,270	1,370	334	636	1854

He then looked at the commercial-diplomatic relationship between Britain and its trading or would-be trading partners on the continent. His survey underscored the importance of Spain as the largest of the Mediterranean wine-producing markets and as the key to the others now that the French treaty was lost. In every case he identified mixed textiles as the British industrial sector that suffered most acutely under the revised conventional tariff of Europe.

However, the deterioration in British exports over the past few years was not steep enough, nor was the outlook in commercial diplomacy encouraging enough, to change the commercial policy of the country. When the Duke of Rutland, a protectionist from the days of the fight over the Corn Laws, brought the current depression to the attention of the House of Lords, Salisbury gave him only circumspect support, confining himself to pointing out how the abolition of all but revenue-producing tariffs had left British diplomats without 'weapons by which they can instil fear of the consequences of refusing the alteration of the tariffs for which they plead'.[25] He backed away from any attempt to restore reciprocal bargaining, or what he called retaliation, admitting that it was not 'immediately practicable'. For that situation he blamed the most-favoured-nation clause inaugurated in 1860. 'We have,' he said, 'wound around ourselves a skein of obligations' that precluded Britain from resorting or even threatening to resort to retaliation when a foreign tariff set out to damage British exports.

Despite the circumspection of Salisbury's critique, the government defended its policy weakly. Granville replied to Rutland and Salisbury with dismissive brevity. The only point in Salisbury's address that he deigned to challenge was the assertion that poverty was increasing. Granville remembered how effectively Chamberlain had used the statistics on pauperism, working-class consumption and taxation to ward off the attack on government policy two years earlier. But without fresh statistics to back him up, his response looked simply like a refusal to recognise the reality of the continuing depression.

Dilke did better towards the end of the year when he defended the record of the government in the commercial negotiations with France. Speaking in the industrial lowlands of Scotland,[26] he contended that British trade had emerged better off under the now Belgian-based conventional tariff than it had been under the conventional tariff of the 1860s except in regard to mixed woollens, printed cottons and cheap cutlery. Yet he admitted that, since the collapse of the Anglo-French talks, Britain no longer possessed an effective voice in shaping the conventional tariff of Europe. He was also obliged to confess that he spoke about the desirability of participation in Europe's commercial treaty-making as an individual and not on behalf of the cabinet.

The debate about commercial policy was listless because the nature of the depression was puzzling. The only certain thing was that it had gone on for a disconcertingly long time, now approaching a decade. Yet it was hard to tell just what, aside from prices, was depressed and how deep the depression was. The Liberal ministry was able to fend off the Conservatives' demand for an inquiry by pointing out that, though falling prices diminished the value of British exports, their volume was hitting unprecedented heights. The phenomenon of unemployment was beginning to impress itself on the British consciousness; but because prices had fallen even faster than wages, the standard of living of the employed working class was rising, as proven by the statistics on consumption of food and drink. Nor was the overseas location of the problems for exports clear. Fair Traders wanted to place the blame for the rising tariffs on continental Europe and looked to the colonies for a remedy. But the answer to the question of whether British exports were improving better in colonial or European markets depended on the years chosen for comparison and varied from industry to industry.

The condition of the major continental economies also perplexed the British, as did the internal impact of the return to protectionism upon France and Germany. The French situation was easier for British free traders to interpret because France slipped deeper into depression after 1882. While French imports measured by weight continued to increase, its exports fell steadily in value as well as weight. Crowe calculated that, 'In spite . . . of cheaper materials, French exports have not yet recovered the position which they held in 1875, nor indeed that which they acquired in 1872, immediately after the most exhaustive war of the present century.'[27] This continuing depression suggested the uselessness if not the folly of higher tariffs. The situation in France also demonstrated that the depression was widespread, not peculiar to Britain, which made it harder to argue that Britain's extraordinary lack of tariffs for bargaining purposes was responsible for its economic plight. At a practical level, Crowe reported in 1884 that the French tariff was doing little damage to British exports except for mixed woollens.[28] Kennedy pointed out a year later that 'many of the difficulties which our traders anticipated when the French Tariff was changed from an *ad valorem* basis to duties by number or weight of goods, have not arisen'.[29] By that time Crowe was able to report a little improvement even in the mixed stuffs of Britain,[30] while producers of stiff woollen stuffs made headway in the French market at the expense of their depressed competitors.[31]

Yet while the evidence from the French experience deepened the British aversion to protectionism, it gained ground in France. The original partners of 1860 were moving ever further apart. In the wake of the unsuccessful negotiations of 1881–82 to renew the partnership, Crowe had been transferred from Berlin to Paris and elevated to the newly created post of Commercial Attaché for Europe. At a party in Paris in the spring of 1884 he came upon Tirard. Now Léon Say's successor as Minister of Finance, Tirard had hardened in his personal hostility to the protectionism that he saw growing around him. Yet he confessed 'with much openness . . . that a great reaction had taken place in French public opinion since 1881, and that the amount of concessions which France had then been willing to make to us far exceeded anything that any Ministry could now venture to submit to parliament.'[32] Like most British observers, Crowe regarded the drift of opinion in France as incompatible with the economic evidence.

The German case was harder to fathom and more disconcerting. There was one dimension of Bismarck's policy that Gladstone might have envied: the unilateral insistence, advocated by doctrinaire free traders as well as by practitioners of *realpolitik*, that each country should set its tariff in its own interests.

Bismarck had distanced himself from the network of tariff treaties. German commercial policy revolved around the autonomous tariff he initiated in 1879. Thereafter, though he negotiated agreements, for example with Switzerland, to retain advantageous terms of access to neighbouring markets, he took care to maintain his freedom of commercial action. He had come to regret as much as the French the clause in the Treaty of Frankfurt that locked them both in a most-favoured-nation commercial embrace.

But the focus of interest in Britain was not on the unilateralism of German commercial policy but on its protectionism. By 1885 it was clear that the tariff of 1879 was not the disaster the Board of Trade had joyfully reported after it first came into effect. Still, its impact across the major sectors of the German economy was uneven, creating a situation that was uncongenial to ideological or partisan debate. Close practical analysis was no more helpful because it raised doubts about the importance of tariffs as a factor in economic performance.

George Strachey, one of Crowe's successors in the British diplomatic and consular establishment in Germany, submitted a pragmatic report in 1885 on the performance of the German economy, sector by sector, since the enactment of Bismarck's tariff.[33] 'Nothing,' he declared, 'could be further from my intention than to get up a case of "fair trade" or to furnish materials for a pamphlet by the Cobden Club.' He argued throughout that the German achievements were rooted less in tariff policy than in 'the people themselves, in the science, in the enterprise, and in the inventive and constructive powers of their mechanicians [sic] and engineers'.

There was evidence in his report to support the case for tariff protection on a selective basis. There had been conspicuous growth in the iron and steel industry, the sector that the tariff of 1879 had been particularly designed to help. Strachey compared the 'jumps of the German output, which commenced with the recent grant of protection', with 'the chronic stagnation, or worse, of Scotland. The Returns of Great Britain for 1884 show a decrease of no less than 11 per cent. against the previous year, while the German production was 6 per cent. larger.' But Strachey never lost sight of the non-fiscal components of the German achievement. It was thanks to the Thomas-Gilchrist process for smelting that German pig iron was catching up in quality with the British product, while the best British pig iron was deteriorating with the exhaustion of the best seams of ironstone. It was thus thanks to 'a considerable advance in structural and technical methods' that the iron masters of Germany had surpassed the producers in Middlesbrough and Glasgow.

Not all the sub-sectors of the German iron and steel industry were happy with the tariff Bismarck had given them. But Strachey concluded that 'the grievances and the inequalities are not unfairly distributed over a number of branches of production.' He summed up his survey of this sector by challenging the contention that free trade was necessary to keep industry open to the bracing winds of competition. 'The iron masters have been undeniably helped [by the Tariff of 1879], and protection, far from causing them to slumber on their successes, has stimulated them to take advantage of the newest and most approved constructive and metallurgical methods.'

Even so, Bismarck's tariff had proven clearly beneficial only for iron and steel. The impact on cotton textiles was distinctly mixed: 'what the Tariff of 1879 gave with one hand it took away with the other, the augmented yarn duties having more than outweighed the benefits derived from the higher rates on finished goods. Germany . . . is largely dependent on England for yarns', making it difficult for German weavers 'to compete with England, and Belgium, and Switzerland, in foreign markets.' The impact of the tariff on woollens, 'the most important branch of the textile industry of the [German] Empire', was still more mixed. Generally German woollens fared quite well: 'while our quantities are declining, the corresponding German figures are growing. The Germans have been driving foreign woollens out of their home market, and are now formidable competitors to France and ourselves abroad.' Furthermore, a 'second augmentation of duties in 1881 has . . . almost entirely destroyed the import of low-priced British north country goods'. Yet in the German market the yarns of combed wool or worsted and especially the lustre and mohair yarns for which Bradford was famous were maintaining themselves well. 'Saxony requires Bradford lustre wefts, as well as [heavy] English cotton yarns . . . and the addition of the high duty to the cost of production makes competition with Bradford in foreign markets almost impossible.'

The situation in Germany as reflected in Strachey's report left those Con servatives in Britain who were sympathetic to but uncertain about the restoration of tariffs for bargaining purposes without clear guidance. Yet his conclusion made bleak reading for the Liberals:

English free-traders who affect intimate acquaintance with the state of foreign political opinion have been in the habit of explaining, within the last few years, that a reaction against protection was setting in abroad, especially amongst the Germans. What has been really happening is the exact reverse of this. The disbelief of the Continent in free trade has been growing, and nowhere more than Germany. . . . The political constellations of the Empire, the highest personal influences, the most powerful industrial and commercial forces, some of the principal press energies, all are on the side of the existing system. The belief is widely diffused that the Tariff reform of 1879 saved Germany from a great ruin, and that the Empire is now on the road to industrial greatness, perhaps to the succession of that hegemony which Great Britain, it is thought, now with difficulty holds in her hands. Protection is in the national air, and it will not be dissipated by foreign arguments, however accurately deduced from the axioms of scientific doctrine.

The difficulty of interpreting the situation on the continent as well as at home induced Salisbury to keep his distance from the Fair Traders and to look instead at alternative responses to the depression. Speaking in the heart of the cotton textile industry at Manchester, he insisted that the trade depression was 'such as this country has not known for many years', extraordinary not so much in its severity but 'for the length and durability of it, and for the absence of any apparent probability of its early close'.[34] He continued to deplore Britain's lack of countervailing duties to combat continental protectionism. He paid more attention than he had done in the past to local experience, to crowd-pleasing effect as *The Times* report showed: 'You know,' he said, 'how the industry of this town is being cramped and fettered and confused by the growing wall of hostile tariffs which shuts you out of most of the markets of the world. ("Hear, hear," and cheers.)' But he deflected attention away from the continental market: 'if you are being shut out by tariffs from the civilized markets of the world, the uncivilized markets are becoming more and more precious to you.' He focused attention on the phenomenon, which Crowe was documenting for the Foreign Office, of European powers seeking to keep trade with their colonies to themselves through restrictive tariffs. The French were enclosing Madagascar. 'Russia is advancing across Central Asia, and shutting out . . . Manchester.' In a further refinement of his argument, Salisbury used this imperial appeal to lift attention above the perplexities of commerce to the higher realms of foreign policy. There he moved with confidence from his experience at the Foreign Office, where the masterfulness of his performance had since been accentuated by the clumsiness of his Liberal successors. 'Why is our Government powerless to do its duty by the commerce of this country?' he asked. 'My answer is, Because it has sacrificed the great name of this country. . . . In all its foreign affairs you will find the stamp of failure.' And he carried his audience through the lengthening list of overseas humiliations to which Gladstone and Granville had subjected Britain, from the Transvaal and Afghanistan to Egypt and the Sudan.

Salisbury resorted to a similar shift of focus when the Earl of Dunraven brought the cause of Fair Trade to the House of Lords. Rather than criticise free trade, Salisbury attacked the 'considerable scepticism' displayed by the government 'as to the existence of this general depression'.[35] Granville came to the debate prepared with updated figures on the positive aspects of the country's performance. But Salisbury knew that, while Granville's statistics might invalidate Dunraven's diagnosis of the depression, they would not persuade many people to doubt its very existence. Salisbury accused Granville of pouring out 'elaborate quotations of statistics, in order to traverse the existence of a thing which anybody, who moves about in England at all, knows to exist as well as he knows that the sun shines in the summer.'

Thereafter Salisbury kept the focus on the depression, so far as economic matters were concerned. When he took office at the head of a minority 'care-taker' government in 1885, he secured the appointment of a royal commission of inquiry into the nature of the depression and prescriptions to ease it. He put the restoration of a tariff for bargaining purposes at the top of his list of reme-dies to be considered.[36] But the testimony that the royal commission obtained early in its proceedings from Kennedy as head of the Commercial Department at the Foreign Office did not point in any clearer direction than Strachey's report on protection in Germany had done. Kennedy downplayed the impact of continental protectionism on British commerce. He said that only in Spain and Russia were continental tariffs 'distinctly prejudicial to English trade. . . . In other countries, Germany, France, and Italy, it does not seem that the British trade as a whole has in the long run been seriously affected, though particular branches of commerce have suffered.'[37] He pointed to other factors, particu-larly the extension of the railways, that had fostered an increase of trade on the continent in which Britain had not shared. The opening, for example, of the St Gothard railway in 1883 enabled German and Belgian goods to reach Italy more cheaply than could British.

Kennedy nevertheless endorsed the use of retaliatory duties. The negotia-tions with Spain had dragged on fitfully, enervated by a conspicuous lack of interest on the part of Gladstone and Granville[38] and by protectionist impulses in Spain. Morier, the British ambassador, was the only participant in the talks who was eager for their success. He managed to secure an agreement at the end of 1884 – not much more than an arrangement Gladstone had rejected two years earlier, most-favoured-nation access to the Spanish market in return for reduction in the British wine duties – only to see the Spanish government renege on it after six months. That action by Spain contributed to the break-up of Gladstone's ministry. After five years of unhappy life, the cabinet was riddled with dissension and almost welcomed a revival in the argument over commercial treaties as a way to end its misery: hence the formation of Salis-bury's minority ministry and the royal commission on the causes of the depres-sion. The refusal of Spain to end its discrimination against British exports renewed the cry for retaliation. Kennedy was therefore asked about the possible effect of an increase in the British duty on Spanish wine. 'I can only express my own personal opinion upon the matter,' he told the royal commission, 'but under the present circumstances of this particular case I think it might have exercised a good influence on those negotiations.'[39]

Salisbury used the retaliation issue in campaigning for the forthcoming general election. He insisted that 'the people must decide whether the neces-sary weapon, a bargaining tariff, ought to be placed in his hands.'[40] To that end he drew attention during the campaign to two of the less popular constraints that resulted from free trade.[41] The first was to prevent Britain from introducing differential duties in favour of the colonies. British interest in colonial markets soared during the 1880s in the face of mounting barriers on the continent. Yet cultivation of the empire could not compensate for loss of the continental market: continental sales formed a far larger proportion of British exports than did sales to the colonies, and the continental proportion continued high. It averaged 38.9 per cent in the 1860s, rising to 41.9 per cent in the 1870s; and though it fell to 35.2 per cent in the 1880s, it was to rise again in the 1890s to 37.1 per cent.[42] Furthermore, the proportion for continental as against colonial imports, which free traders regarded as more important than exports, bulked larger than for exports, and it increased steadily. It averaged 39.7 per cent in the 1860s, 41.8 per cent in the 1870s, 42.2 per cent in the 1880s, and 44.4 per cent in the 1890s. In the face of such figures, Britain still needed somehow to surmount the continental barriers. Hence the second constraint of doctrinaire free trade to which Salisbury drew invidious attention: it ruled out retaliatory use of the wine duties, something he had long favoured and now suggested as punishment for the outrageous conduct of Spain.

The results of the general election proved, however, as ambiguous as the deliberations of the royal commission. The Conservatives did well in urban constituencies, where Salisbury's talk of tariffs may have helped them; but the Liberals made compensatory headway in the countryside. Irish Nationalists emerged holding the balance of power, and Ireland dominated the agenda of the new parliament. Economic issues receded into the background even after the spectre of unemployment had provoked an ugly demonstration along Pall Mall.

The proceedings of the royal commission on the depression continued to obscure the subject they were supposed to illuminate. The stance adopted by spokesmen for cotton textiles was complicated by a preoccupation with competition from India, which the Liberals had denuded of even a revenue tariff in 1882, to Lancashire's relief. The proportion of British cotton piece-goods exported to India reached an all-time high of 43.7 per cent in 1886, though Lancashire lost the trade in coarse yarn and goods to Indian producers.[43] The stance of the Yorkshire woollens industry was even less clear-cut than that of Lancashire cottons. Behrens, now approaching 80 years of age, astonished the royal commissioners by denying that the depression extended to Bradford and the woollens of West Yorkshire. He also reduced the impression of Bradford's dependence on overseas markets by pointing out that more than half of Yorkshire's woollens production was sold within the British home market. Still, it was upon the overseas market that his testimony dwelt. In that regard, armed as usual with statistical evidence, he stressed how well the volume, though not the value or profit, of the British export of woollens had held up. The chairman of the commission asked in surprise, 'Then we may consider that the trade and industry of the district that you represent, or at all events the woollens and worsted trades, are not to be described as depressed?' All Behrens would concede was that 'They have not been so progressive, and were perhaps at a stand-still, from 1874 to 1879, but they never declined with regard to volume.' He went on, 'I am glad to find that we have made progress since 1880; and I believe that we are on the eve of better times.'[44] He put the slow years in the late 1870s down to 'a freak of fashion' that favoured the 'soft and nicely draping goods, which the French were far better able to supply than we were. . . . But since then our spinners and manufacturers have learnt a great deal, and now they are prepared to provide every kind of yarn that we require.'

To what extent, then, had Yorkshire woollens been hurt by the foreign tariffs to which Behrens had paid so much attention for so many year? 'Germany we have lost almost altogether,' he replied, 'except for yarns, for which that country is our best customer. . . . we have done [i.e. exported] more in 1884 to France in weight of stuff than we ever did before.'[45] Yorkshire was also making up for what it lost in Germany with increased sales to the Netherlands and still more to the colonies, particularly Canada and Australia. Asked finally by one incredulous commissioner whether the position at Bradford was 'as good as ever it was', Behrens answered, 'No, I do not say as good as ever, for profits have generally got to vanishing point, but we do a larger trade, and I believe the working population is as well off as ever it was.'[46] Confronted with such a testimony, the commissioners had to ask whether there was any point to their inquiry.[47]

They had already heard from Behrens's Fair Trading former antagonist Henry Mitchell.[48] There were differences in shading in the testimony of the two merchants. Mitchell gave a gloomier though also more impressionistic account than the statistically redoubtable Behrens. He estimated the loss of the trade with France since the expiration of the treaty of commerce as little less than 50 per cent, and the loss of the trade with Germany since the enactment of Bismarck's tariff as close to 90 per cent; he also placed more importance than Behrens on Britain's trade with its colonies. Yet Mitchell agreed with Behrens on much, including the considerable improvement in the Yorkshire woollens and worsteds trade over the past two years. This growth mellowed the relationship between the two men. Soon after Behrens's eightieth birthday, Mitchell moved that the Chamber of Commerce commission a portrait of the old man; it was completed shortly before he died. Afterwards Mitchell carried on Behrens's work as chair of the Chamber's tariff committee. Symbolically this succession marked a closure of the commercial argument in Bradford. Its prosperity was returning despite the loss of the tariff tailored by Cobden and Behrens to fit the needs of West Yorkshire. The recovery suggested that tariffs had less importance than both free and Fair Traders had assumed.[49]

Nevertheless, the gloomy impression Mitchell conveyed of British displacement from foreign markets was borne out by other evidence the royal commission received. Britain's diplomatic representatives on the continent provided a chorus of lamentation.[50] From France came a report that 'Swiss cotton yarn, Swiss and German silks, American agricultural machinery, and some Belgian iron wares, seem to have taken the place of certain goods formerly sent from the United Kingdom.' The report from Italy told of France, Germany, Belgium and Switzerland supplying 'many descriptions of goods to Italy, such as glass, earthenware, cutlery, chemicals, iron wares, machinery, and textiles, which were formerly sent from England'. From the Netherlands came word that 'The trade in machinery (except agricultural) has been largely transferred to Germany in consequence of the greater attention given by the Germans to the consumers' wants, and to provide cheaper articles.' Germany echoed the Dutch reaction. A British representative there relayed a 'very general complaint that English producers are imperfectly acquainted with the requirements of the German market, and unwilling to alter their standard of supply to meet them . . . the day has gone by when the German consumer was content to take the supply of goods which the English dealer thought the best for him . . . the German market has now got a standard of its own, and one not to be despised, which native producers are quite able to attain to.' In other words, British produce was being displaced by German produce in the German market, though not necessarily as a result of the German tariff.

The situation on the continent as portrayed by the Conservative-appointed royal commission made the achievement of the Liberals all the sweeter when, during their brief return to office in 1886, they at last secured an agreement with Spain. Since 1877 when Spain first imposed discriminatory treatment against British goods, France had replaced Britain as the primary trading partner of Spain and German exports to Spain rose close to the former British level.[51] By securing the new agreement without mentioning retaliation, the Liberals discounted Salisbury's threat as unnecessary. On the other hand, the deal involved British payment in the form of a reduced duty on strong wines in return for most-favoured-nation access to the Spanish market: in other words, payment for simple equity of treatment with Spain's other trading partners, the kind of exchange Gladstone did not like to make. Apprehensive about Gladstone's response, the Foreign Secretary Lord Rosebery kept word of it from him until the last moment, when the old man gave in grudgingly. His uneasiness went unnoticed amid the gratification of the business community at the reopening of the Spanish market and the preoccupation of most politicians with Gladstone's offer of Home Rule to Ireland. The discussion of commercial policy in Britain remained inconclusive.

c. The Franco-Italian Tariff War

The Irish question might have neutralised partisan debate on commercial policy at Westminster, but on the continent the commercial treaty network failed to avert a tariff war between two of its members. That war showed how costly retaliation could be. Though especially damaging to the combatants, it hurt non-participants too, including Britain. But it also indicated how the network might be used to overcome the costs of belligerency. In the process, for the first time since the sixteenth century, the centre of commercial policy-setting in Europe shifted from the north-west towards the middle of the continent.

According to Crowe, the conflict began in spring of 1885 when France, extending its protective measures to agriculture, raised the duties it levied at its frontiers on cattle and meat, to the immediate cost of importers in Italy.[52] Crowe held the two countries equally to blame for their falling out because protectionists in both had vowed to withdraw at the earliest opportunity from the treaty that France and Italy reached in 1881. But the danger did not become obvious until the spring of 1887 when Italy moved to increase its general tariff steeply. Behrens was quick to sound the alarm because the proposed Italian tariff included an especially large increase in the duty on woollens. Though meant to protect struggling Italian producers from inundation by French woollens, the duty would fall alike on the pure woollens of France and the heavy mixed woollens of Yorkshire, to the greater detriment of the latter.[53] In effect, said Behrens, 'the new tariff is a differential one in favour of France & Austria but against England.'[54]

Because the acute danger was confined to the woollens industry, this cry of alarm did not attract much attention in Britain. The Irish question further obscured the issue. The Liberal Party had split over Gladstone's proposals for Home Rule, and he was driven from office by an alliance between the dissident Liberals and Lord Salisbury's Conservatives. But though the alliance proceeded to win a major electoral victory, it left the Conservatives dependent on the dissident Liberals, now called Liberal Unionists, for a governing majority in the House of Commons; moreover, it revolved around the single issue of the Union with Ireland. The Liberal Unionists, while opposed to Home Rule, were equally opposed to any deviation from free trade. Salisbury was therefore obliged to suppress the forces of Fair Trade in the Conservative Party, regardless of the power they had gained at the general election and of his personal irreverence towards free trade.[55]

The muzzling of Lord Salisbury and the Conservative Fair Traders did not, however, strengthen the Liberals as spokesmen for free trade. Gladstone had long been their oracle; but his devotion to the Irish question warped and weakened the appeal of his commercial policy after 1886. His preoccupation with Ireland alienated many for whom free trade was a greater issue. When in 1887 Gladstone published an account of the Anglo-French treaty of 1860 which implied that it was still in force,[56] the free-trading *Economist* was provoked to exclaim, 'is his mind so entirely absorbed in the Irish Question that he has no thought to give to other matters? . . . The fact is that [the 1860 treaty] expired in 1882, while Mr Gladstone was Prime Minister.'[57] Exasperated when, despite Salisbury's disclaimers, Gladstone persisted in accusing not just Conservatives but also the Liberal Unionists of protectionist leanings, *The Economist* at the end of 1887 accused him of injuring the cause of free trade and playing into the hands of its opponents.[58]

Meanwhile the reverberations of the Italian tariff widened on the continent. Following the example set by Bismarck in freeing Germany from most of its commercial treaty fetters, Italy denounced its existing tariff treaties, including those with Austria and Switzerland as well as France. Still, Italy had framed its tariff 'with a view to bargaining, as well as . . . for protectionist purposes'.[59] Crowe explained the continental impact of the Italian action in a succession of reports to the Foreign Office: 'The conventional tariff which all states enjoy in Austria Hungary is that appended to the Austro-Italian treaty of December 27, 1878. . . . Most of the states of the continent appear to be waiting upon France so far as action in respect of Italy is concerned; but some are preparing, as I am informed, to take steps for exercising pressure upon Austria.'[60] 'Switzerland, which had been engaged in an exchange of views with Germany as to a new conventional tariff, has interrupted the negotiations at Berlin in order to watch how matters are turning – at Rome, Paris and Vienna.'[61] Switzerland was particularly anxious 'because she is surrounded by neighbours – Italy, France and Germany –, whose tariffs have been gradually raised during the last few year. . . . Swiss opinion now favours retaliation.'[62] These concerns ran thus wide and deep. Yet none of the continental states raised them with the British government.

The Foreign Office was nevertheless alert to the damage the Italian tariff could do particularly to British woollens and metal manufactures. Co-operating with initiatives from concerned interests in Britain, the Foreign Office managed to secure some marginal amelioration in the treatment of British exports to Italy. When a promised Italian emissary failed to show up for meetings with the Manchester and Yorkshire Chambers of Commerce, Kennedy relayed information from them and from Chambers involved in metal manufacturing for presentation by the British embassy in Rome.[63] Behrens arranged with the parliamentary undersecretary at the Foreign Office to send a Bradford merchant familiar with the Italian trade to assist the staff there.[64] The Italian Finance Minister refused to make substantial 'concessions' to Britain without a reduction in the British duty on Italian wines. Britain refused 'because concessions were not asked from Italy, but simply a readjustment of charges, injurious to particular branches of British trade, that took effect upon the lapse of certain [non-British] treaty tariffs'.[65] All the same, the British representations in Rome had some effect. The expert reinforcement from Bradford enabled the embassy to rectify definitions in the Italian tariff that worked against mixed fabrics and curtains from Britain. This tariff nevertheless 'caused a most remarkable decline in British exports of cloth'.[66]

In the spring of 1888, after a year of irritable talks, Italy and France plunged into a tariff war, the first between members of the commercial treaty network since its inception in the 1860s. Britain was protected by its most-favoured-nation arrangements with both belligerents from the full weight of the punitive tariff increases they hurled at each other. For a short while Crowe hoped that Switzerland would keep the Franco-Italian market open by continuing to admit French and Italian goods for exchange there.[67] But the French government, driven by protectionist pressures in the legislature, blocked this route of escape. Customs houses were obliged to insist upon certificates of origin for the most sensitive Italian exports: wine, silk and meat. Diplomatic tensions as well as economic nationalism fuelled the fight between France and Italy. France feared the inclusion of Italy alongside Austria in the alliance formed by Bismarck to keep France from avenging its losses in the Franco-Prussian War.

The economic cost of the tariff war proved high and long-lasting, especially for Italy. French exports to Italy, which had averaged an annual £12 million between 1883 and 1887, fell by nearly half to £6.3 million in the following five years. But Italian exports to France fell from the much higher figure of £17.1 million between 1883 and 1887 to the still lower average of £5.5 millon in the ensuing five years.[68] The large Italian export of wine to France was wiped out. French exports, particularly of textiles, were also hit. However, 'France was able to recoup herself elsewhere (chiefly in the United Kingdom, and as regards woollen goods in Germany) for the loss of much of the Italian market.'[69] The war did not come to an end until the beginning of 1892, when France dropped its surtaxes on products from Italy. Even so, the two countries refused to treat each other on a most-favoured-nation basis until the end of the century.

This commercial war was bound to confirm British aversion to the retaliatory use of tariffs. And that was the use that had most appealed to Salisbury in his search for tools to dismantle the barriers to the entry of British exports into continental markets. In a perplexing variety of ways, the fluctuations in European commerce both fuelled and neutralised the debate on tariff policy in Britain. *The Economist* published worried comparisons of British and continental trade; the Board of Trade likewise refined its comparative statistics. These riveted attention on the decade since the depression set in, too short a time to form an adequate basis for conclusions of enduring validity yet long for comparison with former depressions. The Board of Trade surveyed the value of exports, excluding re-exports, from the principal European countries from 1876 to 1885.[70] Tables 7.2 to 7.6 are derived from that survey.[71]

The Economist concluded from the Board of Trade's survey that, 'there has been a very close correspondence between the contraction and expansion in our own export trade and that of the Continent.'[72] While Tables 7.2 to 7.6

Table 7.2 Exports (Excluding Re-Exports) of the Principal European Countries, 1876–85 (£m)

	1876	1879	1882	1886	1876–79 % change	1879–82 % change	1882–86 % change
Austria-Hungary	49.6	57.0	65.2	56.0	14.92	14.39	−14.11
Belgium	42.6	47.6	53.0	48.0	11.74	11.34	−9.43
Denmark	8.9	7.8	8.9	8.3	−12.36	14.10	−6.94
France	143.0	129.3	143.0	123.5	−9.58	10.60	−13.64
Germany	127.4	138.8	159.5	143.0	8.95	14.91	−10.34
Holland	44.1	48.2	62.3	74.1	9.30	29.25	18.94
Italy	48.3	42.9	46.0	37.8	−11.18	7.23	−17.83
Norway	6.4	4.8	6.7	5.4	−25.00	39.58	−19.40
Portugal	5.1	4.6	5.6	5.6	−9.80	21.74	0.00
Spain	17.6	21.0	30.3	27.5	19.32	44.29	−9.24
Sweden	12.4	10.3	14.1	13.3	−16.94	36.89	−5.67
Russia	52.8	62.8	61.8	53.9	18.94	−1.59	−12.78
Total	558.2	575.1	656.4	596.4	3.03	14.14	−9.14
UK	200.6	191.5	241.5	213.0	−4.54	26.11	−11.80

Table 7.3 Exports (Excluding Re-Exports) of Principal European Countries, 1876–85 (£m) Ranked According to Percentage Change

	Percentage change 1876–86
Holland	68.03
Spain	56.25
Austria-Hungary	12.90
Belgium	12.68
Germany	12.24
Portugal	9.80
Sweden	7.26
UK	6.18
Russia	2.08
Denmark	−6.74
France	−13.64
Norway	−15.63
Italy	−21.74
Average for Continental European States	6.84

indicate that the correspondence was more complicated than *The Economist* suggested, essentially they bear out its generalisation. But where did that leave the debate about free trade and protection? Free-trading Britain apparently fared little better or worse on average than the continental protectionist countries. Were tariffs simply not all that important a consideration in international trade?

Sectoral comparisons drawn from Board of Trade figures had similarly ambiguous implications. The figures for woollens confirmed what Behrens had told the royal commission about the depression by revealing continued British superiority and growth in this sector regardless of the continental tariffs (Table 7.4).

Table 7.4 Exports of Woollens

	1880 £	1882 £	1885 £
Yarn			
Germany	1,637,000	1,701,000	1,812,000
France	1,972,000	1,594,000	1,424,000
Belgium	3,140,000	1,678,000	1,870,000
Total	6,749,000	4,973,000	5,106,000
UK	3,344,000	3,398,000	4,382,000
Manufactures			
Germany	8,558,000	8,879,000	7,918,000
France	14,808,000	16,076,000	13,203,000
Belgium	1,116,000	1,215,000	1,141,000
Total	24,482,000	26,170,000	22,262,000
UK	17,265,000	18,768,000	18,847,000

But the statistics for cottons showed a 'marked decline' for British goods since 1880, 'while Germany, our chief continental competitor, has increased her exports of cotton piece goods, &c., although this is largely set off by a decline in her exports of yarn'. The figures for exports of iron and steel including machinery were also disturbing (Table 7.5).

Table 7.5 Exports of Iron and Steel including Machinery

	1880 £	1882 £	1885 £
Germany	6,866,000	10,513,000	8,059,000
Belgium	3,302,000	4,937,000	3,063,000
Total	10,168,000	15,450,000	11,122,000
UK	37,653,000	43,530,000	32,797,000

Though Britain retained the leadership, Germany was eating into the British share of the market in this field. Contemporary reaction in Britain exaggerated the problem. The best-informed analysis a century later indicates that the British iron and steel industry was holding its own against the Germans.[73] But that was not how it felt at the time. The centre of the agitation for Fair Trade, imperial preference and outright protection shifted from Bradford to Birmingham. During the 1860s the manufacturers of Birmingham had felt that they had 'little to fear from foreigners'. But by the mid-1880s many of them were convinced that a protective tariff was indispensable to their recovery from depression.[74] Unlike the woollens producers of Yorkshire, it was at the cheaper, less value-added end of the product range that the metal manufacturers of the West Midlands were losing market share to continental producers. *The Economist* sought to diminish anxiety about the figures for iron and steel by noting that 'both Germany and Belgium have proportionately lost rather more ground than we have since 1882',[75] 28 per cent for the two continental producers as against 25 per cent for the British. But that was not much of a difference.

Germany had become the test case for protection. Yet the test was obscured by the depression that afflicted the protected and the unprotected alike. *The Economist* opened its 1889 comparison of 'German v. British Trade'[76] with an affirmation of its faith in free trade: 'while this country is at present increasing its trade rapidly, the German export trade is beginning to dwindle, owing mainly to the vicious effects of a rigid protectionist policy, the operation of which can never be deferred for more than a brief period.' But the figures did not warrant such an emphatic conclusion, nor did they attempt to pin the responsibility for the economic performance of Germany on its tariff (Table 7.6). *The Economist* derived its assurance from the margin by which the increase in British exports since 1879 exceeded the German increase: 15.5 per cent as against 13 per cent, again not large. Sectoral statistics followed to amplify the comparison. But they obliged the journal to end more modestly than it began:

Table 7.6 Exports of Home Produce (Excluding Re-Exports)

	1879 £	1881 £	1883 £	1885 £	1887 £
Great Britain	191,531,000	234,022,000	239,799,000	213,044,000	221,414,000
Germany	138,785,000	148,850,000	163,610,000	143,015,000	156,765,000

'although Germany has made more rapid progress in some directions, we have gained most in others, and, on the whole, the result is in our favour' – scarcely a ringing conclusion. It shed little light on the impact of tariffs on trade.

Chapter 8

The Transformation of the Network, 1889–1892

'. . . in this conflict of commercial treaties, to hold your own, you must be prepared, if need be, to inflict upon the nations which injure you the penalty which is in your hands, that of refusing them access to your markets.'

Lord Salisbury at Hastings, 18 May 1892

While British commercial policy froze in face of ambiguous evidence that ran counter to the national predisposition, France moved resolutely towards protection. In order to do so, to regain the freedom to set its own tariff it had to detach itself from its treaties with other European states. The moment was opportune, for most of these were due to expire in 1892. French withdrawal would pull the centre out of the European conventional tariff, but would not necessarily involve complete departure from the network of commercial treaties that Napoleon III and Cobden had inaugurated. That network had established rules that were indispensable to the smooth functioning of European commerce, rules governing, for example, patent rights and international transportation. It also offered simple most-favoured-nation access to the European market, the only kind of access Britain had enjoyed since 1882. Though French protectionists wanted to preserve such access on a selective basis, they disliked indiscriminate most-favoured-nations provisions. Essentially they demanded in every regard freedom to set the national tariff as the nation saw fit.

That freedom was perhaps the only principle on which Gladstone and Bismarck were substantially agreed – Gladstone would just have put it differently. Though it could co-exist with, still it undermined the collective, treaty-made tariff under which the commerce of Europe had grown in the past 30 years. Under this tariff the newer and smaller states of Europe had demonstrated their ability to provide for the material needs of their people. It was the lesser states, particularly Switzerland and Belgium, that reacted with the greatest dismay to the French retreat. They feared that France intended to use its raised tariff to weaken their economies. Yet the interests of each economy and the lack of national weight in the small states kept them from offering the leadership required to preserve the network.

France had provided that kind of leadership when the network was constructed. Britain had let France take the lead then, and was unable to resume it now. Salisbury, Foreign Secretary as well as Prime Minister since 1887, would like to have done so – he would have liked not just to keep down the tariff barriers that disrupted the European market but to revise their definition in terms congenial to British exporters, terms lost in 1882. But he could not do so without the ability to threaten tariff retaliation. The Belgians pleaded with Britain to seize this weapon. Britain was still much the greatest European economic power, but its power was useless for diplomatic purposes so long as it could not be thrown around. The Treasury, however, refused to permit any use of tariffs for bargaining purposes with foreign states.

Without leadership from a major power, the European commercial treaty network was unlikely to survive. By the end of the 1880s all three of the great powers were pursuing national tariff policies, Germany since Bismarck, Britain under the legacy of Gladstone, and now France at the instigation of Jules Méline, leader of the protectionists there. With France pulling out of the tariff treaty network and Britain unable to replace its leadership, all eyes turned on Germany.

Germany was not eager to act. Like France, it was preoccupied with its own affairs, in particular with the Emperor's sacking of Bismarck. His dismissal had little to do with tariffs; all the same the new Chancellor, Caprivi, took a critical look at the fruits of Bismarck's commercial policy. What he saw went some way towards confirming *The Economist*'s indictment of protectionism: the tariff as enacted and increased since Bismarck's day had obviously not saved Germany from the widespread depression. But then neither had free trade saved Britain. And a retaliatory tariff war could only make matters worse, as the Italians were discovering. Caprivi recognised that Germany needed a market in Europe outside its own boundaries that would buy what German industry produced and pay for it with the raw materials and foodstuffs that German industry and its workforce needed. Caprivi also rediscovered what Cobden had grasped in 1860, that the best way to open the European market was through tariff treaties. Working in co-operation with Austria and Italy, his partners in the Triple Alliance, Caprivi began therefore to transform the commercial treaty network that France was abandoning.

It was not simply a reconstruction. The core of the network shifted from Western to Central Europe. The French retreat left Britain with nothing better than most-favoured-nation adherence to a conventional tariff that it could no longer shape. Lord Salisbury eventually sought permission from the electorate for the restoration of a bargaining tariff, but Caprivi's departure from Bismarck's policy only confirmed the British in their aversion to anything redolent of protectionism. When Salisbury left office in the summer of 1892, the commercial leadership of Europe passed incontestably to Germany.

a. The French Retreat

Periodically since 1882 Crowe had reported on the tide towards protectionism in France. The decisive components of its strength came from agriculture. The tariff and treaties of 1881–82 had left agricultural produce largely free of tariff but with no guarantee against its imposition whenever the legislature might so incline. When a tariff was introduced on imports of grain and meat in 1885 and 1887, it gratified the large farming population of France by maintaining domestic prices in the face of cheap foreign imports penetrating ever more widely through the expansion of the railway system. Farmers responded to their new-found security by bringing more land under cultivation. Benefits of this sort appealed to the wine producers of France. Hitherto supporters of a liberal policy, they changed their mind during the 1880s in the face of the massive importation from Spain and Italy while phylloxera blighted French production. Agriculture was now ready to join forces with industry in preserving the economy and social order of France from foreign erosion. As for industry, the depression of the late 1870s continued through the 1880s, with falling prices and profits and stagnant production, especially in metallurgy.[1] The movement in French opinion accelerated with the elections in the autumn of 1889 that expanded the protectionist forces in the legislature to commanding proportions.

Crowe alerted the British authorities to the situation in Paris and its implications for European commerce. France was about to assail the network of treaties and either replace it unilaterally with a tariff – low for the friends of France and high for its enemies – or force its treaty partners to accept a steeply upward revision. The probable reaction elsewhere on the continent only added to the problem. Neighbouring states were expected to retaliate with 'a strenuous assault upon French wine and French woollens under the lead of a coalition of influential powers'. Crowe concluded: 'we are on the eve of a struggle which, no matter how it may be decided – must produce some – aggravation of the French Tariff and . . . may end in the suppression of most favoured nation treatment.' Yet Britain stood helpless. 'Great Britain in this conjuncture, has apparently little to do except to stand by, look on, and hope that France may not favour too much prohibition, or her neighbours prove too violent.'[2]

The current French ministry was headed by Tirard, Britain's antagonist at the beginning of the decade but the last hope for liberalism in France as it came to a close. Tirard tried to deflect the protectionist assault. One way was to tighten the commercial bonds between France and its colonies. Though not a liberal policy, it was less offensive and damaging to other continental states than destruction of the network to which they all belonged. The other tactic of the ministerial liberals was to leave the initiative on tariff policy to the legislature in the hope of playing upon protectionist divisions and liberal anxieties to eliminate the worst proposals and preserve the network. But protectionists in the legislature were too numerous and too well led for Tirard's strategy to succeed. Crowe estimated the protectionist contingent to number at least 300, while there were scarcely 40 'so-called freetraders'.[3] Though the protectionists were indeed splintered into a variety of agricultural and industrial factions, Méline drew them together skilfully and in March 1890 managed to provoke Tirard into resignation.

Méline meanwhile took charge of the tariff commission that the legislature had set up at the beginning of the year. This body prescribed the main features of the impending tariff, relegating the new ministry to the role of moderator. The ministry acted to minimise the damage the tariff might do to sectors that depended on cheap imports, particularly of raw materials. But inquiries launched by the tariff commission placed the nationwide shift in favour of protectionism beyond doubt. All but 13 of the responding 154 Chambers of Commerce demanded an end to the current treaties, and only three supported them. Ninety-nine wanted France to steer clear of treaties altogether.[4] The movement to raise the tariff in France ran in parallel to a similar movement in the Congress of the United States, which produced the McKinley tariff, a decisive step towards higher levels of protection there. By both reaction and emulation, the coming of the McKinley tariff invigorated the forces led by Méline.

In October 1890, after months of manœuvring *vis-à-vis* the tariff commission, the French government proposed a high maximum tariff as the starting point for negotiations with would-be treaty partners. Méline's men forced an immediate change of course. The Minister of Commerce, Jules Roche, was 'instructed to draft an "irreducible minimum Tariff," which would be satisfactory to the Protectionists, who fear lest negotiations with foreign Powers might lead to concessions which they disapprove.'[5] A dual tariff system was emerging, with a maximum tariff to apply to all states that did not make substantial concessions to French commerce and a minimum tariff for those that did. But just how the system would work remained unclear. The minimum tariff was the crucial element. Could it be reduced through diplomatic negotiations? Or would it rule out treaties in future? And how high would it be set? At a level intolerable to other countries? In that case, tariff wars might ensue.

Later that month Roche and Develle as Minister of Agriculture presented the government bill to the Chamber of Deputies. British commentators examined its potential impact on British textiles. The bill was not particularly hard on imports of metal goods and machinery;[6] but textiles were another matter. Crowe reported that the minimum tariff

> kept very much on the lines of the present Conventional Tariff in respect of woollens, but . . . important increases had been introduced into the section of cottons. It seems clear that the framers of the Tariff have endeavoured to

conciliate the States which import French woollens,[7] and Belgium and Switzerland notoriously do; and have been careless to conciliate Great Britain, which is the chief manufacturer of cotton. In other words, the French have a dread of reprisals in the one case, and no such dread in the other.[8]

Still, the immediate concern of the French ministry was not with foreign but domestic reaction. Méline's tariff commission set the pace. The ministry simply 'ask[ed] the Chamber to decide what course ought generally to be pursued'.[9] Yet the ministry proved more powerful that it appeared. While Méline managed to raise the level of agricultural protection, he found himself unable to do so more generally. The government resisted efforts to impose duties on many raw materials and forced the protectionists to compromise on the tariff for manufactures.[10] But that outcome, which was bad enough for the other European states, did not become apparent for more than a year.

The rest of Europe did not wait passively for the French to complete their tariff revision before responding. The calendar in every office responsible for commercial policy was focused on 1892, when most of the component treaties of the existing network would expire. Spain launched a formal inquiry even before the French, hoping to adjust its tariff to the enormous increase in sales its wines were enjoying in the French market, especially during the Franco-Italian tariff war, in marked contrast to the disappointing performance of Spanish wines in Britain after the treaty of 1886. The value of the French import of wine from Spain had risen over the past few years from 7 million to 200 million francs.[11] The Spanish initiative only accentuated the importance of France to the European market. The Spanish newspaper *Impercial* described 'the Treaty which united us with France' as 'the chief basis of the value of our most important commercial wealth'.[12] Once the French set to work on their tariff, the Spanish stepped reluctantly aside to await the outcome.

Aside from the major powers of Britain and Germany, the states whose commercial reaction was of greatest concern to the French government were Switzerland and Belgium. Both were neighbouring suppliers and buyers for the French market, economies of pivotal importance to French and general European commerce. The Franco-Belgian treaty of 1881 formed the basis of the European conventional tariff for industrial goods. Switzerland linked France to Italy and the Austro-Hungarian Empire. In the absence of leadership from Britain or Germany, the possibility of co-ordinated resistance to the French assault on the conventional tariff of Europe depended on these two states.

Neither, however, could afford to defy the French on its own, without assistance. Both had profited from the treaty network and hoped to preserve it, but, in view of the continental drift towards protectionism, they had begun to lose faith in commercial liberalism. In 1887 both gave their industrial and agricultural sectors a modest degree of tariff protection.[13] Belgium was a devotee of commercial rapprochement with its great neighbours, Germany as well as France, but its economy was too closely bound up with the French to risk separate action. It might, for example, withhold its coal which was vital to industries in the north of France; but as the British minister explained to Salisbury, 'any restrictions on the export of this, the most important product of Belgium, which employs over 100,000 men, would be a suicidal policy.'[14] The importance of the French market to Belgium along with the danger the new French tariff was likely to pose to its economy and its powerlessness in the face of that threat brought the Belgian government close to despair. The Foreign Minister, Baron Lambermont, was 'convinced that the application of even the Minimum Tariff proposed by the French Government would be a fatal blow to Belgian trade with France, and that its inevitable effect must be to ruin many industries, and to deprive a large number of men of employment at a time when agitation and Socialism are rife among the working classes . . . but he has little or no hope that the French Government can be induced to modify or mitigate their exorbitant Tariff.'[15] The most Belgium dared do was bluster, and it was afraid to do even that alone. Belgian ministers pleaded with the British to start the agitation.[16] Other European states including France knew that the Belgians would never bite when they hesitated even to bark.

The Swiss were less timorous because they were less heavily dependent upon France. Moreover, the Swiss minister in charge of commercial policy, the Foreign Minister Droz, was arguably the ablest commercial liberal on the continent. But he would have his hands full resisting the Swiss disposition to retaliate if France pegged its minimum tariff damagingly high. The French seemed more likely to heed threats than expressions of sweet reason. Crowe expected the French tariff to display 'a bias . . . in favour of several classes of Swiss goods. States like Holland, from which no reprisals are expected, may be treated with less consideration, and Belgium, which appears at present to hesitate for fear of offending neighbours, will perhaps be treated as a timid and feeble power.'[17] Shortly before the French government presented its proposals for the minimum tariff, the Swiss let it be known that their 'wine duty will be increased . . . by 20 fr., and the duty on French woollens will be raised all round'.[18] When the French government's proposal bore out Swiss fears, Droz could only hope that the French action would 'eventually prove suicidal'.[19] He considered that 'France, already isolated politically, was entering upon a path which must inevitably lead to her commercial isolation also. France was not,' he thought, 'in a position to dictate commercial Tariffs with safety. She could not claim the same importance in the distribution of the trade of the world as Great Britain and Germany.' He 'concluded by professing, in spite of the gloomy prospect all round him, a firm conviction that the principles of free trade . . . would triumph in the long run'.

That was the Gladstonian hope. Yet the great Swiss liberal did not share the Gladstonian notion of free trade. He wanted Switzerland to pursue a policy of 'relative free trade', by which he meant 'duties not exceeding the equivalent of 10 to 15 per cent. *ad valorem*'. That was higher than any British political leader would contemplate until the turn of the century when Chamberlain embraced imperial preference. Droz wanted Switzerland to join Belgium in fighting the French proposals, and he hoped for British encouragement towards this end. But neither Belgium nor Britain would respond. By the end of 1890 Droz concluded 'that there was little hope of any combination on the part of European States to adopt retaliatory measures against the protective French Tariffs, and that it would be hopeless for Switzerland to engage alone in violent Tariff war against that country. Italy had done so, but while undoubtedly doing considerable injury to French trade, had entirely ruined her own.' His regret over the failure to mount a co-ordinated attack on the French proposals was all the greater because he thought such an attack, if widely supported, would have succeeded. 'Had it been possible to effect a combination with Holland, Belgium, Germany, Austria, and Italy to fight the almost prohibitive items of the French Tariff, he had little doubt that France would speedily have been brought to her senses.'[20]

Droz included the Netherlands, though it was only loosely tied to the treaty network, in that list, but not Britain. He knew better than to expect help from that quarter. Lord Salisbury wished to be more forthcoming: nothing would have pleased him more than to place the traditional arts of diplomacy, of which he was a master, at the service of the owners of property whose interests he strove to uphold. But the crucial tool in commercial diplomacy was the capacity to reduce or raise tariffs; and Britain had forsworn its capacity for that sort of action.

Two forces bound Salisbury to accept this national self-denial. One was his domestic political support. Not only was he dependent on free-trading Liberal Unionists for his parliamentary majority; the balance of opinion within his own party favoured free trade. Fair Trade might be popular among the Conservative activists who ran constituency organisations and their countrywide association, the National Union. Indeed, Salisbury had difficulty keeping the enthusiasm of the National Union for Fair Trade in check when it threatened to disrupt the Unionist alliance. He had to restrain his own sympathy with the retaliatory part of the Fair Trading programme. But he recognised that nearly half of his party, including the 'representatives of commercial constituencies',[21] would recoil from any disruption of the national consensus on free trade.

The other fetter on Salisbury's freedom of action came from the guardians of Gladstonian orthodoxy at the Treasury. He received a stern reminder of this constraint shortly before the French government published its tariff proposals. The Foreign Minister of Romania worked out a proposal to replace its existing commercial treaty with Britain with one in which Romania would admit British exports on more favourable terms in return for a pledge from Britain not to restore a tariff on its grain. Romania wanted to develop its commercial relationship with Britain while extricating itself from its most-favoured-nation dependency on Austria. The latter had extended its commercial influence into the Balkans through the construction of railways accompanied by trade treaties. In order to escape from this thrall, the Romanians sought a commercial treaty with Britain that excluded the most-favoured-nation clause. They refused to renew the current treaty or accept any replacement that included it.

The Commercial Department at the British Foreign Office had, however, come to regard the most-favoured-nation clause as the cornerstone of its policy for European trade. Kennedy did not entirely forget the shortcomings that Behrens had pointed out in the terms for most-favoured-nation access laid down in tariff treaties negotiated between other European states. But after 1882 Britain's commercial treaties consisted of little more than most-favoured-nation provisions. Kennedy did not want to jeopardise that. The Foreign Office had given up any hope of including tariff specifications in the treaties it negotiated. The Romanians designed their proposal astutely to get round the British inhibition by asking Britain not to restore a duty that had no realistic prospect of revival. Even Fair Traders backed away from a return to the Corn Laws. Salisbury wanted to comply with the Romanian suggestion, arguing that 'it is very desirable, in behalf of British shipping frequenting Roumanian ports, as well as of British commercial enterprises in that country, and British subjects resident there who are engaged in trade or otherwise employed, that these interests should not be left without the protection of Treaty provisions for their security.'[22] But the Treasury insisted that acceptance of the Romanian demand, 'however harmless in itself, might be construed as a willingness on the part of this country to accept restrictions upon its fiscal liberty in future'.[23] This demand for eternal freedom and independence in fiscal matters left British commercial diplomacy in chains on the eve of the presentation of the new French tariff. Many months later the Treasury softened its opposition to a reformulated Romanian offer,[24] but too late. By then the Romanian government was caught up, like the rest of Europe, in the ramifications of the Méline tariff and was no longer interested in a separate arrangement with Britain.[25]

Though Salisbury accepted the chains that the Treasury laid upon the Foreign Office, he refused to let them completely immobilise Britain at a time when the commercial treaty network of Europe faced either destruction or transformation. He proceeded to demonstrate how much could be done with Britain's existing diplomatic and administrative equipment. Sceptical about doctrine of any sort, he often argued that the choice of policy was less important than how it was pursued. Here he fostered two organisational innovations. One brought about a temporary resolution of the long-standing conflict among the Foreign Office, the Board of Trade, the House of Commons, and Chambers of Commerce over the conduct of commercial diplomacy. The solution advocated by the Chambers of Commerce – the appointment of a Minister of Commerce with a seat in the cabinet – had won majority support in the House of Commons; but ministers familiar with the practice of government insisted that this step would resolve nothing. Kennedy at the Commercial Department of the Foreign Office enjoyed fairly good relations with the Chambers of Commerce, but they regarded him as lacking adequate administrative and political clout. He in turn blamed the uncompromising stance of the Chambers of Commerce, especially in Yorkshire, for the failure to renew the French treaty in 1882. Still, the Chambers could not be ignored. Mindful of the impending expiration of so many commercial treaties, the Association of Chambers of Commerce demanded to be heard.[26] At the same time the government faced the danger of outspoken protectionists on the Conservative backbenches upsetting its parliamentary cohesion. That danger was heightened by the renewed support that Fair Trade was receiving from commercial centres in the provinces.[27]

The Salisbury government therefore arranged for the appointment by the Board of Trade of a Trade and Treaties Committee. Its mandate was to collect, circulate and digest information from the Chambers of Commerce in Britain, British diplomatic missions on the continent and the Board of Trade itself about the evolving French tariff, its wider impact in Europe and its implications for British industry and commerce. The Trade and Treaties Committee was placed under the chairmanship of a Liberal MP with impeccable free-trading credentials who was nevertheless an activist in commercial policy: A.J. Mundella, a former textile manufacturer now on the opposition front bench. Like Behrens, he had gone to Paris in 1860 to assist Cobden in shaping the French tariff, and in his brief term as President of the Board of Trade in 1886 he had helped to secure the commercial treaty with Spain. Now he co-operated with the free-trading Conservative president of the Board of Trade, Sir Michael Hicks Beach, to keep protectionist Conservative backbenchers in line.[28] The Trade and Tariffs Committee was further strengthened by the inclusion of the ablest experts from the relevant departments of state: Kennedy from the Foreign Office and Robert Giffen from the Board of Trade.[29]

The other operational development that Salisbury promoted made fuller use of Joseph Crowe as Commercial Attaché for Europe. It was Salisbury who first assigned Crowe the task of continent-wide commercial surveillance; and Crowe had recently been knighted at Salisbury's behest. Kennedy never reconciled himself to Crowe's advancement and sought persistently to undermine him.[30] But Crowe had unrivalled connections with the makers, high and low, of commercial policy on the continent. No one in the employ of the British government had a keener sense of the political machinations in commercial diplomacy. He pleaded with Salisbury for promotion into the regular diplomatic corps and out of the commercial service, which ranked lower on the continent and was looked down upon in the Foreign Office. But Salisbury had more use for him where he was.

Soon after the French government published its tariff proposals, Crowe asked for permission 'to make a short tour to Berlin, Rome, Brussels and Berne or Zurich' to gauge the prospects 'for combined action against the protectionist tariff now before the French Chamber of Deputies'.[31] Spain was not added to Crowe's itinerary because the Foreign Office was well aware of its wishes, thanks to the work of the preparatory commission that the Spanish government had set up and to able reports from the British ambassador, Sir Clare Ford. The Spanish indicated that their interest in a treaty with Britain depended entirely on further improvement in the British duties on wine. Crowe's three-week tour through other capital cities on the continent excited French suspicions that Britain was 'engaged in promoting or in seconding a commercial league against the Republic'.[32]

If that was Britain's objective, the tour was not encouraging. It left Crowe with the impression that 'France can dare almost anything, as every body is dreadfully afraid of her. . . . All the smaller states that are going to be mortally hit by the new French tariffs are trembling lest such steps as they may be men enough to take should be interpreted as in the nature of declarations of war.'[33] The lesser states were 'all hoping some big powers may yet come & help them to beard France. I could . . . give them a lot of sympathy, which they did not apparently consider enough.' Nor did Crowe himself. A coalition of the lesser states 'could only succeed,' he wrote, 'if a great Power like England were to take it in hand'.[34]

Crowe knew all too well that there was 'no present prospect' of that. There was little Salisbury could do from the Foreign Office beyond alerting the diplomatic staff across Europe to report on local reaction to the tariff that was taking shape in Paris. The response in France to British queries only accentuated the British dilemma. The French Foreign Minister, Ribot, would not even guarantee that the minimum rather than the maximum tariff would apply to British exports. The decision on that issue lay, he said, 'practically with the Chamber rather than the Government'.[35] The French executive was deplorably weak; but so was the government of Britain. Repeatedly Ribot let the British know that the only thing they could do to make the French reconsider was to threaten retaliatory action.

b. A Constructive German Aberration

At Brussels on the first stop in his tour, Crowe learnt that the commercial policymakers of Europe were looking to Berlin. The Belgian Prime Minister told him 'with some satisfaction . . . that Germany and Austria were really preparing to come to an understanding to reduce duties on certain classes of products, which would thus compete more actively than heretofore with similar French produce on neutral markets'.[36] The change of commercial policy in Germany formed the centrepiece of the attempt by the new Chancellor to regularise the conduct of Germany's foreign relations after the devious brilliance of Bismarck. Caprivi was a straightforward soldier, a modest aristocrat who lived strictly on his military income. He had little political ambition for himself and did not welcome, though he loyally accepted, the Emperor's command to take over as Chancellor. But loyalty in Caprivi did not mean subservience. As in high military command, so in the affairs of state he arrived at his conclusions after consulting those he thought best able to advise him and then implemented his decisions with little regard for what he considered to be selfish or short-sighted interests. Authoritarian in his approach to government, he could still reach liberal economic conclusions – a not uncommon combination of tendencies, as Bismarck had displayed at the beginning of his chancellorship.

Within less than a month of becoming Chancellor, Caprivi 'was intensely occupied with a plan for bringing about a customs union for central Europe'.[37] A combination of diplomatic and commercial considerations drove him in this direction. He wanted to remove the deceptive clothing that Bismarck's Reinsurance Treaty with Russia had given to Germany's now basic alliance with Austria. Though Caprivi hoped ultimately to put German relations with Russia on a happier footing, in the meantime the Triple Alliance of Germany with Austria and Italy needed strengthening. In that connection Germany had to rescue Italy from the devastating consequences of its tariff war with France. There was otherwise little German concern with the Italian market. But Germany had economic concerns of its own which were deepened by the antagonistic tariffs that France and the United States erected round themselves. The German iron and steel industry was not benefiting as it had hoped from Bismarck's tariff. While the home market was doing well behind its protective wall, German producers found the competition, particularly from Britain, stiff in the export market. Furthermore, by encouraging domestic consumption and high prices, Bismarck's tariff drew foreign iron and steel (especially British iron and steel) into Germany. The raising of the French tariff threatened to make the situation worse by depriving Germany of the advantage it derived under the Treaty of Frankfurt from access to the current, lower rates of duty France gave to its commercial partners. The tide of opinion on tariffs among German iron and steel producers accordingly changed direction. On the industrial front generally, Caprivi concluded that Germany needed to extend its markets in Central Europe to offset the losses expected from the rising tariffs of France and the United States.

To do so, Germany had to begin with Austria. Austria was not among the few countries to which Germany had specific tariff commitments as distinct from most-favoured-nation agreements. But the German and Austro-Hungarian empires formed the core of the Triple Alliance that Caprivi wished to consolidate. The dual monarchy of Austria-Hungary welcomed his reaffirmation of the alliance through a trade treaty. That essentially political dividend, along with the bipartite reflexes of the dual monarchy in commerce, helped to reduce, though by no means to eradicate, Austria's inveterate protectionism. The interest in tariff reduction came from agrarian Hungary as against more industrial Austria. Germany offered substantial reductions in its agrarian tariff to avert increases and where possible to secure reductions in the Austrian duty on manufactured goods.

The reductions secured on manufactures were fewer and shallower than the Caprivi government and German industry would have liked. While welcoming the German initiative, the Austrian government was responsible for determining the shape of the emerging tariff to a degree that was out of all proportion to the comparative economic weight of the two countries. That pattern was to persist throughout the formative stage of the Central European treaty network when the power of the lesser economies that were willing to join the network was at its height. Still, the reductions on agricultural produce in the Austro-German tariff served German as well as Hungarian interests. The main sources for the imported foodstuffs on which Germany relied, Russia and the United States, had stiffened their barriers to international trade. Poor harvests in Europe and North America worsened the shortage and as a result raised prices. Access to cheaper foodstuffs in and through Hungary eased this situation for Germany, while the high grain prices that prevailed through 1890 and 1891 calmed the fears of the grain-producing Junkers of eastern Prussia.

Britain had been slow to detect the shift in German commercial policy. Berlin was the second stop on Crowe's tour. After meeting the German Foreign Minister, Adolf Marschall von Bieberstein, he was able to send in a full report. German policy as Marschall presented it was still tentative and preoccupied with the French tariff. Marschall did not favour an aggressive policy with the risk of a tariff war. He preferred 'to wait and see how other countries were prepared to meet French advances'. He thought it 'not unlikely that France might induce one at least of the smaller European States to treat for the minimum Tariff'.[38] That would 'enable Germany to avoid the infliction of the French maximum charges, because France would not be allowed to treat Germany worse under the Treaty of Frankfort'. But at the same time Germany was exploring an alternative: to reach agreement with Austria and 'model her relations with other continental States according to the result of the Austro-German arrangement'. Though he expected negotiations with Austria to be 'long and difficult', Marschall left Crowe with the impression that Germany was 'prepared to make important concessions in the hope of enlarging her markets, and that she now holds that it is better to try for these advantages than to venture on reprisals against France.' Crowe expected the German treaties to prescribe 'tariffs measurably less protective than the proposed tariff of France'. He thought that 'The higher the French set their charges the better the chances of those who advocate the German scheme.'[39]

Other states in the collapsing Anglo-French network welcomed the German scheme. Droz saw it as compensating for the losses expected from the French action. He thought of using the Swiss tariff 'as a lever to obtain concessions from the Italians, the Germans, and the Austrians' and thus to create 'a system of comparative free trade . . . in Central Europe'.[40] Liberal though Droz was on commercial issues, there was a vindictive side to his vision. He hoped that the new network would 'lead to the commercial isolation of France'. The Swiss could 'open to Italy and Austria their market for silk and wine, and to Germany their market for woollens; and in this way . . . endeavour to make France suffer for attempting to close her frontier.' Doing so might change the basic diplomatic orientation of Switzerland. If France no longer valued Swiss support, Droz wanted his countrymen to offer 'all the advantages in their power' to the Triple Alliance.

The British government remained preoccupied with the developments in Paris. After soliciting preliminary submissions from the principal Chambers of Commerce, trade associations and 'representative private firms', the Trade and Tariffs Committee hurried out its first report.[41] Though the gathered evidence was impressionistic, it convinced the committee that the proposed minimum tariff

> presents important increases of duty on most of the chief articles of British manufacture exported to France, notably on cotton yarns and tissues and on woollen tissues. Not only have these minimum duties been raised generally to the level of the General tariff of 1881, i.e. about 24 per cent above the present Conventional Tariff, but more complicated classifications have been introduced. . . . In many particular instances, the duties are raised much more than the above mentioned 24 per cent, the extra rates for bleaching, dyeing, printing, embroidering, and generally for all procedures which involve more labour as distinguished from more material, being considerably increased.

The French Chamber of Deputies was expected, under Méline's leadership, to make matters still worse. The British committee feared that the French action would reverse all of Cobden's hopes and excite 'a spirit of commercial war' among the nations of Europe, to the detriment of prosperity and peace.

Salisbury made full use of this report. He sent it to the ambassador in Paris, Lord Lytton, advising him to employ it discreetly in his representations to the French authorities, not hammering at them, yet taking 'advantage of any favourable opportunity to urge, specifically, that the present duties on woollens and cottons should not be augmented.'[42] He also provided Lytton with a summary of the reasons that might be used to stiffen the resistance of the French government to protectionist pressures.[43] Prepared by the Board of Trade, this pointed out that 'Nearly two-thirds of the foreign trade of France . . . is with European countries, and mostly with adjacent countries such as Germany, Italy, Spain, Austria, and England, with which it is provoking commercial war.' Without exaggerating the credit due to the handiwork of Cobden and Napoleon III, the Board claimed that the enormous expansion of international trade in the past 30 years could 'not have been attained without the aid' of that conjoint policy. It bemoaned the demand for retaliation that France was exciting all over Europe. Skating as far from Gladstonian orthodoxy as it dared, it warned: 'Even in this country . . . there are calls for a policy of retaliation.' Salisbury urged the Board to supply the Paris embassy with a more detailed commentary from the Chambers of Commerce. With the Board's concurrence, he despatched Mundella and the secretary of the Trade and Treaties Committee to Paris to brief the embassy and return with word on 'the exact position of the Tariff question in France'.[44]

The French government proceeded meanwhile to denounce all of its existing tariff treaties, though not those consisting simply of most-favoured-nation provisions or guaranteeing international trading rights. Austria-Hungary, Germany, Spain, Portugal and Romania followed suit, putting the entire structure of European tariffs up for revision. Negotiations then proceeded on two rival fronts, French and German. Action on the French front was, however, suspended while the legislature debated the alternative proposals presented by the government and the Méline commission. The delay stretched on longer than any of the French protagonists desired; and the deepening protectionist cast of the tariff as it proceeded through the legislature made the Foreign Minister hesitate to open negotiations with other states. By the autumn of 1891 the determination of the legislature to maintain the minimum tariff without reduction threatened to bring the days of French commercial treaties to a close.[45]

During the suspension of commercial diplomacy in France, the Central European states including Switzerland pushed ahead with their agenda. The lesser economic powers – Switzerland, Italy and Austria in this case – proved of greater importance in the reconstruction of the commercial treaty network in 1891 and 1892 than they had in the original network of the 1860s. Indeed, they were pivotal, as Crowe reported:

> The German Government, hearing that France had denounced her Commercial Treaty with Switzerland, has made distinct overtures to the Government at Berne for the sake of negotiating a Tariff Treaty, with the avowed intention of making a German–Swiss Conventional Tariff the basis of a system of customs duties applicable to all other Powers. Switzerland has

replied to these overtures amicably . . . Switzerland will denounce her Treaty of Commerce with Italy, in order to have the ground clear for negotiation on the wine duties. As Italy has been induced to prolong her commercial obligations to Austria for a year, it is clear that the success or failure of Central European arrangements must now greatly depend on the success of the Austro–German negotiations . . . at Vienna.[46]

France was not blind to these developments. But its ability to escape from the consequences of its self-willed isolation depended here too on the smaller states – Switzerland again and also Belgium, along with the Netherlands, Spain and the United Kingdoms of Sweden and Norway. When the French Foreign Minister made overtures to Switzerland on the basis of the prospective minimum tariff, the Swiss responded coldly, threatening reprisals if it was enacted. The Swiss still hoped to open negotiations on both sides. The commercial line-up on the continent was not driven by unrelieved antagonisms. Hoping for a competitive offer from the French, the Swiss government warned them that the proposals from Germany 'must inevitably lead to the negotiation of a Treaty in which distinctions must practically be made in favour of German as distinct from French products'.[47] Droz wanted to frame the Swiss offers to Germany and Italy in terms that would preserve Swiss bargaining power in talks with France.[48] Italy too attempted to reopen negotiations with the French.[49]

Germany pushed ahead before the French Foreign Minister was free to begin negotiations. Germany and Austria–Hungary had 'practically concluded' their treaty by April 1891. They would not, however, publish it 'until the negotiations with . . . Italy and Switzerland, for which it will form the model, are also published'.[50] The aim, as liberal commentators in France warned, was 'a vast Customs League, created for the sole purpose and with the obvious effect of building up a wall against France and her export trade, of which the French will have furnished the mortar and the stones.'[51] Germany probed deep into the French sphere with an overture to Belgium. The response was more anxious than cordial for fear of the French reaction. An agreement with Germany could not compensate Belgium for what it would lose by a rupture with France. Yet the still commercially liberal French Foreign Minister thought it 'quite natural' for Belgium to 'seek to improve her commercial relations with other countries'.[52] When he declined to discourage Belgium from pursuing the invitation from Germany, talks between the two countries began in Berlin. Germany widened its discussions still further to embrace Serbia, forging what the British minister at Dresden, in a nice turn of phrase, described as 'a fresh link in the chain of interdependency'.[53]

The rapid progress of these Central European talks was interrupted by an angry reaction among the Swiss voting public to the tariff that the French legislature was contemplating. This sentiment, empowered by the uniquely Swiss constitutional provision for a referendum, forced Swiss ministers to suspend their negotiations until the voters could express their will. The strength of the protectionist reaction manifested in the referendum then limited the concessions that the Swiss negotiators could offer to the Germans, Austrians and Italians. The difficulty deepened as the Swiss resistance encountered German demands. Germany pressed for steeper reductions in the Swiss tariff, particularly on silks, than it was willing to make in its own tariff.[54] Unable to resolve these differences in Bern, the German and Austrian negotiators moved their talks to Munich to deal with the Italians.

Britain took no direct part in these manœuvres, but Salisbury followed them attentively. He circulated the reports he received, often from Crowe, to the countries they concerned in order to promote a joint response to the French tariff from the continental states. Salisbury may have been the best informed European leader on commercial issues in 1891 and 1892. The almost daily reports from Crowe gave him a ring-side seat at the debate on the tariff in the French legislature. He encouraged Crowe and other members of the diplomatic service to keep him well informed on commercial manœuvres and diplomacy elsewhere in Europe. He had their despatches organised by country and date and printed for eventual presentation to parliament in three thick volumes.[55]

But he did not draw immediate public or parliamentary attention to these efforts, with ultimately frustrating consequences. Salisbury's aversion to public discussion reinforced the passivity with which the British public responded to the developments in commercial policy on the continent. He had taken steps to keep interested sectors of the industrial and commercial community in touch with those developments through the Trade and Tariffs Committee. But, as he wished, the committee worked quietly without precipitating much parliamentary debate. Salisbury knew that public protests about how much the French tariff might hurt British industry would only encourage French protectionists. He tried to convey this point in the spring of 1891 when he issued one of his infrequent statements to the public on the quickened pace of commercial policy on the continent. Addressing the Associated Chambers of Commerce as the body most likely to speak out, Salisbury warned:

This matter of commercial tariffs is singularly unfitted for the exercise of that magic spell of remonstrance and objurgation of which the people of this country are so fond. The object of a foreign Power in raising its tariffs is to exclude your commodities, and when you tell them in reproachful tones that the effect of their policy will be to exclude your commodities, the only result is they say, 'Thank you, I am very much obliged to you. That is just what I intended.' And they give another turn of the screw to the tariff in order that the effect may be quite unmistakable, and leave you to your reproaches. I, therefore, hope that, whatever other policy may be recommended to Her Majesty's Government by these enlightened Chambers, they will not go back to the somewhat antiquated policy of remonstrance, which will do the very reverse of what they intended.[56]

With these words, fortified by shared experience, Salisbury managed to persuade the Chambers of Commerce to abandon the premise that underlay the commercial policy of Cobden and indeed of Britain generally in the mid-nineteenth century: that the world would follow the example and preaching of Britain by embracing free trade. Behrens had always assumed that, if commercially well-informed representatives of Britain pointed out to their continental counterparts how unfair and economically unjustified were efforts to raise the tariff against British exports, they would see reason and keep them down. But that assumption had proven false. British faith in free trade survived this debunking, but as a commercial policy that was good for Britain, not as one bound to attract other countries.

Retaliatory sentiment spread all over the continent, in Switzerland and now Belgium. Lord Lytton at the Paris embassy hoped that the remaining bastions of liberal commercial sentiment in France – mainly the cities of Paris, Bordeaux, Marseilles and Lyons – might be roused by the spectre of the Méline tariff to ally themselves with the liberally inclined members of the government to bring the tariff down. But this estimate of the strength of this body of opinion and of ministerial spines was overly optimistic. The Trade and Tariffs Committee painted a bleak picture of the French tariff as it stood at the end of April. Wool, silk, flax and skins remained on the free list, 'on account mainly of the magnitude of the exports from France of manufactures from these articles'.[57] But the ministerial bill proposed to raise the duty on yarns and tissues 24 per cent above the current conventional tariff; and the legislature was both complicating the classification of goods and increasing the rates of duty. The prospective changes to the iron and steel manufactures that meant so much in Germany were not great, though here too there were some increases in duty and complications in classification. The main French concern was textiles. The complications there were greatest and the increases in duty highest.

While Méline continued to push the tariff up and the Central Europeans pushed their alternative network forward, the French Foreign Minister looked around for commercial partners. Perhaps one, certainly two would be sufficient to validate the minimum tariff as a basis for preservation of at least the core of the old network. Belgium would certainly join then, if not Switzerland. The most promising possibilities for the initial states willing to sign on were the Netherlands and the United Kingdoms of Sweden and Norway. But the reasons for their interest indicated how far the Méline tariff was reducing the attractions of economic alliance with France. The Netherlands was interested only because its trade with France was 'not of sufficient importance to warrant her opposing the desire of the French to negotiate'.[58] Sweden had 'more interest in navigation than in imports and exports', and hence would 'negotiate for the purpose of getting a Navigation Treaty'.

A rumour that France was approaching Romania prompted Salisbury to revive British discussions in that quarter. The rumour may have been unfounded. In any case Romania had lost interest in a separate agreement with Britain and was waiting for the French tariff to be settled before fixing its terms for participation in the tariff arrangements of Europe. Meanwhile the Romanian legislature hammered out its own general tariff. Britain had some influence on it. Representations from the Trade and Treaties Committee, which devoted its fourth report to Romania, induced the Romanian legislature to reduce the duty 'on several articles in which British commerce is interested',[59] particularly jute cloth and sacks, another branch of the ever sensitive textile trade.

The French tariff as it emerged from the Chamber of Deputies proved a little less protective than expected. The surprise came over plain single cotton yarns, which Lyons weavers and Calais lacemakers 'succeeded in keeping at rates far below those suggested by the Protectionist party and the Government'.[60] The duties on cotton stuffs were also reduced to levels lower than recommended by the government and Méline's committee, 'a result which was hardly to be anticipated a few months ago'. But the improvement did not last long. French cotton spinners rallied at Rouen against the reduction on yarns. As soon as the bill reached the Senate, the protectionists there under the leadership of Jules Ferry pushed the rates above what even Méline had advocated in the Chamber of Deputies – and in the process further delayed the final passage of the tariff.

c. The Continental Line-Up

The referendum in Switzerland, which took place in October 1891, broke the logjam that had held things up through the summer. While the 60 per cent who voted in favour of a high general tariff forced the Swiss negotiators to bargain stiffly, the 40 per cent minority allowed them to go back to work – but not with the French. The Swiss government let the French know that it would not negotiate on the basis of the minimum tariff. Talks were resumed with the central states of Italy, Austria and Germany. They had in fact continued informally through the summer; and a 'complete understanding' had been reached 'in reference to woollens entering Switzerland from Germany'.[61] Crowe learnt that 'The scale has been delicately arranged so as to make the import of French fine woollen stuffs very difficult, even if most-favoured-nation treatment should be conceded to France. . . . On the whole,' he concluded, 'the prospect is that of an understanding of the Central European Powers, and of commercial isolation of France.'

This set of negotiations still had its troubles. Belgium insisted on keeping wine off the table with Germany in order to retain something for bargaining with France.[62] Germany had little to offer Belgium aside from the removal of the railway rates that favoured German over foreign freight. Yet Germany pressed for lower duties than Belgium, with its already low tariff, was ready to concede. There was more trouble in the negotiations between Switzerland and Italy. Swiss exports to Italy had been falling in recent years, while Italian exports to Switzerland had been on the increase.[63] Switzerland needed to make up in the markets of the Triple Alliance what it stood to lose in France.

But the strains in the Central European group never grew as bitter as the feeling directed against France. Protectionists in the French legislature shaped tariff provisions that were certain to repel foreign goods and keep ministers from making concessions in treaty talks. Ferry in the Senate boasted of his contempt for treaties. 'Assez de ces duperies,' he cried, 'restons chez nous.'[64] Even Belgium was reluctant to negotiate with France. Spain dearly wanted an agreement because France had become far and away the best market for its wine, but the French Senate rendered agreement impossible by raising the wine duty to a level that the French government warned would be intolerable.[65] There was a further sting to the French duty on alcohol. Accusing Spain of fortifying its wine with German alcohol, France held up an agreement sought between Spain and Germany, which wanted better access to the Spanish market for its alcohol.[66] That was one of the few clever if malicious provisions in the French tariff. It was on the whole poorly designed for tactical purposes. There was too little difference between the minimum and the maximum tariff to make other states anxious to gain the blessings of the former and avoid the penalties of the latter. As Swiss exporters remarked, 'both Tariffs represent a closed door, and it is a matter of indifference . . . whether the door be double or single barred.'[67]

The Central European bloc reached an almost complete set of agreements at the end of the first week in December. Only the relationship between Switzerland and Italy remained unresolved. The basic treaty in Central Europe, the one between Germany and Austria-Hungary, had been agreed for some time but had been withheld from the public. By waiting to present that agreement alongside the treaties they had reached with Italy, the two German powers gave their action a conservative cast as a corollary to the Triple Alliance. By including Belgium, they minimised the impression of hostility to France. They were intent on opening up the market comprised by the signatory states. The Austrian government looked with gratification at 'a market comprising populations amounting to over 130,000,000'.[68] Within this market the treaties had not so much lowered tariffs as prevented them from rising for a dozen years, until 1903 when the treaties would need to be renewed. As the head of the British embassy explained, 'The great point achieved is a stability of duties.' The achievement was all the more remarkable because Austria had been the *fons et origo* of protectionism. Three times in the past decade the Austrian tariff had been altered, each time upward; and 'each alteration has been regarded in other countries as almost a declaration of commercial war, and has called forth consequent commercial reprisals.' Now, '[t]hough it cannot be said that the protective system is entirely abolished', it was at least diluted. The British chargé summed up the principles of the treaty as: 'Cheapening of the necessaries of life; freedom as far as possible, or binding, of the duties on raw materials; reduction of the duties on all auxiliary substances necessary for industry; and protection of the manufactured articles themselves.' The persistence of protectionism was quite evident within Germany. The British consul-general in Frankfurt insisted that 'The Commercial Treaties which Germany has just concluded do not imply free trade, but a protective Tariff on the part of Germany modified by similar protective Tariffs of the other countries.'[69]

The new treaties had their aggressive side. They were designed to affect France and Russia unfavourably. The negotiators had 'abstained from reducing many of the duties, especially on articles of luxury, which affect French industry'. The duty on certain types of wine was lowered with similar intent, 'to encourage the use of Italian as against French wines'.[70] The crucial reduction in the German tariff so far as Austria-Hungary was concerned, on grain, gave Hungarian agriculture 'an important advantage' over its 'most important neighbouring competitors, Russia and Rumania'.[71] Germany made its concessions generally in order to acquire the privilege, that France had enjoyed since 1860 but was now surrendering, of 'getting the Tariffs of neighbouring countries moulded in a form favourable to French trade'. Germany 'hastened to obtain that advantage for herself . . . by concluding as many Treaties as possible before France was in the field'.[72] There was a further political dimension to these commercial considerations. Caprivi explained to the Reichstag that

in the case of Belgium and Switzerland they had simply been actuated by an earnest desire to live on friendly and neighbourly terms with those countries. It was otherwise, however, with the Triple Alliance. This had been concluded for the preservation of peace, and without the least aggressive aim. But . . . [i]t was their interest to strengthen their allies, so that, if in spite of all their efforts the peace of Europe should be broken, they might be able to bear the necessary armaments.[73]

d. Implications for Britain

The Economist mistook the economic rationale that Caprivi presented for the treaties to the Reichstag as tantamount to a confession that protectionism had failed.[74] But the level of the tariffs established in the Central European treaties of 1891–92 was slightly higher than in Bismarck's tariff of 1879. Protectionism in Germany had come to stay. Where Caprivi took issue with his predecessor was not in his protectionism but in his insistence that Germany must withdraw from the European treaty network and set its tariff independently. The advantage that Caprivi saw in Bismarck's 'autonomous fixing of our Tariff to suit our requirements, and without regard to foreigners, was the assistance given to our home industries'.[75] But that assistance had resulted in an overstocked home market and the production of an excess of goods for which markets proved harder to find abroad when other countries raised their tariffs in line with Bismarck's practice. The remedy that Caprivi offered for this situation lay not so much in reduced customs duties as in arrangements between co-operating states to promote the exchange of goods among themselves.

While the Germans set up their network, the French government was obliged by protectionist forces in the legislature to surrender any hope of reaching agreements on the basis of the minimum tariff with other European states. All France could do now was implement unilaterally by legislation what it could not accomplish through bilateral negotiation. The arrangement to which France had resorted after the breakdown of negotiations in 1882, of giving Britain most-favoured-nation status by legislative action, replaced network diplomacy as the model for French relations with most other European states. The French ministry gained legislative support for a bill to give the minimum tariff for one year to those states that granted France most-favoured-nation status or access to their conventional tariff.

The French withdrawal from tariff treaty-making left the emerging Central European network without a rival. So long as Britain remained unwilling to re-enact tariffs for bargaining purposes, Salisbury could not join the new network. But he could find out how far Britain would benefit from its most-favoured-nation entitlement to the conventional tariff that the new network established. In doing so he could also ascertain how costly the policy of unilateral free trade was to British commerce. Good free traders like *The Economist* challenged his belief that the policy was detrimental. 'While it is true that of late there has been some shrinkage in the volume of our foreign trade,' the journal conceded, still 'there is as yet little to justify Lord Salisbury in attributing this decline to the Protectionist legislation of other countries.'[76] The prospect of a heightened tariff abroad in fact expanded British exports initially as businesses hurried to place their goods inside the country that was about to be protected. In the longer run, admittedly, higher duties had 'some restrictive influence upon our trade,' but higher duties also raised the costs of production in the protected country, and were hence supposed to cripple it when it came to compete in foreign markets. 'Take Germany, for instance. Her manufacturers are so grievously hampered by the dearness of coal and iron, that whereas at one time it seemed as if they would wrest from us a considerable portion of our foreign trade, yet now, notwithstanding all their cleverness and push, if they are holding their own, that is the most than can be said of them.' Even so, *The Economist* implicitly conceded that protectionist tariffs hurt Britain in its most valuable market, the continent, though an imperial slant turned that confession into a boast: 'the very efforts that are being made to shut certain markets against us give us new advantages in other markets, and especially in all new markets such as those which may be opened up in Africa and elsewhere.'

These imperial possibilities led activists in the Conservative Party to a quite different conclusion. Discouraged by the outlook on the continent and excited by the potential of the empire, Fair Traders turned into advocates of imperial preference. Disregarding advice from Salisbury, they carried the National Union of Conservative Associations with them in November 1891 while France debated the Méline tariff and the Germans finalised their treaties. This partisan pressure further encouraged Salisbury to look closely at what was happening in Central Europe and consider what might be done. As soon as the new treaties were presented to their respective legislatures, Salisbury asked the British diplomatic staff to send him detailed reports on the likely bearing of the new tariff on British trade and commerce. If reports did not come in quickly or in as much detail as he desired, he sent out firm reminders.

The responses that he received did not point in any obvious direction so far as British trade policy was concerned. The Central European treaties were designed to benefit only the signatories, not those states that might draw advantage indirectly through most-favoured-nation privileges. Caprivi regarded most-favoured-nation affiliates and particularly Britain as harmful to German interests. The British consul-general in Frankfurt observed that 'The German Government in its endeavour to keep the most favoured nations as much as possible from participating in the reductions granted in the new Treaties, seems in the first place to have thought of Great Britain (along with France), of whose industrial competition Germany entertains great fear.'[77]

The consensus of the reports Salisbury received suggested that the Central European network would do Britain little good but no harm. The report from Austria-Hungary indicated that 'few articles of British import should be affected to any important extent.'[78] A more comprehensive assessment came from Germany, where reports were commissioned from regional consulates as well as from the embassy in Berlin. A lot was at stake here for Britain. In the most meticulous of these reports, Gerson Bleichröder, Bismarck's banker who served as independent consul for Britain in Berlin, estimated that the tariff provisions of the four German treaties – with Austria, Belgium, Italy and Switzerland – would affect almost one-fifth of Britain's exports to Germany.[79] The expectations elsewhere in Germany ranged from an increase of trade with Britain[80] to a diversion of it, concentrating it instead in the signatory states. Bleichröder thought Germany would import more 'raw materials, compounds, and half-finished goods' from its treaty partners, to be finished in Germany and then exported to Britain.[81] On the Belgian side, there were apprehensions of a deluge of goods from Germany, but not such as would hurt imports from Britain. Britain was expected to benefit from the cheaper provision for transport by land and sea that Germany under this treaty accorded to goods coming from Belgium.[82] The only gloomy report so far as Britain was concerned came from Italy. Of all the Central European partners, Italy made the least reduction in its tariff, and it intended to raise the duty on items that it excluded from the treaties in order to protect its infant industries, particularly in textiles and particularly against the competition from Britain.[83]

Italy proved to be the most difficult partner generally in the formation of the new network. Its talks with Switzerland reached an impasse in January 1892 over cotton goods and machinery, shortly before the other treaties came into operation. Italy defended its refusal to improve the terms of entry for these products from Switzerland on the grounds that 'it would be obliged to give the same advantage to British trade under the most-favoured-nation treatment clause.'[84] This failure to reach agreement did not prevent the other treaties from coming into force at the end of the month. Next day, on 1 February, the Méline tariff took effect in France.

The resulting transformation in the ground rules for continental commerce made remarkably little impact in Britain, even on the business community. Already inclined to look outside Europe for new markets, Chambers of Commerce averted their eyes from the continent. Instead, in common with former Fair Traders in parliament, they paid more attention to the market in the colonies. One of the drawbacks of the quiet competence with which Salisbury, the Trade and Treaties Committee and an increasing number of the British diplomatic as well as consular corps on the continent handled commercial diplomacy was that it made little stir at home. Salisbury kept in close touch with the Trade and Treaties Committee and sought its advice before deciding what stance to adopt in the major theatres of negotiation on the continent. He forwarded reports from the committee and from embassies and consulates on the continent to the Chambers of Commerce and the interested press. But this form of transmission muted the message.

There was one part of the continent where Britain could afford to look with complacency; namely France and the efforts it was making to avoid the most damaging consequences of its new tariff. The French government still hoped to turn the minimum tariff into a treaty-based or conventional tariff for at least part of Europe. But these efforts won a meagre response. Only one state, the United Kingdoms of Norway and Sweden, agreed to a treaty on that basis, and then reluctantly, because all that it gained, aside from its crucial navigation clauses, was assurance against differential punishment of its exports to France and the freedom to raise its own tariff as it wished. Otherwise, as the Norwegian *Morgenblatet* put it, 'The French market will in future be even more effectually closed than at present against all the products of our fisheries. . . . Henceforth we must be prepared for the French market becoming of less importance to us.'[85]

The one benefit of the new French system for Britain was that it received the minimum tariff. Though the free-trading Netherlands treated France automatically as a most-favoured-nation, France wanted a treaty with the Netherlands to link this most-favoured-nation treatment with acceptance of the French minimum tariff. But the Dutch refused to make any reciprocal response. Unable to find any state to second the acceptance of its minimum tariff, France settled for much less than it wanted from Belgium and Switzerland. Belgium exchanged its lowest tariff for the French minimum but remained free to withdraw from that agreement at any time and reserved the right to raise the duty on any exports from France that benefited from governmental drawbacks or bounties, indirect forms of compensation for the high tariff.[86] Like Belgium, Switzerland exchanged most-favoured-nation treatment for the French minimum tariff without promising for how long. But the Swiss arrangement depended upon the conclusion before the end of June of a treaty with France involving reductions in the French tariff steep enough to win approval from the Swiss legislature. France and Italy made a truce in their tariff war by exchanging the general Italian tariff for the French minimum. Germany enjoyed access to the minimum tariff under the Treaty of Frankfurt. No agreement, however, was possible between France and Spain because of the punishing duty directed against Spain in the French minimum tariff on wine. As a result, Spain and France hurled their maximum tariffs at each other.

e. The Spanish Sequel

A seismic shift had taken place in the structure of European commercial policy by the end of January 1892. Its implications were clarified over the next six months in negotiations with Spain. Spain had equipped itself to do battle with France with a maximum–minimum tariff of the sort that Spain had introduced in 1877 and France had recently copied. The Spanish Foreign Minister, the Duke of Tetuan, explained that the new tariff would 'contain two columns: the first to be applied to nations not having entered into commercial arrangements with Spain, and the second to those which have done so.'[87] The Spanish ministry, like the French, hoped originally to reduce the second or minimum tariff in exchange for reciprocal concessions from prospective treaty partners. But again as in France, these ministerial hopes were dashed by intransigent protectionism in the Spanish Cortes.

The central concern for Spain remained to bring down the prohibitive French duty on wine in order to preserve the great new market that Spain had acquired while phylloxera ravaged the vineyards of France. Failing that crucial concession from France, Spain would need to expand the market for its wine elsewhere, in Britain and the states of the Central European network. In truth, they constituted a poor alternative to France. British consumption of Spanish wine had not significantly increased since the agreement of 1886; and the Central European states produced wine themselves. Nevertheless, the failure of the French government to reduce its wine duty opened the possibility for a reorientation of Spanish commercial policy away from France towards Britain and Central Europe.

Britain proved able to play a central part in the ensuing set of negotiations in a way that it had not when the Central European network was set up. The British treaty with Spain was not due to expire until the end of June, whereas most of Spain's treaties with other European states expired in February. The desire of these states to enjoy the current conventional tariff, which was much lower than the new Spanish minimum, thus gave Britain a pivotal position until the end of June. Salisbury made full use of this leverage. Though he could not leave London, he used the telegraph to give him tight control over the negotiations in Madrid. His ability as Foreign Secretary to relay telegrams from Madrid to other European capitals further tightened his grip on the process, as did his prime-ministerial authority in dealing with the Board of Trade.

Even so, the Spanish negotiations exposed how the inability to retaliate undermined Salisbury's power. The experience prompted him to appeal at the opening of the general election campaign in Britain for the restoration of a tariff for bargaining purposes. Salisbury was, however, among the few who had followed the commercial diplomacy of Europe closely over the past year and hence fully understood the dynamics of the process. Even so well-informed a journal as *The Economist* displayed ignorance about the current state of European commercial diplomacy. Salisbury appealed to common sense but his appeal was weakened by the lack of common knowledge. The reticence in public which was indispensable to his practice of diplomacy deprived him of the evidence he needed to win electoral consent.

The first step for the Spanish, after creating their two-tier tariff, was to gain acceptance of the minimum tariff from the continental states that wanted to extend their expiring commercial treaties until the end of June. This business went on during the final days of January amid a flurry of activity that included formal completion of the Central European treaties and enactment of the

French tariff. The members of the Central European network did as Spain bade, but grudgingly, none more so than the Germans, who gave their network assertive leadership. Switzerland and Spain reached a provisional agreement, 'subject to reserves under which Spain recovers full liberty of action in regard to duties on foreign alcohol, and Switzerland similar liberty as regards certain articles of no importance to Spain, such as sparkling wines and vinegar'.[88] Belgium put up more of a fight. And when Spain insisted that Germany too must pay the high duties of the minimum tariff on spirits, Germany forced Spain to pay twice the duty laid down in the German treaties with Austria and Italy on wines.[89]

Once these arrangements were in place, Spain invited nine states – the five Central European affiliates, plus Britain, the Netherlands, Russia and the United Kingdoms of Sweden and Norway – 'to send Representatives as soon as possible' to Madrid to settle the commercial arrangements that would take effect when all the treaties expired at the end of June.[90] Spain attached two caveats to the invitation. It excluded most-favoured-nation provisions from the envisaged agreements; and the agreements would apply only to peninsular Spain, not to its colonies. Liberal as well as conservative Spaniards agreed that the most-favoured-nation clause had 'increased imports to Spain, while it has diminished exportation'.[91] Instead of a most-favoured-nation clause, the Spanish wanted to limit each agreement to the items in which the negotiating state was most interested in exchange for the particular concessions the Spanish government sought from that country. What Spain wanted from Britain was reduction of the duties on wine and raisins. The Spanish argued that the duty on the raisins they produced should be brought into line with the duty on currants that Britain had reduced as part of its trade agreement with Greece. Much though British free traders liked to think that their tariff did not discriminate between states, continental Europeans knew better. Still, no matter how just the demand on raisins, the Spanish proposal in 1892 was as bad from the British standpoint as the French proposals made by Tirard a decade earlier. Both expected the British to reduce their customs duties in return for an increase in the tariff on the continent.

Prickly though it was, Salisbury seized the opportunity. He put Crowe on the British negotiating team and handed the Spanish invitation to the new British ambassador, Sir Henry Drummond Wolff, as his first important assignment. He also passed the invitation to the Trade and Treaties Committee, asking for advice on which to base Drummond Wolff's instructions. The committee replied with a sobering report.[92] It rejected the terms in which the Spanish government couched its invitation as providing 'no suitable basis for negotiation'. To begin with, on average the rates of duty in the Spanish minimum tariff, though some 15 to 20 per cent lower than the maximum, more than doubled the rates Britain enjoyed under its current 1886 treaty with Spain.

Some parts of England such as Sheffield and Manchester had a greater interest in trade with the Spanish colonies, which were to be excluded from the treaty, than with Spain itself. Limitation of the treaty to specified commodities would not work acceptably for Britain because British trade with Spain embraced a wide range of goods of ever changing variety according to the advance of technology and whim of fashion. Far from approving of the further reduction Spain sought in Britain's wine duties, the Trade and Treaties Committee advised Salisbury to warn Spain that it must not take the decrease Britain had made in 1886 for granted.

Salisbury strengthened that hint of retaliation in drawing up his instructions for Drummond Wolff. What was more, he induced the Liberal Unionist Chancellor of Exchequer, G.J. Goschen, to make the threat public in his forthcoming budget address. Goschen, though the most orthodox of economists, had recently thought of restoring a registration duty on imports and exports for revenue purposes.[93] From the perspective of the Treasury, he was happy to regain the freedom to raise the wine duty. *The Economist* encouraged his action.[94]

Negotiations began in Madrid once Drummond Wolff and the rest of the British team had arrived. Wolff and Crowe plunged into preparatory discussions with the ambassadors from the network states and, more slowly, entered into formal exchanges with the Spanish authorities. France maintained an unseen but constant presence at the talks. Spain occasionally reminded the participants that its overriding concern was to regain access to the French market.

At the first meeting with the delegation from Britain, the Spanish offered reductions on the tariff of 1886 for a number of commodities, including woollens, cottons, iron and steel goods, and machinery, a list also limited to items not produced in Spain. In return they asked for reduction of the British duty on heavy wines, equalisation of the raisin and currant duty, 'and conditions, not specified, for cattle and fresh fruit'.[95] When Salisbury received a telegraphic synopsis of this offer, he threatened to retaliate: 'we shall return to wine duties before 1886 if our textiles are put in a worse position than now.'[96] He gave the Spanish offer to the Trade and Treaties Committee to develop counterproposals. Meanwhile Goschen made Salisbury's threat public, though in more hypothetical and contingent terms than Salisbury used in the privacy of diplomatic despatches. Goschen told the House of Commons, 'there must not be an impression either in Spain or elsewhere that, if the concessions which were given to this country in 1886 should be withdrawn, it is certain they will retain the fiscal advantages as regards their wines which were given in 1886. There are strong fiscal reasons why we should put a greater duty upon alcohol.'[97]

The principal Spanish commissioner, Reverter, responded bluntly to the British threat. He was, he said, 'indifferent . . . to the duty on wine being raised in England' and 'would rejoice . . . at the negotiations with England falling through, as this would render easy the conclusion of a Treaty with France'.[98] His statement indicated that the British threat would not be enough to preserve the 1886 settlement. The British negotiating team and the Commercial Department at the Foreign Office concluded, not that threats of retaliation were useless, but rather that this particular threat was not enough.

The question for Britain turned into a choice between accepting the minimum Spanish tariff and holding out for better terms with the risk of being subjected to the maximum. For a while Crowe doubted that Britain would have even this choice. 'I very much fear,' he wrote,

> that the policy of Spain is not to prolong Treaties, but to tide over the period during which they will remain in force. If by the 1st July she has entered into no new engagements with the Triple Alliance or with us, she will be in a position to treat us all as she now treats France, i.e., levy upon us all the duties of the Maximum Tariff. She may then go to the French and suggest that the positions being equalized all round, a favourable opportunity has arisen for negotiations. If this should succeed, and France give Spain some privileges as regards wine, the Spaniards might reduce some of their protectionist charges in favour of their new allies, and these advantages would be limited to the one State to which they were originally conceded.[99]

Gradually, however, it came to look as though Salisbury's threat over the wine duties would save Britain from the Spanish maximum. The Spanish negotiations were pervaded by considerations of retaliatory power, and the supreme possessor of such power in this context was France. Its extremely high maximum tariff and the size of its wine market enabled it to demand more generous terms from Spain than Spain's other commercial partners could expect. As Drummond Wolff put it, 'France with her new Tariff is in a commanding position to bargain for concessions.'[100] The Prime Minister and Foreign Minister of Spain confirmed this assessment. France, they told Wolff, could 'give very large concessions owing to her Maximum Tariff . . . while the United Kingdom had very little to give.'[101] The Prime Minister added that both France and Spain had 'a fighting Tariff . . . and if England had deprived herself of such weapons he could only accept things as they were and make the best bargain for his country.'[102] At the same time the tariff armament of Germany and its network associates put them in a stronger position than Britain to demand most-favoured-nation treatment from Spain. When Crowe spoke of the risk that Spain would subject all the other states of Europe to its maximum tariff while giving France the minimum, the German ambassador replied scornfully. Even the ambassador for the free-trading Netherlands threatened to retaliate if Spain discriminated against Dutch goods.[103] Surveying the situation from the Commercial Department at the Foreign Office, Kennedy bemoaned Britain's lack of 'a fighting Tariff or discriminating Customs Regulations' in the face of the threat to the most-favoured-nation clause which had become the cornerstone of his policy.[104]

Within less than a month of the opening of negotiations, Spain withdrew its offer of terms for a lasting treaty with Britain and replaced it with proposals for a provisional arrangement. It offered the minimum tariff for British exports to peninsular Spain, though not to the colonies. In return it demanded maintenance of the existing British tariff on Spanish exports, in other words withdrawal of Salisbury's threat to raise the wine duties.[105] Salisbury relayed the offer to the Trade and Treaties Committee, which observed: 'The Convention of 1886 would, under such an arrangement, remain in force for Spanish goods, while for British manufactures imported into Spain, the duties would be about two-and-a half times the rates of that Convention.'[106] Britain simply could not accept such a worsening of the status quo.

While Spain probed the impasse that its commercial discussions had reached in every direction, its prospective partners sought to maintain a united resistance. Spain secured its first success with Norway and Sweden; but that was for a permanent tariff treaty, the sort of agreement that could not be implemented until the Cortes convened to approve it, perhaps not for another year. When Italy showed signs of succumbing to the blandishments of Spain, Salisbury made sure that the Triple Alliance pressed it back into line. Spain did its utmost to conciliate the French and here seemed on the verge of success, to the dismay of Britain and the Central European network.

In the midst of these negotiations, about which the public had until then known little, Salisbury presented the problem as clearly as he could to the British electorate. The parliament elected in 1886 was hurrying to its dissolution, and a general election would take place during the summer. It was possible, though not likely, that Salisbury's Conservatives and their Liberal Unionist allies would hang on to power by the barest of margins. Salisbury needed to put Conservative activists in the constituencies in good heart for the fight. He could count on a wide measure of tolerance from the Liberal Unionists as each party rallied its particular troops. But these considerations, though of crucial domestic importance, did not entirely govern what he said in his address at the opening of the election campaign to the Home Counties Division of the National Union of Conservative Associations at Hastings. If Britain was ever to regain its effectiveness in the commercial diplomacy of Europe, he had to convince the public of the indispensability of tariffs for bargaining.

Speaking from an experience that every day's events reinforced, Salisbury presented the need for these tools as a matter of logic and common sense: 'this little island lives as a trading island,' he reminded his audience.[107] Britain could not produce enough to feed and employ its population without importing foodstuffs and exporting the products of its great industries. These exports were under fire.

We live in an age of a war of tariffs. Every nation is trying how it can, by agreement with its neighbour, get the greatest possible protection for its own industries, and, at the same time, the greatest possible access to the markets of its neighbours. This kind of negotiation is continually going on. It has been going on for the last year and a half with great activity. . . . what I observe is that while A is very anxious to get a favour of B, and B is anxious to get a favour of C, nobody cares two straws about getting the commercial favour of Great Britain. What is the reason of that? It is that in this great battle Great Britain has deliberately stripped herself of the armour and the weapons by which the battle has to be fought. You cannot do business in this world of evil and suffering on those terms. If you go to market you must bring money with you; if you fight you must fight with the weapons with which those you have to contend against are fighting. . . . The weapon with which they all fight is admission to their own markets – that is to say, A says to B, 'if you will make your duties such that I can sell in your market, I will make my duties such that you can sell in my market.' But we begin by saying, 'We will levy no duties on anybody,' and we declare that it would be contrary and disloyal to the glorious and sacred doctrine of free trade to levy any duty on anybody for the sake of what we can get by it. It may be noble, but it is not business. On those terms you will get nothing. . . . if you intend, in this conflict of commercial treaties, to hold your own, you must be prepared, if need be, to inflict upon the nations which injure you the penalty which is in your hands, that of refusing them access to your markets. (Loud and pro-longed cheers and a voice, 'Common sense at last.')

Salisbury made allowance for the main exception to the commercial policy he advocated: Britain could not apply it to the United States. The United States were more thoroughly protectionist than any European state save Russia and refused to comply with the unconditional most-favoured-nation clause that even Austria respected. British commercial policy had focused on Europe for the past 40 years because of the impediments to entry into the US market: first the Civil War, and then successive postwar escalations in the tariff.

The Power we have most reason to complain of is the United States, [yet] what we want the United States to furnish us with mostly are articles of food essential to the feeding of the people, and raw materials necessary to our manufactures, and we cannot exclude one or the other without serious injury to ourselves. . . . We must confine ourselves, at least for the present, to those subjects on which we should not suffer very much whether the importation continued or diminished . . . if it is a question of wine, or silk, or spirits, or gloves, or lace, or anything of that kind . . . I should not in the least shrink from diminishing the consumption . . . for the purpose of maintaining our rights in this commercial war, and of insisting on our rights of access to the markets of our neighbours. . . . We must distinguish between consumer and consumer, and while jealously preserving the rights of a consumer who is co-extensive with a whole industry, or with the whole people of the country, we may fairly use our power over an importation which merely ministers to luxury, in order to maintain our own in this great commercial battle.

The problem for Britain in common with the other states of Europe was, as Salisbury said, one of access to each other's markets. Even highly protectionist countries on the continent made the dual use of tariffs that he described, to gain access to neighbouring markets as well as to protect the market at home. Spain was trying to do precisely that. There was a risk at the moment that legislative pressure would force France to depart from this European pattern. But no other continental state was tempted to follow Méline's example. Countries like Switzerland wished only to demonstrate to the French how much they would hurt themselves by withdrawal. Germany had abandoned Bismarck's unilateralism and returned to commercial treaty-making. While all the continental states except for the Netherlands agreed on the need to protect their home markets, all save possibly France agreed on the need for market access to each other. Tariffs on the continent were designed to serve both purposes. The question for the British was whether they could devise a tariff that would serve to keep the continental market open to them without damaging the economy at home. European experience convinced Salisbury that Britain could do so with tariffs on luxuries, beginning of course with the existing duty on wine.

The suggestion was a modest one – as was the proposal that Joseph Chamberlain made a decade later for discriminatory use of the registration duty on corn in order to consolidate the empire. Chamberlain made that proposal in the privacy of the cabinet. Salisbury presented his on the hustings; and as Chamberlain was to discover, the publicity made a dramatic difference. It deprived Salisbury's proposal of its intrinsic modesty. The public was startled, unprepared for what he suggested because it had heard little about the confidential commercial diplomacy of the past 18 months. Salisbury's initiative was fiercely attacked, and it drew a disappointing electoral response.

The cheers of the Conservative activists at Hastings had scarcely died down when *The Economist* levelled its guns at the Prime Minister. It sought to present its reply with the practicality and common sense for which Salisbury had appealed. It asked 'whether this war of tariffs in which we are asked to take a part has really worked to the advantage of those nations by whom it has been waged'.[108] As *The Economist* saw it, continental states had learnt the folly of their ways. 'Germany, Austria-Hungary, and other European States . . . after fighting each other for years, have come to the conclusion that the game is a losing one, and modified their tariffs accordingly.' But this was to confuse a war of tariffs such as so far only Italy and France had engaged in with the dual usage of tariffs that Salisbury had described: their deployment to gain access to neighbouring markets as well as to protect the home market. That was becoming almost universal practice on the continent.

There were better grounds for *The Economist*'s claim that the states jockeying for commercial advantage on the continent had 'given neutrals an opportunity of benefiting at their expense'. The Méline tariff was indeed already driving French goods out of neighbouring markets. The replacements came, however, from tariff-equipped Germany, as *The Economist* noted in passing, as well as from Britain with its 'all round commercial neutrality'. Examining Salisbury's argument more closely, it dismissed his talk of tariffs on luxuries as 'only a pop-gun'. If Britain was to engage in the warfare of tariffs effectively, it would have to 'begin by going in for a system of wholesale protection'. There was plenty of evidence to back up this contention. The crucial component in the German tariff of 1879 had been in its extension to agricultural produce, an addition that was deeply repugnant to the British. The most controversial part of the Méline tariff even in France was its application to raw materials. But Salisbury had guarded himself from this criticism by excluding the United States as a major supplier of food and raw materials from his proposal, and also by repudiating any restoration of the Corn Laws. As for its being 'a pop-gun', Salisbury knew from daily experience that much of the commercial warfare in Europe revolved around the luxury items he identified, silks in Italy and France, lace in Belgium and wine everywhere.

Still the impending general election in Britain had little impact on the Spanish negotiations, which moved ahead with a dynamic of their own. The way they developed during the final month before the expiration of the existing Spanish treaties suggested that France was not as completely detached from the treaty network of Europe as had seemed likely at the beginning of the year.

The Salisbury ministry kept its ability to manipulate the wine duties in reserve by saying at the beginning of June that there was no longer enough time for legislative amendment before parliament was dissolved.[109] Spain treated the announcement as a British promise to maintain the existing duty on wine in return for access on the basis of the minimum tariff to the Spanish colonial as well as peninsular market. The inclusion of the colonies met the minimum requirements of the British Trade and Treaties Committee.[110] In line with advice from the Board, Salisbury merely acknowledged the statement the Spanish ambassador made to him about the arrangement. In return, but without making the connection explicit, Salisbury repeated the statement made earlier in the House of Commons that 'since the present Parliament would be dissolved in a few days . . . there was no prospect that the present Parliament would make any alterations in the Tariff.'[111]

The other European states reached similar terms with Spain, always by uni-lateral action on each side, replicating the pattern France had set *vis-à-vis* Britain in 1882. These arrangements involved the Spanish minimum tariff on the one side and a variety of caveats and grudging understandings on the other. All were explicitly temporary, pending the conclusion of bilateral treaties. Germany sought and Italy found a formula to ensure that Spain would not be admitted to all the advantages of the Central European treaty tariff until its minimum tariff was improved. The continental states were as reluctant as Britain to put up with the steep rise in the rates of duty in the Spanish tariff. Spain won acceptance for its *modus vivendi* from other states only after the most reluctant among them, namely France, agreed to it. The French government did not regard acceptance of the Spanish minimum tariff in return for its own as an equitable exchange. The rates in the Spanish minimum were higher than in the French. More seriously, the French minimum would give Spain its primary objective, a lower duty on wine. Before making that concession, the French wanted to ensure that they could find a market in Spain for the textiles they might not be able to sell in Switzerland if the talks in that direction broke down. What induced the French ministry to accept the Spanish proposal was the prospect of a hostile wall of tariffs all along the eastern and southern borders of France with Switzerland, Italy and Spain.[112] While that prospect might dismay the French ministry, it was not enough to secure ratification of a formal treaty from the French legislature. But the ministry could make a temporary arrangement that did not require speedy legislative approval.

Those were considerations on the French side. Other states were more con-cerned about the possibility of a treaty giving Spain access to the French wine market in return for extraordinary privileges for France in the Spanish market, ones that might not be extended to other countries. But the French ministry did not feel strong enough vis-à-vis the legislature to conclude a treaty even along such advantageous lines. The temporary French acceptance of the Spanish minimum tariff signalled the failure of their attempt to conclude a formal treaty, and hence removed the danger that held other states back from accepting the *modus vivendi* offered by Spain. Now, though Spanish producers would enjoy increased internal protection, there would be no inequality between other countries in their terms of access to the Spanish market. Spain stayed on the periphery of the European commercial treaty system, linked by arrangements more limited than most-favoured-nation status.

The arrangements with Spain brought an end to two years of hectic com-mercial diplomacy in which the Anglo-French network of the 1860s was dis-mantled and superseded by a Central European one. The main set of Central European treaties had been completed in April when, after great difficulty,

Switzerland and Italy settled their differences. In keeping with its treaties with Austria and Germany, Italy induced Switzerland to reduce the duties it levied on Italian agricultural produce in return for reductions in the Italian tariff on silks, machinery and other manufactured goods. Similarly, in return for concessions from Germany particularly on wine and citrus fruits, 'Italian duties were lowered to permit an increased importation of German industrial products, especially her chemicals, textiles, machines, and motors, whose value jumped from 134 million lire in 1887 to 203 million in 1900.' Austria too, though a wine producer itself, opened its borders to Italian wines, ever a crucial commodity in these negotiations.[113] Inhibited from bargaining with its wine duties, the British government could not wrest benefits for its industry on the German scale from Italy. Britain still benefited from the Swiss-Italian treaty more than from the other Central European agreements because it lowered the Italian duty on some cotton textiles including items that Britain had marketed successfully in Italy before the raising of its tariff in 1887.[114] Yet the improvement was not enough to reverse the reduction in demand for British cottons, which was at its 'greatest . . . in the important markets of France and Italy'.[115] On balance, Britain did not seem to have either gained or lost substantially from the formation of the Central European network. The settlement with France in January and with Spain in June ensured that it would lose no more from their increased tariffs than any other state. Even so, the squeeze on exports from Britain was tightening across the continent.

And Britain refused to do anything about it. Rejecting Lord Salisbury's advice, it confirmed its acceptance of a peripheral position in European tariff-making at the general election that took place in July. Though Salisbury's remarks at Hastings heartened Conservative activists, the electorate as a whole responded with indifference verging on hostility. Chamberlain, by now the Liberal Unionist leader in the Commons, had long favoured the retaliatory use of tariffs, particularly against Spain. Yet he estimated that Salisbury's words at Hastings cost the Conservative and Unionist forces a dozen seats in the July voting.[116] Whatever the effect on free-trading Liberal Unionists, some of the losses occurred on the Conservative side and in both rural and urban seats. Walter Long blamed the Hastings speech for his defeat in the Devizes division of Wiltshire, while Bradford expelled its Fair Trading Conservative MP, Byron Reed.[117] Though the Gladstonian Liberals had to rely on the Irish for the small majority they won in the new House of Commons, the results certainly did not mandate the basic change in British commercial policy that Salisbury advocated.

The latter's departure from office in August left the principles governing British commercial diplomacy unchanged. Gone was the vigilance with which he had scrutinised the transformation of continental commercial diplomacy over the past two years. His Liberal successor at the Foreign Office, Lord

Rosebery, though anxious to maintain continuity in policy, did not pay as much attention to the changing commercial map of the continent. Word of a possible commercial rapprochement between Germany and Russia arrived shortly before Salisbury left office.[118] He hurried to complete the arrangements for a most-favoured-nation treaty with Romania, where Austrian, German, Russian and British interests jostled for primacy. Britain had nearly doubled its trade with Romania since the Congress of Berlin.[119] Britain had been Romania's largest trading partner for the past two years,[120] and possessed the further advantage of detachment from the competition of Austria-Hungary, Germany and Russia over Romanian wheat. Romania used Britain's offer of most-favoured-nation treatment as a means to resolve those tensions without falling back into subservience to Austria and its German ally.[121] One of Salisbury's last acts at the Foreign Office was to arrange for the signature of this treaty.[122]

The commercial tensions in Europe during the remainder of 1892 reached their peak between France and Switzerland. A settlement worked out that summer between their two governments came to grief in the French legislature. Its rejection of the settlement ignited a commercial war when the two countries raised 'fighting tariffs' against each other. Crowe predicted that 'the closing of the Swiss market to French produce will be . . . a gain to Italy, Germany and Austria.'[123]

But it promised no gain for Britain. *The Economist* concluded that 'no improvement of commercial relations in Europe, as far as the direct action of commercial treaties is concerned, can be expected in the near future.'[124] That conclusion did not imply any change of heart on commercial policy so far as the journal or, for that matter, the country was concerned. In a New Year's Eve message to his prospective successor, Salisbury conceded that henceforth the Conservative Party must avoid any taint of protectionism.[125]

Chapter 9

In Retrospect

Germany had salvaged the network of commercial treaties that Britain and France created but abandoned. Altogether it was a remarkable accomplishment. By 1892 the network, including its most-favoured-nation affiliates, covered all of Western and Central Europe and extended into the Balkans, further than the European Union a century later. The dividends that Germany gained for itself by replacing Britain and France at the centre of the network proved great. As Keynes observed after World War I in his *Economic Consequences of the Peace*, the statistics of the prewar 'economic interdependence of Germany and her neighbors' were 'overwhelming. . . . by the system of "peaceful penetration" she gave these countries not only capital, but . . . organization. The whole of Europe east of the Rhine thus fell into the German industrial orbit.' According to Keynes, the tariff system was crucial to this achievement.[1]

Amid the debate between free trade and protection, the nineteenth-century network defied both schools of thought by promoting access to neighbouring markets as well as protection at home. It held the European market open. Though it preserved whatever protective tariffs the member countries regarded as vital to their separate interests, it kept protectionist pressures from breaking the European economy once again into exclusive fragments. The network also served the more modest function, valued among businessmen, of stabilising tariff rates, and it provided for periodic adaptation of those rates to changing economic and governmental demand when treaties expired and had to be renewed. The process was not smooth or straightforward. Relations between Switzerland and Italy on the one hand and France on the other remained strained during the 1890s. Eruptions of tariff warfare continued thereafter when treaties came up for renewal. The revisions of the fundamental German tariff in the early years of the twentieth century were upward. Nevertheless, the dual policy of the continental network, for access and protection, was rewarded up to 1914 with an expansion of their trade markedly greater than that enjoyed by Britain.[2]

Not long after the German core of the revised network was established, Caprivi placed it in jeopardy by adding treaties with Romania and Russia at a time of falling agricultural prices. His action broke up the alliance between industrialists and agrarian Junkers upon which Bismarck had based the government of the German empire. The Junkers drove Caprivi from office in 1894, and the old alliance was cobbled together again. Germany restored tariff protection to agriculture, leaving Caprivi's chancellorship in that regard as an aberration in the history of the empire. But Germany did not withdraw from the commercial treaty network as Bismarck had done in 1879. On the contrary, it preserved the system and worked inside to revise it as desired. The network thus proved durable. It held up sturdily until World War I, and continued afterwards, though much attenuated.

The network of commercial treaties persisted because it served the interests of the formative states: Britain and France after 1860, Germany after 1892. The crucial mechanism here turned out to be the ironically named most-favoured-nation clause, or rather the way in which it was deliberately subverted by the specific tariff clauses in the treaties to which the provision of most-favoured-nation treatment was connected. Behrens was among the first in Britain to point out how this was done. But from the start the French appreciated how, in the very treaty that inaugurated the unconditional most-favoured-nation clause, a tariff could be shaped to discriminate in their favour. The British wine duties of 1860 proved that point. Thirty years later, one of Caprivi's main reasons for rescuing the network when France abandoned it was to acquire the power to design a tariff that favoured the goods of Germany and its allies over those of Britain and France, regardless of their entitlement to most-favoured-nation treatment. He proceeded to turn Britain and France into *less*-favoured-nations, though they were safe from the full terrors of the general tariff. Less than 20 per cent of the exports from Britain to the major consuming countries with a two-tier, maximum and minimum tariff benefited from the most-favoured-nation treatment to which Britain was entitled.[3]

The genius of the late nineteenth-century European network, as of the late twentieth-century European Union, was that it served the interests of its smaller participants as well as it did those of the formative powers. The supreme example in both centuries has been Belgium. Long after the other states of Europe had forgotten the nineteenth-century network, Belgians remembered it as giving rise to the commercial policy that 'conformed most closely to [our] economic interests'.[4] Paul-Henri Spaak, the Belgian Father of the European Union, recalled that policy in 1955 before negotiating the formation of the European Economic Community. 'La vocation européenne de la Belgique s'affirme,' he wrote, '. . . inspirée par sa position de petite nation au centre d'un continent troublé.' ('The European vocation of Belgium is reaffirmed . . . inspired by its position as a small nation at the centre of a troubled continent.')[5] It was to Belgium that France had first turned in constructing the network of interlocked treaties that Cobden and Napoleon III envisaged. The treaty of 1881 between Belgium and France formed the basis of the conventional tariff of Europe after Britain had departed to the margins of the network. Ten years later it was particularly through the treaty with Belgium that Germany superseded France as the core state of the network.

Just as Belgium has been an eager participant in both European configurations, so in both cases Britain has occupied a position of semi-detachment. Though Britain accepted relegation to the margins, it never abandoned the nineteenth-century network, however much Gladstone was tempted to do so. The price that Britain has nevertheless paid for its marginalisation in the commercial arrangements of Europe has been high. In the nineteenth-century case, marginalisation weakened Britain's hold on the continental market which, so long as the United States preserved its high tariff, was the largest developed economy to which Britain had access. Britain thus increased its reliance on lower-income countries overseas, to its enduring detriment.[6]

Marginalisation was inconceivable to Britain in 1860, given its economic ascendancy not just in Europe but worldwide. What hastened Britain's descent from that eminence in the European context was the unilateral pursuit of free trade, a policy that deprived successive governments of basic bargaining power. At the outset, with full approval from Cobden, Gladstone implemented the agreement with France by stripping the British tariff down towards purely revenue-producing proportions. That left little for Britain to negotiate with, and what little it had it pared down in the ensuing decade. The lucrative returns from the surviving duties provided vital revenue for the Treasury, which therefore resisted their deployment for bargaining purposes.

There was thus a fatal contradiction in Cobden's approach to commercial diplomacy. It only worked once. Afterwards British foreign secretaries had little to bargain with except for the remnants of discrimination in the wine duties, a discrimination that they would not admit yet did not want to forgo. Russell, the first Foreign Secretary to find himself in this predicament, may have been surprised as well as disconcerted by it. But Gladstone had been well aware of what he was doing in 1860. Indeed, he regarded the resulting loss of bargaining power as one of the merits of his scheme. That renunciation would, he hoped, place the British example of complete free trade above suspicion. No longer could British advocacy of tariff reductions by other countries be regarded as a cloak for the advancement of its own industrial interests. The renunciation of bargaining power together with the prosperity that the freedom of trade brought to Britain would surely persuade its trading associates to follow its example.

That faith faded during the long depression that set in after the Franco-Prussian War. But no clear alternative emerged. The peculiar nature of the depression, in which the volume of trade and the working-class standard of living rose, and its extent – it spread across Europe regardless of the restoration of protective tariffs – revived the British debate on commercial policy. But it did not create a new consensus, even among the critics of free trade. Deprived of any mandate for change, British foreign secretaries could not counteract the hostile reconfiguring of commercial policy on the continent.

The British experience of founding and then distancing itself from the network of tariff-reducing treaties in nineteenth-century Europe is rarely remembered nowadays. Yet it sheds light on Britain's ambivalence to the European Union today. There are, of course, fundamental dissimilarities in the two cases. The nineteenth-century network did not have the focused, essentially political objective that the Treaty of Rome gave to the European Economic Community in pursuit of an 'ever closer union'. Nor did the nineteenth-century network possess any agencies for intergovernmental, let alone supranational action like the European Commission, Parliament and Court. All the building blocks of the nineteenth-century network were bilateral treaties which either party could dissolve. The most-favoured-nation clause and synchronous expiration of many treaties gave European commercial diplomacy multilateral implications after 1860; but they were nothing more than implications.

Even so, there are striking affinities between the two cases, not only in the British response. Some, like the jockeying for advantage among the major powers of Europe, are predictable. The subtle affinities are more interesting. Though less coherent and emphatic than in the European Union, there was a political agenda behind the nineteenth-century network. In addition to Cobden's faith in the pacific potential of international commerce, successive British governments valued the improved relationship with France which their commercial alliance fostered. Napoleon III never defined the political objectives behind his commercial treaty-making on the continent, perhaps in order to disguise them. But the British Foreign Office failed to recognise the clearer political objectives in the commercial diplomacy of the new states formed in violation of the peace settlement reached at Vienna after the French wars, of Belgium and Italy as they struggled to demonstrate the capacity and uphold the prestige of their governments, to say nothing of Prussia and the German empire.

Still, the most striking feature that the nineteenth- and twentieth-century stories have in common is the difficulty that Britain has experienced in bringing its resources effectively to bear within the European structures of the day. The nineteenth-century story is particularly noteworthy here because, in retrospect and in comparison with the situation a century later, Britain's ineffectuality in the nineteenth century seems strange. Not only were Britain's economic resources then at their comparative height. The structure that Europe developed after 1860 grew from a British initiative, it was inspired by

British experience and it came close to what Britain sought when it joined the European Community in the next century. It takes more than one comparison to produce a convincing explanation. But the nineteenth-century story suggests patterns of affinity in the British response to Europe, some of which are surprising. One is the aversion, displayed by free-trading Liberals in the nineteenth century and Eurosceptic Conservatives in the twentieth, to any loss of national autonomy in economic policy-making. Another might be classed among the persistent illusions of primacy. Just as Britain was slow to recognise the emergence in the last third of the nineteenth century of Germany as its industrial rival in Europe,[7] so Britain has been slow to recognise the superiority in the last third of the twentieth century of the French as well as German economic performance. The illusion in both cases blunted the critical edge with which Britain examined its own economic policy.

The universally applicable language that British Liberals used in expressing their principles and their inability to present their own national and industrial interests candidly in less elevated terms addled their communication with continental Europeans. 'Libre échange' might translate 'free trade' into French literally; but, as Lord Granville discovered to his dismay, the French words did not convey the same meaning. It was a rare continental European who could embrace a tariff policy devoid of the protective elements that were anathema under the British creed. British free traders sought to avoid any hint of bargaining in their pursuit of tariff reduction for fear that continental Europeans would suspect them of seeking to advance British national and industrial interests – as if continental Europeans would have thought that a bad thing! The high-mindedness of British Liberalism came across to continental Europeans as hypocrisy.

These differences in understanding and communication disabled the British Foreign Office in its negotiations with its continental counterparts in the nineteenth-century commercial treaty network. The spokesmen for Britain refused to grasp, or if they grasped they refused to adapt their conduct to, the way in which continental Europeans interpreted the network of treaties that Cobden and Napoleon III initiated. Unable to accept the working principles developed within the European network, Britain could not improve its terms of access to the continental market. Britain turned away to cultivate other, poorer prospects.

Note on Documentary, Periodical and Archival Sources (with Abbreviations)

Four published documentary and periodical sources are drawn upon extensively in this book: Hansard's Parliamentary Debates (cited here as *Hansard*), the British Parliamentary Papers, the weekly journal *The Economist*, and the daily *Times*. The main archival sources for this study are the Foreign Office (FO) files in the Public Record Office (PRO) and the records of the Bradford Chamber of Commerce.

All the Foreign Office documents cited in the notes can be found under the following listings: PRO/FO10 for Anglo–Belgian trade; PRO/FO27 and 146 for Anglo–French trade; PRO/FO45 for Anglo–Italian trade; PRO/FO64 and 68 for Anglo–German trade; PRO/FO298, 299 and 918 for reports by and correspondence with and concerning Sir Joseph Archer Crowe; PRO/FO425/130, 135, 136, 137 and 138 for the Anglo–French commercial treaty negotiations of 1880–82; PRO/FO881 for printed reports and memoranda.

As usual with the records of the Foreign Office, the documents here were grouped wherever possible under the heading of the particular countries with which they were mainly concerned, the countries being listed in alphabetical order. The documents that could not be so listed in PRO/FO881 were filed between 'France' and 'Germany' under the heading of 'General'. The printed documents dealing with the nineteenth-century commercial treaty network were filed accordingly under this heading, including annual reports from the Commercial Department of the Foreign Office. Most of these papers are quite short; but there are noteworthy exceptions, particularly the three fat volumes – PRO/FO881/6185, 6211 and 6289 – in which Lord Salisbury collected his correspondence with all the states involved in the renegotiation of the network from 1889 to 1892. The Public Record Office also contains papers of Earl Russell (PRO30/22) that are cited in the notes to chapter 3.

The records of the Bradford Chamber of Commerce constitute a tribute to the dedicated and meticulous enterprise of Sir Jacob Behrens. Housed in the West Yorkshire Archives Service in Bradford, they come mainly in two forms. There are, first, the hand-written minutes of the Council of the Bradford Chamber, together with the minutes of its committees including the Tariff Committee. Secondly, the Council published reports of the general meeting each year, to which correspondence between officers of the Chamber and the Foreign Office and Board of Trade was often appended, along with statistical analyses of the woollens trade. Occasional documents which cannot be readily identified under the heading of the Council minutes or the annual reports are cited in the notes to this book with their West Yorkshire Archives Service reference numbers. The West Yorkshire Archives Service also possesses the Annual Reports of the Joint Tariff Committee of the Yorkshire Chambers of Commerce published in the late 1870s and early 1880s.

There are small collections of letters and papers of Sir Joseph Archer Crowe, to which the notes refer, in the Royal Archives (RA) in Windsor Castle, among the Spenser Wilkinson papers in the National Army Museum, London, and in the British Library (BL) among the papers of Sir Charles Dilke (BL Add.MSS.43912) as well as Crowe's reminiscences (BL Add.MSS.41309).

Notes

Chapter 1: Tools for Bargaining

1. Salisbury speaking at Hastings, reported in *The Times* of 19 May 1892.
2. (Oxford: Clarendon Press, 1997).
3. See Paul Bairoch's account of the benefits that continental countries derived from their protective tariffs in his chapter 'European Trade Policy, 1815–1914', in Peter Mathias and Sidney Pollard, eds, *The Cambridge Economic History of Europe*, vol. 8 (Cambridge: Cambridge University Press, 1989).
4. The classic work here remains J. Gallagher and R.E. Robinson's 'The Imperialism of Free Trade,' *Economic History Review*, 2nd ser., 6 (1953).
5. See for example Forrest Capie, 'Tariff Protection and Economic Performance in the Nineteenth Century', in John Black and L. Alan Winters, eds, *Policy and Performance in International Trade* (London: Macmillan, 1983). Capie argues (p. 2) that nineteenth-century 'tariffs were hardly high enough to have the impact often claimed', a conclusion that 'is greatly strengthened when the framework of effective protection is used to show that effective rates were much lower than would normally have been expected'. Ulrich Wengenroth, however, in his close comparison of technology as well as commercial performance in the German and British iron and steel industries, insists that the dual function of the German tariff, to protect the home market and make it easier to expand exports, made it 'enormously effective in assigning shares of the world market': *Enterprise and Technology: The German and British Steel Industries, 1865–1895* (Cambridge: Cambridge University Press, 1994), 267.
6. Most notably J.W. Gaston's article on 'The Free Trade Diplomacy Debate and the Victorian European Common Market Initiative,' *Canadian Journal of History*, 22 (1987), 59–82, drawn from his still more impressive dissertation, 'Policy-Making and Free-Trade Diplomacy: Britain's Commercial Relations with Western Europe, 1869–1886', University of Saskatchewan Ph.D. thesis, 1975. Also Asaana Iliasu, 'The Role of Free Trade Treaties in British Foreign Policy, 1859–1871', University of London Ph.D. thesis, 1965.
7. See chapter 2.
8. The most straightforward appreciation of the tariff network is to be found in Sidney Pollard's *European Economic Integration, 1815–1970* (London: Thames & Hudson, 1974), but Pollard is not particularly interested in the participation of Britain or the political dimension generally. Alan Milward gives the protectionist

movement credit for bringing more Europeans into the political life of their countries, though he minimises the international significance of commercial treaty diplomacy in 'Tariffs as Constitutions', in Susan Strange and Roger Tooze, eds, *The International Politics of Surplus Capacity: Competition for Market Shares in the World Recession* (London: George Allen & Unwin, 1981).

9. See Spaak's preface to Max Suetens, *Histoire de la politique commerciale de la Belgique depuis 1830 jusqu'à nos jours* (Brussels: Editions de la Librairie Encyclopédique, 1955), vii–ix.

10. Sir Roy Denman, *Missed Chances: Britain and Europe in the Twentieth Century* (London: Cassell, 1996), 2.

11. *The World in Depression* (Boston: Little, Brown, 1973).

12. Pre-eminently Timothy H. McKeown in 'Hegemonic Stability Theory and 19th-Century Tariff Levels in Europe', *International Organization*, 37 (1983), 73–91, and J.V. Nye, 'Revisionist Tariff History and the Theory of Hegemonic Stability', *Politics & Society*, 19, 2 (1991), 209–32. Also P.K. O'Brien and G.A. Pigman, 'Free Trade, British Hegemony and the International Economic Order in the Nineteenth Century', *Review of International Studies*, 18 (1992), 89–113. The theory works better for the mid-nineteenth-century tariff relationship between Britain and the United States, as Scott C. James and David A. Lake demonstrate in 'The Second Face of Hegemony: Britain's Repeal of the Corn Laws and the American Walker Tariff of 1846', *International Organization*, 43 (winter 1989), 1–29.

13. For amplification of this argument, see J.V. Nye, 'The Myth of Free-Trade Britain and Fortress France: Tariffs and Trade in the Nineteenth Century,' *Journal of Economic History*, 51 (Mar. 1991), 23–46. See Arthur A. Stein, 'The Hegemon's

Dilemma: Great Britain, the United States, and the International Economic Order', *International Organization*, 38, 2 (spring 1984), 362 for figures on customs revenue as a percentage of total governmental revenue for the UK, France, Germany and the USA from 1820 to 1975.

Chapter 2: Ambivalent Inauguration: The Anglo-French Treaty of 1860

1. W.E. Gladstone, 'The History of 1852–60, and Greville's Latest Journals,' *English Historical Review* (Apr. 1887), 283.

2. Historians have raised doubts about the validity of this impression. Donald N. McCloskey attempted in his article 'Magnanimous Albion: Free Trade and British National Income, 1841–1881', *Explorations in Economic History*, 17 (1980), 303–20, to undermine the assumption that free trade contributed to the growth of the nineteenth-century British economy. Peter Cain challenged that attempt and McCloskey defended it in *Explorations in Economic History*, xxiv (1982), 201–10. Roy Church drew attention to the downs as well as the ups of *The Great Victorian Boom, 1850–1873* (London: Macmillan, 1975).

3. *Effects of the Free Trade Policy Recently Inaugurated in England, as Indicated by its Practical Results*, statement updated by the Board of Trade, 18 Feb. 1860, Public Record Office (henceforth PRO) FO881/902.

4. Quoted in A.L. Dunham, *The Anglo-French Treaty of Commerce of 1860 and the Progress of the Industrial Revolution in France* (Ann Arbor: University of Michigan Publications, 1930), 53. Dunham's work remains the fullest account of the treaty. There is an able reassessment of 'The Origins

of the Anglo-French Commercial Treaty of 1860' by Barrie M. Ratcliffe in the volume of essays he edited in honour of W.O. Henderson, *Great Britain and her World, 1750–1914* (Manchester: Manchester University Press, 1975). Asaana Iliasu in 'The Cobden-Chevalier Commercial Treaty of 1860', *Historical Journal*, 14, 1 (1971), 67–98, draws attention to the international political bearings of the treaty.

5. Dunham, *The Anglo-French Treaty*, 49.

6. Cobden to Chevalier, 14 Sept. 1859, in *ibid.*, 51–52.

7. *Ibid.*

8. Initially Chevalier thought that France too could make its reductions generally applicable, but political realities in France soon forced him to abandon this notion. See *ibid.*, 45 and 50.

9. That is the prevailing impression conveyed by Dunham among others. J.V. Nye, however, claims with regard to the commercial policy of the Second Empire that 'Numerous measures were taken in the 1850s to lower or simplify existing tariffs and the period from 1855 on saw a string of decrees reducing tariffs on such items as wool, materials for shipbuilding, and machinery. In 1857, most of the export tariffs were removed. . . . The entire period of the Second Empire from 1852 to 1870 saw a steady fall in the average French tariffs continuing the drop begun in the 1840s.' Nye, 'Changing French Trade Conditions, National Welfare, and the 1860 Anglo-French Treaty of Commerce', *Explorations in Economic History*, 28 (1991), 463.

10. Quoted by Gladstone to the House of Commons on 28 Feb. 1870, *Hansard*, 3rd ser. 199, 882–83.

11. Raised to the rank of colonel for his service in the royal marines during the French Revolutionary and Napoleonic Wars, Torrens afterwards published essays in political economy

that impressed David Ricardo as well as John Stuart Mill. He was MP for Ashburton briefly before and after the passage of the 1832 Reform Act.

12. The following discussion draws largely upon Douglas A. Irwin's article 'The Reciprocity Debate in Parliament, 1842–1846', in Andrew Marrison, ed., *Free Trade and its Reception 1815–1960*, vol. 1 (London and New York: Routledge, 1998).

13. Lucy Brown, *The Board of Trade and the Free-Trade Movement, 1830–42* (Oxford: Clarendon Press, 1958), 132.

14. Peel in the House of Commons on 9 Mar. 1846; quoted by Douglas A. Irwin, 'The Reciprocity Debate in Parliament', 136.

15. Quoted most recently by Anthony Howe in *Free Trade and Liberal England, 1846–1946* (Oxford: Clarendon Press, 1997), 71.

16. J.V. Nye, 'Changing French Trade Conditions', 469.

17. The following account draws largely on C.M. Kennedy's memorandum of 25 Mar. 1879 on 'How the present Scale of Wine Duties in Great Britain came to be established; and the bearing on it of the Commercial Treaty of January 23, 1860, with France', PRO/FO881/3873.

18. Quoted in Douglas A. Irwin, *Against the Tide: An Intellectual History of Free Trade* (Princeton: Princeton University Press, 1996), 109.

19. Gladstone, 'The History of 1852–60', 300.

20. J.V. Nye in 'The Myth of Free-Trade Britain and Fortress France' disputes this interpretation, which prevails now as it did then. Nye argues that 'France's trade regime was more liberal than that of Great Britain throughout most of the nineteenth century' (p. 25). His argument rests on a dubious statistical base derived by calculating average customs rates 'from tariff revenues as percentages of the value of importables' (*ibid.*).

21. Leader on 'The Misconceptions in

France as to the Commercial Treaty', *The Economist*, 11 Feb. 1860.

22. D.T. Jenkins and J.C. Malin, 'European Competition in Woollen Cloth, 1870–1914', *Business History*, 32, 4 (Oct. 1990), 66–86.

23. All the same cottons yarns, particularly the finer ones, sold well in continental Europe, where they supplied the indigenous weaving industry. R.E. Tyson, 'The Cotton Industry', in D.H. Aldcroft, *The Development of British Industry and Foreign Competition, 1875–1914* (London: George Allen & Unwin, 1968), 104–107.

24. Lancashire responded by making purely cotton fabric that looked and felt like woollens and cost still less.

25. The following account is drawn from *Sir Jacob Behrens, 1806–1889* (London: Percy, Lund Humphries, 1925), based on his unpublished memoirs and translated by Harry Behrens.

26. *Ibid.*, 32.

27. The best contemporary accounts of the nineteenth-century town are by the local historian William Cudworth, and include *Worstedopolis: A Sketch History of the Town and Trade of Bradford, the Metropolis of the Worsted Industry* (Bradford: W. Byles & Sons, 1888). Cudworth's accounts were brought up to date by his twentieth-century successor David James, particularly in his *Bradford* (Halifax: Ryburn, 1990). There is an excellent scholarly treatment by Theodore Kodischek, *Class Formation and Urban-Industrial Society: Bradford, 1750–1850* (Cambridge: Cambridge University Press, 1990).

28. The name is derived from a village in Norfolk where the English woollen textile trade had been based before its shift to West Yorkshire.

29. J.H. Clapham, *The Woollen and Worsted Industries* (London: Methuen, 1907), 37.

30. H.J. Ripley, president of the Bradford Chamber of Commerce, to the Board of Trade, 7 Apr. 1860, Bradford Chamber of Commerce Minute Books.

31. Bradford Chamber of Commerce Minute Books, 19 Apr. 1860.

32. See *The Economist*'s leader for 5 May 1860 on 'The Practical Details of the French Treaty and the Chambers of Commerce'.

33. Report of 6 Aug. 1860 in the Bradford Chamber of Commerce Minute Books.

34. Quoted in *Sir Jacob Behrens, 1806–1889*, 59.

35. Lord John Russell to Crowe, 1 July 1860, PRO/FO/299/11.

36. David Alan Brown, *Berenson and the Connoisseurship of Italian Painting* (Washington, D.C.: National Gallery of Art, 1979), 33.

37. Crowe to Russell, 1 Mar. 1860, copy, Royal Archives (henceforth RA) 1.31/81.

38. Among these Crowe included the Grand Dukes of Baden and Saxe-Weimar and the Prince Regent of Prussia as well as the Duke of Saxe-Coburg-Gotha. 'The kings of Bavaria, Wurtemberg, Hanover & Saxony were conservative and admiring of Austria rather than of Prussia.' Crowe's Reminiscences of Leipzig, British Library (henceforth BL) Add.MSS.41309.

39. Crowe to Russell, 6 Aug. 1861, PRO/FO299/12. Crowe used the terms 'British' and 'English' interchangeably.

40. Cobden to H. Ashworth, 2 Jan. 1860, quoted in Anthony Howe, *Free Trade and Liberal England*, 95–96.

Chapter 3: The Construction of the Network, 1861–1866

1. Asaana Iliasu, 'The Role of Free Trade Treaties in British Foreign Policy, 1859–1871', 201.

2. Marcel Rist, 'A French Experiment with Free Trade: The Treaty of 1860', in Rondo Cameron, ed., *Essays*

    in French Economic History (Home-wood, Illinois: Richard D. Irwin for the American Economic Association, 1970), 287.

3. Léon Amé, *Etude sur les traités de commerce* (Paris: Librairie Guillaumin, 1876), vol. 2, 2–3.

4. E.A. Bowring to E. Hammond, 31 Dec. 1860, and Sir J. Emerson Tennent to Hammond, 11 Jan. 1861, in Select Committee on Trade with Foreign Nations, Appendix no. 6, Correspondence between the Board of Trade and the Foreign Office Respecting the Negotiation of a Commercial Treaty between Great Britain and Belgium, Parliamentary Papers, 1864, vol. 7.

5. Howard de Walden to Russell, 31 Aug. 1861, *ibid.*, 602.

6. James Booth to A.H. Layard, 23 Nov. 1861, *ibid.*, 607.

7. D.A. Farnie points out that the impression of a 'cotton famine' was exaggerated if not completely illusory, that the more important distortion was quite the reverse one of overstocked markets: *The English Cotton Industry and the World Market, 1815–1896* (Oxford: Clarendon Press, 1979), 139–44.

8. The Board of Trade to the Foreign Office, 5 Feb. 1861, quoted in J.R. Davis, 'Trade, Politics, Perspectives, and the Question of a British Commercial Policy towards the German States 1848–1866', Glasgow University Ph.D. thesis, 1993, 310–11.

9. John Darlington, secretary of the Bradford Chamber of Commerce, to the various Chambers of Commerce in the United Kingdom, 19 July 1861, Bradford Chamber of Commerce Minute Books, 22 July 1861.

10. According to *The Economist*, which acquired its information from the Bradford Chamber of Commerce, 'French worsteds and woollen manufactures are now charged in Belgium with a duty of 225 francs per 100 kilogrammes, which is estimated as being about equivalent to 22 per cent. *ad valorem*, and this duty is to be reduced in October next to an *ad valorem* duty of 15 per cent, and again in 1864 it is to be reduced to 10 per cent. . . . English woollens and worsteds are loaded with a duty of 348 francs per 100 kilogrammes, which is calculated as equivalent to a duty of . . . 35 per cent . . . on French woollen yarns the Belgian duty is now 45 francs per 100 kilogrammes, and will in October be about 35 francs, while on English woollen yarns the duty is 116 francs . . . on French silk the Belgian duty is now 4 francs the kilogramme, and after October will be 3 francs, while on English silk it is 11 francs 60 cents. Nor is this all, the Belgian tariff on English goods is specific, and is levied according to a very complicated system . . . the duty on the most important classes of French goods will be levied *ad valorem*, which will give the French merchants another and a great advantage over the English merchants.' *The Economist*, 'England and the Belgian Tariff', 3 Aug. 1861.

11. Report on the Commercial Relations between England and Belgium, 10 July 1862, PRO/FO10/242/32537, Barron's emphases.

12. Lord Howard to Russell, 16 May 1862, Russell Papers, PRO30/22/46/247–50.

13. 19 Jan. 1863, in the Bradford Chamber of Commerce Minute Books for that date, commended in *The Times* of 22 Jan. 1863.

14. Forster in the House of Commons, 17 Feb. 1863, *Hansard*, 3rd ser. 169, 415ff.

15. Report on the Italian economy by L.S. Sackville West, 1 Jan. 1862, PRO/FO45/21.

16. W.G. Grey's report from the Paris embassy, 17 May 1862, PRO/FO881/1276.

17. E. Hammond for the Foreign Office to Sir J. Emerson Tennent at the Board of Trade, 7 Feb. 1863, *ibid.*

18. Sir J. Emerson Tennent to E. Hammond, 3 Feb. 1863, *ibid*.

19. Sackville West to Russell, 11 Feb. 1863, #33, PRO/FO45/40.

20. Those consulted were at Batley, Belfast, Birmingham, Bradford, Bristol, Cork, Coventry, Dewsbury, Dover, Dublin, Dundee, Edinburgh, Galashiels, Glasgow, Gloucester, Halifax, Hawick, Huddersfield, Hull, Kendal, Leeds, Leicester, Leith, Limerick, Liverpool, Manchester, Newcastle, Sheffield, Southampton, Sunderland, Tynemouth, Wolverhampton, Worcester, South Shields, Stoke and Stockton.

21. Mr Liddel to the House of Commons, 17 Feb. 1863, *Hansard*, 3rd ser., 169, 437.

22. *Ibid*., 442–43.

23. *Ibid*., 447.

24. James Booth to E. Hammond, 18 May 1863, PRO/FO881/1276.

25. Sir James Hudson, the British ambassador, to Russell, telegram of 1 Aug. 1863, PRO/FO45/42.

26. Hudson to Russell, 1 Aug. 1863, PRO/FO45/42.

27. Visconti Venosta to Hudson, 1 Aug. 1863, copy, PRO/FO45/42.

28. Russell to Henry Elliot, 28 Oct. 1863, draft no.13, PRO/FO45/39.

29. Elliot to Russell, 19 Oct. 1863, #16, PRO/FO45/43.

30. Much the best study of this subject is J.R. Davis's 1993 Glasgow University Ph.D. thesis, 'Trade, Politics, Perspectives, and the Question of a British Commercial Policy towards the German States 1848–1866', now developed into a book, *Britain and the German Zollverein, 1848–66* (London: Macmillan, 1997). There is an old but still useful study of German as well as French tariff policy in Percy Ashley, *Modern Tariff History: Germany – United States – France* (London: John Murray, 1904). The interweaving of economic and political concerns in modern German history is explored in Harold James, *A German Identity, 1770–1990*

(London: Weidenfeld & Nicolson, 1990).

31. Percy Ashley, *Modern Tariff History*, 43.

32. Crowe to Russell, 15 May 1861, PRO/FO68/118.

33. Crowe to Russell, 3 Oct. 1861, *ibid*.

34. Behrens made the point from an angle that was less flattering to the British than to the Germans: 'Fine woollen cloths cannot be exported to the Zollverein, because the German manufacture is more advanced than our own.' Behrens on behalf of the Bradford Chamber of Commerce to Russell, 7 Nov. 1864, in the Fourteenth Annual Report of the Bradford Chamber of Commerce, 16 Jan. 1865, 21.

35. 28 April 1862, quoted in J.R. Davis, 'Trade, Politics, Perspectives, and the Question of a British Commercial Policy towards the German States 1848–1866', 318.

36. Napier to Russell, 18 Feb. 1865, PRO/FO64/580/22.

37. 31 Dec. 1863, in the Thirteenth Annual Report of the Bradford Chamber of Commerce, 18 Jan. 1864.

38. Report to the Council of the Bradford Chamber of Commerce, Bradford Chamber of Commerce Minute Books 23 Mar. 1864.

39. David James, *Bradford*, 67.

40. The debate was reported in *Hansard*, 3rd ser., 174 (15 Apr. 1864), 1083–120.

41. Russell to Her Majesty's Ministers at the Principal Courts of Europe, 16 Apr. 1864, PRO/FO881/1260.

42. *Hansard*, 3rd ser., 177 (17 Mar. 1865), 1862–64.

43. *Ibid*., 1876.

44. Bradford Chamber of Commerce Minute Books, 30 Nov. 1864.

45. The following discussion draws largely upon the work of Karl F. Helleiner, *Free Trade and Frustration: Anglo-Austrian Negotiations 1860–70* (Toronto: University of Toronto Press, 1973). There is an able, older article on 'The Austro-French Com-

mercial Treaty of 1866' by Dwight C. Long in the *American Historical Review*, 41 (1936), 474–91.

46. Napier to Russell, 12 Jan. 1865, PRO/FO64/580/4.

47. 'The Prospects of Free Trade in Austria', *The Economist*, 7 Jan. 1865.

48. Bradford Chamber of Commerce Council Minute Books, 26 Oct. 1863.

49. Douglas A. Irwin, 'Multilateral and Bilateral Trade Policies in the World Trading System: An Historical Perspective', in Jaime de Melo and Arvid Panagariya, eds, *New Dimensions in Regional Integration* (Cambridge: Cambridge University Press, 1993), 97.

50. Gladstone, 'The History of 1852–60', 299.

51. 'The Board of Trade Tables', *The Economist*, 1 Mar. 1862. Cf. the article in the issue for 14 June 1862 on 'The Marvellous Effects of the French Treaty'.

52. *Hansard*, 3rd ser., 169 (17 Feb. 1863), 445.

53. Memorandum by C.M. Kennedy on Treaties of Commerce with, and between, European Powers, with especial reference to the Trade of the United Kingdom, 17 Sept. 1875, PRO/FO881/2670, 17.

54. 'The Balance Sheet' in *The Economist* for 17 Feb. 1866.

55. Based on the Statistical Abstract for the United Kingdom in each of the last 15 years from 1871 to 1885, 33rd number, Parliamentary Papers, 1886, C.4821.

56. Drawn from Werner Schlote, *British Overseas Trade from 1700 to the 1930s*, translated by W.O. Henderson and W.H. Chaloner (Oxford: Basil Blackwell, 1952), 157–59.

57. Drawn from *ibid.*, 156–57.

58. Drawn from Paul Bairoch, 'Geographical Structure and Trade Balance of European Foreign Trade from 1800 to 1970', *Journal of European Economic History*, 3, 3 (winter 1974), 572.

59. *Ibid.*, 561–67.

60. Peter T. Marsh, *Joseph Chamberlain, Entrepreneur in Politics* (London and New Haven: Yale University Press, 1994), 23.

61. He admitted that 'the duty on rail and bar iron . . . has been subjected to a rate of duty far exceeding that of the other articles in the French tariff', Cobden to the mayor of Birmingham, in *The Economist*, 19 Jan. 1861.

62. D.A. Farnie, *The English Cotton Industry and the World Market, 1815–1896*, 92.

63. Proceedings at the Annual Meeting, 20 Jan. 1862, Bradford Chamber of Commerce Minute Books.

64. David James, *Bradford*, 49.

65. The best account of the impact of the 1860 treaty from the French point of view is Marcel Rist's, 'A French Experiment with Free Trade'.

66. Report by W.G. Grey, Secretary of Embassy, 31 Aug. 1862, PRO/FO425/72.

67. Marcel Rist, 'A French Experiment with Free Trade', 311.

68. 'The Trade between France and England', *The Economist*, 9 Dec. 1865.

69. Report on mixed fabrics in the universal exhibition of 1867, quoted in the Twenty-First Annual Report of the Bradford Chamber of Commerce, 15 Jan. 1872, 35–36.

70. James F. McMillan, *Napoleon III* (London: Longman, 1991), 141.

71. See Robert Tombs, *France, 1814–1914* (London: Longman, 1996), 153ff.

72. '[L]a plus conforme à ses intérêts,' as Max Suetens puts it in his *Histoire de la politique commerciale de la Belgique depuis 1830 jusqu'à nos jours*, 104.

73. *Ibid.*, 101.

74. See G. Luzzatto, 'The Italian Economy in the First Decade after Unification', in F. Crouzet, W.H. Chaloner and W.M. Stern, eds, *Essays in European Economic History, 1789–1914* (New York: St Martin's Press, 1969).

Chapter 4: Dividends in Wartime, 1866–1872

1. Crowe to Russell, 7 July 1864, PRO/FO299/13.
2. Crowe to Clarendon (who replaced Russell at the Foreign Office in the reconstruction of the government following the death of Palmerston), 31 Jan. 1866, PRO/FO68/145.
3. Crowe to Clarendon, 22 Jan. 1866, PRO/FO68/144.
4. James F. McMillan, *Napoleon III*, 110.
5. Quoted in *ibid*.
6. Crowe to Stanley, 21 July 1866, PRO/FO68/144.
7. Crowe to Stanley, 20 Nov. 1866, précis, Royal Archives I/47/96.
8. 'The New Commercial Department of the Foreign Office', *The Economist*, 8 Dec. 1866.
9. Crowe to Stanley, 4 Apr. 1867, PRO/FO299/15.
10. Crowe to Stanley, 29 Jan. 1867, *ibid*.
11. Stanley to Crowe, 4 Mar. 1867, *ibid*.
12. Crowe to Stanley, 29 Apr. 1867, PRO/FO68/147.
13. Crowe to Stanley, 18 May 1867, PRO/FO299/15.
14. Crowe to Stanley, 14 May 1867, *ibid*.
15. Crowe to Stanley, 20 May 1867, *ibid*.
16. Sixteenth Annual Report of the Bradford Chamber of Commerce, 21 Jan. 1867, 20.
17. The Memorial of the Bradford Chamber of Commerce, by Behrens to Stanley, 5 Nov. 1866, *ibid*., 27.
18. Here again the discussion draws largely upon the work of Karl F. Helleiner, *Free Trade and Frustration*.
19. 'Some General Commercial Results of 1867', *The Economist*, 4 Jan. 1868.
20. Richard Roberts and David Kynaston, *The Bank of England: Money, Power and Influence 1694–1994* (Oxford: Clarendon Press, 1995), 158–59.
21. 'The Latest Account of our Import and Export Trade', *The Economist*, 8 Feb. 1868.
22. *Ibid*.
23. Report on the trade and industry of Leipzig for the year 1868, Crowe to Lord Clarendon, 6 Apr. 1869, PRO/FO299/16.
24. Report on the trade and industry of the Rhenish provinces & Westphalia for the year 1868, Crowe to Clarendon, 24 July 1869, *ibid*.
25. Percy Ashley, *Modern Tariff History*, 52.
26. Report on the trade and industry of Leipzig for the year 1869, Crowe to Clarendon, 14 Apr. 1870, PRO/FO299/16.
27. *The Economist* put it ambiguously: 'The duties will still be high . . . they will, nevertheless, be low enough to admit of a pretty extensive opening of Austrian markets' ('The Treaty of Commerce with Austria', 29 Jan. 1870). The Bradford Chamber of Commerce found that the duties on woollen tissues were reduced by 10 per cent but still amounted to 17.5 to 20 per cent *ad valorem*, well above the 15 per cent which otherwise prevailed throughout the European network. Council Minute Books, 29 Mar. 1870.
28. Bradford Reports of Workmen Selected by the Council of the Chamber to Visit the Exhibition, 11–12, West Yorkshire Archives Service, ref. 71D80/17/1.
29. Crowe to Clarendon, 21 Jan. 1870, PRO/FO68/152.
30. Much the ablest account of French tariff policy from this point until the end of the century is Michael S. Smith's *Tariff Reform in France, 1860–1900: The Politics of Economic Interest* (Ithaca and London: Cornell University Press, 1980). For the late 1860s, see pp. 35ff.
31. S.B. Saul, *Studies in British Overseas Trade, 1870–1914* (Liverpool: Liverpool University Press, 1960), 148.
32. Gladstone to John Bright, 27 Dec. 1869, quoted in J.W.T. Gaston, 'Policy-Making and Free-Trade Diplomacy: Britain's Commercial Relations with Western Europe, 1869–1886', University of Saskatchewan Ph.D. dissertation, 1975, 53.

33. Gladstone to A.J. Otway, under secretary at the Foreign Office, 16 Jan. 1869, in H.C.G. Matthew, ed., *The Gladstone Diaries: With Cabinet Minutes and Prime-Ministerial Correspondence*, vol. 7 (Oxford: Clarendon Press, 1982), 11.

34. On this point and much else in this chapter, I am indebted to J.W.T. Gaston's outstanding doctoral thesis, 'Policy-Making and Free-Trade Diplomacy'. For this particular point, see pp. 116–17.

35. Reported by Lyons to Clarendon, 7 Dec. 1869 and 2 Jan. 1870, quoted in *ibid*. 117–18.

36. D.A. Farnie, *The English Cotton Industry and the World Market, 1815–1896*, 164–65.

37. 'The Effects of the French Treaty on the Course of Trade,' *The Economist*, 13 Feb. 1869.

38. 'Business Notes', *The Economist*, 24 Apr. 1869.

39. 'English Exports of Clothing Manufactures in 1860 and 1868', *The Economist*, 15 May 1869.

40. 'Business Notes', *The Economist*, 11 Dec. 1869.

41. Reported in *The Times* of 25 Feb. 1870, 3.

42. This term was more commonly used by the industry on the continent than in Yorkshire.

43. Bradford Reports of Workmen Selected by the Council of the Chamber to Visit the Exhibition, 4, West Yorkshire Archives Service, ref. 71D80/17/1.

44. Bradford Chamber of Commerce, Report of the Deputation appointed by the Chamber to visit the Paris Exhibition, and to report on such portions as might concern the worsted trade in its various departments (Bradford 1867), 8, West Yorkshire Archives Service, ref. 71D80/17/1.

45. Bradford Reports of Workmen, 13.

46. Bradford Chamber of Commerce, *op. cit.*, 10–11.

47 The Memorial of the Council of the Bradford Chamber of Commerce, and of Bankers, Merchants, Spinners, and Manufacturers of Bradford, in Public Meeting Assembled, published in the Nineteenth Annual Report of the Chamber, 24 Jan. 1870.

48. 6 and 15 July 1870, published in the Twentieth Annual Report of the Bradford Chamber of Commerce, 16 Jan. 1871, 13–19.

49. The Board of Trade complained that these figures 'included those [goods] which pass through France in transit as well as French products while the exports from the United Kingdom to France were confined to British and Irish produce & manufactures'. Bradford Chamber of Commerce Council Minute Book, 1 Mar. 1870.

50. *Hansard*, 3rd ser., 199 (28 Feb. 1870), 883.

51. *Hansard*, 3rd ser., 201 (3 May 1870), 110–76.

52. Council Minutes, 29 Mar. 1870.

53. Minutes of the Tariff committee, Bradford Chamber of Commerce, Council Minute Book, 28 June 1870.

54. Quoted in J.R. Davis, 'Trade, Politics, Perspectives, and the Question of a British Commercial Policy towards the German States 1848–1866', 42.

55. Crowe to Lord Granville, 3 Nov. 1870, PRO/FO68/152. Crowe, whose first language was French, used this French spelling of tariff until much later in his career.

56. Robert I. Giesberg, *The Treaty of Frankfort* (Philadelphia: University of Pennsylvania Press, 1966), 143 and 164.

57. Robert Giffen, 'The Cost of the Franco-German War of 1870–71', in *Economic Inquiries and Studies* (Shannon: Irish University Press, facsimile copy of the London 1904 edn), vol. 1, 44.

58. Allan Mitchell, *The German Influence in France after 1870: The Formation of the French Republic* (Chapel Hill: University of North Carolina Press, 1979), 40.

59. Council of the Bradford Chamber of Commerce, 16 June 1871, reiterated

at a General Meeting of members, 3 July 1871, Council Minute Book.

60. Behrens to Russell, 14 June 1871, quoted in Gaston, 'Policy-Making and Free-Trade Diplomacy', 128.
61. Special Council Meeting, 29 July 1871, Bradford Chamber of Commerce Council Minute Book.
62. Special sub-committee report, Council Minute Book, 9 Aug. 1871, and the Twenty-Second Annual Report of the Bradford Chamber of Commerce, 20 Jan. 1873, 17–18.
63. Gladstone to Fortescue, 24 Aug. 1871, quoted in Gaston, 'Policy-Making and Free-Trade Diplomacy', 144.
64. Memorandum of 3 Oct. 1871, quoted in Dunham, The Anglo-French Treaty of Commerce of 1860 and the Progress of the Industrial Revolution in France, 303.
65. Gladstone to Bright, 24 Oct. 1871, in Gaston, 'Policy-Making and Free-Trade Diplomacy', 144.
66. See ibid., 187–94; Anthony Howe, Free Trade and Liberal England, 1846–1946, 162 n. 56.
67. Crowe to Granville, 20 Apr. 1871, PRO/FO299/17.
68. Crowe to Granville, 1 June 1871, ibid.
69. Crowe to Granville, 15 Nov. 1871, PRO/FO68/154.
70. In the words of the summary of this despatch which was given to the Queen. Royal Archives RA I.49/39.
71. Crowe to Granville, 15 Nov. 1871, PRO/FO68/154.
72. Gaston, 'Policy-Making and Free-Trade Diplomacy', 42–43. Lord Odo Russell was a nephew of the former Foreign Secretary and Prime Minister.
73. Ibid., 153.
74. Ibid., 165.
75. Hansard, 3rd ser., 211 (14 June 1872), 1795.
76. Gaston, 'Policy-Making and Free-Trade Diplomacy', 87–92.
77. R.A. Church, The Great Victorian Boom, 1850–1873 (London: Macmillan, 1975), 64.
78. 'The Proposed Commercial Treaty with France', The Economist, 28 Sept. 1872.

Chapter 5: The Impact of Depression, 1873–1879

1. The classic work on Germany's return to protectionism is Ivo Lambi's Free Trade and Protection in Germany 1868–1879 (Wiesbaden: Franz Steiner Verlag, 1963). On the legislation of 1873, see pp. 64–70. Also Crowe to Granville, 25 June 1873, PRO/FO64/784.
2. Ulrich Wengenroth, Enterprise and Technology: The German and British Steel Industries, 1865–1895 (Cambridge: Cambridge University Press, 1994), 46–47.
3. Ivo Lambi, Free Trade and Protection in Germany, 76.
4. A.H. Imlah, Economic Elements in the Pax Britannica: Studies in British Foreign Trade in the Nineteenth Century (Cambridge, Mass.: Harvard University Press, 1958), 176.
5. Sidney Pollard, European Economic Integration, 1815–1870, 26.
6. Percy Ashley, Modern Tariff History, 56.
7. Ulrich Wengenroth, Enterprise and Technology, 130. Wengenroth claims (p. 135) that in the German as well as British iron and steel industry 'The "losing prices" in the export trade thus fairly certainly still lay above the actual marginal costs.'
8. Michael S. Smith, Tariff Reform in France, 1860–1900, 49. Smith covers the phase of French tariff policy dealt with in this chapter on pp. 26ff.
9. 'French Trade since the War', The Economist, 27 Dec. 1873.
10. 'Belgian Competition in the Iron Trade', The Economist, 12 Dec. 1874.
11. 'German Competition with English Commerce', The Economist, 24 Jan. 1874. That extension of the hostility was not overt in Bradford.

12. Reported in *The Economist* for 22 Aug. 1874.
13. P.A. Gourevitch, 'International Trade, Domestic Coalitions, and Liberty: Comparative Responses to the Crisis of 1873–1896', *Journal of Interdisciplinary History* (autumn 1977), 281.
14. Paul Bairoch, 'European Trade Policy, 1815–1914', in Peter Mathias and Sidney Pollard, eds, *The Cambridge Economic History of Europe*, vol. 8, 48.
15. This argument is advanced in *ibid.*, 50–51.
16. 'The Relative Growth of the European Great Powers', *The Economist*, 19 June 1875.
17. 'The Comparative Wealth of France and Germany', *The Economist*, 30 Oct. 1875.
18. Crowe to Derby, 30 Jan. 1875, PRO/FO298/1.
19. Crowe to Derby, 9 July 1875, PRO/FO64/837.
20. Crowe to Derby, 5 Oct. 1875, *ibid.*
21. Derby to Crowe, 6 Nov. 1875, draft, *ibid.*
22. Frank J. Coppa, 'The Italian Tariff and the Conflict between Agriculture and Industry: The Commercial Policy of Liberal Italy, 1860–1922', *Journal of Economic History*, 30, 4 (Dec. 1970), 745 and 749.
23. Tariff committee minutes, 2 Feb. 1875, Bradford Chamber of Commerce Minute Book.
24. Behrens to Derby, 1 Mar. 1875, quoted in J.W. Gaston, 'The Free Trade Diplomacy Debate and the Victorian European Common Market Initiative', *Canadian Journal of History* (April 1997), 68. This article, which draws upon the author's doctoral dissertation, is the most perceptive study of its subject to date.
25. Michael S. Smith, *Tariff Reform in France, 1860–1900*, 44–45.
26. *Hansard*, 3rd ser., 224 (21 May 1875) 724.
27. *Ibid.*, 740.
28. *Ibid.*, 742.
29. The Cobden Club, *Free Trade and the European Treaties of Commerce* [including the proceedings at the dinner on 17 July 1875, correspondence on the prospects of free trade elsewhere, and discussion at a meeting of the Political Economy Society of Paris on 6 Aug. 1875] (London: Cassell, Petter & Galpin, 1875), 6–7.
30. Tariff committee, 6 Aug. 1875, Bradford Chamber of Commerce Minute Book.
31. Memorandum on Treaties of Commerce with, and between, European Powers, with Especial Reference to the Trade of the United Kingdom, 17 Sept. 1875, PRO/FO881/2670.
32. 'The Alleged Differential Duty on Spanish and Portuguese Wines', *The Economist*, 9 Oct. 1875.
33. Tenterden to Derby, 20 Sept. 1875, quoted in J.W. Gaston, 'Policy-Making and Free-Trade Diplomacy', 69.
34. Northcote to Derby, 28 Sept. 1875, quoted in *ibid.*, 71.
35. The best account of Northcote's initiative is in *ibid.*, 71–73.
36. Behrens to Derby, 19 Oct. 1875, *First Annual Report of the Joint Tariff Committee of the Yorkshire Chambers of Commerce* (Bradford: George Harrison, 1876), 19–25.
37. Letter of 6 Nov. 1875, quoted in *ibid.*, 39.
38. Report in *The Times*, 'The Austrian and Italian Treaties', 10 Nov. 1875.
39. Summarised positively in A.L. Dunham, *The Anglo-French Treaty of Commerce of 1860 and the Progress of the Industrial Revolution in France*, 321–24 and more briefly and negatively in Percy Ashley, *Modern Tariff History: Germany – United States – France*, 379.
40. J.W. Gaston, 'Policy-Making and Free-Trade Diplomacy', 77–78.
41. Crowe to Derby, 2 Nov. 1875, PRO/FO64/837.
42. Michael S. Smith, *Tariff Reform in France*, 20.

43. Ivo Lambi, *Free Trade and Protection in Germany 1868–1879*, 83ff.

44. 'Board of Trade Tables', *The Economist*, 8 Jan. 1876.

45. Portugal, however, extended the benefits of its 1866 treaty with France to Britain in April 1876 without securing any revision in the British wine duties.

46. 'Ought We to Reduce our Wine Duties for the Sake of a New Treaty of Commerce with France?' *The Economist*, 12 May 1877.

47. Supplemental Memorandum, January 1878, in 'The British Wine Duties, and their Bearing upon the Revision of the Treaties of Commerce', PRO/FO881/3683, 17.

48. Memoranda by Fred. Goulburn, 29 Sept. 1877, and C.J. Herries, 10 Dec. 1877, in *ibid.*

49. Crowe to Derby, 14 June 1876, PRO/FO298/1.

50. Crowe continued to use this French spelling until the 1880s. See chapter 4 above, n. 55.

51. Crowe to ?Derby, 9 June 1876, PRO/FO298/1.

52. Crowe to Derby, 14 June 1876, *ibid.*

53. Crowe to Derby, 22 Dec. 1876, PRO/FO64/861.

54. J.W. Gaston, 'Policy-Making and Free-Trade Diplomacy', 232. The French press reports were relayed in *The Economist* of 28 July 1877.

55. Michael S. Smith, *Tariff Reform in France*, 52–53.

56. J.W. Gaston, 'Policy-Making and Free-Trade Diplomacy', 269–272.

57. 'English and French Trade with Italy', *The Economist*, 8 Sept. 1877.

58. Draft of Instructions for Delegate Attending Austro-German Commercial Negotiations, in Lord Odo Russell to Lord Derby, 25 Apr. 1877, PRO/FO298/1, partial printed bluebook.

59. David James, *Victorian Bradford: The Living Past* (Halifax: Ryburn, 1987), Introduction.

60. John V. Godwin and Henry Illingworth, General Report of Inquiry into the Relative Conditions of Production in the Worsted Districts of France, 1876, Bradford, 15 Jan. 1877; Twenty-Sixth Annual Report of the Bradford Chamber of Commerce, 15 Jan. 1877, 13ff.

61. Special council meeting, 15 Mar. 1877, Council Minute Book.

62. Translation sent by Dominic Colnaghi, the British consul in Florence, 28 Dec. 1878, PRO/FO45/347/9103.

63. *The Economist* estimated that two-thirds of the fall in the value of exported woollen fabrics was due to the falling volume rather than to the falling price. 'Our Foreign Trade of 1877, Compared in Quantity and Value with that of 1872. II. Exports', *The Economist*, 27 July 1878.

64. 'Woollens, Mixed Fabrics, and Worsted, in the Paris Exhibition', *The Economist*, 21 Sept. 1878.

65. 'The Board of Trade Returns for December', *The Economist*, 11 Jan. 1879.

66. 'Our Foreign and Colonial Trade of Last Year Compared in Quantity and Value with that of 1877. II. – Exports', *The Economist*, 25 Jan. 1879.

67. See above, 12–15.

68. As reported by Crowe in his despatch of 11 Apr. 1878, PRO/FO64/917.

69. *Ibid.*

70. The estimate Salisbury later gave Crowe: Crowe to Lord Odo Russell, 11 Mar. 1879, PRO/FO918/25.

71. Percy Ashley, *Modern Tariff History: Germany – United States – France*, 380.

72. Which Salisbury in turn circulated to the Queen, Lord Beaconsfield (as Disraeli had become) and Northcote: Crowe to Salisbury, 27 July 1878, PRO/FO64/917/25. Crowe was later able to send Salisbury a translation of the proceedings: 'Protocols of the Heidelberg Conference', PRO/FO64/917/31888.

73. Dated 12 Nov. 1878, translated and sent by Crowe to Salisbury, 20 Nov.

1878, PRO/FO64/917/Commercial 31.
74. Crowe to Salisbury, 16 Nov. 1878, PRO/FO64/917/Commercial 29.
75. Russell to Salisbury, 30 Dec. 1878, PRO/FO64/914/79.
76. Russell to Salisbury, 10 Jan. 1879, PRO/FO64/940/5.
77. Crowe to Russell, 15 Jan. 1879, PRO/FO918/25.
78. They included C. Halford Thompson, 'Free Trade or Reciprocity?' *Fraser's Magazine*, new ser., 17 (1878), 89–92; A.J. Wilson, 'Can Reciprocity Help Us?', *Macmillan's Magazine*, 39 (Mar. 1879), 466–80; Alfred R. Wallace, 'Reciprocity the True Free Trade', *The Nineteenth Century* (Apr. 1879), 638–49; Robert Lowe, *The Nineteenth Century* (June 1879), 992–1002; and T.R. Whittaker, 'Free Trade, Reciprocity, and Foreign Competition', *The Westminster Review*, 221 (July 1879), 1–22. I am grateful to Professor Peter Cain for drawing these articles to my attention.
79. See e.g. Lord Grey, 'How Shall We Retain the Colonies?', *The Nineteenth Century* (June 1879), 935–54.
80. Report in *The Times* of 23 Feb. 1878.
81. Bradford Chamber of Commerce Council Minute Book, 20 Jan. 1879.
82. As reported in an article on 'Reciprocity' in *The Economist* of 25 Jan. 1879.
83. This debate was reported in *The Times* of 6 Mar. 1879.
84. *Hansard*, 3rd ser., 245 (29 Apr. 1879) 1393.
85. Salisbury to Russell, 12 Apr. 1879, draft, PRO/FO64/939/19.
86. Crowe to Russell, 18 Feb. 1879, PRO/FO918/25.
87. Crowe to Salisbury, 5 July 1879, PRO/FO64/944/Commercial 24.
88. Crowe to Salisbury, 8 Aug. 1879, PRO/FO64/944/Commercial 31.
89. Russell to Salisbury, 16 May 1879, PPRO/FO64/940/68.
90. Crowe to Salisbury, 14 Aug. 1879, PRO/FO64/944/Commercial 33.

91. Salisbury to Sir John Walsham, 21 June 1879, draft, PRO/FO64/939/39, and Walsham to Salisbury, 5 July 1879, PRO/F0/64/941/102.
92. Crowe to Salisbury, 20 June 1879, PRO/FO64/944/Commercial 16, and Walsham to Salisbury, 7 July 1879, PRO/FO64/941/106 & incl.

Chapter 6: Disengagement between Britain and France, 1879–1882

1. Memorandum on the Commercial Policy of European States and British Trade, 29 July 1879, PRO/FO881/3834.
2. M. de Molinari, discussed in *The Economist*, 8 Feb. 1879, 152.
3. Crowe to Lord Odo Russell, 22 Mar. 1879, PRO/FO918/25.
4. Crowe to Russell, 11 Mar. 1879, *ibid*.
5. J.W. Gaston, 'Policy-Making and Free-Trade Diplomacy', 240.
6. Crowe to Russell, 11 Mar. 1879, PRO/FO918/25.
7. Salisbury to Lyons, 12 Feb. 1879, quoted in J.W. Gaston, 'Policy-Making and Free-Trade Diplomacy', 239–40.
8. Crowe to Russell, 22 Mar. 1879, PRO/FO918/25.
9. *Reciprocity: A Letter Addressed to Mr. Thomas Bayley Potter, M.P., as Chairman of the Cobden Club* (London: Cassell Petter & Galpin, 1879), 16.
10. *Ibid*., 20.
11. J.W. Gaston, 'Policy-Making and Free-Trade Diplomacy', 19.
12. Pierre Tirard, *Liberté du commerce: Du développement de la bijouterie et de l'orfèvrerie par la liberté des titres de l'or et de l'argent* (Paris: A. Lechevalier, 1868), 86.
13. Lord Lyons to Salisbury, 5 Mar. 1880, PRO/FO425/130/215.
14. Lyons to Salisbury, 19 Mar. 1880, PRO/FO425/135/12.
15. Salisbury to Lyons, 28 Feb. 1880, PRO/FO425/130/207.

16. Salisbury to Lyons, 12 Mar. 1880, PRO/FO425/135/1.
17. For a full discussion of the terms of appointment, status and function of British consuls, see D.C.M. Platt, *The Cinderella Service: British Consuls since 1825* (Hamden, Connecticut: Archon Books, 1971).
18. Note by Kennedy on Crowe to Salisbury, 18 Mar. 1879, PRO/FO64/944.
19. Quoted in J.W. Gaston, 'Policy-Making and Free-Trade Diplomacy', 104. On 'Commercial Secretaries' in Russian embassies, see Russell to Salisbury, 2 Oct. 1879, PRO/FO64/941.
20. Quoted in J.W. Gaston, 'Policy-Making and Free-Trade Diplomacy', 106.
21. Crowe to Russell, 29 Apr. 1880, PRO/FO918/25.
22. Salisbury to Russell and Sir H. Elliot, the ambassador in Vienna, 20 Apr. 1880, draft, PRO/FO64/965/Commercial 13 and 26.
23. Lyons to Salisbury, 24 Mar. 1880, PRO/FO425/135/27.
24. George Michel, *Léon Say: sa vie, ses oeuvres* (Paris: Calmann Lévy, 1899), 352. My translation.
25. Memorandum on possible Alterations of the Wine Duties, 26 Apr. 1880, PRO/FO881/4128.
26. Gladstone to Granville, 4 May 1880, in Agatha Ramm, ed., *The Political Correspondence of Mr. Gladstone and Lord Granville, 1876–1886* (Oxford: Clarendon Press, 1962), vol. 1, 124.
27. Gladstone to Dilke, 11 May 1880, quoted in H.C.G. Matthew, ed., *The Gladstone Diaries*, vol. 9, 521.
28. Foreign Office telegraphic circular, 28 May 1880, quoted in J.W. Gaston, 'Policy-Making and Free-Trade Diplomacy', 241.
29. Gladstone to Dilke, 27 May 1880, quoted in *ibid.*, 51.
30. Dilke to Sir Henry Elliot, 31 May 1880, quoted in *ibid.*, 225–26.
31. Say to Granville, 8 June 1880, PRO/FO425/135/140.
32. Dilke's memorandum on an interview with Say, 6 May 1880, PRO/FO425/135/80.
33. Michael S. Smith, *Tariff Reform in France, 1860–1900*, 178.
34. 5 June 1880, quoted in George Michel, *Léon Say*, 357.
35. Granville to Say, 8 June 1880, PRO/FO425/135/146.
36. Granville to Gladstone, 7 June 1880, in Agatha Ramm, ed., *The Political Correspondence of Mr. Gladstone and Lord Granville*, vol. 1, 132.
37. Dilke's memorandum on an interview with Say, 6 May 1880, PRO/FO425/135/80.
38. *Hansard*, 3rd ser., 252 (10 June 1880), 1622ff.
39. Lyons to Granville, 23 June 1880, telegram, PRO/FO425/135/214.
40. Memorandum on French Commercial Negotiations, and the Present Position of the Question, enclosed in Dilke to Adam, 6 Aug. 1880, PRO/FO425/135/2.
41. Dilke to Adam, 6 Aug. 1880, *ibid.*
42. Dilke to Challemel-Lacour, 23 Aug. 1880, enclosed memorandum, 23 Aug. 1880, PRO/FO425/136/33.
43. *The Economist* of 17 July 1880 using figures provided by the South of Scotland Chamber of Agriculture.
44. In a memorandum dated 24 Sept. but not given to Dilke until he went to Paris in mid-October: PRO/FO425/136/105 enclosure. See also Dilke's report to Granville, 12 Oct. 1880, PRO/FO425/136/103.
45. Reported by Dilke to Granville, 12 Oct. 1880, *ibid.*
46. Allan Mitchell, *The German Influence in France after 1870*, 186–88.
47. Remarks by G.M. Wand, Bradford Chamber of Commerce Minute Book, 28 Sept. 1880.
48. Tariff Committee Minutes, 3 Dec. 1880, Bradford Chamber of Commerce Minute Book.
49. S.B. Saul, *Studies in British Overseas Trade, 1870–1914* (Liverpool: Liverpool University Press, 1960), 154.
50. Bradford Chamber of Commerce Council Minute Book, 27 July 1880.

51. David Nicholls, *The Lost Prime Minister: A Life of Sir Charles Dilke* (London: Hambledon Press, 1995), 96.

52. Bradford Chamber of Commerce Council Minute Book, 23 N 1880ff., Thirtieth Annual Report, 17 Jan. 1881, 18.

53. It was well presented by the secretary of the British embassy in Paris in a report of 14 Mar. 1881: F.O. Adams, Report on the Finances of France, Parliamentary Papers, Reports by HM's Secretaries of Embassy and Legation. Commercial. No. 17 (1881). (Trade Reports.)

54. Lyons to Granville, 22 Mar. 1881, PRO/FO425/137/50.

55. Quoted by Lyons to Granville, 10 Mar. 1881, PRO/FO425/137/10.

56. Lyons to Granville, 22 Mar. 1881, *ibid.*

57. Kennedy's memorandum, 11 Mar. 1881, PRO/FO425/137/11.

58. Tariff committee, 16 Mar. 1881, Council Minute Book, Bradford Chamber of Commerce.

59. Dilke to Behrens, 17 Mar. 1881, PRO/FO425/137/29.

60. Quoted at a special meeting reported in the *Bradford Observer* of 29 Apr. 1881.

61. Quoted at a meeting of the Chamber of Commerce in the *Bradford Observer* of 28 Apr. 1881.

62. Mr Tankard at the special meeting reported in the *Bradford Observer* of 29 Apr. 1881.

63. Minutes of a meeting of the whole Membership of the Chamber, Council Minute Book, 28 Apr. 1881.

64. Report of a meeting of members of the Chamber of Commerce in the *Bradford Observer* of 10 May 1881.

65. *Ibid.*

66. Report in the *Bradford Observer* of 17 May 1881.

67. Quoted in the *Bradford Observer* of 7 Apr. 1881.

68. Memorandum by Kennedy, 11 Apr. 1881, PRO/FO425/137/130.

69. Crowe to Salisbury, 9 Aug. 1879, PRO/FO64/944/Commercial 32.

70. J.W. Gaston, 'Policy-Making and Free-Trade Diplomacy', 22.

71. Reports of Mar. 1881 reprinted in the Thirty-First Annual Report of the Bradford Chamber of Commerce, 16 Jan. 1882, 46.

72. *Ibid.*, 53.

73. *Ibid.*, 61.

74. *Ibid.*, 52–53.

75. *Ibid.*, 63.

76. Newspaper report received at the Foreign Office on 25 May 1881, and enclosure in Stephen Watkins to Dilke, 3 June 1881, PRO/FO425/137/271 and 331.

77. E. Brunt to Granville, 17 June 1881 enclosure, PRO/FO425/137/387.

78. Thomas Hall from the Derby Chamber of Commerce to Granville, 17 June 1881 enclosure, and C.H. Hills from the Sheffield Chamber to Dilke, 24 June 1881, PRO/FO425/137/389 and 423.

79. Memorandum of 25 Apr. 1881, PRO/FO425/137/158.

80. Memorandum of 29 Apr. 1881, PRO/FO425/137/165.

81. Minute of 2 May 1880 by Chamberlain and letter of 1 May 1881 from Forster to Granville, in J.W. Gaston, 'Policy-Making and Free-Trade Diplomacy', 253–54.

82. Editorial in *The Economist* of 4 June 1881.

83. *Hansard*, 3rd ser., 262 (9 June 1881), 134.

84. David Nicholls, *The Lost Prime Minister: A Life of Sir Charles Dilke*, 96–97.

85. Lord Lyons to Granville, 10 June 1881, PRO/FO425/137/356.

86. *Hansard*, 3rd ser., 264 (12 Aug. 1881), 1735.

87. Joseph Chamberlain, *The French Treaty and Reciprocity: A Speech Delivered in the House of Commons, on Friday, August 12th, 1881, Revised* (London: Cassell, Petter, Galpin for the Cobden Club), 18. This edition of

his speech contains useful appendices.

88. *Ibid.*, 16.
89. *Ibid.*, 13.
90. Sir A. Paget to Granville, 13 Oct. 1881, PRO/FO425/138/220.
91. David Nicholls, *The Last Prime Minister: A Life of Sir Charles Dilke*, 97.
92. Michael S. Smith, *Tariff Reform in France, 1860–1900*, 190–91.
93. Max Suetens, *Histoire de la politique commerciale de la Belgique depuis 1830 jusqu'à nos jours*, 107.
94. Michael S. Smith, *Tariff Reform in France, 1860–1900*, 186 n. 80.
95. Minutes of a special confidential meeting convened to meet Sir Rivers Wilson (a member of the Commission for concluding a treaty of Commerce with France) and Mr. Austin Lee (Secretary of the Commission), 14 Oct. 1881, Council Minute Book, Bradford Chamber of Commerce.
96. By Michael G. Mulhall, *Balance-Sheet of the World for Ten Years, 1870–1880* (London: Edward Stanford, 1881).
97. Gladstone to Dilke, 2 Nov. 1881, in H.C.G. Matthew, ed., *The Gladstone Diaries*, vol. 10, 155–56.
98. Michael G. Mulhall, *Balance-Sheet of the World*, 41.
99. *Ibid.*, 42–43 and 48.
100. Maurice de Bunsen to Granville, 20 Dec. 1881, PRO/FO425/138/336.
101. Memorandum by Dilke, 28 Dec. 1881, PRO/FO425/138/344 enclosure.
102. Behrens to Austin Lee, 29 Dec. 1881, in the Chamber Council Minute Book, 30 Dec. 1881.
103. Memorandum by Mr. Bateman and Mr. Crowe on M. Sabatier's Report to the Belgian Chamber of Representatives on the Treaty of Commerce between Belgium and France of October 31, 1881, PRO/FO425/138, Appendix 1.
104. *Ibid.*
105. Editorial of 7 Jan. 1882.
106. *The Times* of 11 Oct. 1880, quoted in

107. Lyons to Granville, 3 Jan. 1882, quoted in J.P.T. Bury, *Gambetta's Final Years: 'The Era of Difficulties', 1877–1882* (London and New York: Longman, 1982), 305.
108. Note by Gambetta in Lyons to Granville, 25 Jan. 1882, PRO/FO425/138/397 enclosure.
109. Crowe to Dilke, 26 Jan. 1882, Dilke papers, BL/Add. MSS. 43912.
110. The British Commissioners to Granville, 26 Jan. 1882, PRO/FO425/138/398.
111. Freycinet to Lyons, 8 Feb. 1882, quoted in J.W. Gaston, 'Policy-Making and Free-Trade Diplomacy', 264.
112. Crowe to Dilke, 18 Feb. 1882, Dilke papers, BL/Add. MSS. 43912.
113. Reported by Lyons to Granville, 19 Feb. 1882, PRO/FO425/138/508.
114. Dilke to Behrens, 24 Feb. 1882, PRO/FO425/138/554.
115. Memorandum on the Business of the Commercial Department, 24 June 1885, PRO/FO881/8127.
116. Memorial of the Council of the Bradford Chamber of Commerce to Lord Granville, 4 Apr. 1882, in the Thirty-Second Annual Report of the Chamber, 15 Jan. 1883, 30–31.
117. See T.H. Farrer, *Free Trade versus Fair Trade* (London: Cassell, Petter, Galpin, 1882), 130–31.
118. *Hansard* 3rd ser., 267 (24 Mar. 1882), 1911.
119. Editorial in *The Economist* of 13 May 1882.

Chapter 7: The Quandary over Commercial Policy, 1883–1888

1. To the House of Commons on 24 Mar. 1882, above, 146.
2. Forrest Capie, for example, argues that 'there were two factors operating to keep effective protection down in the course of the century and what

evidence there is lends support to the view that in spite of nominal tariffs rising generally in the late nineteenth century, effective rates were constrained by the growing share of value added in gross output and the continuing tariffs on raw materials and other inputs together with the small scale on which drawbacks were granted.' He adds, however, that 'For some branches of textiles the effective rates were very high though they were falling dramatically.' 'Tariff Protection and Economic Performance in the Nineteenth Century', in John Black and L. Alan Winters, eds, *Policy and Performance in International Trade* (London: Macmillan, 1983), 16–17.

3. E.E.Y. Green, *The Crisis of Conservatism: The Politics, Economics and Ideology of the British Conservative Party, 1880–1914* (London: Routledge, 1996), 32–33.

4. Crowe to Lyons, 25 Oct. 1882, PRO/FO146/2481/2 and 23 Jan. 1883, PRO/FO27/2673; and J.W. Gaston, 'Policy-Making and Free Trade Diplomacy', 23–24.

5. R.E. Tyson, 'The Cotton Industry', in D.H. Aldcroft, ed., *The Development of British Industry and Foreign Competition, 1875–1914* (London: George Allen & Unwin, 1968), 106, 115 and 125.

6. Michael G. Mulhall, *Balance-Sheet of the World for Ten Years*, 53.

7. Crowe to Lyons, 24 Mar. 1883, Report on the Trade of France for the Year 1882, PRO/FO146/2566/6.

8. Allan Mitchell, *The German Influence in France after 1870*, 190.

9. Crowe to Francis Plunkett, 19 Sept. 1883, draft, PRO/FO146/2569/54.

10. Michael S. Smith, *Tariff Reform in France, 1860–1900*, 24.

11. Crowe to Lyons, 22 June 1883, PRO/FO146/2567/27.

12. Crowe to Lyons, 10 July 1883, draft, PRO/FO146/2568/32.

13. Michael G. Mulhall, *Balance-Sheet of the World for Ten Years*, 60–65.

14. German Trade and Industry: Abstract of a Pamphlet on the Industry and Trade of Germany during the First Year of the New Protective Policy, *Parliamentary Papers*, 1882, vol. 72, Commercial Reports, Reports from HM's Diplomatic and Consular Officers Abroad, on Subjects of Commercial and General Interest.

15. Ivo Lambi, *Free Trade and Protection in Germany, 1868–1879*, 228ff.

16. He argues further that the hesitant attitude of British steel industrialists towards the protectionist policies of their competitors prevented them from using 'their collective market power in time and to best effect'. Ulrich Wengenroth, *Enterprise and Technology: The German and British Steel Industries, 1865–1895*, 268.

17. Allan Mitchell, *The German Influence in France after 1870*, 189.

18. Chamberlain to Granville, 30 June 1882, in J.W. Gaston, 'Policy-Making and Free-Trade Diplomacy', 306. The following discussion of the Anglo-Spanish negotiations draws largely upon this thesis. For the shocked reaction to Chamberlain's suggestion, see the entry for 21 July 1882 in *The Diary of Sir Edward Walter Hamilton, 1880–1885* (Oxford: Clarendon Press, 1972), vol. 1, 310.

19. 'Spain and the Wine Duties', *The Economist*, 19 Aug. and 7 Oct. 1882, and 'Our Commercial Relations with Spain', *The Economist*, 14 Oct. 1882.

20. Bradford Chamber of Commerce Council Minute Book, 28 Feb. 1883.

21. *Ibid.*, 28 Mar. 1883.

22. J.W. Gaston, 'Policy-Making and Free-Trade Diplomacy', 307.

23. Report in *The Times*, 30 Mar. 1883.

24. 'Treaties of Commerce with, and between, European Powers, with Especial Reference to the Trade of the United Kingdom', memorandum dated 30 Mar. 1883, PRO/FO881/4779.

25. *Hansard* 3rd ser., 280 (8 June 1883), 12–13.

26. Report in *The Times*, 2 Nov. 1883.

27. Report by Mr. J.A. Crowe on the Trade of France in 1884, 26 May 1885, Parliamentary Papers: Commercial. No. 18 (1885), 155.

28. Preliminary Report on the Trade of the United Kingdom with France in 1883, 23 Jan. 1884, Parliamentary Papers: Commercial. No. 17 (1884).

29. Memorandum on the Business of the Commercial Department, 24 June 1885, PRO/FO881/5127.

30. Report by Mr. J.A. Crowe on the Trade of France in 1884, 26 May 1885, Parliamentary Papers: Commercial. No. 18 (1885), 157.

31. Memorandum by Mr. J.A. Crowe on the Trade of the United Kingdom with France in the Years 1881 and 1882, Parliamentary Papers: Commercial. No. 3 (1884), 23.

32. Crowe to Lyons, 10 Mar. 1884, PRO/FO27/2674.

33. Report by HM's Chargé d'Affaires at Dresden on the Effects of the German Tariff Reform of 1879, and on the Revision of 1885, 10 Sept. 1885, Parliamentary Papers, 1884–85, vol. 81.

34. Report in *The Times* of 17 Apr. 1884.

35. *Hansard*, 3rd ser., 293 (6 Nov. 1884), 1080.

36. B.H. Brown, *The Tariff Reform Movement in Great Britain, 1881–1895* (New York: Columbia University Press, 1943), 62.

37. First Report of the Royal Commission on the Depression of Trade and Industry, Parliamentary Papers, 1884–85, 71, Minutes of Evidence, 8 Oct. 1885, 23.

38. See the reaction to a speech by Granville at the Mansion House in *The Economist* of 15 Nov. 1884, p. 1387.

39. Minutes of Evidence, 8 Oct. 1885, 25.

40. Quoted by *The Times* of 6 Aug. 1885, in B.H. Brown, *The Tariff Reform Movement in Great Britain, 1885–1895*, 62.

41. Speech in south London reported in *The Times* of 5 Nov. 1885.

42. J.W. Gaston, 'Policy-Making and Free-Trade Diplomacy', 2–3.

43. D.A. Farnie, *The English Cotton Industry and the World Market, 1815–1896*, 109–12.

44. Second Report of the Royal Commission on the Depression of Trade and Industry, Parliamentary Papers, 1886, 21, Minutes of Evidence, 25 Feb. 1886, 248.

45. *Ibid.*, 249.

46. *Ibid.*, 259.

47. *Ibid.*, 260: question 6981.

48. Second Report of the Royal Commission on the Depression of Trade and Industry, Parliamentary Papers, 1886, 21, Minutes of Evidence, 28 Jan. 1886, 124–35.

49. Modern scholarship indicates that the recovery to which Behrens and Mitchell referred was restricted to the woollens side of the industry in Yorkshire and that the worsted side did not fare anything like so well. D.T. Jenkins and J.C. Malin, 'European Competition in Woollen Cloth, 1870–1914', *Business History*, 32, 4 (Oct. 1990), 66–86.

50. 'Information Obtained in Connection with the Royal Commission on the Depression of Trade', PRO/FO881/5266.

51. J.W. Gaston, 'Policy-Making and Free-Trade Diplomacy', 24–25.

52. Crowe to Lord Lytton, 22 Dec. 1889, PRO/FO27/2962.

53. Draft letter approved for despatch to the Foreign Office at a meeting of the tariff committee, Bradford Chamber of Commerce Council Minute Book, 23 Mar. 1887.

54. At a meeting of the tariff committee, Bradford Chamber of Commerce Council Minute Book, 8 June 1887.

55. Peter T. Marsh, *The Discipline of Popular Government: Lord Salisbury's Domestic Statecraft, 1881–1902* (Hassocks, Sussex: The Harvester Press, 1978), 129–30.

56. In the *English Historical Review* (April 1887), 296ff.

57. 'Mr Gladstone on the French Treaty of 1860', *The Economist*, 23 Apr. 1887.
58. 'Mr Gladstone on Fair Trade', *The Economist*, 31 Dec. 1887.
59. 'The Italian Tariff', *The Economist*, 20 Aug. 1887.
60. Crowe to Lyons, 20 June 1887, PRO/FO27/2863/60. Crowe reported to the Foreign Office through the British ambassador in Paris.
61. Crowe to Lyons, 20 June 1887, PRO/FO27/2863/61.
62. Crowe to Egerton, 18 Oct. 1887, PRO/FO27/2865.
63. 'The Italian Tariff', two articles in *The Economist*, 20 Aug. and 8 Oct. 1887; Tariff Committee Meeting, Bradford Chamber of Commerce Council Minute Book, 7 Oct. 1887.
64. Tariff Committee Meeting, Bradford Chamber of Commerce Council Minute Book, 18 Nov. 1887.
65. 'The Italian Tariff', *The Economist*, 13 Apr. 1889.
66. S.B. Saul, *Studies in British Overseas Trade, 1870–1914* (Liverpool: Liverpool University Press, 1960), 156.
67. Crowe to Lytton, 3 Mar. 1888, PRO/FO27/2913.
68. Percy Ashley, *Modern Tariff History: Germany – United States – France*, 398.
69. *Ibid.*, 399.
70. Published in *The Economist* of 19 Feb. 1887, 238–39.
71. Prepared by Dr Andrew Marrison, whose counsel on this book has been invaluable.
72. 'The Export Trade of Great Britain and the Continent Compared', *The Economist*, 19 Feb. 1887.
73. Ulrich Wengenroth, *Enterprise and Technology: The German and British Steel Industries, 1865–1895, passim.*
74. G.C. Allen, *The Industrial Development of Birmingham and the Black Country, 1860–1927* (New York: Augustus M. Kelley Reprints of Economic Classics, 1966), 185, 231–32 and 277.
75. 'The Export Trade of Great Britain and the Continent Compared', *The Economist*, 19 Feb. 1887.
76. *The Economist*, 27 July 1889, 959.

Chapter 8: The Transformation of the Network, 1889–1892

1. Again the best work on French commercial policy throughout this period is Michael S. Smith's *Tariff Reform in France, 1860–1900*. With regard to the following discussion, see p. 198ff.
2. Crowe to Lord Lytton, 5 Oct. 1889, PRO/FO/27/2962.
3. Crowe to Lytton, 10 Dec. 1889, *ibid.*
4. 'The Commercial Policy of France', *The Economist*, 21 June 1890.
5. Crowe to Lytton, 13 Oct. 1890, PRO/FO881/6185, 93.
6. 'The Proposed New French Customs Tariffs', *The Economist*, 1 Nov. 1890, 1382.
7. By 'import French woollens' Crowe may have meant 'export woollens to France'.
8. Crowe to Lytton, 21 Oct. 1890, PRO/FO881/6185, 95.
9. Crowe to Lytton, 31 Oct. 1890, PRO/FO881/6185, 99–100.
10. Michael S. Smith, *Tariff Reform in France, 1860–1900*, 205.
11. Sir Henry Drummond Wolff to Salisbury, 20 Apr. 1892, PRO/FO881/6289, 189.
12. 11 Feb. 1890, PRO/FO881/6185, 355–56.
13. Paul Bairoch, 'European Trade Policy, 1815–1914', in Peter Mathias and Sidney Pollard, eds, *The Cambridge Economic History of Europe*, vol. 8, 66–68.
14. Lord Vivian to Salisbury, 13 Feb. 1891, PRO/FO881/6185.
15. Lord Vivian to Salisbury, 24 Jan. 1891, *ibid.*
16. Crowe to Lord Vivian, 16 Nov. 1890, *ibid.*
17. Crowe to Lytton, 13 Oct. 1890, *ibid.*
18. Crowe to Lytton, 18 Oct. 1890, *ibid.*, 94.

19. Charles S. Scott to Salisbury, 30 Oct. 1890, *ibid.*, 520–21.
20. Scott to Salisbury, 27 Dec. 1890, *ibid.*, 525–26.
21. Quoted in Peter T. Marsh, *The Discipline of Popular Government*, 129.
22. Salisbury to the Treasury, 20 Oct. 1890, PRO/FO881/6185, 300–301.
23. R.E. Welby for the Treasury, 14 July 1890, *ibid.*, 296.
24. Welby for the Treasury, 7 Mar. 1891, *ibid.*, 301.
25. Sir F. Lascelles to Salisbury, 30 Mar. 1891, *ibid.*, 310–11.
26. 'The Question of Treaties of Commerce', *The Economist*, 22 Mar. 1890.
27. On the revival of Fair Trade in Yorkshire, see the Bradford Chamber of Commerce Council Minute Book for 19 and 30 Dec. 1890 and 6 Jan. 1891.
28. W.H.G. Armytage, *A.J. Mundella, 1825–1897* (London: Ernest Benn, 1951), 31 and 285–86.
29. The other members included Lowthian Bell, C.E. Bousfield, Frederick Brittain, W.L. Ewart, David Guthrie, Edward S. Hill and Joseph C. Lee, with A.E. Bateman from the Board of Trade as Secretary.
30. See T.G. Ottte, 'Eyre Crowe and British Foreign Policy: A Cognitive Map', in T.G. Otte and Constantine A. Pagedas, eds, *Personalities, War and Diplomacy: Essays in International History* (London: Frank Cass, 1997).
31. Lord Lytton to Salisbury, 10 Nov. 1890, PRO/FO27/3007.
32. Lord Dufferin to Lord Rosebery, 9 Jan. 1893, PRO/FO27/3125.
33. Crowe to Spenser Wilkinson, 4 Dec. 1890, Wilkinson Papers, National Army Museum.
34. Crowe to Sir Edward Malet, 24 Nov. 1890, PRO/FO881/6185, 252–53.
35. Lytton to Salisbury, 11 Dec. 1890, *ibid.*, 120.
36. Crowe to Lord Vivian, 16 Nov. 1890, *ibid.*
37. J. Alden Nichols, *Germany after Bismarck: The Caprivi Era, 1890–1894* (Cambridge, Mass.: Harvard University Press, 1958), 140.
38. Crowe to Sir Edward Malet, 24 Nov. 1890, PRO/FO881/6185.
39. Crowe to Wilkinson, 12 Dec. 1890, Spenser Wilkinson Papers, National Army Museum.
40. Crowe to C.S. Scott, 1 Dec. 1890, PRO/FO881/6185, 523–24.
41. First Report of the Trade and Treaties Committee, 24 Jan. 1891, FRO/FO881/6185, 163–65.
42. Salisbury to Lytton, 12 Feb. 1891, *ibid.*, 160.
43. *Ibid.*, 160–63.
44. *Ibid.*, 165–66.
45. Crowe to Lytton, 23 and 26 Oct. 1981, PRO/FO881/6211, 100.
46. Crowe to Lytton, 29 Jan. 1891, PRO/FO881/6185, 526–27.
47. Crowe to Lytton, 24 Feb. 1891, *ibid.*, 529–30.
48. C.S. Scott to Salisbury, 13 Mar. 1891, *ibid.*, 530–32.
49. Crowe to Lytton, 27 July 1891, *ibid.*, 249.
50. Paget to Salisbury, 8 Apr. 1891, PRO/FO881/6185, 265.
51. Reported in translation from the French journal *Débats* by Crowe, enclosed in Lytton to Salisbury, 13 Apr. 1891, PRO/FO881/6185, 185.
52. Lord Vivian to Salisbury, 23 Sept. 1891, PRO/FO881/6211, 32–33.
53. G. Strachey to Salisbury, 29 May 1891, PRO/FO881/6185, 269.
54. Charles S. Scott to Salisbury, 11 and 13 Aug. 1891, PRO/FO881/6211, 462 and 465.
55. PRO/FO881/6185, 6211 and 6289.
56. 4 Mar. 1891, quoted in C.J. Fuchs, *The Trade Policy of Great Britain and her Colonies since 1860*, trans. C.H.M. Archibald (London: Macmillan, 1905), 71.
57. Third Report of the Trade and Treaties Committee, 24 Apr. 1891, PRO/FO881/6185.
58. Crowe to Lytton, 2 June 1891, PRO/FO881/6185, 223.
59. Sir Frank Lascelles to Salisbury, 20 July 1891, *ibid.*, 348.
60. Crowe's report enclosed in Edwin H.

Egerton to Salisbury, 21 July 1891, *ibid.*, 346.

61. Crowe to Lytton, 20 Oct. 1891, PRO/FO881/6211, 98.
62. Lord Vivian to Salisbury, 13 Nov. 1891, *ibid.*, 35.
63. Charles S. Scott to Salisbury, 24 Nov. 1891, *ibid.*, 469.
64. Quoted by Crowe, who called the words 'strong and almost untranslatable', to Egerton, 25 Nov. 1891, *ibid.*, 111.
65. Crowe to Egerton, 6 Dec. 1891, *ibid.*, 118.
66. Sir Edward Malet to Salisbury, 2 Jan. 1892, *ibid.*, 176.
67. Charles S. Scott to Salisbury, 8 Dec. 1891, *ibid.*, 471.
68. As reported in two despatches from E.C.H. Phipps to Salisbury of 8 Dec. 1891, *ibid.*, 5–8.
69. Report by Consul-General Oppenheimer on the New German Treaties and British German Commerce, 13 Feb. 1892, *ibid.*, 204.
70. Nichols, *Germany after Bismarck*, 147.
71. Phipps to Salisbury, 11 Dec. 1891, PRO/FO881/6211, 11.
72. Memorandum presenting the German perspective by H. Farnell, 11 Dec. 1891, *ibid.*, 170.
73. Précis of a Speech by General Caprivi in the Reichstag during the Debate on the Commercial Treaties, delivered on 10 Dec. 1891, *ibid.*, 172–74.
74. 'The Central European Customs Union', *The Economist* of 12 Dec. 1891.
75. Précis of Caprivi's speech on 10 Dec. 1891, PRO/FO881/6211, 172–74.
76. 'Protectionist Tariffs and our Foreign Trade', *The Economist*, 28 Nov. 1891.
77. Report by Consul-General Oppenheimer on the New German Treaties and British German Commerce, PRO/FO881/6211, 202.
78. Report by Mr. Phipps on British Trade with Austria-Hungary (as to Imports from Great Britain and Colonies) in so far as Affected by the New Treaties, 21 Dec. 1891, PRO/FO881/6211, 13–17.
79. *Ibid.*, 235.
80. Report from Charles S. Dundas at Hamburg, 25 Feb. 1892, *ibid.*, 213.
81. *Ibid.*, 243.
82. Report from Conyngham Greene at Brussels, 23 Jan. 1892, *ibid.*, 57–58.
83. Report by Rennell Rodd enclosed in Lord Dufferin to Lord Salisbury, 11 Jan. 1892, *ibid.*, 297–98.
84. Charles S. Scott to Salisbury, 12 Jan. 1892, *ibid.*, 474.
85. Extract of 16 Jan. 1892 translated and enclosed in Consul-General T. Michell to Salisbury, 2 Feb. 1892, *ibid.*, 457.
86. Crowe to Egerton, 5 Feb. 1892, *ibid.*, 154.
87. Sir Clare Ford to Salisbury, 8 Dec. 1891, *ibid.*
88. Charles S. Scott to Salisbury, 25 Jan. 1892, *ibid.*, 479–80.
89. Sir Clare Ford to Salisbury, 30 Jan. 1892, *ibid.*, 427–28.
90. W.A.C. Barrington telegram to Salisbury, 16 Feb. 1892, *ibid.*, 434.
91. Drummond Wolff to Salisbury, 1 Apr. 1892, *ibid.*, 451.
92. Eighth Report of the Trade and Treaties Committee, 11 Mar. 1892, PRO/FO881/6289, 161–64.
93. E.H.H. Green, *The Crisis of Conservatism: The Politics, Economics and Ideology of the British Conservative Party, 1880–1914*, 51.
94. 'Commercial Relations with Spain', *The Economist*, 7 May 1892.
95. Drummond Wolff telegram to Salisbury, 4 Apr. 1892, PRO/FO881/6289, 171–72.
96. Salisbury telegram to Drummond Wolff, 5 Apr. 1892, *ibid.*, 172.
97. Report in *The Times*, 12 Apr. 1892, reprinted in *ibid.*, 178.
98. Wolff to Salisbury, 14 Apr. 1892, *ibid.*, 186.
99. Confidential Memorandum on the General Negotiations, 13 Apr. 1892, *ibid.*, 185.

100. Wolf to Salisbury, 14 Apr. 1892, *ibid.*, 186.
101. Wolff telegram to Salisbury, 22 Apr. 1892, *ibid.*, 186.
102. Wolff to Salisbury, 20 Apr. 1892, *ibid.*, 189.
103. Memorandum by Crowe, 28 Apr. 1892, *ibid.*, 192–93.
104. C.M. Kennedy, Minutes on the Commercial Negotiations with Spain, 4 May 1892, *ibid.*, 195.
105. Wolff telegram to Salisbury, 23 Apr. 1892, *ibid.*, 187.
106. Twelfth Report of the Trade and Treaties Committee, 29 Apr. 1892, *ibid.*, 194.
107. Reported in *The Times*, 19 May 1892.
108. 'Lord Salisbury's Advocacy of Tariff Wars', *The Economist*, 21 May 1892.
109. A.J. Balfour, in *Hansard*, 4th ser., 5 (3 June 1892), 555.
110. Board of Trade to Foreign Office, 10 June 1892, Drummond Wolff telegram to Salisbury, 15 June 1892, and Drummond Wolff to Salisbury, 13 June 1892 (received at the Foreign Office after the telegram of 14 June), PRO/FO881/6289, 233–4, 245 and 247.
111. Salisbury to Wolff, 20 June 1892, *ibid.*, 250.
112. Crowe to Lord Dufferin, 26 May 1892, *ibid.*, 58, and Crowe to Phipps, 22 June 1892, PRO/FO27/3087.
113. Frank J. Coppa, 'The Italian Tariff and the Conflict between Agriculture and Industry: The Commercial Policy of Liberal Italy, 1860–1922', *Journal of Economic History*, 30, 4 (Dec. 1970), 753.
114. Memorandum of 25 May 1892 enclosed in Lord Vivian to Lord Salisbury of the same date, PRO/FO881/6289, 73.
115. D.A. Farnie, *The English Cotton Industry and the World Market, 1815–1896*, 181.
116. Chamberlain to Balfour, 19 July 1892, in R.T. Shannon, *The Age of Salisbury, 1881–1902* (London: Longman, 1996), 380.
117. *Ibid.*, 379.
118. Sir Edward Malet to Salisbury, 6 Aug. 1892, PRO/FO881/6289, 68.
119. Percy Sanderson, Report on Roumanian Trade, Agriculture, and Danube Navigation from 1881–1890, 5 Feb. 1892, Parliamentary Papers, 1892, lxxx.
120. 'The Foreign Trade of Roumania', *The Economist*, 19 Dec. 1891; extract from the *Curierul Financiar* of 1 May 1892, PRO/FO881/6289, 134–35.
121. Among the many letters to this effect is A.G. Vansittart to Salisbury, 15 June 1892, *ibid.*, 141.
122. Telegrams from Salisbury to Vansittart, 29 July and 2 and 12 Aug. 1892, *ibid.*, 151 and 154.
123. Crowe to Lord Dufferin, 26 Dec. 1892, PRO/FO27/3089.
124. 'Commercial Treaties and Tariffs', *The Economist*, 10 Dec. 1892.
125. R.T. Shannon, *The Age of Salisbury, 1881–1902*, 350.

Chapter 9: In Retrospect

1. John Maynard Keynes, *The Economic Consequences of the Peace* (New York: Harcourt, Brace and Howe, 1920), 17–18 and 65–66.
2. Paul Bairoch, 'European Trade Policy, 1815–1914', in Peter Mathias and Sidney Polland, eds, *The Cambridge Economic History of Europe*, vol. 8, 70, 88–90.
3. Andrew Marrison, ed., *Free Trade and its Reception 1815–1960* (London: Routledge, 1998), vol. 1, 231–32.
4. Max Suetens, *Histoire de la politique commerciale de la Belgique depuis 1830 jusqu'à nos jours*, 104.
5. Preface to *ibid.*, vii–ix.
6. Cf. Ulrich Wengenroth's insistence that the captains of the British steel industry 'had long overestimated the demand from the colonies and less developed countries in South America and Asia and had

simultaneously underestimated the developments on the Continent': *Enterprise and Technology: The German and British Steel Industries, 1865–1895*, 270.

7. The widespread impression that Germany attained industrial equality with Britain before 1914, particularly in iron and steel, is challenged by Ulrich Wengenroth in *ibid.*, 264ff.

List of Secondary Sources
Books, articles and theses referred to in the notes

Allen, G.C. *The Industrial Development of Birmingham and the Black Country, 1860–1927*. New York: Augustus M. Kelly Reprints of Economics Classics, 1966.

Amé, Léon. *Etude sur les traités de commerce*. Paris: Librairie Guillaumin, 1876.

Armytage, W.H.G. *A.J. Mundella, 1825–1897*. London: Ernest Benn, 1951.

Ashley, Percy. *Modern Tariff History: Germany – United States – France*. London: John Murray, 1904.

Bairoch, Paul. 'Geographic Structure and Trade Balance of European Foreign Trade from 1800 to 1970', *Journal of European Economic History* 3, 3 (winter 1974).

——. 'European Trade Policy, 1815–1914', in *The Cambridge Economic History of Europe*. vol. 8., Peter Mathias and Sidney Pollard (eds). Cambridge: Cambridge University Press, 1989.

Behrens, Sir Jacob. *Sir Jacob Behrens, 1806–1889*. Translated by Harry Behrens. London: Percy, Lund Humphries & Co., 1925.

Brown, B.H. *The Tariff Reform Movement in Great Britain, 1881–1895*. New York: Columbia University Press, 1943.

Brown, David Alan. *Berenson and the Connoisseurship of Italian Painting*. Washington, D.C.: National Gallery of Art, 1979.

Brown, Lucy. *The Board of Trade and the Free-Trade Movement, 1830–42*. Oxford: Clarendon Press, 1958.

Bury, J.P.T. *Gambetta's Final Years: 'The Era of Difficulties', 1877–1882*. London and New York: Longman, 1982.

Capie, Forrest. 'Tariff Protection and Economic Performance in the Nineteenth Century', in *Policy and Performance in International Trade*, John Black and L. Alan Winters (eds). London: Macmillan, 1983.

Chamberlain, Joseph. *The French Treaty and Reciprocity: A Speech Delivered in the House of Commons on Friday, August 12th, 1881, Revised*. London: Cassell, Petter, Galpin for the Cobden Club.

Church, Roy. *The Great Victorian Boom, 1850–1873*. London: Macmillan, 1975.

Clapham, J.H. *The Woollen and Worsted Industries*. London: Methuen, 1907.

The Cobden Club. *Free Trade and the European Treaties of Commerce*. London: Cassell, Petter & Galpin, 1875.

Coppa, Frank J. 'The Italian Tariff and the Conflict between Agriculture and Industry: The Commercial Policy of Liberal Italy, 1860–1922', *Journal of Economic History*, 30, 4 (Dec. 1970): 742–69.

Cudworth, William. *Worstedopolis: A Sketch History of the Town and Trade of Bradford, the Metropolis of the Worsted Industry*. Bradford: W. Byles and Sons, 1888.

Davis, John R. 'Trade, Politics, Perspectives, and the Question of a British Commercial Policy towards the German States 1848–1866.' Ph.D. thesis, Glasgow University, 1993.
——. *Britain and the German Zollverein, 1848–66*. London: Macmillan, 1997.
Denman, Sir Roy. *Missed Chances: Britain and Europe in the Twentieth Century*. London: Cassell, 1996.
Durham, A.L. *The Anglo-French Treaty of Commerce of 1860 and the Progress of the Industrial Revolution in France*. Ann Arbor: University of Michigan Publications, 1930.
Farnie, D.A. *The English Cotton Industry and the World Market, 1815–1896*. Oxford: Clarendon Press, 1979.
Farrer, T.H. *Free Trade versus Fair Trade*. London: Cassell, Petter, Galpin, 1882.
Fuchs, C.J. *The Trade Policy of Great Britain and her Colonies since 1860*. Translated by C.H.M. Archibald. London: Macmillan, 1905.
Gallagher, J., and R.E. Robinson. 'The Imperialism of Free Trade', *Economic History Review*, 2nd ser., 6 (1953): 1–15.
Gaston, J.W. 'Policy-Making and Free-Trade Diplomacy: Britain's Commercial Relations with Western Europe, 1869–1886.' Ph.D. thesis, University of Saskatchewan, 1975.
——. 'The Free Trade Diplomacy Debate and the Victorian European Common Market Initiative', *Canadian Journal of History*, 13 (1979): 59–82.
Giesberg, Robert I, *The Treaty of Frankfort*. Philadelphia: University of Pennsylvania Press, 1966.
Giffen, Robert. 'The Cost of the Franco-German War of 1870–71', in *Economic Inquiries and Studies*, vol. 1. London: George Bell, 1904, 1–74.
Gladstone, W.E. 'The History of 1852–60, and Greville's Latest Journals', *English Historical Review* (April 1887), vol. 2, 281–302.
Gourevitch, P.A. 'International Trade, Domestic Coalitions, and Liberty: Comparative Responses to the Crisis of 1873–1896', *Journal of Interdisciplinary History* (autumn 1977): 281–313.
Green, E.E.Y. *The Crisis of Conservatism: The Politics, Economics and Ideology of the British Conservative Party, 1880–1914*. London: Routledge, 1996.
Grey, Lord. 'How Shall We Retain the Colonies?', *The Nineteenth Century* (June 1879): 935–54.
Hamilton, Sir Edward Walter. *The Diary of Sir Edward Walter Hamilton, 1880–1885*, D.W.R. Bahlman (ed.), 2 vols. Oxford: Clarendon Press, 1972.
Helleiner, Karl F. *Free Trade and Frustration: Anglo-Austrian Negotiations 1860–70*. Toronto: University of Toronto Press, 1973.
Howe, Anthony. *Free Trade and Liberal England, 1846–1946*. Oxford: Clarendon Press, 1997.
Iliasu, Asaana. 'The Role of Free Trade Treaties in British Foreign Policy, 1859–1871.' Ph.D. thesis, University of London, 1965.
——. 'The Cobden-Chevalier Commercial Treaty of 1860.' *Historical Journal*, 14, 1 (1971): 67–98.
Imlah, A.H. *Economic Elements in the Pax Britannica: Studies in British Foreign Trade in the Nineteenth Century*. Cambridge, Mass.: Harvard University Press, 1958.
Irwin, Douglas A. 'Multilateral and Bilateral Trade Policies in the World Trading System: An Historical Perspective', in *New Dimensions in Regional Integration*, Jaime de Melo and Arvid Panagariya (eds). Cambridge: Cambridge University Press, 1993.
——. 'The Reciprocity Debate in Parliament, 1842–1846', in *Free Trade and its Reception, 1815–1960*, Andrew Marrison (ed.), vol. 1. London: Routledge, 1998.
——. *Against the Tide: An Intellectual History of Free Trade*. Princeton: Princeton University Press, 1996.
James, David. *Victorian Bradford: The Living Past*. Halifax: Ryburn, 1987.
——. *Bradford*. Halifax: Ryburn, 1990.
James, Harold. *A German Identity, 1770–1990*. London: Weidenfeld & Nicolson, 1990.

James, Scott C., and David A. Lake. 'The Second Face of Hegemony: Britain's Repeal of the Corn Laws and the American Walker Tariff of 1846', *International Organization*, 43 (winter 1989): 1–29.

Jenkins, D.T., and J.C. Malin. 'European Competition in Woollen Cloth, 1870–1914', *Business History*, 32, 4 (Oct. 1990): 66–86.

Keynes, John Maynard. *The Economic Consequences of the Peace*. New York: Harcourt, Bruce and Howe, 1920.

Kindleberger, Charles. *The World in Depression*. Boston: Little, Brown, 1973.

Kodischek, Theodore. *Class Formation and Urban-Industrial Society: Bradford, 1750–1850*. Cambridge: Cambridge University Press, 1990.

Lambi, Ivo. *Free Trade and Protection in Germany 1868–1879*. Wiesbaden: Franz Steiner Verlag, 1963.

Long, Dwight C. 'The Austro-French Commercial Treaty of 1866', *American Historical Review*, 41 (1936): 474–91.

Lowe, Robert. 'Reciprocity and Free Trade', *The Nineteenth Century* (June 1879): 992–1002.

Luzzatto, G. 'The Italian Economy in the First Decade after Unification', in *Essays in European Economic History, 1789–1914*, F. Crouzet, W.H. Chaloner and W.M. Stern (eds). New York: St. Martin's Press, 1969.

McClosky, Donald N. 'Magnanimous Albion: Free Trade and British National Income, 1841–1881', *Explorations in Economic History*, 17 (1980): 303–20.

McKeown, Timothy H. 'Hegemonic Stability and 19th-Century Tariff Levels in Europe', *International Organization*, 37 (1983): 73–91.

McMillan, James F. *Napoleon III*. London: Longman, 1996.

Marrison, Andrew (ed.). *Free Trade and its Reception, 1815–1960*, vol. 1. London: Routledge, 1998.

Marsh, Peter T. *The Discipline of Popular Government: Lord Salisbury's Domestic Statecraft, 1881–1902*. Hassocks: The Harvester Press, 1978.

——. *Joseph Chamberlain, Entrepreneur in Politics*. London and New Haven: Yale University Press, 1994.

Mathew, H.C.G. (ed.). *The Gladstone Diaries: with Cabinet Minutes and Prime-Ministerial Correspondence*. vol. 8. Oxford: Clarendon Press, 1982.

Mathias, Peter and Sidney Pollard (eds). *The Cambridge Economic History of Europe*. vol. 8. Cambridge: Cambridge University Press, 1989.

Michel, George. *Léon Say: sa vie, ses oeuvres*. Paris: Calmann Lévy, 1899.

Milward, Alan. 'Tariffs as Constitutions', in *The International Politics of Surplus Capacity: Competition for Market Shares in the World Recession*, Susan Strange and Roger Tooze (eds). London: George Allen & Unwin, 1981.

Mitchell, Allan. *The German Influence in France after 1870: The Formation of the French Republic*. Chapel Hill: University of North Carolina Press, 1979.

Mulhall, Michael G. *Balance-Sheet of the World for Ten Years, 1870–1880*. London: Edward Stanford, 1881.

Nicholls, David. *The Lost Prime Minister: A Life of Sir Charles Dilke*. London: Hambledon Press, 1995.

Nichols, J. Alden. *Germany after Bismarck: The Caprivi Era, 1890–1894*. Cambridge, Mass.: Harvard University Press, 1958.

Nye, John Vincent. 'Revisionist Tariff History and the Theory of Hegemonic Stability', *Politics and Society*, 19, 2 (1991): 209–32.

——. 'The Myth of Free-Trade Britain and Fortress France: Tariffs and Trade in the Nineteenth Century', *Journal of Economic History*, 51 (March 1991): 23–46.

——. 'Changing French Trade Conditions, National Welfare, and the 1860 Anglo-French Treaty of Commerce', *Explorations in Economic History*, 28 (1991): 460–77.

O'Brien, P.K., G.A. Pigman and G. Allen. 'Free Trade, British Hegemony and the International Economic Order in the Nineteenth Century', *Review of International Studies*, 18 (1992): 89–113.

Otte, T.G. 'Eyre Crowe and British Foreign Policy: A Cognitive Map', in *Personalities, War and Diplomacy: Essays in International History*, T.G. Otte and Constantine A. Pagedas (eds). London: Frank Cass, 1997.

Platt, D.C.M. *The Cinderella Service: British Consuls since 1825*. Hamden, Connecticut: Archon Books, 1971.

Pollard, Sidney. *European Economic Integration, 1815–1970*. London: Thames & Hudson, 1974.

Ramm, Agatha (ed.). *The Political Correspondence of Mr. Gladstone and Lord Granville, 1876–1886*. Oxford: Clarendon Press, 1962.

Ratcliff, Barrie M. 'The Origins of the Anglo-French Commercial Treaty of 1860', in *Great Britain and her World, 1750–1914*. Manchester: Manchester University Press, 1975.

Rist, Marcel. 'A French Experiment with Free Trade: The Treaty of 1860', in *Essays in French Economic History*, Rondo Cameron (ed.). Homewood, Illinois: Richard D. Irwin for the American Economic Association, 1970.

Roberts, Robert, and David Kynaston. *The Bank of England: Money, Power and Influence 1694–1994*. Oxford: Clarendon Press, 1995.

Tombs, Robert. *France, 1814–1914*. London: Longman, 1991.

Saul, S.B. *Studies in British Overseas Trade, 1870–1914*. Liverpool: Liverpool University Press, 1960.

Schlote, Werner. *British Overseas Trade from 1700 to the 1930s*. Translated by W.O. Henderson and W.H. Chaloner. Oxford: Basil Blackwell, 1952.

Shannon, R.T. *The Age of Salisbury, 1881–1902*. London: Longman, 1996.

Smith, Michael Stephen. *Tariff Reform in France, 1860–1900: The Politics of Economic Interest*. Ithaca and London: Cornell University Press, 1980.

Stein, Arthur A. 'The Hegemon's Dilemma: Great Britain, the United States, and the International Economic Order', *International Organization*, 38, 2 (spring 1984): 355–86.

Suetens, Max. *Histoire de la politique commerciale de la Belgique depuis 1830 jusqu'à nos jours*, with a preface by Paul-Henri Spaak. Brussels: Editions de la Librairie Encyclopédique, 1955.

Thompson, C. Halford. 'Free Trade or Reciprocity?', *Fraser's Magazine*, new ser., 27 (January 1878): 89–92.

Tirard, Pierre. *Liberté du commerce. Du développement de la bijouterie et de l'orfèvrerie par la liberté des titres de l'or et de l'argent*. Paris: A. Lechevalier, 1868.

Tyson, R.E. 'The Cotton Industry', in *The Development of British Industry and Foreign Competition, 1875–1914*, D.H. Aldcroft (ed.). London: George Allen & Unwin, 1968.

Wallace, Alfred R. 'Reciprocity the True Free Trade', *The Nineteenth Century*, vol. 5 (Apr. 1879): 638–49.

Wengenroth, Ulrich. *Enterprise and Technology: The German and British Steel Industries, 1865–1895*. Cambridge: Cambridge University Press, 1994.

Whittaker, T.R. 'Free Trade, Reciprocity, and Foreign Competition', *The Westminster Review*, 221 (July 1879): 1–22.

Wilson, A.J. 'Can Reciprocity Help Us?', *Macmillan's Magazine*, 39 (Mar. 1879): 466–80.

INDEX

ad valorem duties, 21–22, 68, 102, 105, 118, 122, 126, 131, 133, 139–140, 142–143, 150, 157

agriculture, 67, 77, 91–92, 94, 95–96, 126–128, 137–138, 151–152, 164–165, 174–177, 183, 203, 205, 208

Albert, Prince, 25–26

Alsace–Lorraine, 80–81, 89–91, 151–152

Anglo–French (Cobden's) treaty of 1860, 3–7, 8–29, 32, 38–39, 42, 45, 47, 54–55, 57–59, 61–62, 70ff., 82ff., 102, 114, 117ff., 148, 155, 165–166

articles de Paris, 58

Australia, 141, 163

Austria, 8, 11, 14, 24–26, 29, 32, 41–45, 49–53, 61, 63ff., 75, 81, 83, 93, 94, 97–99, 101, 104, 107–109, 112–113, 117, 119, 123–124, 126, 128, 137, 140–142, 155, 165–169, 173, 176, 178–179, 181ff., 193–194, 197, 201, 203, 205–206

Austria Hungary *see* Austria

Austro-Prussian War, 63ff.

Bagehot, Walter, 17

Balance-Sheet of the World, 140–141, 150–151

Balkans, 26

Baltic sea, 19

banks, 52, 65, 68–69, 74, 84, 95, 141

Barron, H.P.T., 34–35

Bateman, A.E., 143

Bateman, Lord, 115

Bavaria, 42, 44

Beaumont, Somerset, 51–52

beer, 77, 105, 112, 128

Behrens, Jacob, 1, 18–23, 26, 33, 50–52, 57, 67, 74, 79, 82, 94, 96, 101–102, 104, 114–115, 122, 130–132, 134–135, 142, 146, 154, 162–163, 165–166, 169, 179 180, 188, 208, 212

Belgium, 4, 26, 28–37, 40, 43, 45, 48–49, 54, 59–60, 66, 69, 75, 81, 85, 90–92, 97–98, 137, 139–141, 143, 155–156, 159, 161, 164, 168–170, 172–173, 176–178, 181, 186, 188, 190–191, 194–195, 197, 208–210, 212

Birley, Hugh, 78–79

Birmingham, 38, 95, 127, 130, 154, 170

Bismarck, 41–45, 63ff., 80ff., 88–89, 93, 112–113, 115, 117, 151–152, 157–159, 163, 166–167, 172–173, 182, 192–193, 202, 208

Bleichröder, Gerson, 193–194

Board of Trade, 8, 21, 28, 30ff., 46ff., 71, 75–76, 82–83, 86, 95, 100, 125, 135, 143, 152–153, 158, 167, 169, 180, 185, 196, 203, 212

Bordeaux, 58, 74, 188

Bradford, ix, 17–23, 30–31, 33–34, 36, 38–39, 43, 46, 58–59, 67, 69, 74–77, 79, 82, 96, 101, 108–109, 114, 116, 127, 130–131, 133–134, 138, 140, 142, 146, 150, 154, 159, 162–163, 166, 170, 205, 212

Bremen, 86

Bright, John, 9, 71, 83

budget of 1860, 6, 15–16, 99, 126–127, 130

business classes/community, 5–6, 10, 15–23, 51, 78, 108, 113, 116–117, 149, 164, 194

Calais, 189
Canada, 141, 163
Caprivi, Count von, 7, 173, 182–183,
    192–193, 208
Cavalcaselle, Giovanni Battista, 24
Chamberlain, Joseph, 57, 125, 135, 138,
    149, 153–154, 156, 178, 202, 205
Chambers of Commerce, 5, 19–21, 33,
    37–39, 43, 46ff., 50–51, 72, 74–75, 78,
    83, 85–86, 95–96, 101–102, 106–107,
    114–115, 123, 132–133, 135–137, 143,
    149, 152–154, 166, 175, 180, 184–185,
    187–188, 194, 212
chemicals, 22, 38, 60, 106, 151, 164, 205
Chevalier, Maurice, 9–10, 21, 78
China, 9, 32, 54, 69, 82
Civil War, American, 5, 18, 32, 35, 54, 58,
    62–63, 68, 70, 73–74, 91–92, 201
Clarendon, Lord, 71, 79
coal, 16, 20, 66, 69, 72, 77–78, 84, 87,
    106–107, 139, 177, 193
Cobden, Richard, 1, 6, 8–28 passim, 31,
    33–34, 45, 47, 51–53, 57, 59, 61–62, 67,
    71, 78, 80–81, 83, 85, 88, 95, 98, 101,
    105–106, 109–110, 114, 117–120,
    124–127, 146, 163, 172–173, 180,
    184–185, 187, 209–211; see also Anglo-
    French treaty of 1860
Cobden Club, 96, 120, 158
colonies, 32–33, 35, 45, 140, 148, 154,
    156–157, 160–163, 174, 194, 197–198,
    200, 203; see also imperial preference
Commerce, Minister of, 48, 86, 95, 180
common market, concept of, 3
comparative advantage, 59–60
compensation see reciprocity
Conservative Party, 3, 12–13, 67, 74, 88,
    106, 119, 122, 127–128, 137, 149, 156,
    159, 162, 164–166, 178, 180, 193, 200,
    205–206, 211
Corn Laws, 6, 9, 12, 45, 70, 79, 92, 155,
    179, 203
cottons, 17–18, 21, 29, 31–32, 35, 37, 42,
    57, 63, 65–70, 73–74, 77, 79, 85, 94, 102,
    106, 115–116, 119, 126, 142–144,
    150–152, 156, 159, 160, 162, 164, 169,
    175–176, 184–185, 189, 194, 198, 205;
    see also India; Lancashire; Liverpool;
    Manchester
Crowe, Sir Joseph Archer, 23–26, 34,
    42–43, 62–66, 68–69, 84, 87–88, 93–94,
    102, 106, 108, 111–115, 119, 122–124,

142–145, 150–151, 157–158, 160,
    165–167, 174–175, 180–181, 183ff.,
    197–199, 206, 212–213
currants see fruit

Delbrück, Rudolph von, 69, 89
Denmark, 53, 84, 141, 168–169
Derby, Lord (earlier Lord Stanley), 64,
    66–68, 93–94, 96–102, 104, 106–108,
    111, 114
depression, royal commission on, 161–164,
    168
Dilke, Sir Charles, 80, 125–127, 129ff.,
    148, 153–154, 156, 213
discriminatory duties see wine
Disraeli, Benjamin (eventually Lord
    Beaconsfield), 12, 39, 96, 109, 111,
    115
Droz, Swiss foreign Minister, 177–178,
    184, 186
dumping, 90, 110
Dundee, 116, 138
Dunraven, Earl of, 160
Düsseldorf, 87, 93, 102, 108, 123

The Economist, 17, 22, 34, 50, 54, 58, 64,
    72–75, 87, 91–93, 105, 109–110, 136,
    144, 147, 153–154, 165ff., 173, 192–193,
    196, 198, 202–203, 206, 212
Egypt, 118, 151, 160
electorate, British, 2, 347, 352, 356
equity, 36
Europe, Concert of, 100
European Community/Union, 3–4, 53,
    207–208, 210–211

Fair Trade, 79, 95, 110, 114, 118, 120, 127,
    130–131, 133–134, 136–137, 148–149,
    153–154, 156, 158, 160, 163, 165, 170,
    178–180, 193–194
Ferry, Jules, 189–190
flax see linens
Ford, Sir Clare, 181
Foreign Office (British), 5–6, 19, 21, 23,
    26, 30ff., 46ff., 64, 66–67, 74–76, 82, 86,
    87, 94–97, 99–101, 105–106, 108, 111,
    117, 122–126, 131–132, 134, 143, 145,
    148, 155, 160–161, 166, 179–181, 196,
    199–200, 205, 210–212
Forster, W.E., 31, 33, 36, 46–47, 71, 79, 82,
    94, 114, 135
Fortescue, Chichester, 83

France, *passim* throughout; *see also* Anglo-French (Cobden's) treaty of 1860
Franco-Prussian War, 80ff., 88, 130, 167, 209
Frankfurt (city), 66, 193
Frankfurt, Treaty of, 81, 83, 102, 104, 117, 130, 137, 158, 182–183, 195
free trade, 3, 5–9, 39, 46, 48–49, 53–54, 118, 126, 138, 140, 146, 148–150, 154, 157–162, 165–166, 168, 173, 177–178, 188, 201, 209, 211; *see also* liberals, economic; unilateralism
Frère-Orban, 29
fruit, 38, 40, 60, 112, 197–198, 205

Gambetta, Léon, 121–122, 126, 129, 132, 134, 139–142, 144–145
Germany, *passim* throughout; *see also* Zollverein; Prussia
Genoa, 37
Ghent, 29, 31, 35, 37
Giffen, Robert, 180
Gladstone, W.E.G., 2, 6, 8–12, 15, 28, 33, 39, 51–52, 54, 67, 71–72, 78, 80–81, 83–86, 88, 99, 122, 124ff., 140–141, 143, 146, 148–150, 153–154, 157, 160–161, 164–166, 172–173, 177, 185, 209; *see also* budget of 1860
Glasgow, 135, 158
gold standard, 4, 54, 86, 90
Goschen, G.J., 198
grain, 42, 58, 71, 91, 103, 112, 151, 174, 179, 191, 202, 206; *see also* Corn Laws
Granville, Lord, 117, 125, 136, 153–154, 156, 160–161, 211
Greece, 197

Hamburg, 19, 86
Hanseatic ports, 50, 53, 86
Hastings, 172, 200–202, 205
hegemony, 45
hegemonic stability theory, 3–4
Hicks Beach, Sir Michael, 180
Holland *see* Netherlands
hops, 71
House of Commons *see* Parliament
House of Lords *see* Parliament
Howard de Walden, Lord, 30–31, 34
Howe, Anthony, 3
Huddersfield, 22
Hull, 20
Hungary *see* Austria

imperial preference, 170, 178, 193
India, 9, 18, 32, 94, 151, 162
iron and steel, 17, 26, 42–43, 57–58, 60, 65–66, 68–69, 72, 77, 87, 89, 91, 93–94, 99, 102, 106–107, 109–110, 112–116, 126, 132, 135, 138, 143, 150, 152, 158–159, 164, 166, 169–171, 175, 182, 188, 193, 198
Ireland, 162, 164–165, 205
Italy, 11, 14, 20, 25, 32, 36–40, 45–46, 48–50, 52–53, 60, 62–65, 84, 94, 97–102, 104–105, 107–108, 112–113, 125, 129, 134–135, 137, 139, 141–142, 150, 153, 155, 161, 164ff., 173–174, 176, 178, 182, 184–187, 189–190, 194–195, 197, 200, 203–207, 210, 212

Japan, 82
Junkers *see* Prussia
jute, 116, 138, 189

Kendal, 95–96
Kennedy, Charles M., 95, 97–100, 117, 123–124, 132, 134–135, 146, 155, 157, 161, 166, 179–180, 200
Keynes, J.M., 207
Kindleberger, Charles, 4
Königgrätz, 63–64

Lambermont, Baron, 177
Lambi, Ivo, ix, 152
Lancashire, 17–18, 35, 37–39, 57–58, 67, 72, 74, 79, 85, 94–95, 162
Latin Monetary Union, 53, 74
Layard, A.H., 46–47, 49
Leeds, 17, 19–20, 22
legislature, French (including Chamber of Deputies and Senate), 70, 85, 111–112, 121–122, 126–127, 129, 132–133, 135–136, 139, 144–146, 157, 174–175, 181, 184ff., 202, 206
Legrand, Pierre, 151
Leipzig *see* Saxony
Liberal Party (British), 3, 8, 12, 94, 106, 119, 149, 153, 156, 159–160, 162, 164–165, 205, 211
Liberal Unionists, 165–166, 178, 198, 200, 205
liberals, commercial/economic, 2, 6, 17, 30, 42, 49–50, 59–60, 70, 95, 104, 106–107, 110–111, 113–114, 118–119, 139, 142, 146, 174, 176–177, 182, 184, 186, 188

linens, 29, 38, 68–69, 73, 77, 106, 116, 143, 188
Lister, S.C., 20, 114, 131
Lister, Villiers, 100, 105, 123–126
Liverpool, 18, 20, 94
Lloyd, Sampson, 95–96, 114
London, City of, 4, 17, 90
Low Countries, 20
Lowe, Robert, 48, 71, 74, 79, 84, 86
Luzzatti, Luigi, 101–102, 109
Lyons (city), 58, 74, 90, 188–189
Lyons, Lord, 72, 79, 83
Lytton, Lord, 184–185, 188

machinery, 75–78, 92, 106, 135, 139, 150–151, 164, 169, 175, 194, 198, 205
Mallet, Sir Louis, 51–52, 68–69, 82–83, 86, 95–97, 99–100, 105, 111, 119–120, 123
Manchester, 23, 46, 78–79, 136, 160, 166, 198
Marseilles, 74, 141, 188
Marschall von Bieberstein, Adolf, 183
McKinley tariff, 175
Méline, Jules (including the Méline tariff), 151, 173, 175–176, 179, 184–185, 188–189, 193–194, 202–203
metal manufacturing see iron and steel
Methuen treaty, 1703, 59–60
Metternich, Austrian chancellor, 41
Mexico, 70
Miall, Edward, 62
Middlesborough, 135, 158
Mill, John Stuart, 12, 15
Milner Gibson, 39, 54
Mitchell, Henry, 114–115, 131, 133–134, 163
Monk, Charles, 136
Morier, Sir Robert, 153, 161
most-favoured-nation clause, 1, 6–7, 28, 35–37, 39–40, 43–45, 52–53, 69, 72, 81–82, 101–104, 106–107, 110, 113, 117, 119, 130–131, 135–136, 140, 142–143, 145–146, 148–149, 153, 155–156, 158, 161, 164, 167, 172–174, 179, 183, 185, 190, 192–195, 197, 199–201, 204, 206–208, 210
Mundella, A.J., 180, 185

Napier, Lord, 28, 45
Napoleon III, 1, 8–9, 11, 13–15, 21, 23, 25–28, 50, 52–53, 58–61, 63–64, 70, 81, 88, 90, 121, 130, 146, 153, 172, 185, 209–211

Nationalverein, 25–26, 43, 64
navigation see shipping
Netherlands, 29, 32, 35, 45, 49, 53, 60, 62, 81, 97, 102, 137, 141–142, 145, 150, 155, 163–164, 168–169, 177–178, 186, 188–189, 195, 197, 199, 202
network, European commercial treaty, 1, 3–5, 7, 17–18, 22–4, 28–62, 70–72, 74, 80, 82–84, 88–89, 90, 96, 100, 103–104, 109 ("the economic union"), 117–118, 120–121, 130, 132, 136, 146, 151, 155, 158, 164–165, 167, 172ff., 207, 209–212
North German Confederation, 64
Northcote, Sir Stafford, 96, 99, 100, 102, 106, 111, 119
Norway see Sweden and Norway, United Kingdoms of

overproduction, 89, 106

Palmerston, Lord, 8–9, 11–12, 14, 33–34, 36, 46, 50, 86
Paris exhibition: of 1866, 69, 75, 78; of 1878, 109
Parliament (British), 5, 9, 115, 124, 127–129, 136–137, 143, 146, 156, 160, 180, 187, 198, 200, 203–204
Peel, Sir Robert, 8, 10–11, 13, 16, 59
phylloxera, 102, 129, 132, 138, 150, 174, 196
Portugal, 29, 52–53, 59–60, 74, 79, 82–83, 85–86, 97–99, 104, 119, 125–126, 128–129, 139, 141–142, 145, 153, 155, 168–169, 185
potteries, Staffordshire, 39, 135
Pouyer-Quertier, Augustin, 70, 81, 85, 107
protectionism, 9, 79, 88, 94, 102, 105–106, 110–115, 117–118, 120–122, 125, 127–128, 130, 132, 135–136, 139–141, 146, 149, 151, 155, 157–158, 160–161, 165ff., 172ff., 206–207
Prussia, 19, 25, 29, 32–34, 36, 40–45, 48, 52–53, 61, 63ff., 75, 79ff., 92–93, 103, 112, 183, 208, 210; see also Zollverein; Germany

rags, 50, 134
railways, 26, 53–54, 58, 60, 65, 68–70, 89, 91, 151, 161, 174, 179, 190, 194
raisins see fruit
raw materials, 22, 53, 65–66, 71, 84–85, 106, 151, 175–176, 191, 194, 201, 203
reciprocity (including compensation), 9,

12–13, 15, 31, 33, 38–40, 43, 45–46, 49,
    52, 74, 81, 84, 110, 114–115, 119–120,
    128, 130–132, 143, 156, 195–196
retaliation, 72, 79, 82, 111, 114, 119–120,
    129, 131, 133, 135, 137–138, 153, 156,
    161–162, 164–167, 172, 174, 177–178,
    181, 184–186, 188, 191, 196, 198–199,
    205
revenue, customs, 2, 6, 15, 17, 40, 55, 71,
    81, 84–85, 88–89, 98, 100, 104–105, 118,
    120–121, 125–126, 128, 145, 162, 198,
    209; see also wine; spirits
Reverter, principal Spanish commissioner,
    198
Rheims, 75, 134–135
Rhine/Rhineland, 26, 53, 66, 80–81, 87,
    94, 207
Ribot, French Foreign Minister, 181
Ripley, H.W., 22, 33, 46, 48, 96, 114
Ritchie, C.T., 138
Roche, Jules, 175
Romania, 107, 178–179, 185, 189, 191, 206,
    208
Rosebery, Lord, 164, 205–206
Roubaix, 59, 69–70, 75–78, 108, 110,
    134–135
Rouen, 70, 189
Rouvier, Maurice, 141–142, 144
Ruhr, 66, 69, 87, 89, 110, 112
Russell, Lord John, later Earl, 11, 14, 18,
    24–25, 28ff., 40ff., 67, 86, 209, 212
Russell, Lord Odo, 85, 88, 113, 116,
    122–123
Russia, 26, 43, 62, 76, 81, 84, 91, 93, 97,
    108, 111–112, 119, 138, 140–141, 150,
    155, 160–161, 168–169, 182–183, 191,
    197, 201, 206, 208
Rutland, Duke of, 155–156

Sackville West, L.S., 38
Salisbury, Lord, 2, 5, 111–113, 115–117,
    119–120, 122–125, 149, 153–156,
    160–162, 164–167, 172–173, 178–181,
    184, 187–189, 192–194, 196–198, 200ff.,
    212
salt, 65
Salt, Titus, 20
Saxe-Coburg-Gotha, 25
Saxony, 23, 26, 43–44, 62–66, 68, 75, 80,
    84, 87, 89, 94, 109, 159
Say, Léon, 122, 124–129, 132–133,
    144–146, 151, 157
Scheldt, 32–33, 35, 53, 60

Schleswig-Holstein, 26, 41, 44, 62
Sedan, 81, 135
Serbia, 186
Sheffield, 130, 150, 198
shipping, 8–9, 12, 38, 52, 74, 78, 85, 141,
    150, 179, 189, 194–195
shoddy, 101, 134–135, 138, 142–143
silks, 18, 29, 34, 38, 42, 58, 66, 70, 74,
    77–78, 82, 91, 102, 109, 114, 139, 164,
    167, 184, 187–188, 202–203, 205
Slagg, John, 136
Smith, Adam, 122
socialism, 177
Spaak, Paul-Henri, 4, 208
Spain, 6, 29, 34, 53, 74, 76, 79, 82–83,
    85–86, 97–99, 104–105, 107–108, 111,
    119, 125–126, 128–129, 131, 135, 137,
    139, 141–142, 145, 147, 153ff., 161–162,
    164, 168–169, 174, 176, 180–181,
    185–186, 190, 195ff.
South America, 62, 69, 91
spirits, 11, 15, 29, 84, 99, 106, 112, 197,
    202; see also wine
sovereignty, 3, 211
Stanley, Lord see Derby, Lord
Strachey, George, 158–159, 161
statistics, 50, 54, 59, 91, 96–99, 156, 160,
    162–163, 167–168, 207, 212
sugar, 71, 112
Sweden and Norway, United Kingdoms of,
    45, 53, 60, 62, 75, 84, 92, 97, 137, 141,
    155, 168–169, 186, 188–189, 195, 197,
    200
Switzerland, 34, 45, 53, 60, 62, 81, 84, 92,
    101, 104, 135, 137, 142, 145, 158–159,
    163–164, 166–167, 172, 176–178, 184ff.,
    194–195, 197, 202, 204–207

Tariff reform, 92
Tenterden, Lord, 100
Tetuan, Duke of, 195
textiles, 10, 26, 39, 43, 51, 59–60, 66, 68,
    70, 74, 80, 87, 90, 92, 94, 99, 106–107,
    109–110, 114–116, 118, 120, 122, 129,
    136–139, 142–145, 150, 152, 155, 164,
    167, 175, 180, 188–189, 194, 198,
    204–205; see also cottons; linens; silks;
    woollens
Thiers, Adolphe, 24, 70, 73, 81–83, 85, 107
The Times, 24, 36, 144, 160, 212
timber, 50, 60, 71
Tirard, Pierre-Emmanuel, 121, 129ff., 151,
    153, 157, 174–175, 197

tobacco, 112
Torrens, Robert, 12
Trade and Treaties Committee, 180,
    184–185, 187–189, 194, 197–198, 200,
    203
Triple Alliance, 182–184, 190–191,
    199–200
Turkey, 108, 111

unemployment, 156, 162
unilateralism (in free trade), 2, 10, 44–45,
    60, 83, 85, 88, 100, 118, 127, 146,
    157–158, 192, 202, 209
United States, 3–5, 7, 18, 20, 54, 65, 68,
    84, 89, 91, 103, 112, 120, 127, 130, 134,
    138, 140–141, 151, 164, 175, 182–183,
    201, 203, 209; see also Civil War,
    American

Vienna settlement, 13, 25, 29, 37, 210

wages, 68–69, 76–78, 80, 89, 106, 108, 131,
    138, 156
Ward, John, 34
Wengenroth, Ulrich, 152
wheat, see grain
Whitwell, John, 96
wine, 2, 9–11, 14–15, 29, 33, 37–38, 40, 42,
    50, 52, 55, 58–60, 67, 74, 78–79, 82–86,
    99–100, 102, 105–107, 109, 111, 118,

120, 122, 125–129, 131–133, 135–140,
    142, 146–148, 150–151, 153–154,
    161–162, 164, 166–167, 174, 176–177,
    181, 184, 186, 190–191, 195ff.,
    208–209
Wolff, Sir Henry Drummond, 197–199
Wolverhampton, 135
woollens, 17–20, 30, 34, 38–39, 54, 57,
    59–60, 63, 66–70, 73, 74–79, 82–83, 85,
    91, 94, 96, 98–99, 101–103, 105,
    108–109, 114, 116, 119, 126, 130–132,
    134–137, 142–144, 146, 151, 156–157,
    159, 162–163, 165ff., 174–177, 184,
    188–190, 198, 212; see also worsteds
working classes, 10, 20, 58, 70, 122, 138,
    149, 156, 163, 173, 177, 210
worsteds, 20–22, 35, 67, 75, 78, 82, 95, 103,
    109–110, 130, 134
Württemberg, 42, 44

Yorkshire, West, 9, 57–58, 67, 79, 83, 85,
    101–103, 108, 130, 134–135, 138, 146,
    162–163, 180; see also Bradford; Leeds;
    woollens
Yorkshire Chambers of Commerce, Joint
    Tariff Committee of, 94–95, 116, 134,
    166, 213

Zollverein, 3, 19, 41–45, 50–51, 60–61,
    63ff., 80, 84, 89